Shree Gurujee and his RSS

Editor
Aanand Aadeesh

Price : Rs. 800/-

Printed & Published by
MD Publications Pvt Ltd
11, Darya Ganj
New Delhi-110002
E-mail : contact@mdppl.com
www : www.mdppl.com

To

THE SACRED MEMORY

of

MY PUJYA PARENTS

SHRI ASHA RAM JI

AND

SMT. BRAHM DEVI JI

Intent And Acknowledgement

THE present volume, being published during Gurujee's Centenary Year, is not intended to be a chronological history of RSS or for that matter even a planned and systematic biography of Shri Gurujee, the legendary second Sarsanghchalak of RSS. The articles contained here in have been selected with a view to understanding Gurujee as a man, as an ideologue and as an architect of RSS. The very first article *Hindutva Symbolizes Universal Salvation* is the essence of the RSS ideology of Hindutva as propounded by Gurujee in consonance with the age old Indian philosophy as enunciated by an unbroken chain of great saints, seers and scholars of our ancient nation.

To a casual reader, some of the articles may appear to be a little incongruous with the central theme, but, I am sure, a closer look will convince the perceptive readers of their relevance and significance in the over all matrix of the book.

Hindus have a hurt psyche - first being the target of the attacks of barbarous and fanatic foreign Muslim invaders and later on of wily European imperialists. During this prolonged period of slavery and subjugation, Hindus were subjected to not only discrimination but also atrocities and religious persecution. A large chunk from amongst them was converted to Islam or Christianity under coercion, capitation and allurement. A number of their own weaknesses like casteism and narrow regionalism further contributed to the erosion of their self esteem and weakened the Hindu society.

Motivated and malacious propaganda was unleashed on an unprecedented scale to distort India's glorious past and undermine her contribution to world civilisation and culture. The Aryan Invasion Theory was concocted and India was denied her due for her significant contribution in the field of Science, Technology, Art, Philosophy, Literature, Yoga, Medicine etc.

Unfortunately, the situation has not much changed even after the sinful partition of the country. Forces inimical to India are again at work. Hindu baiting seems to be the order of the day. No stone is being left unturned to denigrate and divide the Hindu society in independent India.

Our country is passing through a crucial period. Anti-national communal forces aided and abetted by power hungry politicians of various hues and colours are once again raising their ugly head. Casteism and Regionalism is all out to shatter apart our social fabric. International situation is extremely volatile and the terrorist threat is a real challenge to the civilised society and human culture. With in the RSS fraternity also there is a wide spread feeling of disgust among the followers whose common strain is that the political leadership has miserably failed them. How else one can explain the way they conducted themselves during the past one decade or so, keeping their own cadre at an arms length and relying totally on time-servers who have no stakes in party programmes and policies, projecting a few expert toe-touchers as conveners of this 'think tank' or that 'wing', nominating the hand picked self-seekers to Rajya Sabha or some other plum-positions. The go-betweens seemed to have a heyday. It is a classic case where, instead of providing collective leadership, they collectively failed in implementing their own policies and programmes in their zeal to please their own whims or their coalition partners' and a few of them promoting their relatives - actual or adopted - forgetting that they owe their position courtesy their cadre.

For the honest and dedicated majority of workers, more disturbing still has been the conduct of some of the comparatively young gentlemen swearing by the mother-organisation - most of them the so called intellectuals or opinion builder journalists- floating trusts over night, manipulating allotment of prime land on concessional rates anywhere from Dadar to Delhi to Dehradoon and/or garnering generous advertisements from government departments or corporate houses for souvenirs published for their selfish gain and claiming the patronage of some of organisations high-ups. However, the most heart rending has been their act of washing their dirty linen in full public view exposing the despicable inter/intra party squabbles and damaging the RSS image.

Fortunately, the RSS is made of a different stuff and the core stubbornly refuses to be corrupted. Where as excessive interference or indulgence in day today affairs is counter productive, the leadership of present Sarsanghchalak Shri Sudershan and Sarkaraeyavah Shri Mohan Bhagwat can ill-afford to rest on their oars. Uninterrupted introspection, periodic course correction and eternal vigilance is the price, the Swayamsevaks and through them the society demands if the dream of Dr Keshav Rao Hedgewar and his worthy successor Shri Gurujee is to be realised.

The life and work of Shri Gurujee, I believe, is the beacon of hope in such disparaging and diabolical times.

Hence this Compendium.

All this has been possible only because of the learned authors whose illuminating and informative articles have been incorporated here in. On the basis of my personal knowledge, I can confidently vouchsafe that most of them have lived an era with RSS and had had the good fortune of working and growing under the benign shadow of Gurujee. Others too are deeply inspired by Gurujee's personality and philosophy. All are eminent scholars, their commitment to truth and objectivity sacrosanct.

Where as I can only bow my head to the versatile genius of late Poojya Gurujee, Pt. Deen Dayal Upadhyaya and Dattopant Thengdi, I cannot really sufficiently express my indebtedness to Sarvashree V. Sundaram, P. Parmeshwaran,

Dr M. Rama Jois, S. Gurumurthy, K. Surya Narayan Rao, Rakesh Sinha, Shripati Shastri, Dr Satish Mittal, Prof. Devendra Swaroop, Atul Rawat, Prof. Shivaji Singh and Prof. V.G. Bhide.

I must also express sincere thanks to my worthy friends Shri Lalit Kumar Vidyarathi and Shri Rajendra Swaroop Goyal for translating on my request the articles of Shri Gurujee and Dr. Satish Mittal. I know how difficult it is to capture the essence and substance of an idea through the idiom of a foreign language.

I also owe my heartfelt thanks to Shri Vijay Gupta, the Managing Director of M.D. Publications for so generously and painstakingly bringing out the book in such a fine and presentable form.

I cannot but appreciate the sincerity and strenuous hard work put in by Shri Parmod Kumar Kaushik in preparing the computerized press copy.

To my wife Sarla, for her generous co-operation so very essential in such a selfless endeavour and to our sweet playful little grand-daughter Dhaani Aanand, for her occasional innocent and invigorative intervention, I can only say - very well done !

January 14, 2007
(Makar Sankranti) **Aanand Aadeesh**

(722, Neelkanth Apartments, Sector 13, Rohini, Delhi-110085, Phone: 011- 65722744)

Contents

1

Hindutva Symbolizes Universal Salvation

Gurujee Madhav Sadashiv Golwalkar

(English Rendering by L.K. Vidyarthi)

THE first essential characteristic of a nation is land, which as far as possible has a physical boundary and forms its basis of evolution, progress and prosperity. The second essential quality of a nation is a social group inhabiting it and development of a respectful emotional attachment to it like that of a son to a mother - providing security and well-being.

We do not regard society as a mere social-gathering, a conglomeration gathered at a place. A society evolves its own way of life, which gives it a form through its own ideals, attitudes, emotional reactions, sentiments, faith and tradition. Such an evolution of society - its people having come together with a will of their own, aspirations, sharing its ups and downs, common friends and foes - results into a well-organised entity. These people - sons and daughters of the country they live in - form what we call a Nation.

Sacred-Bond

If we apply the above definition of Nation - readily agreed to by learned people of the world - to our own country, we come to the conclusion that our great nation - stretching in the north from the Himalayas, Himalayan ranges in the

North-West and the North-East to the groups of islands in the Southern Seas - is one great entity. Our well-developed and well-organised society has been inhabiting this land as its progeny for thousands of years. It is this social-group that has been named as Hindu in modern times. It is primarily Hindus who are devoted to their motherland, created its culture and tradition, evolved ideals of life. It is they who built its social norms, noble attitudes, sacred duties and obligations. It is their ancestors who made this country "dynamic, living and divinely oriented organism worthy of our reverence and worship. It is they who shed their blood to preserve its individuality and sanctity. It is Hindus who have performed this sacred duty since times immemorial. Our thousands of years' history bears eloquent witness to this outstanding and splendid achievement. This leads to incontestable conclusion that it is Hindus who have all along been treating themselves as true sons of India. Lives of great heroes of this ancient land established and exemplified their mother-son relationship.

This togetherness at the altar of motherland had tied each one of us - from Kashmere to the Cape of Comarin - its cities, villages', forest-dwellers - into an unbreakable bond. Every one of these different groups - having their own specific mode of worship, different from others - are variegated expressions of the great Hindu society and the off-springs of this great Nation.

Stream of cultural csonsciousness

We, Hindus, have placed a noble ideal before us - to know 'the ultimate truth'. Befitting this ideal, we have evolved our 'Dharma', our way of life, which is uniquely broad-based and broad-minded, enveloping and absorbing every aspect and stage of human existence. We have evolved a distinct way of life, attitudes, sentiments and sensibilities. We call it "Hindu-Culture". It enables everyone of us to cultivate nobility of thought and action, instills in us purity of character, forbearance, fortitude and a passion for sacrifice. It empowers us to achieve the highest goals of human-existence. Our culture imports divinity to worldly aims of our life and permeates every sphere of our daily-life. To cite one example: To us every woman is like our own mother - even a girl-child is addressed as mother. Even in our vernacular languages, the word for mother (ma) connotes this sentiment. This means that with the exception of one's wife, every woman - of any age, position or status - is aspected as 'mother'. Our culture has, thus, a very distinct-identity, a uniqueness of its own. Inspite of the vitiating influence of the hundreds of years of foreign rule and the immorality seeping into the conduct and behaviour of the so-called high society, the ordinary man in villages and cities continues to show examples of high moral character as enjoined by our scriptures. In our hearts, we Hindus have nurtured a culture, a code of conduct which is chaste, noble and distinctive. It is this culture which has given us a name, an identity which is entirely our own. Through the ages, we have thrown an unending line of great seers, saints, heroes and emancipators of mankind, who have created a glorious tradition and guided us in the search of "The Supreme Being" and in achieving the pinnacle of fame, honour and material-prosperity.

To cater to the material needs of our people, our great ancestors have produced a social-system which organised the means of production and technique of distribution of economic wealth and riches through multiple institutions and created a political order which ensured security of life and limbs. The continuity of these social, political and economic systems through the centuries, produced commonality and similarity of our reactions to adverse and advantageous situations. Consequently there has been flowing of diverse community interests into one stream of commonality.

Whenever there was a clash of interest - under a false notion of one's separate identity, exclusive existence - we came to battle each other and fragmented ourselves. We were, then, overpowered by foreigners. Decline and fall of Hindu kingdoms was the inevitable result. There were times when one kingdom was arraigned against a foreign invader, while the other one treated the same foreigner as a friend and ally. The fall of the Prithviraj Chauhan's dynasty illustrates this point.

As against this, whenever our interest converged, even if for a short period, treating foes and friends according to our shared interests, there emerged such a power-packed force which brought the enemy to his knees. Thus the great Hindu society provides all the essential components of a Nation. Therefore, it is our firm conviction that it is this Hindu culture and civilisation that provides a true picture of our nation. In short this is our concept of "The Hindu nation".

Hindutva - A Divine Dispensation

Hindutva is not an 'ism' or a debating point. Whenever we made an exposition of our idea of a nation and refer to 'Hindu Dharma and Culture', the so-called secularists feel disturbed and apprehensive. They start asking why do we mix religion and politics. We can cite the example of Stalin, who made all sorts of insinuations against God and religion and said that it is an opiate for poor masses. Even he once conceded that mere economic and political interests and aspirations of a people of a country do not constitute a nation, nation; is a psychological notion - a product of shared interests.

In modern times Swami Vivekanand, the most widely acclaimed leader of Indian Renaissance declared in unambiguous terms that - India is a Hindu nation and cited Guru Govind Singh and Shivaji as shining symbols of great Hindu Ideals. He said that only those hearts that beat in unison are true sons of India.

Therefore our firm conviction is that our concept of Hindu nation is validated through reason, sentiment and historical perspective. And this is the true and logical fact of life. This is not a matter scoring points in a debate but a short term discussion of some temporal political and economic theories.

This is our life-breath.

Some people even opine that politics is like a comely dancing nautch-girl who dresses herself with different ideological garments to attract the attention of men. She changes her dress at will. "Nripaniti Varanganaiva Aneka-Rupa". In comparison to politics, life's canvass is much larger and broader. To import-primacy to politics over life's diverse activities is against the grain of Indian soul.

Politics is divisive in nature and breeds intolerance. Verily, we have forgotten the pure art of showing due consideration to views other than ours. It should be our endeavour that various ideological groups come out with their own agendas about Nation' progress and advancement, regroup themselves in arriving at a common solution and action plan.

It is erroneous to think we achieve ever-lasting good through politics. The great kings like Mandhata are a forgotten name today. 'Gyaneshwari' proclaims that even Puranas carry tales of those who have perished. On the other hand, there have been many who did not hanker after power, yet served mankind even if they had to suffer pain and hardships. It were they who sustained society, while those who occupied seats of power indulged in aggrandizement creating dis-harmony and disorder.

I fancy a state, where administration is responsive, life is safe and secure, wealth is evenly distributed. Peace prevails in every nook and corner. Every Indian develops traits of spotless character, good-conduct and self-effacement. Pure qualities of patriotism, self-confidence and self-reliance permeate every fibre of our being. I am the least concerned with who is occupying the throne. Everybody aspires to be at the top. Such ambition makes me feel at sea. I would always aspire to be the stone in foundation which shoulders and sustains the majestic temple rather than a part of the highest edifice where even crows can station themselves.

Loyalty to Nation-At stake

When we declare that we are a 'Hindu Nation', people at once raise the question of the status of Muslims and

Christians who live in India. Are they not born and brought-up in this country? How could they turn into foreigners, with the change of their religion? It depends upon their attitude? Do they continue to hold on to the fact that they are the sons of the soil? The fact that we treat them as such will not answer the question. We are not so narrow-minded as not to regard a person the son of the soil, only because he has changed the mode of his worship. Everyone is free to worship his own God. We, who are a part and parcel of the RSS have imbibed the essence of 'Hindutva'. We respect the sentiments of those who follow a different religious path. We do not regard a person true Hindu, if he lacks in tolerance. However, the problems is how do they, who have taken a different religious route, feel about this 'Motherland'. Undoubtedly India is a native place for Muslims and Christians. However, do they feel indebted to this 'mother'? Do they feel grateful that mother India has brought them up with love and care? Do they feel that they have inherited great Indian tradition, that they are a product of the time-tested culture of this land? Do they regard the service of motherland as their prime duty, sacred task and great fortune?

Do they regard any other country as their sacred mother land? They call themselves 'Sheikhs' and 'Sayyids'. Both these are Arabic clans. Why should Muslims of India regard them as their ancestors. Muslims have disengaged themselves from our ancient moorings and identified themselves with foreign invaders. Therefore, it is not a question of the change in Religion. It is a question of Nation's Identity, Nation's soul.

Once a very senior American professor posed this question, "Muslims and Christians are sons of this country. Why don't you regard them as one of you?" In reply I too asked a question, "Suppose a person of this country migrates to America and wants to become a true American, but fails to acclaim the greatness of American heroes like Lincoln, Washington and Jefferson and their likes, would you regard him as a national of America?" The American professor said emphatically, "No"

Then I asked why should we not apply this norm in deciding the Nationality of a person living in this country? You want us to treat them as Nationals who oppose our traditions, show scant respect to our past heroes and deride our nation's honoured ideals. Mere birth and upbringing do not entitle a man to be regarded as truly national. He has to inculcate the sentiment of belonging to its culture and tradition, of honouring its heroes-past and present both. Such a mental make-up is a necessary component of Nationality.

Mere nativity does not create a sense of National-identity. Common traits of character and conduct and a feeling of oneness does. The new-comers have to bring such a radical change in their out-look as if they are reborn to Nation's culture and tradition.

There is one example from England also, regarded as an ideal Democracy - which is very illuminating. About a hundred years ago, a number of Germans immigrated to England and acquired its citizenship. They were treated as natives of England. One of them became an ICS officer, was sent to Indiā and posted in Madhya Pradesh. When thē First World-War broke out in 1914, he was arrested and imprisoned as there was a nagging doubt about his loyalty to England - an adopted country. Was this not a mature reaction? This is true nationalism.

The above contention applies to our own country, too. No doubt all of us are born in this country, have prospered in like manner, but this does not lead inevitably to shared values (of life), code of conduct and quality of life.

Religious Dogmatism

Our appeal to Muslims and Christians of our country is that they ought to give-up their allegiance to a culture and mentality foreign to us and merge their identity in the mainstream of national life.

It is common knowledge that the number of Muslims which came from abroad was quite small. Now their number has increased enormously. This has not been a natural growth. It is an increase in the manner of increase in the number of fishes. It is a result of conversion of a section of the native population. We can trace the source of this phenomenon, when one part of Hindus converted to Muslims and another to Christians. The rest continued to cling to their Hindu identity. Let us ponder why did some of us give up our ancient culture and tradition. Was conversion a spontaneous out-come, a consequence of awareness that the adopted religion was better and superior. History does not record any such example.

On the other hand history is replete with examples of forced conversion either through the use of brute-authority or inducement in the shape of more power or higher status in the administration. Such people - converted ones - liked to curry the favour of the rulers, by imitating their way of life and lastly embracing their religion. They even copied their dress. Often crafty methods were resorted to. Like when a piece of cow's meat or a tasted piece (Jhutha) of bread was thrown into the waters of a lake from where the villagers drew water for drinking and preparing meals. Next morning the Padari (Christian preacher) or the Mullah (the Muslim Holy-man) presented themselves and declared that villagers have become impure by drinking impure water. The only way out for them was to give up their religion and get themselves converted. In this way in northern India villages after villages were converted into Muslim or Christian religion. Thus Christianity was spread in the west-coast. It was black mail - pure and simple. The real aim was to establish the supremacy of foreign-power through increase in numbers. It was not propagation of faith, but a shrewd political move with religion as a cover. The foreign invaders not only enslaved them politically, dominated them socially, but also changed their religion - their faith. This in a way is foreign domineering. The foreign-power dominates a people not only politically, economically and culturally but also religiously.

It is our bounden duty to bring them back to their original

and ancient-culture and tradition - their heritage. For long they have experienced the disadvantages of religious enslavement. Like freedom loving people, they must cast-off the burden of oppression (political) and exploitation (religious), reverting back to their old culture and tradition. Let them be one with the main currents of national life. Enslavement of every kind, form and shape is against natural tendencies and is fit for wearing off. It is a clarion call to our mis-led brothers to come back to their ancestral homes and hearths. We shall celebrate their home-coming in the manner of the festival of lights. There are no restrictions here, no boundaries to keep one brother away from the other. It is my fervent wish, my prayer that they evaluate themselves, their own real status and condition and then re-adopt their old way of life - participate freely in Hindu institutions - regarding conduct, marriage, house-building, dress, last-rites etc. Let them feel one with Hindu-culture and tradition (which is as multi-faceted as any, yet presents a one single-body).

There are people who lay stress on unity in political and economic institutions. To them I say we stress on shared-equality in cultural and religious spheres along with unity of thought in political and economic matters. We would welcome every one with open arms. The doors of our sacred places and temples are unlatched. Our age-old culture and heritage is so cosmopolitan and broad-based as to let in anyone who seeks to benefit from it. This breath-of-vision is our attitude to life and its diversity.

False-sense of unity

In their hearts several people feel the same way as we do. Pt Jawahar Lal Nehru in his foreword to the famous book "Sanskriti key Char Adhyaya" by eminent Hindi poet, Shri Ram Dhari Singh 'Dinkar', has expressed his deep love and admiration, for this culture (Hindu) which he calls 'Bharatiya Culture'. He devoutly desired that the power of assimilation so characteristic of ancient culture and civilisation, again becomes operative. He mentions two stages of this faculty of assimilation. During the first stage Shakas and

Hunas, who entered India as foreign invaders, merged their separate identity into Bhartiyata - Indianness, giving up their original religion and social practices. They started calling themselves 'Rajputs'. They became one of us of their own free will. We had the courage and strength for assimilation and we took them into our social and cultural life. We also benefited from this contact. The second stage was ushered in when the more volatile and aggressive invader stepped in. For security and survival, we caged ourselves with inhibitive practices. We went into a cell, safe-guarding our identity by keeping a safe distance from the foreigner.

It is unfortunate that Shri Jawahar Lal Nehru confined himself to only two stages in our history. There is the third stage - a tragic one. There were those who surrendered themselves completely. They lay prostrate before the invader. They could not face the aggressor boldly. They adopted the customs and rites of the ruling invader for survival. The tragedy is that those who meekly submitted to the aggressor were, once, quite vocal about their love for and devotion to Hindu culture and tradition. Fifty or sixty years back a Hindu minister in the state of Hyderabad under Muslim ruler used to offer 'Namaj' in the manner of a devout Muslim. This is abject surrender. The first stage may be characterised as 'Aggression' the second as 'conservatism', but the third one is 'meek surrender'. Even today we appear to be almost in the third stage. The army vocabulary consists of 33 per cent words of the English language and another 33 per cent are words of Persian origin. This type of mixture in language and numerology does not necessarily lead to unity and harmony in relationships. It is definitely aimed at pleasing the (foreign) ruler. It was nothing but meek submission before power and authority. The rulers, on the other hand, continued to look down upon natives. This 'self-surrender' was a way to escape the wrath of the aggressor.

Freedom of worship

Once again 'The Hindu' will have to cultivate the aggressive attitude (Purusharth). A new dynamism has to be infused in Hindus. We must also make clear to others that they have a responsibility to this nation - a duty to perform. They have a national obligation - showing due respect to its social-customes and tradition, honour its great men and be proud of its great heritage. He is completely free to choose his personal religion, faith and spiritual inspiration. He can follow any path that fulfils his desire for salvation. After fulfilling his obligation to the society and discharging his duties to Nation, if some-body feels that the study of and devotion to 'Koran' or 'Bible' touches his inner-self or that a particular mode of worship is more mentally satisfying, we can have no objection. (Temple, mosque, church do co-exist). In all other aspects of life, he must feel and act one with the mainstream of national ethos. This is the only true, just and correct way to national integration.

Our glorious past bears witness to this broad-outlook on life. Our doors to people of other countries have always been wide open, allowing free and uninterrupted access. However, all these coming from distant places, behaved within the parameters set by our social, cultural norms. Many centuries ago, a number of Persians - now known as Parsis - were forced out of their country to escape persecution at the hands of barbaric hordes from Arabia and Turkey, carrying with them "Holy-Fire" and 'Holy-book - Azewesta". They set sail for India and anchored at the port of Surat. The king, Yadava Rana, accorded them a hearty and open-armed welcome. He asked for guidance from the Shankaracharya of Dwarika Peeth as to what kind of treatment be given to new settlers - Parsis. The Parsis were enjoined to give up beef-eating, showing respect to "The cow" revered as mother and as a symbol of Nation's piety and live amicably with the natives. The followers of Zaruthust i.e. Parsis have been honouring their commitment up-till-now.

They have identified themselves completely with the national life (Their contribution to Nation's progress and prosperity has simply been outstanding - much more than their proportion in India's population).

Once Pt. Jawahar Lal Nehru said in Jabalpur that he saw no reason why we should not assimilate Muslims, when we could do it with Shakas and Hunas. For a harmonious national life, this is the only true path.

This is our view also and this is how we look at our relationship with non-Hindu natives of this land. We believe that this is the most reasonable, just and practical solution.

Inspite of such a logical attitude and feeling of togetherness between Hindus and non-Hindu natives of this country, many people are entertaining a wrong notion that in 'the Hindu Nation', there will be no honoured and respectful place for Muslims and Christians. No notion is more dangerous and stupid than this. It is not only defaming but also insulting to our great and all embracing cultural ethos - a boon to humanity. It is widely known that Shivaji - who initiated Hindu-awakening had Randulla Khan as one of his trusted commanders. Even later on in the battle of Panipat in 1771, where life and death battle for resurgent Hinduism took place, Ibrahim Gardi was the head of the artillery of Hindu army. How can we turn our back to these historical truths and age-old traditions. It is strange that in the face of such clear and emphatic examples, some people still feel that in the event of India being declared a Hindu Nation, non-Hindus will come to trouble.

Firm foundation of National unity

Present political leaders often refer to 'National integration'. What is this sentiment? What are those eternal-springs of national life which can be a true source of unity? Who can ensure progress and lead to respectable place in human affairs?

The first sentiment that fill our hearts is the emergence of pure devotion and reverence for the land of our birth.

The second principle is the feeling of brother-hood and companionship which give birth to the intense feeling that every and each one of us is the son of the great and glorious motherland.

The third component of nationalism is the sense of belongingness to the mainstream of national life - a consequence of shared history, tradition, ideals, aspirations, heritage. If we are called upon to describe this "belongingness", this shared consciousness in one word, it is "Hindutva". It provides a firm foundation to the greatness of the temple of nation.

When we declare that every ounce of our energy - Sangh's - is directed to re-emergence and re-invigoration of the ever-young Hindu way of life, many ask us." How do you define 'Hindutva'? No doubt it is an onerous task. Once a gentleman said, "I can pin-point Muslim and Christian identity, but definition of Hindu defies logic." He was right. We can point out 'The Sun' and 'The Moon', which are visible to eyes. "The Supreme Being" who created them is indescribable 'He' is infinite, without a beginning, without an 'end'. But this does not mean that he is incomprehensible. He exists.

Only because 'He' is beyond descriptive symbols and is indefinable, it does not mean that 'He' is a 'non-being'. Shri Ram Krishna Paramhamsa said that God is the only Being who is chaste, virgin and pure because 'He' is untouched by human-description. Speech could not impurify Him. We can define motion, but 'The Supreme Being' who is here, there and everywhere is indefinable. He is known as 'Truth' and is infinite.

All embracing Hindu

We, Hindus, regard Him as The fundamental entity - foundation of our existence. Therefore it is in the realm of possibility that Hindu-society, too, evolved as an all-encompassing consciousness, repository of varied forms, ideas, attitudes, sentiments and sensibilities, yet there has been an under current of intimate relationship which binds them and unites them as a cultural whole. We can define various view-points and diverse streams of thought. The characteristics of different races can be pin-pointed, but Hindutva which represents them, is beyond description. Time and again its definition has been attempted, but failure has been the results. How can one limit the unlimited? Definition is a process of confining 'an idea' within boundaries. Definition restricts. "Truth" is comprehensive, all-pervasive, unbounded and inclusive. It is indefinable. The civilisations and societies which have evolved and advanced during the past few centuries had definite aims and exclusive characteristics. They are shorn of splendid varieties of Hindutva. Therefore they are definable.

The story of the evolution and progress of Hindu culture and civilisation goes back into hoary past. It can not be dated. In a way "Hindutva had no beginning. It is timeless. To define such a society is as impossible as defining "Eternal Truth". The development of language - the word-power - is a much later development. Hindu-consciousness has existed since time immemorial. We existed even before 'naming' of the matter and spirit began. We knew the inner meaning of 'nature' and 'soul'. We were Aryans (men of honour, of distinguished birth) and enlightened ones. We were well-conversant with laws of nature and the significance of 'soul' in human body. We built-up a unique social order. In it we included every aspect of human endeavour designed to make human-beings happy and contented. At this point of time most of the world was inhabited by human-beings who could be called two-legged animals. Therefore no particular name was given to us. Often to give us a separate identity - distinct from others - we were addressed as 'Arya' and the rest 'Malechh' - a low-born. After a period of time, when different sects, and different religions came into existence in other countries and communities opposed to us sprang-up, it was felt that our people should be specifically identified by giving us 'a name'. Many names were given to us over a period of time in the same way as the Ganges is given a different name at different places, namely Gangotri, Bhagirathi, Jahnavi or Hugali. The term 'Hindu' identifying us as a distinct nation and people is derived from 'Sindhu'. A long history and tradition has so sanctified it that it has gained wide currency and is a respected term.

Trans-migration of soul - our guiding light

Thus, though the word 'Hindu' is indefinable, its existence as a truth is a widely acknowledged reality. Hindu society is a living truth, which we feel within every drop of our blood. Though we can pin-point its distinct quality which sets it apart from others, yet we make attempt to discover its main traits which impart it unique fragrance - a flavour of its own.

To a Hindu, life is not aimless. His great aim of life cannot be measured in terms of power, authority, status, name and fame. His supreme object is realisation of the divine state of being - inherent in his soul - awakening into the realm of truth - which is eternal, and initiating into a state of supreme bliss. Since human life is short and transient, the achievement of this highest state of mind within such a short span of life is not considered feasible. Man's knowledge of human body is also inadequate, even though he has been using the various faculties of human-body throughout his existence. How can he, then, take the measure of 'the Supreme Being' who is indestructible and who permeates every fibre of his being. The law of cause and effect reveals that every action performed by us is a consequence of some 'cause'. This cycle (of cause and effects) is all the time evolving, expanding and culminating into a Divine-state. Therefore, the present state of 'being' in respect of human-beings is not the full story of his existence. Man's distinctiveness (from animal and other forms of nature) lies in the fact that he, too, expands his attributes and reveals his inherent divinity. He will continue to take birth, till he achieves perfection - the Supreme Divinity. If he continues to make honest and sincere efforts, he will be attaining higher and higher state of bliss in different births.

For the merger of man's soul into the supreme-being - the eternal truth - this theory of the transmigration of soul is a great-hope and inspiration. This theory is the guiding light-house of Hindutva. It nurses the eternal hope. It means all is not lost with the present state of passing away of the body; that our soul will continue to take new forms, new shapes, new bodies. Thus we have eternity before us to reach our goal, to do our duty, to fulfil our destiny. In this wide world it is only Hindus who have continued to hold the torch of hope and aspirations. This fundamental truth is inherent in all our scriptures, holy books and philosophical musings - both past and the present.

Timeless culture

Our idea of Hindu nation is not a mere repository of political and economic rights. It is basically a cultural entity. Our age-old cultural values are its life-blood. Its rejuvenation will bring into true focus the cross-currents of our national life and lead to a triumphant solution of all our outstanding problems and guide our endeavours in right directions. Now-a-days this cultural regeneration is described in derogatory terms as 'reactionary' and 'revivalist' clinging to blind-faith. Re-emergence of harmful customs is certainly reactionary. It may lead to a stage which results in fossilization of social-customs. Conversely the re-awakening and re-energising the true values of life can never be reactionary. It is sheer intellectual bankruptcy which regards "Renaissance" as reactionary, simply because it pertains to old-values. Thus re-awakening simply means we imbibe those eternal values of life which are time-tested and have nurtured our national life - invigorating it for thousands of years.

We are often called upon to define 'Hindutva', Hindu-culture. No doubt it is indefinable, but we feel it in every fibre of our being. Some people debar it completely from their lives, because it cannot be defined. Is their view logical? To cite an example: medical science has made great advances in saving life. However the most learned among the modern scientists have failed to state in unambiguous terms, "What is life?", yet this has not deterred them in making use of medical science in preserving and saving lives. Life continues to manifest itself in all its bewildering variety. It acts and reacts. This is all we need to know and be convinced that it (life) does exist.

In the same way Hindu culture - faith, aspirations and values of life - is a living reality, playing a vital role in our scheme of things; even though it can not be defined and pin-pointed as per rules of logic and mathematics. In fact, it is these imperceptible Hindu ideals which shape our consciousness in a much more significant way than material things and objects which are measurable and definable.

Our culture - even though indefinable - has left a lasting imprint on every aspect of our life. In all our dealings, we can trace the impact and influence of Hindu culture. Pt Jawahar Lal's life presents us with an illustration of this impact. His outlook on life was scientific and logical. To him God, religion, soul, birth and rebirth were meaningless, unscientific ideas. (Wahiyat i.e., worthless, was the word he often used). Unfortunately his ailing wife, who was sent abroad for treatment, passed away on foreign soil. As per Hindu custom her body was cremated. How to dispose of her ashes? As an agnostic, Nehru would say, "It is only an ash - a material to be thrown into the field - where it might act as a manure. To a materialist treating ash 'as sacred object' is sheer non-sense. At the most it could be said, return to earth from where it was issued forth (A human body is a combination of earth, fire, water, wind and firmament).

Nehru was on the horns of a dilemma. The agnostic in him would prefer ash to be mingled in the foreign soil as a routine matter and proceed back to India. But the age-old Hinduism in grained in his blood urged him to take the sacred remains (ashes) of his beloved wife back to India, proceed to Allahabad and immerse it in the waters of the Ganges - the holy river. The ancient wisdom triumphed. Her sacred ashes were taken to Allahabad and immersed in the holy waters of Triveni - the confluence of the sacred Ganga and Jamuna and imperceptible Saraswati. Afterwards Nehru, himself averred - His modern views, education and training, all were in revolt in his mind, yet there was something deep in him - an indescribable perception - which forced him to bring the (sacred) ashes to Triveni for immersion."

Society - A manifestation of the Supreme Being

The first and the foremost quality of the human-mind is the desire to reach the Eternal Reality, to be one with it or in simple language - to reach the Supreme Being, God.

But is the Supreme Being approachable? How can we reach Him? Does He have a form, a shape? What are his qualities? All this we endeavour to know, so that we can comprehend Him, through meditation and merging ourselves - individual souls - into the Supreme Being. Describing Him as formless and non-attributed will not solve our problem. Therefore different forms of worship were evolved. People created idols representing Him, built temples and installed His images so that they could reach Him through idols. However, we Hindus who are a dynamic people felt that image-worship is inadequate. We need a living-force, not one who listens, but does not answer. These symbols react, smile, shed-tears only when devotees with extraordinary attributes pray before them. For ordinary people idols are speechless, inactive symbols of God. Therefore, we need a living God, who makes us perform our duties and awakens our inherent-strength and dynamism.

Thus the realisation of the Divine Being, through service of mankind was made central in our lives by our seers and saints of antiquity. Holy brotherhood of mankind is manifestation of God (Janta Janardan). Ram Krishna Paramhamsa's - the great saint - inspiring message of divine-worship through service of the suffering humanity elevates and uplifts our souls. His eminent disciple, Swami Vivekananda laid great stress on his master's philosophy of life. However it was not easy to comprehend the concept of entire humanity as a solid reality. It was observed that many among those who started with the service of mankind as their object, suffered from sloth and inactivity. Therefore, realising the limits and constrictive nature of human mind and intellect, our ancient seers and prophets opined that, notwithstanding lofty concept of service of mankind, we should confine ourselves, with our limited capabilities, to serve those whom we can comprehend and keep contact with. They said that our great Hindu-society is that all-encompassing entity (virat Purush) - a reflection of God Himself. They did not use the word 'Hindu'. In 'Purush Sukta' He is unambiguously stated to be one whose eyes are the sun and the moon, stars and the sky are his navel, Brahmans his face, Kshatriyas his arms, Vaishyas his thighs and shudras, his feet. This means that Hindu-society which formed this four-fold social-order is in the image of the 'Supreme Being - cosmic personality (Virat Purush)'.

ब्राह्मणोऽस्य मुखमासीद् बाहू राजन्य:कृत:।
ऊरू तदस्य यद्वैश्य पद्भ्यां शूद्रो अंजायत।।

Man is God

This vision of humanity as "The Supreme Being" is the central theme - the heart and soul of our conception of Hindu society as a great nation. It has permeated our way of thinking and given birth to unique ideals of our cultural heritage.

Thus we regard every one of us to be an inseparable part of the Supreme Being. Consequently everyone of us is a measure of His holiness and worthy of service. The very idea of discrimination between one person and another is repugnant to us. Service of man has been accorded the same importance as the worship of God.

There are thousands of hungry and destitute human beings around us, deprived of the basic necessities of life. The tales of their suffering can move the heart of even the most insensate among us. Verily, the Supreme Divinity is He who has assumed the form of the deprived, the down-trodden, the poor, the hungry. God has provided us with this opportunity to redeem ourselves through the service of the suffering humanity. Ram Krishna Paramhamsa calls Him, *"Daridra Narayan"* (God, the Poor and Deprived.).

When we are imbued with this spirit of service, we begin to feel that our riches, wealth and worldly-goods, even though incalculable, do not belong exclusively to us. We are infused with the quality of non-possession. Whatever we have is for the service of society - our living God. We are His instruments. Then our entire life becomes a divine-gift to service. Our Upanishad says (Yajurveda-40-1)

ईशावास्यमिदं सर्वं यत्किञ्चित् जगत्यां जगत्।
तेन त्यक्तेन भुञ्जीथा मः गृधः कस्यस्विद् धनम्।।

(यजुर्वेद, 40-1)

(Ishavasyamidam servam yethkinchit Jagatiyam Jagat
Ten Tyakten Bhunjitham Ma Gridhah Kasyaswidam Dhanam.)

Meaning "This entire universe is infused with the spirit of Divinity. Whatever remains with you after offering to Him is to be used by you. Do not Covet what belongs to others."

It is, therefore, befitting that we strive to strike a balance between individual-dynamism and social obligations. The enterprising individual will have all the freedom to grow and progress, at the same-time the means of producing wealth are shared equally between "the haves" and "the have-nots". To achieve this goal, restriction will have to be put on individuals. The notion of individual liberty will have to be tempered with social-equality. The notion of personal freedom, however noble, can not be allowed to usurp social-good. It has a limited application. To use wealth for personal comforts, to accumulate it for future security and safety is allowed within bounds. It can not be allowed to impinge on the freedom of others. On the other hand every one will have free and uninterrupted access to the fruits of a happy and prosperous existence.

The genius of Hindu-thought prepares its components - Hindu individuals - to adhere to this balanced view of life. It educates them, makes them cultivate this outlook as a true-joy of life. It teaches us that material benefits are not the be-all and end-all of our existence. They have a limited value. They do not lead to eternal bliss on their own. To attain divine-bliss, we will have to rise above mere materialism. Then we will discover the inner meaning of life. Then and then only we partake of that divine-happiness which fills us with its radiance. Then we shall be able to feel that each one of us is in His image - a divine manifestation–capable of partaking the fruits of his creation with all its attendant pleasures of life.

The unity of inner-self

Man is not a two-legged animal and a mere bundle of carnal-desires. An animal does not lead an organised and systematic life, full of love and affection. Man does. With regard to animal instincts in human-beings, it can be stated that man does not kill man because in that instance if 'A' wanted to kill 'B', then some 'C' might appear and kill 'A' himself. Therefore to prevent destruction of each-other, a system has to come into operation. A compromise has to be arrived at. However this does not explain a man's desire to sacrifice himself in the service of other or to share the sorrows and sufferings of his fellow human-beings. Verily, there are instances in the history of mankind, when we find persons who have given up their lives with a smile and with love in their hearts. We have such an example in the person of sage Dadhichi in our ancient literature, who of his own free will donated his body so that a mortal-weapon - Vajra - could be fashioned out of his ribs to enable Indra - King of gods - to destroy the demon, Vritrasur. The sage's abode was a forest. He did not have any worldly-desire or ambition. What inspired him to offer his own life? Let me cite an example from modern times. It happened in Kolkata. Two children were playing in the street. Accidentally they fell into an open-mainhole. A gentleman was passing by that way. He witnessed the incident. Without losing time, with his coat on his body, he jumped into the gutter and saved the lives of the children. Unfortunately he himself was caught in the mire, could not pull himself out and died. What was it that inspired him to give-up his life to save another? Materialism can not fathom this altruism.

There is only one explanation. We are all embodiment of the same living truth, which establishes an inner and able relationship. Hindu-philosophy calls it "Ekatmta" togetherness of souls. We are not bound to, and serve each other through out-ward objects, but because our 'souls' are bound by inner and intimate relationship. In Brihadaranyak Upanishad the sage Yagyanvalkya addresses Maitrey (His wife):

न वा अरे मैत्रेयि पत्युः कामाय पतिः प्रियो भवति
आत्मनस्तु कामाय पतिः प्रियो भवति।

(Na va Arey Matreyi Patyawah Kamya Patiha Priyo Bhavanti, Atmanastu Kamya Patiha Priyo Bhavati.)

Meaning 'O Maitreyi, a wife does not love her husband because he is her husband, but because they are soul-mates. All persons are equal because of the same soul residing in them. Thus at the level of "The Supreme Being" called "Parmatma" by Hindus, we are all equal constituents of Him. At the worldly level, the same supreme soul takes myriad forms.

According to Hindu philosophy of life, this duality in universe is created by the imbalance in the harmonious relationship between the three attributes of life namely Godly (satya), Worldly (Rajas) and Evil (Tamas). If harmony could be achieved between the three attributes, then the universe disappears merging into the Supermind. Therefore, divisiveness, inequality and diversity is ingrained in human nature. We have to live with it, keeping it within limits and weeding out envy, hatered and biased consequences of inequality. This should be our sincere endeavour.

Glorious Hindu Nation - an eternal ideology

We dedicate ourselves to bring glory and greatness to our nation. It is our supreme object. We ought to realise the true significance of this grand notion of the re-emergence of the magnificent Hindu nation for which we aspire and pray daily in our Shakha prayer. The next step is in what way we can contribute to accomplish this prime object of our life and to maintain its continuity.

Ordinarily the achievements in the material world constitute a nation's greatness. No doubt a great nation's material prosperity is a prime virtue. The physical needs need to be satisfied. However, it is only a part of a Nation's glory - not the full-glory. We must ponder over this.

Every nation has its own ethos - its soul, a melody of life of its own. Its forward march is attuned to these ethos. Since hoary past the Hindu nation has preserved its individuality. To us the material-comforts of life accumulation of riches (Arth), satisfaction of physical-desires (kaam) is only a part of life. Our sages pointed out two more goals of life - spiritual urge (Dharma) and deliverance from human-bondage (Moksha). This four-fold objective of life is a special characteristic of Hindu society. It also consists of four stages of life (Brahmacharya, Grihastha, Vanprastha and Sanyas). Thus accumulation of wealth, satisfaction of physical-desires, spiritual duty, merger with the Supreme Being formed the four supreme destinations to be reached through the medium of inner-strength (Pursharth). All the world over Hindu-society has been famous not only for its riches, but more for its spiritualism and divinity. This was the reason that we were regarded as moral and spiritual leaders of the world. Our ultimate goal of life has always been deliverance from human body and merger of soul with the supreme divinity namely 'Moksha'.

If we give up this longing, there will be no difference between us and the animals. It also leads to the conclusion that man's vision of an accomplished life is different from other beings. If the satisfaction of hunger and other physical desires is the test of identity, then men have to be considered at par with animals. Therefore we aim at gratification of the spirit, the fulfilment of spiritual desire. Only then, we can regard our existence as a nation, a splendid achievement. Therefore when we begin to think of our nation's greatness and success, then we refer to not only its capacity to satisfy the physical needs of the individual but also think of his mental make up. By and by we attempt to raise his mental abilities, so that he may reach that stage, where all his rights and requirements as a human-being are given to him, namely he is allowed to merge himself with the Supreme Power. It is, therefore, enjoined that the man must, first, live-up to the spiritual-ideal and then this higher-spiritual state will lead him to the fulfilment of his physical urges.

All encompassing Dharma

When we say that we want to protect Hindu Dharma and also to transform it into a powerful agent, we do not merely refer to its outward form, namely its application in world-affairs. Some of us wear sacred thread, some do not, some worship idols, others do not. These out-word forms are valued by those who believe in them. They are only outer-indicators of our all-encompassing religion. They are not identified with Hindu-religion in all its entirety.

Our definition of 'Dharma' is bi-focal. First, proper reforming and re-fashioning of mind, then bringing together men of diverse nature into one harmonious relationship, aiming at sustaining and maintaining an effective social-organisation.

Let us discuss the first aspect. We know that a man's individuality is a true reflection of his mind and soul. This mind is like that animal who runs after many things. It also possesses the ability to achieve harmony of diverse entities. Ordinarily he does not evaluate things in their true-perspective - what is right? What is wrong? He can stoop to any level to gratify his desires. The possibility that he will raise his faculty of discrimination to a higher-level, is remote. Therefore our minds have to learn how to exercise restrain, how to cultivate self-control and to instill in ourselves nobler values of life. Shrimad Bhagwad Geeta and other sacred books of Hindus speak of this quality giving many instances. There are five regulations (yamas) for our souls and five rules of conduct (Niyamas) for our body. Both are complimentary to each other:

यतोऽभ्युदय निःश्रेयस् सिद्धिः स धर्मः।

(वैशेषिक दर्शन 1.2)

(Yato Abhudaya Nishreyas siddiha so Dharmoh)

(Vaisheshik Darshan. 1.2)

It means 'Dharma' is that attitude of life which helps man exercise control over his desires and enables him to identify himself with the supreme Divine and Eternal Truth while enjoying the fruits of a prosperous world. The second aspect refers to that capability which unifies men and sustains them as a part of society:

धारणात् धर्ममित्याहु: धर्मो धारयते प्रजा: ।

(Dharnat Dharmityahu Dharmo Dharyati Prajah.)

The harmonious togetherness of both these aspects refers to 'Dharma' as the establishment of a well-organised social order in which each and every individual feels in harmony with others and is filled with the spirit of sacrificing for the good of others, for making life of each one of us full of material comforts and happiness and leading us towards evolution of a spiritual life, making us realise the ultimate truth.

This is a common experience that 'wants' are endless. The more you try to satisfy them, greater grows their demand. It is like pouring oil into the fire which leads to higher and stronger flames. Tolstoy has written a very instructive story entitled, "How much land does man require"? There was a farmer who was promised as much land as he could cover on-foot in a dayfrom morning till the setting of the sun. He will have to be back to the spot by the sun set from where he started (in the morning). The desire to grab more and more land made him run so-far that he could not come back by the appointed hour. The super-human effort exhausted him so-much that he fell dead by the time he reached the starting point. Mere seven feet long and two and a half feet wide earth was required to bury him. This is the measure of worth for human beings.

This is also well-established that a man with bundles of unsatisfied desires can never achieve real happiness even if he commands vast resources. In America criminality and mental-illness are reaching frightful proportions. Hundreds of thousands of Americans need sleeping-pills before they go to bed. This phenomenon is a pointer to a serious flaw in their philosophy of life. The lack of attention to spiritual needs of man and giving undue importance to politics and economic needs is responsible for this sad situation. The spiritual urge in man is that basic element which elevates the human soul, and produces equilibrium that provide avenues for attainment of peace and happiness, brings consumation to the soul of man.

Dharma - a way of life

Our view of life (Darshan) has described the highest state of our being and its explicit exposition:

न वै राज्यं न राजाऽऽसीन्न च दण्डयो न दाण्डिकः।
धर्मेणैव प्रजाः सर्वा रक्षन्ति स्म परस्परम्।।

(महाभारत-शांतिपर्व 59-14)

(Na Vai Rajyam na Rajaaseena Cha Dandayo No Dandikoh; Dharma naiva Prajah serva Rakshanti smah Parasparam.)

(There was no kingdom, no king. There was no one to be punished, no punishment. Dharma was the protector. It is through Dharma that each-other's right is protected.)

Dharma (Right-conduct) is the repository of right action, thought and behaviour. It establishes common bonds of life and regulates self-interest, maintains harmony of relationships without any outside influence. If man develops altruism, he will give-up possessiveness and greed and everyone will perform his obligations to society. He will live and act for common good.

Thus Dharma is the truest quality of human life:

आहारनिद्राभ्यमैथुनं च सामान्यमेतत्पशुभिर्नराणाम्।
धर्मो हि तेषामधिको विशेषो धर्मेण हीनाः पशुभिः समाना।।

(हितोपदेश, कथामुख-25)

(Aahar Nidra Bhaya Maithunam cha samanyam Aitat Pashubhiha Naronam,
Dharmo Hi Jeshamodhiko Visheshano Dharmateieenak Pashubhiha Samanak.)

(Hunger, sleep, fear and gratification of sexual-desire are common qualities of man and animal. It is Dharma which distinguishes man from animal. Without it, he, too, joins the category of animals.)

The evolution and blossoming of Dharma in human life, enables man to reach the highest stage of human mind's composite and harmonious existence. This is like cooperation between a blind and a lame man. The lame man can walk sitting on the shoulders of the blind man. The blind man can see, find the right direction, through the eyes of the lame man. Both, thus, compliment each other. This spirit of comradeship removes sourness - a consequence of inequality. The personal good is identified with the social-good. The conflict between them becomes in-operative with the realisation of the existence of the same spirit in both and consequent harmony of relationship and feeling of comradeship. The individual becomes a living component of the social-personality. Individual and society are, thus, complementary to each other, strengthening the bond between each other and achieving social-good.

The natural corollary to above contention is whether the objective of the RSS - re-energising of Hindu nation and organising Hindu-society for such a regeneration - is compatible with the welfare of mankind.

Welfare and well-being of Humanity

It should be made clear at the outset that modern thinkers are not the first ones who spoke of and endeavoured for the welfare and happiness of mankind. The ancient seers and prophets of Bharatvarsha pondered deeply over this important and vital issue long before the advent of modern age. Our hearts had been aglow with the idea of the unity of mankind of a world free from inequality and conflict. From times immemorial we had been striving, praying, "All live happily - free from worries:

सर्वे भवन्तु सुखिन: सर्वे सन्तु निरामया:

(Survey Bhavantu sukhinah, survey santu Naramayah.)
All may live peacefully and happily.

While the western world has not gone beyond the ideal,

'maximum good of the maximum number', Hindu nation expanded the ideal of the welfare and happiness of mankind to include every living organism (animals, birds, plants) in the universe. It had been unimaginable to think of any living-thing in distress. The well-being of the entire universe has been our noble objective.

Today humanity is facing a crisis. The forces of discord and destruction are on the rampage. The mankind is divided and sub-divided into small and big nations. Everyone is trying to feather his own nest. It is a matter of every-day experience that the two groups trying to cater to their own interests often clash with each other. This hampers the growth of fellow-feeling. This makes the welfare of mankind an impossibility.

Modern-day wars and clashes and its attendant suffering and destruction have compelled the thinkers of the world to conclude that narrow-nationalism (and excessive nursing of self-interest to the exclusion of others) is the greatest impendiment in the welfare and well-being of the mankind. They, often, declare that Nationalism ought to be totally obliterated from the world. Communism regards this type of internationalism its basic ideology.

On the other hand there is another school of thought which regards the roots of nationalism so deeply ingrained that it is well-nigh impossible to efface it. The Soviet Union which had discarded nationalism in favour of international Communism soon realised that patriotic fervour inspires a people to sacrifice all for their nation. Its rejection deprives people of that noble spirit which acts as a source of perennial inspiration. Undoubtedly Russia made notable advances in economic affairs in the first flush of revolution. Their five-year plans succeeded to some extent. Gradually the zeal began to subside. Their source of inspiration almost dried-up. To run the factories, the labourers were compelled, using brute-force. When during the second world-war German force's tanks were flinging forward into the Russian territory, crushing everything before them, international Communism failed to inspire the Russian people. Their resistance crumbled.

This opened the eyes of the Russian leaders to the dangers of excessive dose of Communism. They soon realised that the dormant sentiment of nationalism could be re-energised if they go back to their inspiring past, invoke its glorious achievements and heroic deeds. (Leningrad again reverted back to Peterograd). It should be clear now that the concept of sacred motherland, piety, culture and tradition are essence of nationalism. It is these noble and elevating thoughts and ideals which inspire a whole generations to serve the motherland and suffer for it willingly.

Unfulfilled desire

Our firm conviction is that nationalism is that pure and uplifting sentiment which should not be, cannot be destroyed. Therefore, how to reconcile the welfare of the community with the well-being of the mankind? There was a time when imperialism was regarded as panacea of all ills. It was thought, bringing small states under one umbrella, their conflicting interests would be harmonised. Yet the imperialist nation was interested in furthering its own selfish-interests. The nations under it felt suffocated and soon revolted against oppression, exploitation.

"League of Nations", an experiment in international coopration, was started after the first world war. Its aim was to avoid conflicts and wars between different member nations. But within two decades it disintegrated as a result of clashes between nations' over-weening ambitions. It led to the second world-war - the fiercest ever - defacing the earth. After this catastrophic great war "The United Nations Organisation" came into existence. It has failed to create an honourable fellowship between defaulting nations. It has become a battle of wits. The powerful nations have turned it into a debating society and a means to strengthen their over-lordship. It has become a battle ground for warring nations. The ominous shadow of the third-world war is looming large, which might lead to disastrous consequences. The sudden and tragic end of human race cannot be ruled out.

We, thus, see that nations are still not ready to act in

unison in the spirit of comradeships for the good of all. On the other hand the feeling of a separate and exclusive nationalism is getting deep-seated. New countries are appearing on the world horizon.

The whole world is besotted with conflicts and clashes of various kinds and nature among the nations.

In short, the conclusion is inevitable that the sentiment of Nationalism is deep-seated and permanent. All attempts at achieving harmony of interests of various nations have been unsuccessful. On the other hand the world is on the edge of atomic annihilation. What is the way out? The challenge has not been squarely met. No solution is in-sight. All the thinkers of the world are struggling with this problem for long without success.

Togetherness - A natural sentiment binding individuals in a society

We, Hindus, can provide a solution to the problem of conflicting nations. Our key to the solution is not based on materialism. Every experiment, attempt uptill now at finding a solution has been based on principles, beliefs of economic-fundamentals and materialism. But materialism fails to fully explain and comprehend man's inner urge to work for the betterment of humanity and his constant striving towards universal-brotherhood: Why should we love each other? Why should we be filled with sympathy and kindness as quarrelsome individuals. From the materialistic point of view, every one has a distinct personality of one's own - an individuality of his own, mutually exclusive is our own existence - without attachment, without love. Such a materialistic person lacks inner spiritualism - self-control which inspires a person to set a limit to his own self-interest and possessive instinct. Without this noble intention and sacred inspiration, no plan can be implemented effectively, however good the intention. Only, the nobility of inspiration can provide an attractive alternative to power-drunk countries, who regard their self-interest as over-riding. This has been man's destiny till to-day - history's relentless verdict.

As against this self-centred mentality, Hindu seers and philosophers have directed their energy towards a nobler goal than materialism. They delved deep into the mystery of human-nature and discovered the eternal-truth which permeates the universe. All living things are His manifestation. He is called by many names addressed in different ways - Soul, God, Reality, Truth or Nothingness (Shunya). From time to time, we, Hindus, intensely experienced Him and were inspired to strive towards the well-being and happiness of fellow-men. The idea that the soul, which resides in us, also inhabits our fellow human beings, makes us react to the sorrows and happiness of the others as we would react to our own. This pure feeling of brotherhood - like-mindedness born out of the sameness of inner-urges, is the true source of fellow-feeling and unity of mankind. Therefore the extent and limits of the concept of unity of mankind and welfare of humanity are fixed by this awareness of the fundamental unity of souls - awareness of the inner bond that strengthens and secures this intimate inter-relatedness.

The feeling of kindred souls is the only power that can do away with conflicts and dissensions which are inevitable consequences of materialism, broaden human-outlook, reconcile diverse interests and aspirations with the happiness of mankind.

Not extinction, but co-existence

Now we discuss the second question, how can one retain one's distinctiveness, in the midst of complex social-organism? Will it result in dispensing with Nation's own individuality and moulding them into a separate identity wholly self-centred? Or, will it allow a nation to retain its individuality, yet co-existing with others, making collective efforts towards human welfare and achieving a state of happiness.

Our seers have, definitely, shown the path to true happiness. Nations, like individuals, have separate identities. All over the world both nations and individuals have developed their own characteristics and play their own part in affairs of the world. Different social-orders are proceeding towards a goal in their own typical way and according to their own nature. Thus, the disappearance of nation's distiguishing traits will destroy the nature-ordained diversity and pleasures of self-expression. It will block the all-round development of human race, leading to totalitarianism and despotism.

A man attains true-happiness, aims at perfection only through the blossoming of his natural sensibilities. Therefore search for unity and harmony in the welter of individual diversity has been the unique contribution of Indian culture (read Hindu Culture) to world-thought. This distinguishing feature of Hindu-civilisation and culture - unity in diversity - is often cited as an example. It is a product of our sincere efforts to properly, evaluate the principles and view points which strive for unity of mankind, which try to define human progress and happiness. In short we aim at co-operation and co-existence between nations, not the disappearance of their distinctiveness. The world with its bwildering, beautiful variety enchants us. The very idea of stateless one world which dispenses with the distinct characteristics of an individual and a nation is repugnant to us. We dream of a world-state which will come into existence as an organisation of self-sustaining, independent countries. It will keep inter-dependence as well as individual enterprise through a centrally controlled system.

Incomparable Hindu Genius

The sacred task that the RSS has set-about to accomplish is organising Hindu-society in such a way as to maintain its distinct character and genius – as stated in the previous paragraph. It is a clarion call - Mapreface, - not only to reinvigortate the nation but also to aim at integration of different nationalities and welfare of mankind. It is Hindu's noble thought only which can bring about true-unity of mankind and provide a firm foundation to the brotherhood of man. Thus this true knowledge of inner self-human soul provides equal and unincumbered opportunity to every one to progress according to his own nature and also to strive towards a blessed-state for one world.

This knowledge is safe in our hands. We say with conviction that it is a divine gift which destiny has conferred on Hindu society. It is also our sacred duty that we keep this divine treasure of knowledge safe and secure, make it available to other nations for their own benefit. If a person or society forgets this sacred task, it harms both itself and others. Therefore, it is a divine dispensation to Hindus that they perform the holy-task.

What gives us the exclusive authority to be the divine agent? This may appear, in the first instance, self-glorification and self-indulgence, yet this is the established truth. It can be verified. Look at historical events and processes in other countries. History is a witness - generations after generations of Hindu seers, philosophers and sages have arisen to unravel the mysteries of human soul. Delving deep into soul's inner chambers, they discovered this synthetic philosophy of life, empowered it and perfected it. This perennial source of knowledge of inner-self and fulfilment of spiritual urges is there for all to know. It is Hindu Nation's spirit of sacrifice and its experience of centuries of striving. On the other hand the world outside India did not try to fathom this knowledge of 'soul'. They kept themselves busy in the study of physical world and remained out-ward looking. Since their mental-faculties remained glued to the physical and material world, they could not discover the mysteries of inner-world, thus the western world remained ignorant of this knowledge of the self - particularly, 'The Transmigration of Soul'. Inspite of their achievements in unearthing the secrets of the material world, they remained, largely, oblivious of the knowledge and experience of inner-soul.

Non-duality of the living (the personal) and non-living (impersonal)

It was not knowledge for the sake of knowledge - a dull, dry and uninteresting thought - confined to their abodes in the forest - a theoretical exercise - a mere intellectual guess.

It was a dynamic - a living-reality which took our ancestors - traders, scientists, teachers, thinkers-rulers, mendicants - to distant lands with the message of universal brotherhood. Wherever they stepped out, they taught the people spiritual values of life and art of achieving material prosperity. They created in them a feeling of fellowship. Hindu's spiritual empire spread far and wide. They presented themselves as a self-confident, self-reliant, self-empowered society.

Long before Columbus discovered America, we had reached distant lands - China, Japan, Combodia, Malasia, Vietnam, Indonesia and other countries of far-east. In the north, we reached Mangolia and Siberia. Our political power dominated the far-eastern countries for about 1400 years. For more than 700 years the Shailendra-dynasty - an impregnable bulwark against Chinese imperialism, thrived and prospered. For centuries the local people in Siam and Comboja, never felt disenchanted. There were no revolts, no opposition. Had there been even the slightest indication of oppression and exploitation, this could not have been possible. On the other-hand, the local people always felt indebted, had great respect for us and faith in our integrity. They even aspired to spend their last days on the banks of the holy Ganges and die there. (The magnificient monuments like Angkor-wat tell the story in unmistakable terms). This fact stands in great contrast to rivers of blood that flowed when the Christian and Arab armies - addressed as world-conquerors - smashed through countries after countries. The pages of history are full of such bloody records. Even today the culture and civilisation of several nations has Hindu influence writ large on them. They have Hindu names (Sukarna), Hindu appearance (Bali-islands) and feel intense pride in their Hindu-heritage, (Garuda-Lord Vishnu's vehicle is Indonesia's Air-line)]. In Philipines, in the big hall of the central court is a big marble statue of Manu - our first law-giver. The words engraved are "The world's first great and wise law-giver - Manu".

For centuries, such famous, great personalities have taken

birth in our country. Each of them is a shining, brilliant star on the firmament of world-thought. Even today Hindus are producing bright sons like Ram Krishna Paramhansa. He identified himself not only with the suffering humanity; but felt one with all living and non-living beings. There is an instance in his life - he cried with pain when he saw a man lashing cruelly a cow. The marks of the lash appeared on his back. On another occasion, the marks of the cloven-hoofs of a bull grazing in a grassy-field appeared on his chest. Our ancient as well as present day great men have reached a stage where all differences disappear and one identifies one-self with the entire universe-living and non-living both. There is no duality for them. This is their noble message to the world.

Our glorious Heritage

It is sad to note that our present generation is not only disinterested in our glorious heritage, but trying to run it down. It has become a fashion to deride it and to mould our society according to Western norms. To artificially impose ideals and social systems of other countries on us and not to attend to natural growth and progress of our own culture and civilisation will result in our decline. There are signs of this decay. Our disorganised society - Hindu-Samaja - has become a victim of various inimical forces and foreign philosophies - view-points and thought-processes. A nation rendered weak through self-deprecation, rejection of its long-held cultural ethos can never assume the role of a world-teacher. How can a man lead others, who himself lacks self-confidence and leadership qualities.

It is imperative that we should present ourselves as a strong, vigorous and self-sustaining nation-desirous of regaining past-glory. Only then we will be able to impact our splendid knowledge to the world, achieve the unity of the world and fulfil our duty towards the upliftment and betterment of the world. The RSS has taken upon itself this age-old sacred duty and is determined to achieve this national-objective. As a first-step it is striving to unite diverse elements of Hindu-society and to create an invincible force in spiritual as well as material spheres.

Uninhibited Aggrandizement

Some countries boast of being developed and modern nations. The main thrust of their life is material-prosperity. Unfettered competition is the first characteristic of their materialistic outlook. Everybody is busy in adding to his material opulence. The second characteristic of this attitude is what we call "an open society".

Let us consider this concept of uninhibited liberty. The simple and straight meaning of this concept is - everyone is free to enjoy liberty in his own way. There are no limits. There is no control over his physical-desires (Vasana in Hindi), family ties, social-relationships and food-habits. In his writings, conversations, conduct and thinking, this concept of un-restricted freedom of choice is reflected. This excessive freedom, this licentiousness can never lead to true-happiness of mankind. The first and the most powerful ill-effect of this mentality will lead to social-disintegration and anarchy. Western world's basic philosophy of life contained in 'the theory of social-contract' has failed to stem the tide of disintegration, since this theory is a kind of compromise between the clashing interests. When a person starts regarding social-ties only as a contract and not a sacred bond, then it pre-supposes that any one party is at liberty to severe ties if they fail to serve his interests.

This logic - freedom to break the contract-strikes at the very root of social institutions and organisations. "In a disintegrating society individual's well-being suffers" becomes a truism. When we regard society as a living force and individuals its important components then and then only the concept of social-unity can have a lasting influence on individuals' minds. Only then he will be able to control his basic instincts and identify himself with the welfare of society. Hindu way of life endorses this concept of the sacredness of social-bonds.

Materialism

One very important element of the modern society is competition. It is a matter of common experience that the competitive spirit does not remain a healthy spirit over a long period of time. Healthy competitive spirit degenerates sooner or later, it is its nature. It is quite feasible that a person tends to acquire supremacy over his rivals when he aims at outsmarting them in producing more and better in comparison. He tries to run his rivals down. This tendency to score over other competitors has spread to sports and games, too. When in reality, the aim of sports and games is pure physical enjoyment, strengthening the body and inculcating mental toughness. Winning and losing do not matter much. However our observation is that in this sphere, too, the feeling of brotherhood and honest attempts is missing. To win by hook or crook, spoils the spirit of the game. If this is the result of competition in sports, then in matters of selfish-gains, the situation is worse. According to thinkers of the western world, the competition is the surest way to raise the standard of life.

To this western-mind, a man's happiness is achieved through the satisfaction of his sensual desires and so raising the standard of living means accumulating more and more materials for attaining sensual-pleasures. Such a person gets engrossed in materialism at the expense of noble values of life. The intense desire to possess wealth is the next step. For this, acquiring power and authority becomes a necessity. The insatiable thirst for sensual pleasures is not confined to individual's only. It has infested nations - extending beyond boundaries. Stronger nations indulge in exploitation and oppression of weaker nations in order to fill their coffers. This gives birth to conflict and destruction. When this process starts, it has no end. All moral ties get shattered. Human sensibilities ebb away. The quality of life and moral values which sets human beings apart from animal and plant will-disappear. This process of decline in human life and qualities is romanticised as competition, progress, freedom of choice etc.

Play of power and pelf

The rise of American Nation is a terrible reminder of this danger. A large number of Europeans migrated to America in search of 'power and pelf'. Natives of America almost perished as a result of this onslaught. The dreadful stories of persecution, torture, murder by the white people makes one's hair stand on end. The surviving Red-Indians - small in numbers are mere show-pieces. America is not the only example. Australia, South-Africa, south-America etc. are others. Wherever these white people (Europeans) went, they left a trail of murder and destruction. Some time back further tales of inhuman atrocities of South-Americans by whites came to light.

The Communist Soviet Russia and China are no better. The language and form may be different, but implementation of their plans follow the same pattern. Possession and acquisition of riches, attack on weaker nations, exploitation and slaughter of thousands is their in-human game-plan to acquire power and influence.

All these remind us of the description of 'Asuras', evil-forces, in Bhagwat Gita word for word. The so-called civilised and modern Nations are veritable homes of 'Asuras'. The conclusion is inevitable that in the name of "open society" and "spirit of competition", the modern world has pushed the goal of happiness, peace and prosperity of human race a great distance away.

Insatiable worldly desires

It is common knowledge that striving after pleasure and happiness is fundamental to human nature. He aims at life-long happiness, not a temporary one. Like other living-beings, he, too, seeks pleasure through senses. In the beginning the satisfaction of physical needs, mental-urges give him happiness. It cannot be denied that this feeling of satisfaction is experienced only for a short-period. It is transient. The feeling of dissatisfaction gets intense and intenser as man tries to attain more and more physical comforts. His hunger for carnal desires is insatiable. The inadequacy of bodily wants increases in proportion to one's attempts of satisfying them. The more one tries to accumulate material objects, the more dissatisfied one feels at one's failure to gain true happiness. The intenser his attachment to physical-pleasure, the greater is disenchantment. Our scriptures have declared unambiguously: *'Na Jatu Kamaha Karmanamupubhogen Shamayti'.* (Mahabharat, Aadi-Parva-75:50). Carnal pleasures do not come to an end with satisfaction. The sage, Bharthrihari, says "Trishna Na Jeerna, Vayameva Jeerna" (Vairagya Shatak-7). The man grows old, but his thirst for bodily pleasure is unquenchable. This is man's real misfortune he finds himself ensnared into.

Permanent Remedy

This short introspection proves that blissful state is in the inner-self - the soul - and not in any outside agency. Hindu-philosophy presents the sure remedy. A man will leave the musical-concert, however engrossed he may be, if he hears the news of the death of a close-relation. If the music is soulful then the man will be oblivious of his miseries, being deeply immersed in the melody. But the effect is contrary. The same melody which was a source of pleasure, becomes distasteful. It is, thus, clear that the real source of happiness is the inner-self, not material objects which appear to be so. Unknowingly man continues to cling to desire for material-happiness, like that canine who continues to lick a dry piece of bone and feels great pleasure in tasting the blood issuing forth from his own mouth. The same kind of pleasure is felt coming from bodily-pleasures. Obviously the physical-happiness stays for a while and then leads us to dark chambers of disenchantment and unhappiness.

Eternal Bliss

What, ultimately, is the source of bliss - unending, inner happiness? Let us consider. When we are enjoying a particular type of pleasure, its awareness disappears from our minds. Therefore, the true happiness is experienced only by our inner self and not through any material outside.

Therefore, to obtain eternal bliss, we shall have to reach a state of mind where materialism is dispensed with altogether.

It is a matter of common experience that a disturbed mind can never get solace. A calm and quiet state of mind can enjoy real happiness. For peace of mind and a tranquil mental condition, it is necessary that 'wants' of different kinds do not raise their head. The bed of a lake is invisible if its surface is beset with dancing waves. We cannot, also, see our own reflection in it. But as soon as the waves disappear, stillness reappears on the surface. The lake regains its transparency. In the same way an undisturbed mind becomes aware of the inner-most recesses of the human mind. As long as the mind is disturbed - full of worries - its power of awareness of reality is dimmed. As soon as awareness returns, man's mind regains its ability to attain a state of bliss. This means we can reach the state of pure-enjoyment without the help of any outside agency, if we can inculcate in ourselves a calm and peaceful state of mind. (We reach this peace of mind through meditation, state of consciousness).

When man realises that true-happiness is in his inner soul and not outside in the plethora of material objects, he becomes inward-looking and his attachment to outside world will gradually ebb-away (subside). He will be a liberated soul. He will attain the highest state of liberation - peace of mind. Such a man will not hanker after physical-desires, because his longing for material-comforts will have completely subsided. Inner-calm and peace-will radiate his face, since he will have discovered the true source of eternal bliss. This bliss is boundless and lasting. In comparison the physical needs pale into insignificance. This is the state of mind which man ought to aim at. To attain it, he must strive ceaselessly. It is this we call 'Moksha', the highest state of divine-happiness.

The yoga-way

The great sage Patanjali has postulated in his "Yoga-Sutra" that a man, rich and prosperous, of pure character, holy-nature should not be envied, but acclaimed with joy.

Following one's own instincts and inner urges, one should go forward in life. Envy and unhealthy competition should be avoided. A man should wisely acquire wealth, possessing the knowledge of what is right and what is wrong. He should have the wisdom to know when to enjoy, how to enjoy and the proper proportion of enjoyment; otherwise there is the danger that he might deprive others of their share of joy. It may lead to man's losing his sense of balance and destroying his own happiness. Patanjali says that somebody's suffering should arouse in us compassion and sympathy. We should try our best to lessen the sorrows and sufferings of human beings. This noble attitude of mind leads to peace and tranquillity of mind, blessed life and ultimately results in attainment of inner bliss.

The western civilisation's other characteristic is untrimmed freedom, which is antagonistic to co-existence. Our old scriptures describe an age when there was total anarchy, no system of organised societies, no rules of orderly-behaviour, no control. It resulted in fights, conflicts and enmities. Its awful consequences were anxiety, fear, hatred. Then it was felt that rules of conduct and behaviour should be formed to bring order, peace and tranquility in life. Social and moral codes (shastras) were formed.

Modern societies have come into existence two-three centuries ago; hence are a recent products. Therefore any conclusion about various aspects of human life on the basis of their dazzling material prosperity, technological achievements will be hazardous. The right and proper perspective of life can be obtained on the basis of time-tested experiences of human race. A true partnership of divergent views and variegated experiences of mankind through the centuries will bring true-happiness.

Pure and perfect stream of life

Our national life's millions of year's old experience and knowledge reveals that never-ending desire for satisfaction of carnal desires, and wild and uncontrolled competition for their fulfilment, cannot settle the issue. Our ancient-wisdom has taught us to exercise self-restraint and self-control to secure the progress and advancement of society and individual both. To develop self-control, four-fold action is recommended. The four-fold path namely Dharma (Right conduct), Arth (self-interest), Kama (Desire for bodily pleasures) and Moksha (salvation) is designed to achieve a life of self-fulfilment, self-restraint, harmony and equality. An orderly existence reminds us of our duty to both–the individual and the society. Dharma is that inspiration which guides us towards achieving true happiness. It enables us to exercise control over various aspects of life, namely Artha (political and economic activities) and Kama (Desires).

The main object of the awareness of Dharma is to create in us an intense longing for "Moksha" - *salvation of soul.* Moksha is the ultimate aim of our life and our endeavour to attain perfection. All our sensibilities and desires exist for and are regulated by Dharma on one side and Moksha on the other. It is like the river which is kept within bounds by its two banks, but spells disaster if it is flooded and breaking its banks over flows. The same is true of the stream of human life. The stream of life flowing between Dharma and Moksha is an inexhaustible source of a blessed existence for both-man and society. It is this system that maintains balance between peace of mind and satisfaction of carnal-desires. It, ultimately, guides a person to reach the state of 'supreme-bliss. Neither the life nor the body exist for their own sake, but as instruments to subserve a higher purpose, a supreme good which is more mental, ethical and spiritual. The RSS has taken upon itself the task of organising Hindu-society to accomplish the sacred task of fulfilling the dream of universal happiness. The emergence of 'Hindutva' in full bloom is the surest key to open the doors of a healthy, happy and blessed world.

(Shree Gurujee, the propounder of this philosophy, needs no introduction. Well-known educationist and former Deputy Director of education, L.K. Vidyarthy, the translator, is son of great martyr and freedom fighter Shri Ganesh Shankar Vidyarthy's sister.)

2

The RSS Founder, His Legacy And Gurujee

Aanand Aadeesh

THE advent of Rashtriya Swayamsevak Sangh on the auspicious Vijayadashmi Day of 27th September, 1925 was as enigmatic an event as astonishing and exceptional was the idea of its founder Dr Keshav Rao Hedgewar who by no stretch of imagination could be considered at that point of time as one cut-out for such a unique experiment with no parallel in the annals of recorded history. All other organizations before and after him were founded by either an outstanding well known and resourceful personality or by a group of such persons. The Congress, the Communist Party, the Hindu Mahasabha, the Forward Bloc, The Socialist Party, The Kisan Mazdoor Praja Party, the Bharatiya Jana Sangh etc. can be cited as examples in support of this argument. It was therefore natural for the common man to consider RSS as just an assemblage of a handful of youngsters training themselves in martial arts to display their physical prowess and to act as a volunteer force to discipline the crowds on the occasion of festivals or annual sessions and public meetings of political parties.

They knew Dr Hedgewar as an honest, strong built youngman of sterling character and a fiery freedom fighter with some background of underground revolutionary activities, yet it was beyond the wildest of their imagination to find in him the promise of an epoch making greatman.

The seed Dr Hedgewar sowed had no name, no written

constitution, no designated head, no office, no flag and no funds for months, even years together. Yet it caught the imagination of the young and up-coming and evolved in due course of time despite the initial hiccups, handicaps, ridicule and opposition. The credit must go to the iron will power and doggedness of Dr Hedgewar and band of his dedicated young followers. Never given to displaying his intellectual superiority or snobbery, he believed in frank and fair heart to heart dialogue with his colleagues who too felt quite comfortable in his company. Difference in age and education did not stand in their way. They never for a moment realized that they were not equals. After all their leader was extraordinarily ordinary in demeanour and dealings. He was a down to earth pragmatist. Never tense, always relaxed cutting or chewing his betelnuts even in extremely taxing times. They all marched forward hand in hand with no distinction between leader and the follower - all incensed with an aroma of complete camaraderie.

Keshav's Formative Years

Born in a poor, practicing purohit (Priest) family of Baliram Hedgewar on Hindu New Calendar day (Varsh Pratipada), Sunday, April, 1, 1889, Keshav could hardly claim to have inherited anything spectacular. Their ancestral village of Kundkurti stood at the Triveni of Godavari, Vanjara and Haridra rivers. It also signified tri-junction of Marathi, Telugu and Kannada speaking areas. His great grandfather left his ancestral village in Nizam's Hyderabad and shifted over to Nagpur. Keshav was fifth of the six children - three sisters and three brothers. The brothers were well built, tall and dark complexioned. Mahadev, the eldest brother was an athlete, fond of Bhang and short tempered. Keshav had to bear the brunt of his anger quite often. Keshav was also inflicted with small-pox in early childhood and carried his pock-marks for the rest of his life.

Nagpur was ravaged by a severe plague in 1902. Baliram Hedgewar, as a priest, had to perform obsequies of several plague victims in a row for days together. As ill-luck would have it, Keshav's father Bali Ram and mother Revti Bai were both struck by plague, died and were cremated together on the same pyre. Keshav, hardly 13 years old, was orphaned only to bear the thrashings of his brother Mahadev for not preparing Bhang for his consumption. He had to fend for himself in regard to his food, cloth and education. The days when he had to sleep empty stomach and wear torn cloths were not a few. This also seems to have proved to be the single most factor responsible for moulding Keshav into a man of indomitable will-power - indeed a man with muscles of iron and sinews of steel. The fiery streak of a revolutionary had begun to manifest itself in Keshav's activities even at that early stage of his life. The only source of solace and support used to be his distant uncle Abaji Hedgewar, a revenue collector at Ram Payli village, near Nagpur.

Spurned at home, most of Keshav's time was now spent with his friends-engaging himself in long sessions of running races, swimming and discussing the contemporary social and political condition of the country as the boys of his age could comprehend then. Naturally, Shivaji the great was their role model.

Keshav, like many other teenagers of Nagpur, felt drawn towards Dr Munje, the most outstanding public figure of Nagpur then. Dr Munje proved to be a pillar of great strength in Keshav's personal life and a guide of some substance in matters of his patriotic revolutionary activities. Lokmanya Bal Gangadhar Tilak's Nagpur visit of 1908 seems to have put the final seal on Keshav's future course of life - a life wedded to the cause of Mother India's emancipation, a life full of unimaginable perils, untold sufferings and sacrifices. The first test came sooner than expected. Keshav was rusticated from his Neel City Schol for greeting the English inspector of Schools with full throated Vande Mataram. All attempts of the placid well-wishers to wean away Keshav from his chosen path, failed. Even the national school 'Vidya Graha' of Yavatmal, being run under the stewardship of great patriots like Aurobindo Ghosh and Surendra Nath Bandopadhyaya, which Keshav subsequently joined for his matriculation examination, got locked due to the high-handedness of CID officer Cleveland.

Quite undeterred, Keshav appeared for the Praveshika examination of the Calcutta National Vidyapeeth from the Amravati Centre in 1909. Since independence of Mother India was his one and only consuming passion, Keshav completely immersed himself in revolutionary activities. He was in regular touch with a Bengali Revolutionary named Madhav Dass Sanyasi who later on left for Japan, and through him with Anusheelan Samiti of Calcutta which was his next destination now. All this while he saved some money by taking up private tuitions and also teaching in a coaching school. Dr Munje too, in whose house Keshav was staying then, like all other nationalist leaders and revolutionaries of Nagpur, inspired him to join National Medical College in Calcutta. This fact has been corroborated by the well-known revolutionary Ram Lal Vajpayee, who later on settled in America, in the pages of his autobiography - Shri Keshav Rao Hedgewar, the founder of RSS was sent with the financial assistance of Dr Munje and Daji Saheb to Calcutta more with the object of receiving training for revolutionary work under the supervision of Shri Pulin Behari Dass, rather than prosecuting higher studies. Soon after reaching Calcutta, Keshav became a full-fledged member of the Anusheelan Samiti and was given the code name of Kokan, perhaps signifying his Konkan (Maharashtra) connection.

The next few years were momentous. Ominous black clouds of First World War had started hovering over the sky. The young Keshav verily aspired to take advantage of British discomfiture, as and when it occurred. Soon he became quite a familiar young face of Calcutta's public life. Often he even used to attire himself in typical Bengali style. Be it Prabhat Pheries, Boycott Delhi Durbar of 1911, Damodar river floods of 1913 or Makar Sankranti mela at the confluence of Ganga with Ganga Sagar, Keshav was always found in the vanguard of volunteer force. He had the good fortune of receiving filial affection from renowned nationalists like Sir Ashutosh Mukherjee, the illustrious father of Bhartiya Jan Sangh Founder Dr Shyama Prasad Mukherjee, and guidance of Amrit Bazar Patrika Editor Moti Lal Ghosh, besides close company of Pulin Behari Dass, Trailokya Nath Chakravarti, Shyam Sunder Chakravarti and Moulavi Liaquat Hussain. No wonder Imperial Intelligence personnel were always closer on Keshav's heels. It is another matter that on all such occasions he proved too smart for them. He successfully completed L.M.S. in 1914 and after another two years of internship returned to Nagpur in 1916 as a qualified doctor - more than that a recognized fiery freedom fighter.

Ostensably for a change, but in reality to rejuvenate and rededicate himself to the cause of Mother India, Dr Hedgewar stayed with Lokmanya Tilak for a few days at Pune and thereafter visited Shivneri, the birth place of Shivaji Maharaj, his role model.

Freedom Fighter

The Nagpur Congress session of 1920 was a grand success. Dr Keshav Rao, as incharge of Housing and Food sub-committee for the big volunteer force of over 1000 youth, impressed one and all with his amazing organizing capabilities and sense of discipline. In his own way he, alongwith a few other youngmen, tried invain to impress upon the Congress leadership to declare complete Independence as its goal.

With a view to placating the Muslim mind and ensuring their support for the freedom struggle, the Congress openly supported their demand for the restoration of Khalifat in far-off Baghdad (Turkey) which had catastrophic consequences for India and its unity. Soon after followed the non-co-operation movement in which Keshav too participated with full vigour. He was charged with sedition. His brief yet powerful defense speech delivered on August 19, 1921, in the court of Semely was manifestation of his intense patriotic feelings. He thundered - I tried to excite feelings of affection in my people for our poor mother land, I tried to impress upon them the principle that India is for Indians. If an Indian cannot preach these patriotic principles without being seditious and cannot talk plain facts without rousing feelings of enmity between Indians and Europeans here, if things have come to this pass, the Europeans and those who call themselves the government of India should beware that the time for their graceful exit is passing.

A stung Semely sentenced Keshav to one year's rigorous imprisonment with the remark - His statement is more seditious than his speech.

In the evening of July 12, 1922, the day Keshav was released on completion of his jail term, he was garlanded among others, by Moti Lal Nehru, Hakim Ajmal Khan, Dr Ansari, Vithal Bhai Patel and Rajaji who were that day present in Nagpur in connection with the Congress Working Committee meeting.

His mentor Dr Munje's joy knew no bounds in this hour of Keshav's glory who was now one of the front ranking local leaders.

Dr Keshav Rao might not have been terribly impressed with the Congress support to the Khalifat movement, but the fact remains that like many other well intentioned nationalists he too had willingly suspended his disbelief in the communal minded Muslim leadership of Mullahs and Maulvis and underestimated their capacity to misguide their uneducated poor religious brethren. Otherwise he would not have participated in the Congress movement. Swami Shradhanand's speech from the pulpit of Delhi's Jama Masjid should be sufficient to illustrate this longing of a large section of national leadership in the interest of Hindu-Muslim unity to frustrate the dirty designs of the foreign rulers who had for long been successfully playing their card of 'Divide and Rule'. Ironically only Mohammad Ali Jinnah, who was a nationalist then, had opposed this move to support the restoration of Khalifat and Congress support to this demand. Subsequent broad day murder of the same

Swami Shradhanand in Delhi's Chandni Chowk proved how venomous the cobra of Muslim communalism was.

The Khalifat Movement was foredoomed to be a failure. For one thing, Turks under the dynamic leadership of modern minded Kamal Pasha and the Arabs, in the hope of getting rid of Turkish overlordship, rejoiced at the demise of the institution of Khalifa. For another, fanatic Indian Muslim leadership - political as well as religious - got hysterical over the issue and engaged itself in rousing the dormant communal feelings of Muslim masses. The support of the nationalist leadership to the Khalifat cause only fanned the flames of this fanatism. The foreign rulers could not ignore this civil strife like situation without risking their own safety and security.

The frustrated Muslim leadership provoked its followers to indulge in unprecedented violence against hapless Hindus. In 'The History of the Congress' Dr Pattabhi Sita Ramayya admits - the bane of the year (1924) was the outbreak of communal troubles in various places, specially at Delhi, Gulbarga, Nagpur, Lucknow, Shahjahanpur, Allahabad, Jabalpur and, worst of all, at Kohat. The Kohāt riots really broke the backbone of India.

Disenchantment

If greatman like Gandhiji admitted his blunder and went on 21 days fast, up-coming youthful freedom fighters like Dr Hedgewar felt cheated and totally disenchanted with this policy of appeasement.

A new slogan of Pan-Islamism got afloated and the slogan of 'Allah-ho-Akbar' began to rent the air. Hindu temples were desecrated, cows were openly slaughtered and women were unabashedly molested. Instead of remorse, they regaled. The Servants of India Society report on the Moplah atrocities concluded - One thousand Hindus were killed, twenty five thousand Hindus were forcibly converted and thousands of Hindu women were dis-honoured and abducted. Even Jawahar Lal Nehru in his autobiography admitted - Even

Western educated Muslims who had no genuine religious feelings began to grow beard and observe external Islamic rituals... Many a Congressmen was a communalist under nationalist cloak.

Nagpur was no exception. All of a sudden in 1923 they had started objecting to the playing of music in front of Masjids. Anti-social elements amongst the Muslims seemed to have been given a free hand. Their leadership always looked the other way round and Hindus as usual were given to stupor. Ram Lal Vajpayee has described the pathetic situation thus - In a town with lakhs of people an ordinary Pathan from Kabul enters, beats up the helpless poor and goes away with his loot unhindered... slums have sprung up all around the Hislop College. Drunken Muslim rowdies have made it their habit to abuse us when we pass that way to reach the college. We do not react. An arrogant British soldier kicks a poor man in front of thousands and walks away. No body reacts. When educated people like us go to the gymnasium for body building, others look upon us with contempt. One is really at a loss as to what could be done with such a society.

In the Belgaon session of the Hindu Mahasabha in 1924 Pandit Madan Mohan Malviya commented that but for the weakness and fear enveloping the Hindus, many Hindu-Muslim clashes could have been averted. Similarly Swami Shradhananda felt that the only solution to the problem was for the Hindu leaders to organize their own society.

Destiny seems to have designated Dr Hedgewar to accomplish this seemingly impossible task. Not that no attempts were made in this direction before. Hindu youths had increasingly started taking interest in physical exercises and wrestling as a result of which Akharas (Gynamsia) in large numbers were sprouting up almost all over the country. Voluntary organizations like Mahaveer Dal and Arya Veer Dal - youth wings of Sanatan Dharma Sabha and Arya Samaj respectively - were being activated. But their presence was visible mostly during the festival days and Melas like

Kumbh at Haridwar and Prayag. Even Akharas were functioning on caste lines.

Even as Dr. Hedgewar's mind was engrossed in searching a lasting solution to the problem, he kept himself abreast with the on-going socio-political activities, particularly in and around Nagpur. He was closely associated with Dr Munje's brain child - Rifle Association and other revolutionary activities. Veer Savarkar's analytical - historical treatise 'Hindutva', with its inspiring and lucid exposition, struck sympathetic chord in his heart. But this in no way diminished his sincere regards for Gandhiji. He knew Gandhiji belonged to that rare breed of greatmen who practised what they preached. And that alone was enough to place Gandhiji on a much higher pedestal. In fact Dr Hedgewar himself belonged to this exalted class.

Analysis

By now Dr Saheb had drawn his own conclusions. Although he was closely associated with both the revolutionary and the liberal Congress movements, yet he was conscious of their limitations. Revolutionaries deserved all praise for their intense patriotic feelings and readiness to sacrifice their all for the freedom of India. Yet they were vulnerable to certain pitfalls - the unmatched might of the British rulers, lack of unity among their ranks, Resource crunch, presence of some black-sheep and absence of consistency in their ranks.

The liberal Congress rank and file on the other hand were a house divided amongst themselves, both vertically as well as horizontally. There was total absence of discipline and disregard for cleanliness in public life was all too apparent in their personal conduct. They made compromises with all sorts of forces and were prone to black mail by the bully. Yet it had mass appeal, all India presence and towering leadership.

Dr Hedgewar wished to invent an instrument (organization) which could separate chaff from the grain.

The country, he felt, needed the best of both - Revolutionary spirit as well Congress' liberalism - minus their shortcomings. He was in search of a panacia for all the ills the nation was suffering from. Difficult, yet not impossible, he thought.

And he succeeded. Rashtriya Swayamsevak Sangh was the Amoghastra (invincible weapon) he invented.

But Dr Hedgewar's commitment to the cause of country's freedom was so abiding and uncompromising that even after he had founded the Rashtriya Swayamsevak Sangh, he continued to take active part not only in all the Congress lead movements but also in underground Revolutionary activities.

After considerable consultations and deliberations with his friends, Dr Hedgewar set the following objective before the Rashtriya Swayamsevak Sangh:

Hindus must be organized to be able to stand up to anti-social and anti-national elements - whichever class or community they hail from and be radicalized to hasten the departure of the foreign rulers.

In reality both the evil forces - separatist communal and anti-national elements among Muslims and the cunning English rulers were intertwined as each one was supporting and sustaining the other one.

Dr Hedgewar knew that the hype of superior prowess and dare devilry of these two oppressors was a mere myth. All the bully's behave the same way as long as they are not challenged. The malady lay in lack of unity and self confidence among Hindus who as a consequence of prolonged period of slavery and oppression had become oblivious of their glorious past and brave deeds. Internal dissensions and mutual acrimony based on caste considerations was the curse eating into the vitals of our society. Thus, the only course of redemption, Dr Hedgewar realized, was to awaken the Hindu conscience and imbibe in them the spirit of unity and courage. It was this challenging task of re-charging and re-animating the Hindu society that Dr Hedgewar accepted.

According to him Hindu did not denote to any specific mode of worship; it is way of life, a value system. Hindu symbolizes the great perennial Indian cultural and civilizational stream manifest through different schools of thought propounded and propagated by our great philosophers like Patanjali, Kanad, Gautam, Valmiki, Vyas, Buddha, Mahaveer, Shankaracharya, Guru Nanak, Kabeer, Ravi Dass, Chaitnya Mahaprabhu, Swami Vivekananda, Maharishi Dayananda etc. Hindutva is inclusive not exclusive and therefore, provides the best basis for the genuine Commonwealth of religions and is synonimous with Humanism.

RSS is born

A little more than a dozen youngmen assembled in Dr Hedgewar's mud-house on the auspicious occasion of Vijayadashmi, 1925 to launch an organization with the sole purpose of giving a new and desirable direction to the prevailing depressing social situation and prepare them for winning a prolonged war of Independence with peaceful means if possible. If not, by whatever means available. The Swayamsevaks would constitute the core group of this movement.

Prominent among the participants, besides Dr Hedgewar, were Balaji Huddar, Bhauji Kawre, Vishvanath Kelkar and Annaji Sohni. All of them were enthusiastic, public spirited, disciplined, selfless and dedicated youngmen. As for celebrities, there was none. And resources! No resources. Not even a pen, paper or pencil. Yet the capital they had in the form of Dr Hedgewar's sterling character, courage, exceptional organizing acumen, self-sacrificing nature, honesty and integrity stood them in stark contrast.

In the initial stage, there were no daily Shakhas, the members were required to attend some Vyayamshala (Gymnasium) regularly and meet for discussion and consultations on Sundays. In due course of time, they began to assemble daily, for the first few months in a primary school and later on in Mohite-ka-wada. Slowly but steadily was evolved the threefold schedule - physical, mental, intellectual and emotional. The Swayamsevaks used to assemble at an appointed time and place for one hour daily. After physical exercises and plays they would sit in a circle and discuss about the social and national problems.

Martand Rao Jog imparted physical training where as Dr Hedgewar and Kelkar sharpened their intellect. A prayer - a hybrid of Marathi and Hindi verse was also adopted. The uniform too was the same as that of the Nagpur Congress Session's volunteer force in 1920 - Khaki shirt, knee long Khaki shorts and Khaki cap with two buttons.

In fact, Dr Hedgewar adapted several techniques adopted from different organizations like Bharat Scouts and Guides, Military, Akhadas and other voluntary out-fits.

The name Rashtirya Swayamsevak Sangh was approved on April 17, 1926 and Dr Hedgewar was duly designated Sar-Sanghāchalak the same year on December 19. The first Officers' Training Camp was held in May 1927 where in the number of participants was not even one score (It was seventeen to be exact). The Gurudakshina function was introduced in 1928 and the offerings totalled 84 rupees (yes, rupees eighty four only). The founders mud-house was all that could be called RSS office, if any, till 1930.

Thus slowly and steadily, yet surely, the Sangh was evolving as it was growing.

Extraordinary Organizer

Dr Hedgewar's organizing capabilities were now coming to the fore. He was a living example of one lamp lighting up another and yet another, making a long row. One inspired soul seemed to inspire his compatriots. His rapport with his comrades was very warm and intimate. He evinced keen interest in their studies and personal problems. Their interest was uppermost in his mind. His own transparent life, blameless character, self-effacing nature and commitment to the cause endeared him even to those who were outside the Sangh orbit. Verily he was an Ajatshatru. He had an aura of magnetic touch around him. Otherwise he was always conspicuous by his commonness. Not many could believe that they were living with a Yug Bhagirath determined to change the course of history. He had decided to remain a life long celibate and not to take up any full time job or professional practice. His preoccupation with his social and organizational responsibilities did not allow him such luxuries. Even then to meet his bare necessities of life he took up some part time jobs - sometimes coaching work, sometimes medical examinership attached to an Insurance Company. But this allowed him only to meet bare necessities of life. Poverty, his proverbial bosom friend never betrayed him all through his life.

This did not, however, deter him from participating and helping in revolutionary activities. His help in arranging shelter for Sardar Bhagat Singh's friend Rajguru at Bhayyaji Dani's Farm at Umrer is one of several such examples. Simultaneously he participated in Jungle Satyagraha (Local version of Gandhiji's salt Satyagraha) on July 21, 1930 alongwith Appaji Joshi, Dada Rao Parmarth and several others. He was sentenced to nine months rigorous imprisonment and was released from jail in 1931.

By now the network of Shakhas had already spread not only in several neighbouring towns and a few villages of Nagpur, but also in a few far off places of Vidarbh and Marathwada. The Vijayadashmi function of 1932 witnessed its first impressive parade by some 1200 Swayamsevaks in uniform which provoked the British Governor-in-Council to issue orders on December 15, 1932, prohibiting government employees from participating in RSS activities. Again it goes to the acumen of Dr Hedgewar that the move was assailed in the assembly by members of all shades of opinion.

The Wardha District winter camp of December 23-25, 1934 stands out as a mile stone in the annals of early RSS history for two reasons - First some 3000 Swayamsevaks stayed together for three days and participated in all the programmes from morning till evening. The camp was held at Seth Jamna Lal Bajaj's Farm. Second, Incidentally Gandhiji was also staying in a near by building and he came to visit the camp along with Mahadev Desai and Meera Ben at 6 a.m. on December 24 and was highly impressed by the discipline and total absence of any sort of caste bias among the Swayamsevaks. The next day Dr Hedgewar, accompanied by Appaji Joshi and Bhopatkar called on Gandhiji in his Ashram and exchanged views. Gandhiji's remark - I thought I was the only organizer in India, but there is another and he is Dr Hedgewar - gladdened the hearts of RSS founder and his colleagues who now threw themselves into RSS work with added zeal and enthusiasm.

However, the time at the disposal of Dr Hedgewar was short, the task was stupendous and the means minimal. What was in abundanace was his resolve and readiness to offer each drop of his blood to realize his cherished goal. Naturally, thence onward there was steady growth of RSS shakhas.

The Swayamsevaks were ever-ready whenever the society was confronted with any challenging situation. Dr Hedgewar saw to it that the Swyamsevaks did not involve themselves in any petty personal or political controversies. He deliberately kept them aloof from politics and, thus, succeeded in getting support from varied sections of the people. At the same time he was informally yet definitely preparing future pracharaks from amongst his more promising young Swyamsevaks. Baba Sahab Apte, Bhayyaji Dani, Dada Rao Parmarth, Bala Saheb Deoras, Eknath Ranaday, Yadav Rao Joshi, Moropant Pingle, Digamber Paturkar and later on Madhav Rao Mule, Bhau Rao Deoras, Vasant Rao Oak and Abaji Thatte (the list is not all inclusive) constituted the first team of pioneers who in due course of time spread the movement in all the nooks and corners of the country.

Dr Hedgewar deputed ten of these young Swayamsevaks to Northern India for further studies alongwith Shakha work. Shakhas started functioning in a few big cities like Delhi, Lahore, Kashi, Pune, Patna and Calcutta. With the spread of Shakha network, spread the name and fame of Dr Hedgewar; his own aversion for the same notwithstanding.

By about the same time Gurujee Madhav Rao Golwalkar returned to Nagpur from Sargachhi Ashram, since Swami Akhandanandji had passed away and Gurujee, in the absence of his Deeksha Guru and his guidance, found no point in staying in his Ashram. Instinctively Dr. Ji and Gurujee now felt more and more drawn towards each other. Through that, naturally, Gurujee came closer to RSS. When in 1938 Dr. Hedgewar set out on a visit to Lahore, he took Gurujee along with him and asked him to address one of the meetings of Swayamsevaks there. In fact, conscious of his failing health Dr Ji had started delegating more and more of his responsibilities to Gurujee thereafter. That year the route march by more than 3000 swayamsevaks in full uniform in Nagpur and presided over by renowned Punjab Hindu leader Dr Gokul Chand Narang confirmed that RSS had come to stay.

To meet the demands of multiplying Shakhas and expanding RSS work all over the country, a 10 day long meeting of leading RSS leaders of yore was held at Sindhi in February 1939. Prominent among them were Dr Hedgewar, Gurujee, Appaji Joshi, Bala Saheb Deoras and Krishna Rao Mohirir. Many of the RSS conventions and practices were reviewed and revised. Operational and procedural changes were also approved and introduced. It was in this conclave that the present Sanskrit prayer was adopted. Shri Gurujee played an important role in these deliberations and his imprint was quite discernable. Dr Hedgewar too was all praise for him and felt relieved after the conclave. On 13th August, 1939 (Guru-Poornima Day) he announced the appointment of Shri Gurujee as the Sarkaryawah (General Secretary) of RSS.

Suddenly the international political situation deteriorated and the Second World War broke out on 1st September, 1939.

On the national scene, in its Lahore Session of 1940, the Muslim League became all the more belligerant and aggressive. It openly declared that they would carve out their own Islamic state of Pakistan by all means and manners.

That was also the year when over 1400 Swayamsevaks representing almost all the provinces of the country participated in the month long officers' training camp of RSS in Nagpur. It was the beginning of resurgent Hindu Nation's response to the communal anti-national Muslim League and its foreign ruler patron. A few years more, and RSS would be strong enough to face the twin challenges, young Swayamsevaks thought.

They would not only boldly thwart the evil designs of Muslim League aimed at the vivisection of Mother India but would also throw out the colonial powers - lock, stock and barrel!

Whom God loves......

God, however, willed otherwise. Dr Hedgewar's physical health was causing great concern. He could make to the camp only once and could speak hardly for a few minutes with signs of great fatigue and discomfort all too visible on his face. He was running 103 degrees temperature.

Two of the leading lights of national status to call on Dr. Hedgewar during his last few days were Dr Shyama Prasad Mukherjee, that illustrious son of illustrious father Sir Ashutosh Mukherjee and Netaji Subhash Bose, the tallest of all Indian revolutionaries.

Dr Shyama Prasad Mukherjee who later on founded the Bharatiya Jan Sangh, called on Dr Hedgewar on May 20, 1940 and requested him to depute 100 RSS Pracharaks to help organize Hindu Raksha Dal so that the hapless innocent Hindus could repulse the horrendous atrocities being perpetrated on them by the fanatic Muslims in Bengal.

Netaji Subhash Chandra Bose came to see Dr Saheb on June 20, 1940, the night before Dr Hedgewar breathed his last. Perhaps Netaji wanted to share his future plans with him and if possible, evolve a common strategy for Country's independence. Sadly, Dr Hedgewars condition was precarious and he was in an unconscious state. Netaji Subhash, his eyes shut, stood there for a few minutes in deep silence and anguish. The sole witness to this spectacle was a serene and saintly looking scholar - Gurujee Madhav Rao Golwalkar who too stood in silence for what felt like forever, waiting for some miracle to happen and wake up Dr Hedgewar. But that was not to be. In a voice chocked with emotion Netaji Subhash expressed his grief to Gurujee who like his Shadow was always by the side of Dr Saheb during his days of illness. With folded hands the rarest of rare Indian revolutionaries offered his parting Namaskar to Dr Hedgewar and left on his onward journey to fame and immortality. And so did Dr Hedgewar, the rarest of rare organizers of modern India, as he breathed his last the next morning at 9.27 a.m. of June 21, 1940, leaving behind his imperishable foot prints on the sands of time and thousands of bereaved Swayamsevak followers and friends in grief, yet in no way grounded. Dr Hedgewar's legacy was there to shine their perilous path and so was Shri Gurujee, the newly nominated Sar-Sanghchalak to complete the unfinished task of organising Hindus to take Mother India to the pinnacle of eternal glory -

परम् वैभवन् नेतुमेतत् स्वराष्ट्रम्.....

Comes Madhav

Like his mentor the new Sarsanghchalak too belonged to a very ordinary lower middle class family of practising priests whose original surname was Padhye and who had shifted to Nagpur after migrating from Knokan via Paithan. Madhav was born on Phalgun Krishna Ekadashi (Vijya

Ekadashi), Vikram Samvat 1962, i.e. February 19, 1906 A.D. and was the only surviving child out of nine children born to his parents. His father Sadashiv Rao Golwalkar was a lower division clerk in the Post and Telegraph Department but later on became a primary school teacher in a most backward village of Chhattisgarh. Madhav was naturally the pupil of his mother Taiji's eyes who, though unlettered, was a very pious house wife and an ideal mother capable of inculcating healthy and desirable Sanskars in her son. Once in Pune Shri Gurujee had recalled - I used to be woken up early in the morning. My mother used to busy herself with house hold chores, but at the same time chant Stotras (Hymns) and the names of gods. Tai's melodious voice would fill my ears and heart. What a deep and noble impact those melodious lines sung in the peaceful and elevating moments of the morning must have made on my young mind!

Many of the fine personality traits - inner urge for knowledge, razor sharp memory, punctuality, purity of heart, dedication to duty, readiness to work and suffer for others, forbearance etc, that got manifest in his later life, were quite discernable even in his early childhood days and must have been the result of the excellent samskars he imbibed from his poor but cultured and caring parents.

Madhav passed his High School examination from Jubilee High School at Chandranagar in 1922 and Intermediate from Hislop College, Nagpur in 1924. Subsequently he passed his B.Sc. in 1926 and M.Sc. in Zoology in 1928 from Benaras Hindu University. It's scenic surroundings, well equipped library, vast and wide play grounds and gymnasium and a rich library stacked with over one lakh reference books on practically all subjects, provided extremely favourable opportunities for the all round development of young Madhav Rao. Evidently the sylvan surroundings of the Kashi Vishvavidyalaya left lasting impressions on his young mind. He had ample opportunities to quench his insatiable thirst for knowledge on the fount of that treasure-trove of treatises on Indian scriptures, oriental and occidental philosophies, science, literature, history of peoples of different countries and above all biographies of greatmen of all ages, regions, and religions. The life and works of the great saint, savant and sentinel of Hindu culture Swami Vivekananda fascinated his imagination the most during that prime of his youth. He seemed attuned more to a life wedded to spiritualism rather than a life of materialism. As early as on February 28, 1929, in a long letter written to his friend Babu Rao Telang, the tempest raging in the young mind of Gurujee surfaces in all its fury and is quite revealing - Now I am trying to cultivate a sense of renunciation in every atom of my being even while living in the ordinary world, sharing in the sorrows of a common man's life and discharging all its responsibilities with diligence. Now I shall not go to the Himalayas, rather Himalayas shall come to me, its serene silence will dwell with in me. Now it is not necessary to go anywhere for attaining that serenity.

Madhav Rao's brief stint with the aquarium of the fisheries department in Chennai (Madras), three years (1930-33) on the faculty of Benaras Hindu University, graduation in Law and even undertaking coaching work and practice as an advocate for a while and then suddenly in 1936 disappearing from his house without telling anybody and joining Sargachhi Ashram in far off Bengal as a disciple of Swami Vivekananda's Gurubhai Swami Akhandanand, all indicate about the state of mental turmoil young Madhav Rao was passing through. Married and settled life of an ordinary house-holder was out of question. While in Sargachhi Ashram, he reflected and meditated a lot and practised yogic exercises to be adept in Dhyaan (Meditation), Dhaarna (concentration) and Samaadhi (state of realization). This mastery over art and science of Yoga kept him in good stead all through his later life. But he was not yet definite about the direction and destination of his life. Nor was he clear about the mission of his life. On the one hand, Himalayas with all it's loftiness, solitude and serene heavenly climes beckond him and on the other echoed in his ears perpetually the clarion call of Swami Vivekananda to consider only Mother India and her sons and daughters as the deity worthy of our worship in the present times. Let us live, and die for them. That done, all other gods will be pleased to shower their choicest blessings on us in full measure.

The New Sarsanghchalak

On his return from Sargachhi Ashram, subsequent upon the demise of his Deeksha Guru Swami Akhanandanandji in January, 1937, Gurujee had prolonged meetings and frank discussions with Dr Hedgewar who as always, implored and emphasised upon him to take a dispassionate view of his future course of action and ultimately succeeded in prevailing upon him that the right pursuit for a young scholar with a spiritual bent of mind like Gurujee could only be service of Mother Land rather than attainment of Moksha (Individual salvation), which after all, concerns only the self, the 'I'. Does not Geeta teach us that true Karmayog has to be Nishkaam (non-selfish and impersonal)? The appeal, more than the argument, emotional yet logical worked miraculously well. Once convinced about the soundness of RSS ideology and effectiveness of its methodology, Gurujee made RSS his life's mission and never ever looked back or wavered from his chosen path even for a fraction of a second till his last breath. He lived and died for the cause. It must have been a Bheeshma Pratigya indeed! Gurujee used to wonder - I never knew how Doctorji could enter my sternly rational and inaccessible mind. He did not particularly impress as a scholar, but his sheer truthfulness and utter sincerity gripped the mind... Right from the beginning my inclination was towards both - spirituality on the one hand and the task of national regeneration on the other. During my stay in Benaras, Nagpur and Calcutta I realised that if I stayed with the Sangh, I would be able to do this work more effectively. So I dedicated myself to the Sangh work. I think what I am doing is in consonance with Swami Vivekananda's philosophy, guidance and method of work. No Other great personality's life or teaching has influenced me so much. I believe by doing the Sangh work, I am carrying out only his work.

But the story does not teminate here. It only begins. Despite his scholarship, sagacity and sincerity, Gurujee at the time of his nomination to the exalted position of Sarsanghchalak was only 33 years old youngman, literally quite unknown outside the small RSS fraternity. He was not even remotely associated with the current political / public activities. No wonder, with in a few days of Dr Hedgewar's passing away, efforts were made by a few so-called RSS sympathisers and even by a handful of ambitious and envious seniors to raise controversy to create confusion so as to provoke rank and file not to accept Gurujee's leadership. But the vast majority of senior colleagues and the overwhelming majority of grassroots swayamsevaks nipped the evil in the bud. In the homage offering ceremony on the thirteenth day of Dr Hedgewar's death, Shri Gurujee was officially declared as the new Sarsanghachalk as per the wishes of the departed soul. Dr. Hedgewar's aged uncle Shri Abaji Hedgewar's emotional speech silenced the critics into numbness - ndeed our Doctorji has not left us at all; we still see him in the form of Shri Madhav Rao Golwalkar. Now onwards, every directive from him is to be obeyed as-if it was Doctorji himself. Whatever doubts and misgivings remained harboured in the minds of Gurujee's detractors, got evaporated after listening to his forceful speech, punctuated with extreme humility, but full of rare aplomb - Doctorji has entrusted to me the onerous responsibility of the Sarsanghchalak. But this is verily the Vikramaditya's throne. Even if a rustic boy sits on it, he will dispense only an even handed justice. He who cannot bow down to a greatman like Doctorji can achieve nothing in his life. I feel very proud to offer my worship to such a great soul... However, real worship is to try to become like the object of worship itself - *Shivo Bhutva, Shivam yajet* - to worship Shiva is to become Shiva himself. That is the special feature of our Dharma.

Gurujee left no one in doubt about his resolve when he declared - Our organisation is an impregnable citadel. Doctorji has made its ramparts so srong that those who seek to breack them, will have their own heads broken. He remained true to his Sanskrit quote and for the next 33 long momentous years he continued to suck out all the poison that had accumulated in our national life in the form of disunity, disharmony, dishonesty, inequality, casteism, regionalism and above all selfishness, virtually paralysing our entire social fabric.

Still the task ahead demanded Herculean efforts to realise Dr Hedgewar's dream of organising Hindu society into an impregnable and invincible force capable of defeating the designs of anti-national and communal elements and winning back her lost freedom. What Dr. Hedgewar achieved in a short span of 15 years of RSS existence was a tribute to the founder's superb organising skills and patriotic zeal. What he bequeathed was a beautiful yet very tender and nimble sapling. Outside the three provinces of Madhya Bharat, Vidarbha and Maharashtra, the RSS presence was at best symbolic. The total number of regular shakhas stood at about 350 and the Swayamsevaks accounted for about 20,000-25,000 souls including about 250 activists - most of them teenagers or in their early twenties. Even Shri Bala Saheb Deoras, who was considered as one of the front ranking activists then and later on succeeded Shri Gurujee as Sarsanghachalak, was hardly 24 years old school teacher. The present day well entrenched Pracharak system also had not been properly institutionalised. The resources too were as meagre as worthy of any mention. What to talk of jeep or a motor car, there were hardly any motor cycles with the whole of organisation. Those were the days when a cycle was considered a luxury, a telephone connection an extravaganza. Shri Gurujee himself, when he was sent to Calcutta for a month for RSS work, was given princely amount of Rs. 20 (Rs. twenty only) to pay not only for both ways railway fare but also for meeting his lodging, boarding and local travelling expenses. And Lo! on his return to Nagpur he deposited back 3 paise that remained unutilised. The Swayamsevaks by and large belonged to economically poor or at best lower middle class families. Once, in his rare moments of recapitulation of utter lack of financial resources those days, Shri Bhau Rao Devras, who is credited with spreading the RSS net-work in UP, confided with the writer of these lines - 'only if our organisation and Swayamsevaks could be in a position to arrange Rs. 5000-7000, Doctorji's life could have perhaps been saved by providing him with better medical care and facilities. By God's grace, the RSS with all its lofty ideals and great goal was running on a pittance, and that too due to poor swayamsevaks' willing contributions.

Making of a Gurujee

But the limited sweep of the organisation, lack of resources and his own anonimity did not dis-hearten Gurujee. In fact he looked to the brighter side - the unblemished inspiring personality, exemplary courage of conviction and sterling character of Dr. Hedgewar, committed and dedicated band of colleagues, discipline of Swayamsevaks and flawless ideology and efficacy of unique organisational methodology. Gurujee knew what he had and what he had to attain, where he stood and where he had to reach and what he had inherited, and what he had to bequeath.

Above all he, more than anybody else, was conscious of his own shortcomings and limitations. Like all perfectionists, he could not brook laxity or incompetence on anybody's part. He was short tempered and given to sharp-tongue. He expected all others to be above board in their dealings as he himself was. However, he soon realised that this detracted people rather than attract. It did not take him long to make amends and acquired sweet and loving disposition so very necessary for building up a team of dedicated followers, without compromising with his fundamental principles. Soon he transformed himself into a fountain of love and offection whose laughter and transparent personality had a magic effect on his followers and opponents alike. He resolved to take only minimum vegetarian meals necessary to keep body and soul together and that too only once a day at lunch time, acquired complete control over his sleep, hardly ever enjoying sleep for more than 3-4 hours in 24 hours. Earned no money, no property, not even a bank account, no family-life, infact no personal aspiration and ambition. For the next 33 years that he lived, railway compartment was his abode (Gurujee toured all over the country at least twice in an year), Swayamsevaks his family and Bharat Mata his goddess, the object of his daily worship. A complete metamorphosis. A hermit, a Maharishi in spotless white; a man of destiny who became synonymous with the conscience of the concept of Hindu Nation. Only a namesake of RSS founder Keshav, Madhav rose to the heights of Yogeshwar Krishna by dint of his selfless service, sacrifice and self control.

Consolidation and expansion of the shakha work was Gurujee's prime concern. After a careful thought, a detailed plan to prepare a nation wide network of full time Pracharaks exclusively devoted to the Sangh work, was drawn and implemented. His highly sentimental speech delivered on the Varshpratipada Day of 1942 touched the chord in the hearts of patriotic young swyamsevaks. The speech made in the extremely volatile national and international situation, is not only an index of Gurujee's anxiety over the limited strength of the organisation, but also a highly emotional out-pouring from the deepest recesses of the heart of a man in a hurry. He exhorted - It is our great fortune that we are born in these dangerous times which we must view as most auspicious. The golden moment that arrives in the history of a nation after centuries, is coming our way. If we sleep at such a crucial hour, no one would be more unfortunate than us. He only achieves immortal fame who stands up four square in the face of adversities. Let us, therefore, face the present adversity with serenity and determination. Consider it as an excellent opportunity to bring out the best in us. Rejuvenation of a fallen nation should be possible at the most with in one generation. But what is our condition? Even after 17 long years of strenuous efforts, our work has remained far too limited. The Sangh stands by the truth and it will certainly succeed and redeem its plege. Once we give our word, we shall have to prove its worth even if we have to sacrifice ourselves in the process. So keep aside all your thoughts about family and your personal fortunes for a period of at least one year. Adopt the life of treading on a razor's edge. Be prepared to be hard to yourself. Concentrate all your time, all your thought and all your energy on this very task. We have to be vigilant about this and steel ourselves for achieving the success of our cause.

Expanding Horizon

Young, dynamic and inspired swyamsevaks in hundreds responded to this appeal and went to far off places to spread the shakha network. There was a phenomenal increase in the RSS strength - qualitatively as well as quantitatively. In the 1942 movement period shakhas sprang up all over the country, more so in the northern provinces of Delhi, Uttar Pradesh, Punjab, Sindh and parts of Haryana and Rajasthan under the inspring stewardship of Gurujee. Besides the young pracharaks, prominent public figures like Baba Saheb Ghatate of Nagpur, Bhai Parmanand of Punjab, Lala Hari Chand of Delhi, Barrister Khanchand Gopaldas of Sindh, D.D. Chaudhary of Karachi, Prem Nath Dogra of Jammu, Giri Raj Sharma and Bachh Raj Vyas of Rajasthan, Barrister Narendrajeet Singh of Uttar Pradesh, Babu Padam Chand Jain of Calcutta and Krishan Vallabh Narayan Singh (Babua Ji) of Bihar, among others contributed immensely to the expansion of RSS during those eventful years and remained pillars of great strength all through their life. Professor Rejindra Singh (Rajju Bhaiyya) whom Bala Saheb Devras nominated his successor as Sarsanghchalak, Professor Balraj Madhok, Lala Hans Raj Gupta, Bhai Mahaveer and several others got attracted towards RSS during the tumultuous years before independence. During the years before and after the sinful partition of the country, huge crowds would gather to listen to Gurujee's clarion call to face the challenge of anti-national forces unitedly. He minced no words and declared that country's freedom and nation's integrity cannot and must not be negotiated. There was an unprecedented upsurge in RSS activities and popularity. Still by no reckoning, howsoever liberal, could it be deemed to be strong enough to convert the 1942 movement into a successful all India mass up-rising against the British Rulers or to match their machinations of aiding and abetting Muslim Communalism demanding partition of Mother India. Of course, it could and did opt for the second best option available, that is awakening the spirit of intense patriotism and nationalism and to check-mate the Muslim intransigence and wait for the right movement to give them a determined and decisive blow. The heroic role of RSS during that period is a saga of courage and chivalry of epic proportion. But for the RSS role, one really shudders to imagine what would be the magnitude of the barbaric massacre of peace loving Hindus on August 16, 1946, declared by Jinnah as a Direct Action Day or in the strife torn areas of the proposed Pakistan after the June 3, 1947 announcement by the imperial power to vivesect the country. When the true and unbiased history of that period of our country will be recorded, it will surely echo Gurujee's modest one liner - If I disclose all that happened then, listeners' hearts will burst forth with the words 'All glory to the Sangh'.

Comparisions of greatmen, as has rightly been said, are odious but the fact must be recorded that if Dr Hedgewar laid the foundation of RSS, Gurujee built the majestic edifice.

Agni Pariksha

Any how, more litmus a test was awaiting. Instead of appreciating, the powers that be felt extremely zealous. The prime-minister of whatever remained of independent India, Pt. Jawahar Lal Nehru who was always under the spell of Mountbettans and took pride in delcaring that he was a Hindu by accident, got unnecessarily apprehensive of the increasing RSS popularity. Unnecessarily, because RSS was a cultural non-political organisation and, therefore, no where in the race for political power. May be Nehru nurtured a guilty conscience for succumbing to the Muslim League intransigence and Mountbatten's pressure and conceding the country's division on communal lines resulting into the worst ever massacre of lakhs of innocent Hindus and an uncertain future to crores of those who some how escaped as refugees in their own homeland. He was also, perhaps, afraid of people's wrath.

The Communists who had blatantly betrayed the freedom struggle, had also supported the partition of the country. Besides, Sangh has always been a red-rag to the Communist bull. After all their philosophy of Dialectical Materialism stood no chance in the face of time-tested sound and profound philosophy of Vedanta which RSS espoused. Hence they have always played a page to the Nehru royalty; their so-called intellectuals thriving on government largesse.

In Mahatma Gandhiji's dastardly and heinous murder by Nathu Ram Godse on January 30, 1948, they thought, they had found a golden opportunity to crush RSS by falsely implicating the organisation. A viscious propaganda was unleashed and soon on February 2, 1948 RSS was banned under an ordinance. Thousands of innocent swayamsevaks were incarcerated behind the bars and subjected to unheard of third degree methods. Even a great saintly leader like Gurujee was shamelessly humiliated in jail by the so-called law enforcing agencies so as to extract a confessional statament and prove their baseless and trumpeted charges of RSS involvement in Gandhiji's murder. Lakhs of Swayamsevaks and their sympathisers outside the jail became the victim of government atrocities and target of Congress and Communist goonda elements.

And all this despite the fact that as early as on February 27, 1948 i.e., well with in a month of Gandhiji's assassination, Sardar Vallabh Bhai Patel, the then Home Minister of India, in a letter written to prime minister Jawahar Lal Nehru, had clearly stated that - I have kept myself almost in daily touch with the progress of the investigations regarding Bapuji's assassination case. All the main accused have given long and detailed statements of their activities. It also clearly emerges from the statements that the RSS was not involved in it at all.

It was virtually a war between good and evil and an unequal war for that

रावण रथी, विरथी रघुवीरा !

(Ram on foot, fighting the mighty Ravan riding a chariot)

When all the pleas for truth and justice fell on deaf years, a country wide satyagraha was launched on December 9, 1948 in which, breaking all previous records, more than 70,000 (seventy thousand) swayamsevaks courted arrest compelling the government to lift the unlawful ban on July 12, 1949 and releasing Gurujee from Betul Jail the next day.

Finest Hour

For the next 5-6 months Gurujee was on a countrywide whirldwind tour consoling the hurt feelings of innocent rank and file of RSS and inspiring them to work with renewed zeal and enthusiasm. He received unprecedented ovation wherever he went. The over-whelming public response by more than 5 lakh people to the felicitation function held on August 23, 1949 at Delhi's Ram Leela Grounds was a historic event. B.B.C. reported - Shri Gurujee is a shining star that has arisen on the Indian firmament. The only other Indian who can draw such huge crowds is Nehru. Even at that height of popularity, Gurujee was his sagacious self. No anger, no rancour. He advised his followers - Let us close this chapter of the ban on the Sangh. Do not let your minds be overcome with bitterness for those who, you feel, have done injustice to you. If the teeth were to bite the tongue, do we pull out the teeth? Even those who have done injustice to us are our own people. So we must forget and forgive. Just as a man who wakes up from sleep, works with renewed energy, we too must devote ourselves with renewed energy to the task to which we have dedicated ourselves - the task of putting an end to separatism, narrow mindedness and such other divisive factors?

RSS under the leadership of Gurujee was once again

engaged in its mission of national rejuvenation through Hindu organisation and consolidation which alone could provide the basis for universal peace and progress because of its philosophy of

वसुधैवकुटुम्बकम् *(The world is one big family).*

An ordinary mortal under the spell of such an enviable popularity and strength could have been lulled into inaction or lured by political power, but not Gurujee. He politely spurned Sardar Patel's overtures for RSS to work hand in hand with Congress Sewa Dal. True to its character and declared motto, RSS believes that nations are built on the strength of people's power and not on political power. Although conceding to the request of Dr Shyama Prasad Mukherjee, he deputed a few of his trusted pracharaks and activists like Deen Dayal Upadhyaya and later on Atal behari Vajpayee, Kusha Bhau Thakre, Jaggan Nath Rao Joshi, Sunder Singh Bhandari, P. Parmeshwaran, Nanaji Deshmukh, Lal Krishna Advani, Kedar Nath Sahni etc., to work in the Bharatiya Jana Sangh, Gurujee always cautioned the Swayamsevaks against the very slippery ground of power-politics. During one of his discourses he highlighted its limitations thus - Politics is a very small segment of national life. It can never cover its entire gamut... The truth is that political power should be guided by the people and not the otherway round... our society is still in the grip of casteist and provincial differences, disorganised and weak and suffers from an amnesia of identity. It has also become greedy of material objects of enjoyment. So long as our people are not devoted to the nation as a whole and imbued with sterling character, how can even democracy succeed? Had our life depended upon mere political power, we would have been finished the moment foreigners committed aggression on us. We will live so long as we keep this cultural stream full and flowing. If the people have firm faith in our culture, who can ever rule over us? Hence the primary task is to unite the entire society on that enduring and life giving basis.

With in 8-9 years of Gurujees ascendency to the exalted office of Sarsanghchalak, RSS came to be recognised as a highly disciplined and very potent all India organisation. During the remaining 24 years of his life he devoted all his energy not only to consolidation and-expansion of RSS but also spreading the message of Hindutva in different walks of life, facing heroically all sorts of canards of calumny and motivated criticism. Lack of resources needed for such a gigantic task also could not hinder his onward march. It has became a second habit with swayamsevaks to voluntarily and promptly come forward to people's succour at the time of national calamities like floods, drought, earthquake epidemic etc. In times of national crisis like foreign aggression, the RSS is always in the foreront, a fact recognised and appreciated even by its worst critics and opponents.

Creative Genius

However, Gurujee's unique contribution in the form of inspiration and encouragement provided to some of his best and trusted Pracharaks and Swayamsevaks like Dattopant Thengadi, Bala Saheb Deshpande, Eknath Ranade, K.R. Malkani, Krishna Chandra Gandhi, Shiv Shankar Apte and later on Ashok Singhal to go and work in such varied fields as Labour, Vanvasi Kalyan, Education, Students, journalism etc. will surely be recorded in golden letters. Only a reformist in Gurujee could think of Vishva Hindu Parishad and only a visionary in him could dream of the Vivekananda Rock Memorial.

One has only to see and objectively assess the magnitude and impact of organisations like Vidya Bharati, Sewa Bharati and Vanavasi Kalyan Ashram or the grandeur and import of the new centre of pilgrimage Vivekanand Shila Smarak at the Conflunce of three Seas to appreciate the work and wisdom of RSS Swayamsevaks. Can one find better example of creative work and that too without government or corporate patronage; rather inspite of them! A living monument of peoples power.

To the opponents who charged RSS of trying to infilterate all fields of national life, Shri Gurujee's blunt reply was yes we want to dominate every aspect of our national life with our ideology. In response to the query of one of his close friends and the then chief minister of earstwhile Madhya Bharat, Pt Ravi Shankar Shukla, Gurujee minced no words when he replied that such a big countrywide organisation had not been built merely for engaging little children in games: 'We certainly have a specific purpose behind it. We want to make an impact of the Sangh's nationalistic ideology on every aspect of the nations life and we have never hidden this purpose.'

He had further elaborated this theme during the historic session of RSS Pracharaks at Sindhi on March 14, 1954 - during the past few years some activities have been started alongwith the Sangh work. For instance, some news papers, schools, dispensaries etc., have been started by Swayamsevaks. This has not been done for business purposes. These are either instruments for propagating the cause of the Sangh or complementary sub-activities. Social service projects have also been launched at a number of places... This is our Hindu nation. Our aim is not only its protection and preservation but also its expansion and evolution.

Regarding organisation's expectations from persons deputed to work in such other fields, Gurujee's candid advice was - A living close contact with the source must be maintained at all costs. And then wherever you go, you have to work there to establish the ideal and ideology of the Sangh in that field and in the process, strengthen the people's faith in the Sangh. You have been sent into these various activities to conquer them on the strength of our ideology and individual integrity and character.

Strange though, yet on a close and dispassionate scrutiny no other two greatmen are found closer than Gurujee and Gandhijee. Both were ascetic in the true sense of the word.

Both contemplated and commented on almost all aspects of human life. Both immersed themselves in the service of the society and became one with the mission of their life. There was no diacotomy between the principles and practices of both. Both could attract people on such a massive scale and produced a galaxy of renowned and worthy colleagues because of their own transparent personality and self-abnegation. Not I, but thou (मै नहीं, तू ही तू), as Gurujee put it.

Shri Gurujee sincerely believed that if India has to reach the pinnacle of glory and lead the strife torn world to the path of universal peace and prosperity, She must awaken the spirit of time-tested Dharma, (Quite distinct from religion or way of worship), assimilate the essence of science coupled with spirituality and test all her policies and programmes on the touchstone of human welfare here in this world and salvation here-in-after (अभ्युदय-नि:श्रेयस). That India had successfully done it in the hoary past and can achieve it in not very distant future, was Gurujee's firm conviction. Never for once did Gurujee walk the talk or criticise his friend in the organisation or foe in opposition by name - howsoever serious a lapse or painful a provocation. He believed in the process of self course-correction through persuation and force of conviction. Never did he once play to the gallery - press or political power. And never did he act the ring master cracking his whip to scare his flock into submission. And yet crores of his followers did as he desired, virtually worshipped him and the countrymen at large admired him. He had not acquired Himalayan heights for nothing.

What Gurujee achieved was in the realm of super human. Yet he never claimed Godhood and discouraged all those who tried to treat or address him as such. In this connection I am reminded of a very interesting episode of 1957. Shri Gurujee was in Meerut in connection with the 'Zonal RSS Swayamsevaks' meet. Before the evening public function, a few prominent personalities from different walks of life were present at Lala Rameshwar Dayal's Kothi for exchange of views with Gurujee over a cup of tea. The writer of these lines, a young college student then, was incharge of arrangements. Among the dignitaries was Shri Pitambar Dass, the All India President of the Bharatiya Jana Sangh. Those were the days when the communists, basking in the reflected glory of Congress lead by Jawahar Lal Nehru, were indulging in all sorts of wild and viscious propaganda against RSS. During the discussion Shri Pitamber Dass recalled how during the 1948 ban on RSS the Communists stooped so low that they levelled even a personal charge against Gurujee for smoking one cigarette a day after lunch while in Shivni Jail. To the delightful amazement of all present, Gurujee took it very casually and commented - "In fact I feel obliged to them for at least once conceding that after all I am also like any other commoner and not a monster as they have always been projecting me". And then,on a philosophical note, added - These poor fellows like their demi-god Marx can never understand and appreciate the significance and symbolism behind our Lord Shiva consuming Bhang and in our own times Swami Vivekananda sharing an untouchable's Hukkah on the out-skirts of Varanasi while on his pilgrimage to the Himalayas."

The Communist animosity against RSS is understandable. After all it is RSS that by successfully awakening and organising nationalist forces has contained their forward march and had earlier been instrumental in-stone-walling the invasion of their Chinese masters beyond Tibet - thus shattering their dream of ruling over the shores of Indian ocean.

Immortal Gurujee

Shri Gurujee was always on the move with no signs of fatigue for all these long years. Not that he was not at all affected by the sad demise of his parents or many of his contemporaries like Dr Shyama Prasad Mukherjee, Lal Bahadur Shastri, Dr Hedgewar, Baba Saheb Apte, Dr Raghuveer, Pt Deen Dayal Upadhyaya and several others.

In particular, the death of Deen Dayal Upadhyaya under mysterious circumstances had left a deep scar on his heart. Yet Gurujee knew no rest. One wondered whether there was a perennial reservoir of energy behind his lean and frail physical constitution.

But nature spares none. It surreptitiously and silently follows it's own schedule. Gurujee, for the first time, could not address the Varsha Pratipada function of Nagpur held on April 7, 1970 owing to indisposition which unfortunately later on proved to be an alarm bell. On confirmation of Cancer on July 1, the same year he was operated upon by the renowned Cancer specialist Dr Prafull Desai in Tata Memorail Hospital, Mumbai. Now the footsteps of the inevitable were quite audible. But Gurujee dreaded Her not the least. Who could know it better than the Vedantic philosopher in Gurujee that man is mortal but the soul is immortal. The hurricane speed with which he continued to work for the next three years was proof enough that he knew the end was fast approaching. With RSS prayer on his lips, Gurujee left for his heavenly abode at five minutes past nine on the night of June 5, 1973.

Shri Gurujee, the Vivekanada incarnate was no more. What was left was a flood of tears in the eyes of millions of his compatriots and countless countrymen and, of course, the heavenly radiance that always heralds the departure of a pious soul amidst chanting of

वासांसि जीर्णानि यथा विहाय, नवानि गृहणाति नरोऽपराणी।
तथा शरीराणि विहाय जीर्णा न्यन्यानि संयाति नवानि देही।।

नैनं छिन्दन्ति शस्त्राणि, नैनं दहति पावकः।
न चैनं क्लेदयन्त्यापो, न शोषयति मारुतः।।

Today a net work of Shakhas in more than 30,000 villages, towns and cities spread all over India from Kashmir to kanyakumari and Kachh to kamroop under the leadership of over 2500 full time dedicated team of Pracharaks, over 75,000 social service projects being run by its activists, besides about a hundred huge and not so huge sister organisations of RSS constitute the world's most multi-splendoured and extra-ordinary living memorial to Gurjuee the Great.

Napoleon Bonaparte's famous quote - Men of genius are meteors destined to burn themselves out in lighting up their age - is fully applicable in the case of Shree Gurujee.

What better and more befitting an epigraph to the haloed memory of Shri Gurujee can there be than what he himself wrote about Mahatma Gandhi, for a booklet published by Rashtrothan Sahitya, Bangalore (Karnataka) on November 8, 1969 -

The chilld came into this world like any other human being but grew to towering heights of greatness by his sheer efforts and the qualities of his overwhelming love for one and all; and verily became a Mahatama. Gandhiji was never tired of emphasising character, moral values and self-restraint. Gandhiji lives in the hearts of men as eternal image of affection and adoration chiefly because of his unflinching adherence to the spiritual and moral values and his endless efforts to live upto them in his own life. His life demands of us a deep appreciation of the eternal values of life manifest in his conduct and determined effort to make them a living inspiration for generations to come. It is an inspiration for selfless and dedicated service to the society, for a life of virtues, sweetness and harmony which would make one-worthy of adoration by the entire humanity.

(The writer has about a dozen books to his credit.)

3

Shri Gurujee: The Peerless Patriot

V. Sundaram

RIGHT from the dawn of history Bharat has produced great saints and sages, great beings who made the supreme discovery that the God they sought for many years was no different from their own selves.

Each generation has been blessed by these enlightened souls who spread only goodness throughout India and had the power to grant a divine boon i.e the boon of perfect wisdom.

Shri Guruji Paramapoojaniya Madhava Sadashiva Golwalkar-the second All-Bharat Chief of the Rashtriya Swayam Sevak Sangh (RSS) belonged to this sacred and glorious tradition. Through his selfless life and example, he gave us all this message: When the Mysterious Unity between the soul and the Divine becomes clear, you will realise that you are none other than God. You will see all your actions as His actions; all your features as His features; all your breath as His breath. He taught us all that the priceless gift of intelligence can be brought to bear upon each of the chief centers of consciousness in the human constitution. Individuals, who cherish this privilege enough to conduct a series of experiments with truth in daily living, will assuredly gain a great awareness of the dignity of being human. The orbit of the sacred is revolutionary; it is radically subversive to the status quo of one's previous somnambulistic existence. This is the vision of a perfect being; this is the vision Guruji Golwalkar gave to Bharat and to every Indian. Guruji Golwalkar succeeded Dr Keshav Baliram Hedgewar, the great founder of the Rashtriya Swayam Sevak Sangh (RSS), who passed away on 21 June 1940. From 1940, till his Mahanirvana on 5 June 1973, Guruji as the chief of the RSS for 33 years, converted it into a mighty national force for the protection, preservation, consolidation and advancement of Mother India. He was a man of great vision, unsurpassed courage and unrivalled judgement. He had a clear, definite and clairvoyant vision of a renascent India of the future. With unshakable faith in his mission, he came to the firm conclusion that it was impossible for Bharat to become strong and confident enough to realise its destiny unless every walk and dimension of life was informed and animated with the pure ideology of Hindutva -the bedrock of the RSS.

When this great Nation was getting threatened by the rising forces of militant Islam and government sheltered Christianity soon after the First World War, Dr Keshav Baliram Hedgewar, who was a staunch supporter of the Congress and a fighter for India's freedom, realised the urgent national need to start a national-level cultural organisation to re-establish the glory of Hindu Rashtra.

When the Khilafat Movement was at its height under the leadership of Mahatma Gandhi after 1920, Mahatma Gandhi made some disparaging remarks about the Hindus by stating that 'an average Hindu is a coward and an average Muslim is a bully'.

Khilafat Movement stood for Pan-Islamism. This encouraged several Muslims in different parts of India to start an anti-Hindu rebellion in 1923. They slaughtered cows, attacked Hindu processions, molested Hindu women and desecrated Hindu temples. It was against this dark and horrendous background that Dr Hedgewar thought of creating a new organisation to strengthen the hands of Hindus. He was not interested in merely training an army of 'Yes' men. It was his dream that an organisation should be created consisting of lakhs and lakhs of self-sacrificing and self-inspired young men willing to lead a disciplined life in the cause of the country.

The great RSS was born on the sacred day of Vijayadasami in 1925. About 15 to 20 young men gathered in the doctor's house on that day. Chief among them were Bhauji Kawre, Anna Sohni, Viswanath Rao Kelkar, Balaji Huddar and Bapurao Bhedi.

Dr Hedgewar declared to the gathering - We are inaugurating the Sangh today. All of us must train ourselves physically, intellectually and in every way so as to be capable of achieving our cherished goal'. His mission was to charge the people with the true spirit of national character and cohesion. All those habits, superstitions and tendencies which had divided, disrupted and devitalized the nation during the last several centuries had to be eradicated on a war-footing. Sublime and life sustaining values had to be nurtured and cultivated. This was a gigantic task of character moulding, man-making and nation building. This called for a mighty national organisation. The answer was the RSS.

In order to sustain and stabilize this vision, the 'Shakha' technique was evolved by Dr Hedgewar. The name of the Sangh, its flag, its prayer, its pledge, its morning hymn, its exposition of thought, the several aspects of its methodology- each one of these conveyed and proclaimed one message - the message of unadulterated devotion to national integrity and national identity. And finally, a child of this motherland nurtured in this soul-stirring philosophy was born - the Swayam Sevak.

The responsibility of presenting before the people of India this glorious mission and vision carrying the living message of what Bharat stands for and how it proposes to achieve its goal of all-round national regeneration devolved on all Swayamsevaks.

Dr Hedgewar transformed himself into a model Swayam Sevak. His 'Shakha' model became the most effulgent and enlivening model and thousands of Swayamsevaks were inspired by his example during his lifetime to follow him with undivided devotion and dedication.

Vivekanand Reborn

Madhava Sadashiv Golwalkar was born in Nagpur on 19 February, 1906. His father was Sadashiva Rao and mother Lakshmibai. He was called lovingly as Madhu by his parents. His mother-tongue was Marathi. As his father was posted in Hindi-speaking areas, Golwalkar became very proficient in Hindi right from his childhood days. At the same time he also developed his mastery in English as well. As a school student he was known for his extraordinary memory. In 1924, after completing his intermediate college education, he went to Banaras Hindu University to do his B.Sc. He was quite thrilled to see the mighty library of Banaras Hindu University. When he was not attending his classes, he was in the library. He became a voracious reader filled with an insatiable thirst for knowledge. He took his M.Sc Degree in Zoology in I Class from Banaras Hindu University.

In 1929, Guruji left for Madras to do research work in the Government Aquarium. He had to return to Nagpur that very year on the retirement of his father for want of funds to pursue his research. In August 1931, Golwalkar became a lecturer in Zoology at Banaras Hindu University. He became a very popular teacher. He got the name of Shri Guruji from his beloved students of Banaras Hindu University who held him in very high regard. Throughout his later life he came to be known as Shri Guruji. Pandit Madan Mohan Malviya noticed the extraordinary talents of Guruji and predicted a very great future for him. Through Bhaiyyaji Dani, a Swayamsevak from Nagpur, Guruji came into contact with Dr Hedgewar. Guruji was appointed as Palak of the Shakha in Banaras. In February 1933, on the expiry of his teaching term, he returned to Nagpur. He then pursued his legal studies and took his B.L. Degree in 1935. He started associating himself actively with the RSS.

After closely watching the extraordinary work and intellectual versatility of Guruji in Nagpur, Dr Hedgewar started entrusting him with more and more responsible tasks. In 1934 Guruji discharged the duties of 'Sarvadhikari' of Sangh Siksha Varga in Akola with tremendous verve, skill and dedication. When his mother brought up before him his marriage proposal and said that if he did not marry, their Golwalkar family lineage would become extinct, Guruji replied with humility and reverence. In the present situation it is necessary that, for the welfare of the society, if the family lineages of not only me, but several others like me are terminated, I will not in the least be worried'.

Right from 1929, Guruji's power of discrimination was truly sparking and awake. In a letter to his friend Telang on 29 March, 1929; Gurujee wrote 'I have no desire to attune myself to a mundane human life. What I want is to stretch this string of life to create a still purer tune. While doing so, mental strain cannot be avoided. This means that it does not matter if one has to live apart from the common world. The important thing is that the string of life must not be out of tune with that heavenly music. Now I shall not go to the Himalayas, rather Himalayas shall come to me; it's serene silence will dwell within me. Now it is not necessary to go anywhere for attaining that serenity.'

On the one hand the pathetic plight of the Hindu society and of an enslaved nation tortured him. On the other, he was tormented and pulled by his inborn spiritual thirst for self-realisation. In 1936, Guruji quietly left for Sargachhi Ashram in search of a spiritual guide. Guruji involved himself actively in the service of Swami Akhandananda. It was Swami Akhandananda, who gave the final verdict - 'It seems Golwalkar would work in association with Dr. Hedgewar'. Swamiji also gave his personal belongings like 'Kamandal', etc. to Guruji. Swami Akhandananda passed away in February 1937. On his return to Nagpur, Guruji's life took a new and revolutionary turn. From 1938 onwards, Guruji identified the work of RSS as the sole mission of his life. Guruji declared: 'Like spirituality, organisation of the nation has also been my inclination from early days. I believe that I would be in a better position to achieve it successfully by being a part of the Sangh. Hence, I have dedicated myself to the activities of Sangh. From the point of view of the insight and practical approach of Swami Vivekananda, my decision is appropriate'.

Just as Ramakrishna Paramahamsa Identified and understood the inherent and potential spiritual genius of Vivekananda even as a very young man, Dr Hedgewar correctly and exactly assessed the powerhouse that was latent in Shri Guruji. An important meeting of Sangh workers took place at Sindhi in February 1939 where Dr Hedgewar and his other senior prominent co-workers were present. The meeting lasted for ten days to have a detailed discussion on many subjects - like the progress of Sangh work, the Shakha system of work, the commands used therein, the prayer and so on - in order to take some final decisions on the basis of the consensus. These changes were considered necessary for the purpose of giving a uniform pattern and form to the daily programmes of the Shakha throughout the country. At this meeting Shri Appaji Joshi who was considered the Chief Lieutenant of Dr Hedgewar and another important Lieutenant Shri Balasaheb Deoras were present. Shri Gurji was also invited as a new colleague. It was at this meeting that Dr Hedgewar had the opportunity of closely watching the personality, character, attitude and aptitude of Shri Guruji. Several far-reaching decisions were taken on the future of the Sangh at Sindi and Shri Guruji played a stellar role in laying a solid foundation for the future. It will not be too much to say that Dr Hedgewar came under the magnetic spell of Shri Guruji.

Dr. Hedgewar finds a successor

After the Sindi meeting Dr Hedgewar sent Shri Guruji to start the Sangh work in Calcutta. Shri Guruji toured all over Calcutta for nearly a month, tirelessly propagating the ideals of the Sangh among the people. Without much money for transportation or other expenses, single-handedly Shri Guruji walked from place to place, covering a distance of almost 25 to 30 miles everyday. As a result of his determination, the first Sangh Shakha in Calcutta came into existence on Varsha Pratipada Day (The Hindu New Year Day) in 1939. But soon thereafter he was called by Dr Hedgewar to return to Nagpur to serve as 'Sarvadhikari' of a historic training camp which was to take place in Nagpur.

In the light of Shri Guruji's leadership qualities displayed as Sarvadhikari, he was appointed 'Sarkaryawaha' (Secretary-General of the Sangh) for a short period of ten months. During this period the work was expanded quite fast in Vidarbha, Madhya Pradesh and Maharashtra. Hundreds of Shakhas were set up in these areas. Even in distant places like Punjab, Delhi, Karachi, Calcutta, Lucknow, etc work was initiated by dynamic Sangh workers. The Sangh was soon assuming an all-Bharat proportion and character. The total number of Swayamsevaks had crossed a figure of 1 lakh volunteers. Dr Hedgewar was constantly on the move exhorting and inspiring the Swayamsevaks.

The II World War started on 3 September 1939. Dr Hedgewar had gone to Rajgir in Bihar for taking rest and treatment. From there he sent a circular letter calling upon all Sangh workers to speed up the Sangh's strength by converting three per cent of the total population in the urban areas and one per cent of the total population in the rural areas into young Swayamsevaks. Shri Guruji took immediate action to translate Dr Hedgewar's dream into a reality. Unfortunately Dr Hedgewar passed away on 21, June 1940. Even before his passing away, he had clearly indicated his mind to Appaji Joshi that Shri Guruji will be his successor. Soon after Dr Hedgewar's death, at a function to pay homage to his hallowed memory, it was officially announced that Shri Guruji will be the Sarsanghchalak of the RSS. At that very function, Dr Hedgewar's aged uncle Shri Abaji Hedgewar in his speech said: 'Indeed our Doctorji has not left us at all; we still see him in the form of Madhava Rao

Golwalkar. Now onwards every directive from him is to be obeyed as if it was from Doctorji himself'.

Soon after accepting his new responsibility as Sarsanghchalak of the RSS, Shri Guruji stated - He who cannot bow down to a great man like Dr Hedgewarji, can achieve nothing in his life. I feel very proud to offer my worship to such a great soul. Worship with sandal paste and flowers is of a low order. The real worship is to try to become like the object of worship itself. *'Shivo Bhutvo, Shivam Yajet'*, to worship Shiva is to become Shiva himself. Doctorji has entrusted to me the onerous responsibility of the Sarsanghchalak. But this is verily going to occupy a Vikramaditya throne. Even if a rustic boy sits on it, he will dispense only an even handed justice. Today an ordinary individual like me is destined to sit on it, but Doctorji will inspire even a person like me to say the right things. Our great leader's hallowed merit will make me do only the right things. Now let us set ourselves to the task with full faith and confidence and take it forward with redoubled vigour and enthusiasm.

From that day in 1940 till his passing away on 6 June 1973, Shri Guruji was the supreme commander of the RSS and converted it into a mighty and powerful organisation for national rejuvenation and national reconstruction based on our timeless Hindu Dharma.

The Great Leap

The period from 1940 to 1947 was a time of cataclysmic world events and great national events. The widespread escalation of the II World War in Europe and elsewhere, the Quit India Movement and the imprisonment of Mahatma Gandhi and other national leaders, the total suppression of the Quit India Movement by the strong arm tactics of the Government of India, these events had convinced Shri Guruji that unless the Sangh was converted into a strong national organisation, the nation's backbone could never be straightened or strengthened. A large portion of the country remained untouched by the Sangh. The Government of India was keeping a close watch on the activities of the Sangh. Shri Guruji showed great statesmanship by carefully complying with Government regulations and restrictions by adopting an elastic policy. At the same time he took very effective steps to increase the number of 'Shakhas' in those areas where 'Shakhas' were already functioning. He also took vigorous action to bring in new areas and new States within the orbit of activities of the Sangh. He was able to do this by undertaking extensive tours throughout the country starting from 1941. To begin with, there were only a few notable full-time 'Pracharak's (teachers), like Babasaheb Apte and Dadarao Paramarth. Shri Guruji came out with the plan of sending 'Pracharak' exclusively on a full-time basis to all parts of the country. Wherever Shri Guruji went, he carried his highly emotional appeal which touched the heart-strings of the young and dynamic Swayamsevaks in all parts of India. Shri Guruji endeavored to bring home to them the fact that the Sangh was not a leisure time activity, but something which demanded more and more of their time and energy. In a historic speech in the history of the RSS on 'Varsha Pratipada Day'- in 1942, Shri Guruji declared; 'It is our great good fortune that we are born in these dangerous times which we must view as most auspicious. The golden moment that arrives in the history of a nation after centuries is coming our way. If we sleep at such a crucial hour no one would be more unfortunate than us. He only achieves immortal fame who stands up foursquare in the face of adversities. Let us therefore face the present adversity with serenity and determination. Even after 17 long years of strenuous efforts, our work has remained far too limited. The Sangh stands by the Truth and so it will certainly succeed and redeem its pledge.

This appeal went home. Hundreds of young Swayamsevaks came forward from many places to work full time. There were many who gave up their jobs, ideas of marriage, family relationships, etc and took the decisive plunge inspired by the soulsttirring message of Shri Guruji. Some householders too expressed their willingness to devote full-time to Sangh work. One such worker was Shri Bhaiyaji Dani who went to Madhya Bharath as 'Pracharak'. From June 1942, 'Pracharak's' began to be sent to various provinces, and the work acquired a new momentum and dimension.

When the Quit India Movement came in August 1942, Shri Guruji had the courage to declare that the RSS was a cultural, non-political organisation. If any of the Swayamsevaks Participated in the Quit India Movement, it was done in their personal capacity. This was made clear to everyone. Shri Guruji felt that the most important thing for the Sangh was to set up a wide network of 'Shakhas' and increase its organisational power. Only through such an approach it would be possible for us to awaken and build up the disciplined might of our people in order to achieve the larger objective of enhancing the glory of Bharat.

Shri Guruji worked day and night and toured the country several times to broaden and widen the base of the RSS and by the beginning of 1947 the RSS had become a strong national organisation. It is not therefore surprising that RSS was able to play a very important role in helping millions of Hindu refugees to move from the newly created State of Pakistan to India safely at the time of partition. The first Government of independent India relied heavily upon the RSS and its 'Swayamsevaks' to deal with the problem of law and order and refugee rehabilitation in the disturbed months after independence. The outstanding leadership provided by Shri Guruji in those stirring days and troubled times is indeed a glorious chapter in Indian history.

Country Betrayed

In May 1945, the II World War came to an end. The British Government in India realised that their days in India were coming to an end. The Congress was divided on the question of partition. Rajaji had resigned from Congress on this issue. Jinnah was proudly proclaiming the 'Two-Nation Theory' stating that Muslims could never live in India because he considered Congress a Hindu party. The Congress officially at this point of time struck to its anti-Pakistan stand.

Lord Wavell and his successor Lord Mountbatten were surreptitiously supporting Jinnah's demand for a separate Muslim State of Pakistan. In those dark days, Shri Guruji took a bold and unequivocal stand on the question of united India or what he called Akhand Bharat. He clearly declared in all his speeches throughout India and more particularly in the affected States like undivided Punjab, Rajasthan, United Provinces, Bihar and Bengal that there can be no question of any negotiation or discussion on the issue of a United India. In 1945-46 he used to attract milling crowds who wanted to hear his inspiring words on the issue of Akhand Bharat.

All the leading Congress leaders (with the singular and salutary exception of Mahatma Gandhi), who were released from prison in 1945, after years of imprisonment, had become far too eager to capture positions of power and pelf. Despite this disturbing trend, under the influence and inspiration of Mahatma Gandhi, the Congress in its session officially rejected Jinnah's demand for partition in 1945. Soon after the session, Gandhiji declared; 'Partition can take place only over my dead body'. These words came as a succour to millions of Hindus in undivided Punjab and elsewhere. Therefore, they took it for granted that partition of India would never take place.

In order to intimidate and pressurize the British Government on the one hand and the peace loving Hindus of India on the other, Jinnah in a true Jihadi style, announced 16 August, 1946 as the 'Direct Action Day.' On that fateful day, riots were incited by Muslim leaders belonging to the Muslim League all over the country. More particularly, barbaric massacres and genocide took place, on this day in places like Calcutta, Dacca, Noakhali, striking terror in the hearts of the Hindu. Naturally, there was a counter reaction. In Bihar, Congress leaders forcibly suppressed such a rebellion. However, the Congress party and its leaders came to realise that it would be better to agree to Pakistan rather than invite a civil war and terrible blood shed. It is clear now from what happened after independence that the Congress was fully confident that after agreeing to Jinnah's demand for Pakistan, in post-independent India, taking advantage of the system of adult franchise granted to illiterate millions, they could create any number of secular pockets in India, assuring minority vote banks in the name of 'secularism'.

In those terrible days, the Sangh had became a powerful force in Punjab. Shri Guruji in all his public meetings spoke against the creation of Pakistan. He was personally touring all the affected areas to maintain and boost up the public morale. In those terrible times, he toured the whole of Punjab and Sind quite often. The local Congress leaders in all these areas became very envious of the rising force of the Sangh and the growing popularity and moral influence of Shri Guruji. Shri Guruji told the Congress leaders not to accept partition in a meek and tame manner. He often used to say that Hindu society was capable of tackling the Muslim League goondaism. He exhorted the Hindus and told them not to be unduly disturbed by terrorism, atrocities and threats of killing. In a famous speech at Nagpur on Vijayadasami day in 1946 he said: I do not think it is manly to talk about non-resistance. In these days of strife, how can non-resistance ever benefit the country? I feel a violent struggle is unavoidable. You may well refrain from resistance, but will that stop the aggressors from indulging in their black deeds? Do not forget that the sacrificial goat at the Kali temple is an embodiment of non-resistance. We are not to become such sacrificial goats. Self-defence is the natural, legitimate right of every in dividual and of every society. So to say that one should not take the law into one's own hands merely because security is the Government's responsibility, is basically illegal'. Shri Guruji, as one who had taken a degree in law, knew clearly that there was a provision in the IPC to kill another man in self-defence. Shri Guruji declared in Punjab on 1 June, 1947 - We do not know Pakistan, nor do we accept it. We must take a stand, wherever we are, we should put up an organised resistance. If we fear to go into that fiery ordeal, and leave our motherland, history will say that these people felt no pangs of pain over the cutting up of their dear motherland.

Despite the fervent appeals of great men like Shri Guruji, partition was announced on 3 June, 1947. Shri Guruji directed all the Sangh Swayamsevaks to act as a protective shield to all the Hindus in Punjab and Sind, who were going to move into India soon after this announcement. Violence was let loose by the Muslims against innocent Hindus in different parts of Punjab and Sind. Even in such a state of anarchy and lawlessness, Sangh's training camps were held in Phagwara and Sangrur in Punjab in the third week of July 1947. In this traumatic hour, the Sangh Swayamsevaks proved to be the only ray of hope of succor and survival to the Hindus. Several eminent international writers of books and articles on partition have paid great tributes to the Sangh Swayamsevaks and to Shri Guruji for the extraordinary courage and strength of character shown by them under very trying conditions. At the instance of Shri Guruji, the Punjab Relief Committee was set up to provide all-round relief to the uprooted Hindus. Shri Guruji came to be revered as the sole saviour of the Hindu Society.

In September 1947, on the instruction of Shri Guruji, RSS volunteers were posted at the Bhangi Colony in New Delhi to give security to Mahatma Gandhi who was staying there. A that time, neither Nehru nor Patel, or any of the Congressman, raised any objection to this arrangement. On 16 September, 1947 Mahatma Gandhi addressed about 500 members of the RSS at the Bhangi Colony. The late Shri Jamanlal Bajaj had taken Mahatma Gandhi to the camp and Gandhi said: 'I am very impressed by their discipline, complete absence of untouchability and rigorous simplicity inspired by the ideal of service and self-sacrifice, it is bound to grow in strength.

Nation First

Shri Guruji was noted for his burning patriotism for Akhand Bharat and he had spoken strongly against the partition of India right from 1943.Responsibilities often gravitate to the person who can shoulder them. Many people today may not be aware of the fact how Shri Guruji was deputed by Sardar Patel on a political mission in a special plane to Srinagar to meet Maharaja Hari Singh of Jammu & Kashmir and the stellar role he played in the accession of Jammu and Kashmir to the Indian Union after independence.

This indeed is an interesting story about the historic role played by Shri Guruji as a responsible and patriotic citizen at a crucial time in our national history.

Soon after independence, the most serious challenge to the freedom and integrity of independent Bharat was posed in Kashmir. The British government declaration of 3 June, 1947 left the princely rulers of independent Bharat to join either Bharat or Pakistan or remain independent. Hari Singh, the Maharaja of Jammu & Kashmir, was in an awful fix. In view of the marked Muslim majority in the State, he was a little hesitant. Lord Mountbatten flew to Kashmir in the third week of June, 1947 in a bid to persuade the Maharaja to join Pakistan. The Maharaja resisted the pressure. R.C. Kak, the then Prime Minister of Kashmir, however advised Maharaja Hari Singh to remain independent. Amidst these conflicting pulls, the Sangh leaders in the State of Jammu & Kashmir began exerting every possible influence to persuade the Maharaja to declare his accession to Bharat before the deadline of 15 August, 1947.

The State Sanghchalak of the RSS Pandit Prem Nath Dogra, submitted several petitions and followed them up with personal interviews with the Maharaja. The Sangh also persuaded several social, political and cultural organisations in the State to pass resolutions urging the Maharaja to join Bharat without delay. At the same time, Shri Badridas, Sanghchalak of Punjab, whom the Maharaja held in high esteem, rushed to Srinagar to meet and advise him.

However, forces inimical to Bharat would not let Maharaja Hari Singh have his way.

When 14 August, 1947 (one day prior to independence) came, the postal authorities in Srinagar hoisted the Pakistani flag in their office, because the post offices in the State came under Sialkot Circle which was to become part of Pakistan from that day. Promptly, the Sangh Swayamsevaks and sympathizers saw to it that the postal authorities pulled down the Pakistan flag.

On the next day, 15 August 1947, the Indian tricolour flew over most of the houses and shops in Kashmir. The tricolour had been prepared in thousands in the Sangh Karyalaya. Meanwhile the pro-Pakistani Muslim elements in Kashmir intensified their propaganda to pressurize the Maharaja to join Pakistan. Large scale smuggling of arms into the State to foment internal rebellion started taking place from the month of August 1947. At the diplomatic level at the Centre, too, Sangh had made certain strategic moves in the crucial mid-October days in 1948.

Sardar Vallabhai Patel, knowing the mind of Maharaja Hari Singh, had pitched upon Shri Guruji to talk to the Maharaja. Patel knew that Shri Guruji commanded the implicit and full confidence of the Maharaja.

At the instance of Sardar Patel, Shri Guruji flew to Srinagar on 17 October, 1947. He explained to the Maharaja, the futility of entertaining any idea of retaining Kashmir as an Independent Kingdom, and advised him to join Bharat straightaway. Consequently, the Maharaja expressed his readiness to sign the instrument of accession to Bharat.

Shri Guruji returned to New Delhi on 19 October, 1947 and reported to Sardar Patel about the Maharaja's readiness to accede to Bharat. Unfortunately there was a sudden and massive invasion of Kashmir on 23 October, 1947 by Pakistani tribesmen which was instigated by the government of Pakistan and the Maharaja appealed to government of India for help, agreeing to the accession of the Sate to Bharath and the flying of Indian troops to save Kashmir-all these historic events following in lightning succession.

Within the city of Jammu itself, the local Muslims numbering about 20,000 were a in a rebellious mood. The fate of Jammu City and the entire countryside in Jammu, with no troops on hand, was in precarious state.

The young men of Sangh rose to the occasion. They faced the pro Pakistani Muslim elements inside and repulsed their repeated attacks and shattered their designs. But for the Swayamsevaks' valiant efforts, Jammu could never have been saved and without Jammu, there was not the ghost of a chance to save Srinagar even by Indian forces. This inspiration to defend our motherland against the Pakisan maruaders was provided by the Swayamsevaks and not by the indecisive government of Pandit Jawaharlal Nehru.

On the contrary, it was Pandit Nehru who stopped the Indian Army from driving out the Pakistani invaders from a portion of Kashmir by taking the matter to the United Nations. Nehru took this disastrous and abrupt decision against the advice of Major General Kulwant Singh, Corps Commander, General Thimmiah and General Cariappa of the Indian Army. He did not trust his countrymen. He had greater faith in the machinations of Lord Mountbatten and his British officers. The country is still paying the price for that inexcusable political blunder.

Shri Guruji had a good equation with Mahatma Gandhi who addressed the RSS Swayamsevaks at Bhangi Colony in New Delhi on 16 September, 1947 where they were posted to keep guard at various points.

R.S.S. Banned

Mahatma Gandhi was assassinated at Birla House on 30 January 1948. Nathuram Godse, the assassin, was immediately arrested. Later he was tried and sentenced to death. On that fateful day at 5 P.M. Shri Guruji was in Madras, sipping a cup of tea with his friends. When he heard the terrible news, he sent telegrams to Patel and Nehru assuring them of all help at that time of trial and tragedy. Shri Guruji immediately flew to Nagpur. On 1 February, 1948, hundreds of goondas gathered outside Shri Guruji's house in Nagpur and started pelting stones. On the same day, Shri Guruji was arrested by the police on the charges of Gandhi's assassination under sections 320 and 120 of the Criminal Procedure Code.Was it not a lurid example of Nehru's callous thoughtlessness and unrestrained lust for power? Was he not trampling all justice and godliness with his great secular foot? This happened within six months of the attainment of our independence and Nehru's famous 'Tryst with Destiny'. It was indeed a tryst with tyranny; it was indeed a tryst with terror; it was indeed a tryst with treachery. Pandit Nehru clearly showed that he could beat the record of his beloved Stalin in post-independent India.

On 2 February, 1948, it was officially announced that the Rashtriya Swayamsevak Sangh (RSS) was banned. Sangh workers and Swayamsevaks were arrested throughout the country. There were more than 40,000 arrests. The atmosphere of the whole country was poisoned by the effete Congress party with anti-Sangh rumours, with charges and venomous tirades against the Sangh and Shri Guruji. On 5 February, 1948, when his lawyer-friend Dattopant Deshpande went to see Shri Guruji, Shri Guruji handed over to him a written statement saying that the RSS was disbanded and asked him to get it published. Shri Guruji said in that statement. 'It has always been the policy of the RSS to be law-abiding and carry on its activities within the bounds of law. Therefore, since the Government has declared the RSS an unlawful body, it is thought advisable to disband the RSS till the ban is there, at the same time denying all the charges levelled against the organisation'.

The tragedy of post-independent India was that the press was not officially muffled by the Government of India. The press gagged and strangled itself with its own notions of nationalism and secularism. The only newspaper which gave a full account of Shri Guruji's statement on the disbandment of the RSS was Pakistan's Dawn on 6 February. The Government of India led by the Congress party thought that the life of RSS had come to an end on 2 February, 1948.

On 7 February, 1948, the Government of India suddenly withdrew the charge of conspiracy of murder and issued a new ordinance ordering Shri Guruji's internment under the National Security Act. He was kept in a solitary prison. Newspapers were denied to him for the first one-month. Shri Guruji displayed unwavering faith and mental fortitude during his stay in prison.

It is clear that Nehru was no champion of civil rights or human rights. After our independence, he functioned like any other petty politician. From his attitude towards the RSS and Shri Guruji we get the lesson - We can vaccinate ourselves against smallpox; there is no vaccination available against small minds, particularly in high places.

At that point of time, Shri Guruji was not aware of the capacity of the Congress party for infidelity and Intrigue. The Nehru government, in a most uncivilised way, ordered the arrest of Shri Guruji on 1 February, 1948 and charged him with the assassination of Mahatma Gandhi. To crown it further, the same mindless and soul-less government withdrew the charge of conspiracy for assassination against Shri Guruji and issued a new ordinance ordering his internment under the National Security Act on 7 February, 1948.

On 6 August, 1948 Shri Guruji was released subject to certain restrictions placed on his activity. Shri Guruji immediately wrote to Nehru and Patel protesting against his unwarranted and illegal detention without assigning any reasons. He also jokingly commented about the restrictions placed on him by saying - I have been transferred from a small jail to a bigger one. Only my prison walls have been extended. He also wrote another strong letter to Nehru in October 1948 requesting to lift the ban on the RSS - I am sure you are convinced that the allegations against the RSS have been found to be without foundation in facts. It is therefore a case of simple justice, which we have a right to expect from a government which we have always considered our own.

Sardar Patel sent a reply to Shri Guruji stating there can be no doubt that the RSS did service to Hindu society. In the areas where there was the need for help and organisation the young men of the RSS protected women and children and strove much for their sake - 'I am strongly convinced that the RSS men can carry on their patriotic endeavour only by joining the Congress and not by keeping separate or opposing.'

At the same time, Nehru wrote to Shri Guruji stating that the RSS was a communal and anti-national organisation. He indirectly seemed to share the view of Patel that the RSS should merge with the Congress.

Reigning Rough Sea

Was it not a moment of great national disgrace that the Prime Minister Nehru and the Deputy Prime Minister of Independent India Patel, whose government had baselessly charged Shri Guruji with the assassination of Mahatma Gandhi and arrested him on 1 February, 1948 and detained him illegally for six months till 6 August, 1948, should now somersault and invite Shri Guruji to join the Congress party in October 1948 even while the trial against Nathuram Godse was still on and he was to be hanged only in November 1949? Were they not guilty of perfidy and travesty of truth? Was it not a sordid act of great national betrayal by both Nehru and Patel? Nathuram Godse only liquidated the body of Mahatma Gandhi. Nehru and Patel spiritually destroyed Mahatma Gandhi and all that he represented for ever. Secular Spiritual Baptism even at that time perhaps meant joining only the Congress party and no other political party.

On 13 Ocotber, 1948 all restrictions on Shri Guruji's activities were unilaterally removed. Shri Guruji went to New Delhi and met Sardar Patel on 23 October, 1948. Sardar Patel insisted that the RSS should merge with the Congress.

Shri Guruji gave him a firm 'no' stating that the RSS was a cultural organisation and not a political party. Emotionally upset by Shri Guruji's spirited reply, Sardar Patel spoke imperiously to Shri Guruji stating that no more discussions were possible and he could go back to Nagpur. Sardar Patel failed to realise that he was dealing with a Maharishi and not with a Congress mercenary who would sell his soul for a mess of pottage. Unsurpassed courage of conviction was the footstool of the virtues upon which he stood. Shri Guruji then moved like a hurricane to show his 'Vishwaroopa' form, even as Lord Krishna did to Arjuna at Kurukshetra, to both Nehru and Patel and indeed the country.

Shri Guruji, a man of indomitable courage and invincible faith, categorically told Nehru and Patel that he would not be cowed down by their intimidation or threats. Enraged by the firm stand of Shri Guruji, Jawaharlal Nehru and Sardar Patel the close political followers of Mahatma Gandhi, who fought with the weapons of non-violence and truth all his life, strangely decided to let loose the forces of State violence and Congress-orchestrated untruth against Shri Guruji and the RSS.

On 2 November, 1948 Shri Guruji called a press conference in New Delhi and distributed two lengthy statements refuting every single charge against the Sangh. He made it clear in his statement that he would not be lured by the offer of Nehru or Patel to join the Congress party. Government of India reacted by issuing a threat to Shri Guruji that unless he returned to Nagpur he would be arrested. It became clear to Shri Guruji that a national Satyagraha by the Swayamsevaks all over India was the only solution open and that was the only way of making the Government of India under Nehru and Patel see reason. On the night of 13 November, 1948 Shri Guruji was arrested under the notorious Bengal State Prisoner's Act of 1818 and sent to prison. This very Act had been strongly condemned by Nehru and Patel before independence as a 'black law'. That 'black law' suddenly became 'white' under the 'inspiring' leadership of Pandit Nehru in post-independent India.

Shri Guruji sent a letter to all the Swayamsevaks soon after his arrest in which he wrote: This state of affairs is humiliating. To continue to submit meekly to this atrocious tyranny is an insult to the honour of citizens of free Bharat and a blow to the prestige of our civilised free State. I therefore request you to stand up for our great cause. Truth and justice are with us. Let the skies reverberate with the call 'Victory to Bharat' and rest not till the goal is reached. *Bharat Mata ki Jai.* The whole nation was electrified by the resounding message of Shri Guruji.

Nehru and Patel wrongly calculated that Shri Guruji and the Sangh could be intimidated into total silence. Nehru particularly was of the view that any Satyagraha movement consisting of inexperienced youths launched by Shri Guruji would peter out in a few days. Nor did he or Patel expect the number of Satyagrahis to cross a few thousands. This wrong perception was made clear by Nehru at a public meeting at Jaipur in the first week of November 1948 when he said: This is a Duragraha of the urchins of the Sangh. The government will use all its might to crush this agitation. In this context it will not be out of place to mention that Nehru spoke almost the same language against the Government of China when he was in Ceylon on the first day of the Chinese invasion in October 1962. We will throw out the Chinese. The harsh and bitter truth is that by the time he returned to New Delhi, Chinese had over-run the greater portion of Arunachal Pradesh and were on their way to Guwahati.

In a public meeting in Gwalior on 5 December, 1948 Sardar Patel said: 'some people say the Sangh is going to start a Satyagraha. But these people can never conduct a Satyagraha, their Satyagraha will never succeed, because their minds are unclean. We had advised them to join the Congress and had tried to bring about a change of heart among them but they have chosen the path of confrontation. I warn them, we are ready to face such challenges'.

Yevgency Yevtushenko, the great Russian poet, had double-dealing men like Nehru and Patel in view when he came out with the following lines of poetry. -

'NERO, apparently thought
He was a poet.
HITLER thought that he
Would redeem the world from woe!
The man thinks:'I am so generous'
The shallow man: 'I am profound'
Sometimes God will sigh: 'I am a worm'
The worm hisses: 'I am God'.

Shri Guruji gave a call for total Satyagraha on 9 December, 1948. As he was in prison, he nominated Sarkaryavaha Shri Bhaiyayaji Dani to lead the Satyagraha movement by holding Shakhas all over the country. From that day, the Satyagraha gained momentum. Shouting slogans like Bharat Mata Ki Jai ! and 'Long Live Sangh',batches of Swayamsevaks all over the country came out to hold Shakhas and the police took them into custody. The nationwide Satyagraha launched by Shri Guruji led to an animated and heated discussion among all sections of society in India about the illegal ban imposed by the Government of India on the RSS. In many places, apart from Swayamsevaks, even the common people not belonging to the RSS started putting up posters with the demand - Prove the charges against the RSS or lift the ban'At the same time, lakhs and lakhs of copies of pamphlets legally refuting the charges against the RSS and explaining its just and nationalist demand were distributed from Kashmir to Kanyakumari. There was a great enthusiasm among the Swayamsevaks for pushing the Satyagraha movement to its logical conclusion regardless of consequences. The Government of India had never imagined that more than 80,000 Satyagrahis would come forward to offer Satyagraha and would be cheerfully willing to be thrown behind bars. It became virtually impossible for the police administration in all the States to deal with this very large number of "cultural prisoners" Simultaneously in many of the places the Swayamsevaks went on a hunger strike causing great worry to the government at various levels. The inhuman lathi charges on peaceful Satyagrahis in Madras City was condemned by eminent men like T.R. Venkatrama Sastri of the Liberal Party and Swami Venkatachalam, a Member of Parliament.

Shri Guruji was still continuing in prison. There was no sign of the Satyagraha movement stopping and of the enthusiasm of the Swayamsevaks abating. In January 1949, G.V. Ketkar, editor of the Pune based daily 'Kesari' met Shri Guruji in Sivani Jail twice and suggested to him that if the Satyagraha was suspended, it would pave the way for public spirited men like T.R Venkatrama Sastri for initiating some moves for getting the ban on the RSS. lifted. Shri Guruji agreed and gave a written directive for suspending the Satyagraha and finally on 22 January, 1949, the suspension of Satyagraha was formally announced. The saga of the country wide Satyagraha, that was started on 9 December, 1948 on the call of Shri Guruji came to a remarkably successful conclusion.

Satyameva Jayate

A wave of public sympathy for the RSS swept throughout the country. For a change, this was also reflected in the media. On 22 January, 1949, 'The Tribune' from Ambala remarked. 'The RSS leader has paved the way for eventual settlement by calling off the movement without any conditions. It is now for the Government of India to honorably withdraw the ban. Let the Government of India remember that a policy of suppression will never succeed in killing an organisation'. Likewise, 'The Statesman' of Calcutta paid a personal tribute to Shri Guruji for the manner in which he conducted the agitation and stated that the ban on the RSS was causing the youth power to go to waste by keeping them behind bars'.

Realising that the public opinion was going against the Government of India, a request was made to Shri Guruji to prepare a written Constitution for the RSS and to send it to Government of India for information. (It may be noted that till then RSS was functioning in a most disciplined way without even a written Constitution). Accordingly, some leading office bearers of the RSS met T.R. Venkatrama Sastri in Madras and got a draft Constitution ready for the RSS in June 1949. It was finalized by Shri Guruji and forwarded to Government of India for their information.

In the meantime, angered by the authoritarian and dictatorial attitude of the Government of India, T.R. Venkatrama Sastri had prepared a long statement to the press and sent it to them on 6 July, 1949 with request that it should not be published till 13 July, 1949.Government of India was rattled by this move. T.R. Venkatrama Sastri's publication of his indictment in all the newspapers in India and abroad would have brought great shame to the government in the eyes of the people and so it was decided to lift the ban just a day prior to its proposed publication on 13 July, 1949. Yet, 'The Hindu' of Madras carried the entire statement of T.R. Venkatrama Sastri on its 13 July issue which fully exposed the Government of India. Reacting to Government of India's objection that The RSS Constitution was right enough, but the leaders of this organisation cannot be trusted to function within its scope', T.R. Venkatrama Sastri in his strong statement said:'Apart from being illegal, it would be hard on any organisation to say that in anticipation of a not unlikely unlawful action on the part of its members, it is not allowed to begin its work. A government or a State can be characterised as 'Fascist', but not a private organisation like the RSS, to which no one is compelled to belong. One may join it, or refuse to join it, or having joined it, may resign at will'.

On 12 July, 1949 the ban on the RSS was removed unilaterally by Government of India.Shri Guruji was released from Betul Jail on 13 July, 1949. The Government of India covered themselves with deathless shame and Shri Guruji with immortal glory in the pages of history.

After nearly 18 long months of illegal incarceration with out any charge, Shri Guruji was released unconditionally from Betul Jain on 13 July, 1949. When he arrived at the Nagpur Railway Station at noon, more than 30,000 people gave him a tumultuous welcome. Thousands of people shed tears as they saw Guruji's father garlanding his own son who had come out successfully out of the fiery ordeal. Four days later, Shri Guruji went to Madras to thank T.R.Venkatrama Sastri personally for having taken the trouble to draft a Constitution for the RSS, for having taken the initiative to meet Patel and Nehru and strongly advice them to lift the ban on the RSS and to release Shri Guruji from prison and finally for issuing a very strong statement against the Government of India for having acted in such a dictatorial manner in the first few months of independent India, which he thought was cruel mockery of freedom.

After several months of orchestrated fraud, untruth and falsehood enacted with the full might of the State, the government itself came out candidly with the truth in the Bombay Legislative Assembly on 14 October, 1949. In replies to questions raised by Lallubai Patel from Surat, the Minister for Home and Revenue, Government of Bombay, said:

a) That the lifting of ban on RSS was unconditional.

b) Its leader Golwalkar had given no undertaking to the government.

Thus it can be seen that the Congress cowards in New Delhi smartly transferred the dirty responsibility of making the above truthful but very unsavoury statements from their point of view, to the Congress Government of Bombay. It became clear to all concerned, the whole of India and the wider world outside that the Government of India had tried to arm-twist Shri Guruji and to crush the RSS. The real eye-opening fact was that not even a single Swayamsevak of the Sangh was charge-sheeted or prosecuted anywhere in the country on any of the politically and baselessly trumpeted charges against the Sangh, including the charge of 'assassination of Mahatma Gandhi'. The whole dishonesty of the Government of India right from the start can be seen from a letter sent by Sardar Patel to Pandit Nehru on 27 February, 1948, less than a month after Mahatma Gandhi" assassination on 30 January, 1948 'I have kept myself almost in daily touch with the progress of the investigations regarding Bapu's assassination case. All the main accused have given long and detailed statements of their activities. It also clearly emerges from the statements that the RSS was not involved in it at all'. Even after sending this letter, Government of India, which meant Nehru and Patel-did not have the grace to release Shri Guruji till August 1948.

Superb Statesman

As Shri Guruji had been out of touch with the Swayamsevaks all over India from 1 February, 1948 till July 12, 1949 when the ban on the RSS was removed, it became very much necessary for Shri Guruji to undertake a nation wide tour. Shri Guruji's All Bharat Tour began in August 1949 and lasted till January 1950. Wherever he went, he received spontaneous and tremendous ovations. The overwhelming public response to the function at Delhi on 23 August, 1949 Attracted world-wide attention. The BBC reported on the radio. Shri Guruji is a shining star that has arisen on the Indian firmament. The only other Indian who can draw such huge crowds is Pandit Nehru. The Indian Press too flashed the highlights of this function. History may have but few examples of lakhs and lakhs of people giving a leader without any Government authority, such a rousing reception wherever he went. Shri Guruji rose to Himalayan heights of magnanimity, forbearance and statesmanship by giving this message at all his public meetings - Let us close this chapter of the ban on the Sangh. Do not let your minds be overcome with bitterness for those who you feel, have done injustice to you. If the teeth were to bite the tongue, do we pull out the teeth? Even those who have done injustice to us are our own people. So we must forget and forgive. This was Guruji's Sanatana Dharma in action in answer to

Nehru and Patel's low-level politics marked by hatred, jealousy, prejudice and arrogance of unbridled power.

The post-independence era has witnessed many a campaign launched by the Swayamsevaks for upholding and refurbishing aspects of national faith and veneration in various spheres of life. Dr Hedgewar's views of the future set-up of Bharat after the attainment of freedom was in tune with the essence of our national ethos. The jottings that he put down on the day the Congress adopted 'Complete Independence as its goal in 1930 are clear and emphatic: The Hindu culture is the life-breath of Hindusthan. It is therefore clear that if Hindusthan is to be protected, we should first nourish the Hindu culture. If the Hindu culture perishes in Hindusthan itself, and if the Hindu society ceases to exist, it will hardly be appropriate to refer to the mere geographical entity that remains as Hindusthan. Mere geographical lumps do not make a nation. The Sangh will cooperate with the Congress in the efforts to secure freedom, so long as these efforts do not come in the way of preserving our nation's culture.

Shri Guruji in his penetrating and perceptive analysis of the directions in which the post-independence Bharat was being led by the Congress and other rulers said: Today we find everywhere attempts to recast our life pattern in the mould of an American, English or Russian way of life. How can we call it swantatra (freedom) which has no 'Swa' (our national genius) in it? Then it is only para-tantra. If Lenin is kept as the ideal, it becomes Lenin-tantra and not Swantantra. In fact preservation and propagation of our national life values i.e. our Sanatana Dharma and *Samskriti*, have always been held in our historical traditions as the raison d'être of Swantantra.

Taking these as our firm guidelines, the Swayamsevaks have been trying to manifest the nation's pristine genius in diverse fields of national endeavour for the last 58 years of our independence. They have always kept before them the following message of Dr. Hedgewar and Shri Guruji.

'Wherever and in whatever position you are, do not forget that you are a Swayamsevak. Always and everywhere consider yourself as a Sangh Pracharak-devoted to carrying the message of Sangh'.

On 2 August, 1954; 100 Sangh Swayamsevaks stormed the Portuguese enclaves of Dadra and Nagar Haveli. The attack was led by Vinyak Rao Apte, Pune Sanghchalak. They attacked the main police headquarters at Selvassa and forced the 175 soldiers there to surrender unconditionally. The national tri-colour flag was hoisted and the region handed over to the Central Government on the same day. Like-wise the first to unfurl the national flag over the Panaji Secretariat in Goa in 1955 was a Swayamsevak working as a teacher in Goa. He was put in prison in a Lisbon jail for full 17 years till 1972-well after Goa was liberated in 1961. One cannot help surmising that Government of India was not interested in his earlier release only because he was a Swayamsevak.

Shri Guruji was the first public leader to give out the news of illegal occupation by Chinese Government of large chunks of our strategic Himalayan borders in 1960. In 1960 when Pandit Nehru and Chou-En-lai were jointly touring our country singing the lullaby of 'Hindi-Cheeni Bhai-Bhai', Shri Guruji's was the lone voice laying bare the dragon's teeth hidden behind that enchanting slogan. Nehru had romantic love for Chou-En-lai and ignored the timely warning of Shri Guruji.

When Pakistan attacked Bharat in 1965, Lal Bahadur Shastri, the then Prime Minister, personally rang up Shri Guruji who was then touring Maharashtra and requested him to be in New Delhi for the All Leaders Conference the following day. Shri Guruji placed the entire RSS at the disposal of the Government of India to fight the invaders and to safeguard the integrity of our motherland. In Delhi, for the entire period of 22 days of war, police duties like traffic control and patrolling were transferred to Swayamsevaks to free the police for more pressing tasks.

Right from the beginning of the war, everyday, hundreds of Swayamsevaks daily reported at the General Military Hospital, Delhi to offer blood. The military looked upon the Sangh as a friend in need. Likewise during the Bangladesh War in 1971, the Swayamsevaks of the Sangh played a vital role in assisting the Government of India in their war efforts against Pakistan.

During the Emergency in 1975-77 imposed by Indira Gandhi, like a dictator in the line of Hitler and Mussolini, our country was plunged in dark internal slavery and every single cherished value of free and democratic life was smothered. Indira Gandhi repeated the mistake of Nehru and Patel and imposed a ban on the RSS. In those dark days, the Swayamsevaks rose as one man in the cause of the people. Winston Churchill's heroic words can be applied to the Swayamsevaks and the RSS: Let us therefore brace ourselves to our duties and so bear ourselves that if Bharat Mata and Hindu Dharma last for a thousand years, men will still say this was their finest hour'.

Shri Guruji had a clear vision of the ideal conditions in every sphere of national life. Bharat could never be strong to fulfill its destiny unless every aspect of the nation's life was informed with the pure and inspiring ideology of the Sangh. Shri Guruji pioneered the creation of many fields of such constructive activity. Through his tremendous drive and initiative, he created several powerful nationwide organisation like Vishwa Hindu Parishad, Vivekananda Rock Memorial, Akhila Bharatiya Vidyarthi Parishad, Bharatiya Mazdoor Sangh, Vanavasi Kalyan Ashram and the Shishu Mandir educational institutions. To the political field Shri Guruji gave two priceless jewels like Dr Shyama Prasad Mukherjee and Pandit Deen Dayal Upadhyaya.

On 5 June, 1973 Shri Guruji passed away peacefully in Nagpur after a lifetime of ceaseless activity for the advancement of the glory of Bharat Mata and victory of Bharat without losing sight of the ultimate ideal of achieving Akhand Bharat. Like Swami Vivekananda, he embodied the spirit of India. In my view he was amongst the greatest of our nationalists. The best tribute to him was paid by R.K. Karanjia of 'Bitz' of Bombay: "He had no axe to grind, and in the pursuit of his ideals languor was not in his heart, weakness was not in his word, weariness was not on his brow. It would be good if other political leaders emulate his example of dedicated life and win the respect and confidence of his followers'.

Essence of R.S.S.

A nation is a soul, a spiritual principle. Two things that in truth are but one constitute this soul or spiritual principle. One lies in the past, one in the present. One is the possession in common of a rich legacy of memories; the other is present-day consent, the desire to live together, the will to perpetuate the value of the heritage that one had received in an undivided form.

Man does not improvise. The nation, like the individual, is the culmination of a long past of heroic endeavours, selfless sacrifices and glorious deeds of devotion. Of all cults, that of the ancestors is the most legitimate, for the ancestors have made us what we are. A heroic past, great men, glory in song, tradition and legend- this is the social capital upon which one bases a national idea. To have common glories in the past and to have a common will in the present; to have performed great deeds together, to wish to perform still more-these are the essential conditions for being a people. One loves in proportion to the sacrifices to which one has consented, and in proportion to the ills that one has suffered. One loves the house that one has built and that one has handed down. The Spartan song-"We are what you were; we will be what you are"-is, in its simplicity, the abridged hymn of Hindutva today. If Hindutva vanishes, what will Bharatvarsha be? She will become a geographical expression of the vanished past, a dim memory of a perished glory. We have to avert this grim national tragedy at any cost. How can we forget that our history, our literature, our art, our temples and monuments, all have Hinduism writ indelibly across them?

Sri Guruji was pained that Hindus should have been reduced to the position of "non-Muslims" in post-independent India. Even before Independence, he wondered why India alone should be described as a "sub-continent" when even much bigger countries like USA, USSR and China were not described in that manner. He said he had no doubt that our country was being dubbed a "sub-continent" only to prepare the public mind for its Partition. Consistently, Sri Guruji took a strong stand against the Partition of India. He stood for Akhand Bharat throughout his lifetime.

Sri Guruji always ridiculed the idea of India being a "nation in the making" and said that proponents of this theory appeared to be only "patriots in the making". Wherever he went he quoted chapter and verse to show that Bharatvarsh had been a "Rashtra" since Vedic times. He was quite amused that Shaivites and Vaishnavites of Kanchipuram should refer their religious ritualistic disputes- whether the temple elephant should bear a "U" tilak or a "Y" tilak- to the British Privy Council, which knew little about India and nothing about Hinduism.

A little before the Partition of India when Sri K. Ponniah, Editor of The Sindh Observer asked him if it would really matter if India was partitioned, Sri Guruji said that at that rate it wouldn't matter if somebody lost his nose. At that point of time when somebody said that it didnot matter if all Hindus became Muslims in one stroke, Sri Guruji replied; "It wouldn't matter even if all the Hindus died. Because they would live as ashes, and science has proved that matter is indestructible and that even matter has only some electrical charges."

When Sri Guruji was asked to define the RSS in one word, he said; "Hinduism can be defined in one word, 'Om'. But it would take years of study to understand its significance. Likewise RSS can be understood only by attending Shakha everyday."

Once making an emotional appeal to workers to complete the RSS work in the manner and measure required, he quoted an example from the famous biography of Dr. Samuel Johnson written by his Secretary Boswell; "Doctor, how many fish in a chain will take it reach from here to the moon?" Dr. Johnson was nonplussed by this question. Goldsmith himself replied; "Only one fish will suffice-if it is sufficiently big!" Sri Guruji said that similarly even a single day would suffice for the completion of RSS work-if only all the Swayamsevaks of the Sangh worked with every atom of their strength with unshakable faith in the ultimate victory of 'Sanatana Dharma'.

Sri Guruji consistently held the view that a proper history of India had not yet been written. In this context he stated:" It is ridiculous to divide our national history into Hindu period, Muslim period and British period. History can't be named after rulers; a proper history has to be a history of the people. And so, our entire history is Hindu history." This is the quintessence of Hindutva. Bal Gangadhar Tilak, Aurobindo Ghosh, Vir Savarkar, Dr. Hedgewar, and Sri Guruji have all built up this great edifice of Hindutva. 'Hindutva' is not just a word. It is history of a great culture and civilization called Sanatana Dharma. Hinduism is only a derivative, a fraction or a part of Hindutva or Hinduness.

Often Sri Guruji would also add:"Our history books tend to revolve round Delhi. But Delhi is not India. And in many periods of Indian history, other kingdoms have been bigger than the kingdom of Delhi. Because of these lop-sided history books, our people know little about the Cholas, the Cheras, the Pandyas, the Hoysalas, the Pulakeshins. How many people have even heard of Kharvel of Utkal, one of the greatest kings of Bharatvarsha, who controlled much of Southeast Asia? Or of Lachit Barphukan, hero of the successful Assamese resistance to Mughal attacks?"

Saga of Sacrifice

Under Sri Guruji's inspiring, fearless and indomitable leadership, RSS grew by leaps and bounds. In town after town the Sangh Pracharak would arrive with a few letters of introduction to the local leaders, whether belonging to the Congress, the Hindu Mahasabha, the Arya Samaj or whatever. They would put up themselves in the local bhavan of any of these organisations or in a temple or with any well-wisher. His job, often as a teacher, would bring them in touch with many students and teachers. Any existing local Hindu volunteer organization would promptly merge with the new RSS Shakha. With help from local well-wishers and guidance from their seniors in the RSS, the Shakha would grow in to a social magnet, attracting promising youngmen and local VIPs alike, regardless of their caste, class or sect. Soon it would be the strongest organisation in town. Before long it would produce energetic young men to carry the message of Sangh to other towns and even villages. At a time when RSS was growing like wildfire, Sri Guruji said: "If I were to spend just one day in each Shakha, even a life-time would not suffice to cover the whole country."

Swami Akhandananda, one of the 16 monastic direct disciples of Ramakrishna Paramahamsa, discerned in Sri Guruji all the potentialities of a Vivekananda re-born. Dr. Hedgewar, the founder of the RSS saw in him a worthy leader of the Sangh. While casting off their mortal coil, both these mahatmas had an innate satisfaction-Swami Akhandanandaji for having handed over the torch of spiritualism to a worthy disciple and Dr. Hedgewarji for leaving the Sangh in strong safe hands. As a disciple of the former and successor of the latter, Sri Guruji combined in himself both the roles-both in one, both at once. In him were fulfilled the missions of both blended into one. He established through his example that apparently divergent messages of these two illustrious souls were in reality not only compatible but perfectly identical too. By a lifetime saga of sacrifice and service to Bharatvarsha, Sri Guruji demonstrated that society is merely a manifestation of the Vishavaroopa. Emphasizing the importance of unity in society amongst the Hindus, Sri Guruji wanted all the Hindus to keep the following poem of William Wordsworth in mind every moment:

"Dust as we are, the immortal spirit grows like harmony in music; there is a dark Inscrutable workmanship that reconciles Discordant elements, makes them cling together in one society".

There are two types of people in this world. Those who come into a room and say, "well, here I am!" and those who come in and say "Ah! There you are!" Sri Guruji did not consider himself a separate entity, independently of the Sangh. His life was a yajna, an eternal sacrifice at the sacred feet of the jana (people), the manifestation of Janardhana (God). Sri Guruji's most precious offering in this Yajna was his own ego. For Sri Guruji innate humility was just as much the opposite of self-abasement as it was of self-exaltation. He wanted every Swayamsevak to give up the pursuit of individual salvation in favour of an endeavour for corporate self-realisation of the Sangh.

While replying to a civic address at Madurai in December 1949, Sri Guruji aptly observed: "A post box receives letters, at times very important ones. But the box has no reason to be flattered by them. It is only an intermediary through which letters pass to proper persons in the proper places. The honours which you have bestowed on me I will pass on to those countless workers whom I am privileged to represent." On another occasion, dismissing the idea that RSS would suffer incalculably in his absence, he stated with fervor and conviction: "No particular individual is indispensable. Men may come and men may go, but the society goes on forever. With me or without me, the Sangh will continue to work and grow because of their inner necessity and intrinsic work."

Carlyle in his famous work 'Heroes and Hero Worship' wrote: "It is well said, in every sense that a man's religion is the chief fact with regard to him. No great man lives in vain. The history of the world is but the biography of great men. The hero can be poet, prophet, king, priest or what you will, according to the kind of world he finds himself born into." These stirring words are totally applicable to Sri Guruji. He would have made his mark anywhere. He was a saint, a sage, a seer in the great Hindu tradition of sages like Vashishta, Bharadwaj, Shankracharya, Yagnavalkya, Vishwamitra, Angirasa and others going back to the dawn of history.

We have to live up to his legacy that can help human beings in all corners of our globe to rejuvenate our spirit not to conquer one another, but to conquer oneself; not to destroy, but to build; not to hate, but to love; not to isolate oneself, but to integrate everyone into one global society and to achieve much more in the future to enrich human civilization to result in the maximum welfare of the maximum number or as in Sanskrit it is called: Loko samasto sukhino bhavantu & samasta janaanaam sukhino bhavantu.

(The writer is a retired I.A.S. officer and eminent thinker.)

4

From Yuva Sanyasi To Rashtra-Rishi

P. Parmeshwaran

I first met Shree Gurujee in a winter camp at Salem in 1946. I was a student doing my honours in the University College, Thiruvananthapuram. We were all seated in a hall, to be addressed by Shri Guruji. Being the first occasion, I was all expectation, if not trepidation. As Shri Guruji entered the hall, my eager eyes took him in. He was young, dynamic and had the appearance of a Yuva Sanyasi dressed in white dhoti and kurta over which he wore a coat. He held a staff with a metal head in hand. Brilliant, piercing eyes which directly entered into your very soul; dense, dark, flowing hair and beard completed the serene majesty of his unique personality.

Each one of us got introduced to him by turn. To each one, he asked a few questions. From the answers, he could easily size up the caliber and capacity of each one. Every one got some suggestion and guidance through this informal question and answer session. At the end we were pleasantly surprised that Shri Guruji could call everyone by his name. But what appeared strange was that this meeting of the ground level workers with the highest in the organisation was full of mirth and laughter, even while serious matters of organisation were raised, discussed and answered. All felt homely, as if they were meeting the head of the family. It took about one whole hour though we felt as if it was not even half that time. At the end when Shri Guruji stood up and left us, the living image of his unique personality was indelibly carved in everybody's heart. It was to remain there for all time to come as an object of sweet remembrance and respectful adoration.

Shri Guruji was about 40 years of age at that time. I was hardly 20. Thereafter, it was my good fortune to meet him at least twice every year and some times even more, till he passed away in the year 1973. Every meeting was a unique experience, each in its own way.

Just as the first meetings engraved on the mind, one of the last meetings also remains undimmed. The year may be 1970 or 1971. The venue was Calicut. Shri Guruji had come for a baithak of senior karyakartas. He had grown old with silvery hairs and white beard. The staff in hand was substituted by a kamandalu. We were told that it was gifted to him by his revered guru Swami Akhandananda Ji. From the dynamic Yuva Sanyasi that he was in 1946, he had grown and evolved into revered Rashtra Rishi. We were reminded of the galaxy of our ancient Vedic sages. Age and experience had matured him into a loftiness beyond human. He seemed to be in a hurry. As the moment of departure came, we lined on either side with folded hands to have another look at him. Shri Guruji with his graceful glance and an occasional word or two moved swiftly ahead as if he was conscious that the time left was short and the mission ahead was beckoning him to hurry up. Yes, the life's journey was moving forward towards its final end. It was as moving and unforgettable a moment as the first meeting was.

From 1940 to 1973, was a tumultuous period in our nation's history. It was through these momentous 33 years that he led the great organisation committed to his care by Dr. Hedgewar, steadily, swiftly and carefully ahead. A minor error, a small slip, a slight error would have landed the organisation in irreparable chaos or calamity in those eventful and challenging period. But he never slipped, never erred. To err is human, says the old proverb. By that standard Shri Guruji was super human. From the time of taking over from the founder to the time of handing over to his successor, Shri Guruji was wisdom and alertness incarnate. The organisation grew from strength to strength, spread over the whole of the country and even abroad wherever Hindus lived. Every area of national life was illumined and electrified by the mantra of Hindu Rashtra. Along with the growth of the movement, Shri Guruji, the one-time little known professor of the Benares Hindu University, emerged and evolved into the stature of the Rashtra Guru, revered and respected by one and all. Irrespective of any other consideration, he won universal acceptance. But he never compromised on principles or minced words in giving expressions to his convictions. Even those politicians who were never tired of criticizing him in place and out of place, paid rich tribute to his services to the nation, when the Parliament adopted the condolence resolution at his passing away.

Shri Guruji's mighty personality had combined in itself two great streams of our ancient national life-the spiritual and the national. It was there in its seminal form right from the beginning of his life. In later life, both the currents mingling into one became a mighty flow. He had inherited the timeless spiritual tradition of Sanatan Dharma from Shri Ramkrishna Paramhansa, Swami Vivekananda and Swami Akhandananda Ji Maharaj, who was his deeksha guru. From Lokamanya Tilak, Veer Savarkar and Dr. Hedgewar he had inherited the nationalistic stream which became inseparable part of his very constitution. Though at times, the spiritual dimension gained dominance over the other, Shri Guruji could never break away from the nationalist moorings. At first it was an uneasy co-existence which later evolved into one harmonious, single, sacred flow as in the case of Swami Vivekananda and Shri Aurobindo. The spiritual and the national so intermingled that they became identical and inseparable. Worship of the motherland became worship of the divine mother. It was the message of the sublime spiritual nationalism that he has bequeathed to us. Being fully assured that therein lies India's unique contribution to the rest of the world. For Shri Guruji, the work of Sangha was nothing but the selfless sadhana for fulfilling this world mission of Bharat. The Bhagirathi of Sangh sadhana flows on undeterred to its divinely destined goal.

Sister Nivedita, in her foreword to the complete works of Swami Vivekanand, wrote in 1906. "What Hinduism needed, amidst the general disintegration of the modern era, was a rock where she could lie at anchor, an authoritative utterance in which she might recognize herself." Similar words may be used to describe the message that Guruji gave to his countrymen during three decades as Sarsanghchalak of the RSS.

Like Swami Vivekanand, Guruji's ideas have come down to us mostly through the lectures he delivered and the letters he wrote on innumerable occasions. He neither had the time, nor the inclination to sit down and write any book, though his skill, ability, scholarship and mastery over the language for the task was unquestionable. To the question why, in spite of his thorough knowledge of history, he did not write down a book on history, Guruji's reply was typical; "We are here to make history. It is for others to write." In his endless travels and meetings with people from all strata of society - rich and poor, intellectuals as well as illiterate - and in his daily lectures and discourses, Guruji dealt with every aspect of life, both in their practical and philosophical dimensions. He was eminently qualified for such a daunting task.

These viewpoints have a unique significance. They are not mere philosophical treatises. Guruji was not just an academic philosopher. No doubt, he had mastered the crux and complexities of Hindu philosophy. But, as a down-to-earth, practical leader of men, guide and philosopher of a multi-faceted countrywide movement, he had tested his philosophical wisdom by experience and experiment in his everyday life and contact. He never lost touch with ground realities and burning problems. As such, his viewpoint, while remaining deeply rooted in the Hindu spiritual tradition, had intense practical relevance.

Shri Guruji never got struck in the problems and travails of the day. Though he never failed to give practical guidelines for the immediate problems of the organisation and Hindu society. He had always kept a long-term perspective and never swerved from the national and spiritual angle. Even while guiding politicians who approached him for advice, Guruji never counselled expediency or unprincipled compromise. He belonged to the tradition of the rishis who were the safe custodians of unerring wisdom.

All this was possible because he lived and worked during what could be termed a 'Yuga-Sandhi'. He belonged as much to the glorious traditions of the past as to the future, with its immense possibilities. He was born into a family enriched by rigorous and austere religious practices. His parentage left a deep and indelible impression of uncompromising spiritual values, of rigorous and austere religious practices and observances. His education at the then most famous Benares Hindu University, where the atmosphere was throbbing with the living presence of M.M. Malaviya, moulded him in a manner not possible elsewhere.

The rare privilege to come under the spiritual magnetism of Swami Akhandananda, a direct disciple of Ramakrishna Paramahamsa and the gurubhai of Swami Vivekanand, gave Guruji a unique opportunity to nourish his in-born spiritual tendencies to the fullest extent. Besides, Guruji came into intimate contact with Dr. K.B. Hedgewar, who was the very personification of dedication to Hindu nation. The touch of Hedgewar gradually transformed and finally decided the direction of Guruji's momentous life. In him, we find the combination of Aurobindo and Lokamanya Tilak, the father of Indian unrest. This was a rare combination pregnant with tremendous possibilities.

As Guruji's life unfolded through various stages, the world witnessed the presence of an organiser, a transformer, a philosopher and a prophet, all rolled into one. Dattopant Thengadi, with his intuitive perception, described Guruji as

The great sentinel, with genuine poetic inspiration. Thengadi sang the glory of Guruji in the following couplet:

O mighty master! To the tune of thy finger
The oceans dance and mountains move
Crowns are raised and melted down
Thou art supreme - here and above

The mission entrusted to Guruji, as the head of the RSS, was to bring about national regeneration. This required a restatement of the tenets and practices, views and objectives of Sanatana Dharma in terms of the new Yuga Dharma, in manner both intelligible and applicable to the modern generation. Moreover, this had to be done in the context of the emerging world situation. No country, much less an important one like Bharat, could live in isolation. The way Bharat shaped itself was relevant to the shaping up of the world. Guruji knew it too well. Though his prime concern was national resurgence and reconstruction, Guruji knew that Bharat had a global role to play.

The international situation that presented itself at that time was one of great peril.there seemed no option left before the world. It was in the grip of two conflicting systems and ideologies, Capitalism and Communism, each claiming to be the sole custodian of a world redeeming philosophy and a model of humanity.

Many people falsely believed that the Hindu regeneration movement had nothing to offer to mitigate the distress or to resolve the dilemma faced by the world. To them, the approach of Guruji was based on narrow Hindu sectarianism, whereas the situation demanded an alternate worldview, which could provide hope and cheer for the future of all humanity.

Shri Guruji unambiguously stated that much before Capitalism and Communism were even thought of, our forefathers in India had been thinking about the whole world and its welfare. The prayer on their lips was

Lokassamasta Sukhino Bhavantu (Let the whole world be happy). While the West based its philosophy on principles of competition and conflict, and envisaged survival only for the fittest, the Hindu paradigm visualized the entire world as one family.

The highest that the West could promise was the greatest good of the greatest number. According to Guruji, the different Western views were incapable of offering a way of life wherein not only human beings but also the entire creation will find a safe and secure place to occupy. This is inherent in their philosophy, whether it is Capitalist or Communist. Both are compartmental, and not comprehensive, because they are based on gross materialistic approach.

Neither Capitalism, nor Communism could provide a lasting and peaceful solution because both were essentially materialistic. It was only the Hindu approach based on a spiritual view of things that could provide the real alternative. Spirituality does not compartmentalize. It does not reject material needs and the other requirements of man. It only locates and evaluates them in an overall context. It gives a new vision of life, which includes both material welfare and spiritual enlightenment. Materialism does not ensure full growth of man. It dwarfs him by abolishing the spiritual dimension altogether.

For the materialist, whether a Capitalist or a Communist, man is essentially a body with or without a soul. Spirituality, in contrast, envisages man as an embodied divine spark or soul. It encompasses both the aspects and envisages a perfect or an integral man. Guruji called him poorna manav. This concept of poorna manav, which Guruji invoked was the cornerstone of philosophy of integral humanism, elaborately propounded by Pandit Deendayal Upadhyaya. 'Integral humanism' was a restatement of the Hindu social philosophy based on Sanatana Dharma in the context of the existing situation. This is posited not merely as another alternative or just a third way, but as the real way ahead for the humanity sandwiched between Capitalism and Communism in those days.

Shri Guruji was of the Firm view that neither Communism nor Capitalism could ever unite the world. The reason he gave is fundamental. Materialistic philosophy which considers man as basically a physical animal and which considers the fulfillment of material desires and wants as the supreme need of man can only generate competition and conflict and not Unity and Harmony. The reason is simple. At the material plane, there is only diversity and difference. They foster concepts of separatism and exclusivism. For people who see only at the level of material reality there is nothing that unifies or integrates. There is no reason why they should think of co-operation. It is only when we look beneath the apparent diversities that we come to realize that there is an underlying unity though subtle which unites all these gross entities into one integrated whole.

Shri Guruji stated:

"From the materialist point of view we are all gross entities, each separate and exclusive in itself, who can have no bonds of mutual affinity or affection. There can also be no inner restraint in such beings which can make them control their selfishness from running amuck in the interest of the humanity as a whole.

"After all, any arrangement evolved for achieving world welfare can be fruitful only to the extent the men behind them would mould their individual and national conduct in tune with the welfare of humanity. Without that supreme urge, any scheme, however good its purpose may be, will only provide one more alluring mask for the aggrandizement of power-drunk nations. That has been the uniform verdict of history right up to the present times.

"Our ancient Hindu philosophers, therefore, had turned their gaze to a plane higher than materialism. They delved deep into the mysteries of the human soul, well beyond the reach of material science, and discovered the Ultimate Reality which pervades all Creation, the one great common principle present in all beings whatever the name we may give it - Soul, God, Truth, Reality or Nothingness. It is the occasional realization of this common entity that inspires us to strive for the happiness of others. The 'I' in me, being the same as the 'I' in the other beings, makes me react to the joys and sorrows of my fellow living beings just as I react to my own. This genuine feeling of identity born out of the community of the inner entity is the real driving force behind our natural urge for human unity and brotherhood. Thus it is evident that world unity and human welfare can be made real only to the extent mankind realises this common Inner Bond which alone can subdue the passions and discords stemming from materialism, broaden the horizon of the human mind and harmonise the individual and national aspirations with the welfare of mankind."

Shri Guruji was of the considered view that the Bharateeya system was the only one which ensured individual freedom without compromising social development 'The West relies on two systems: Democracy and Communism. Democracy, as we see, has led to the growth of selfishness and set up man against man. There is no peace to man. Spirituality has no chance to grow there. The self-praise and the condemnations of others which are normally indulged in during elections kill spirituality.

Communism on the other hand has led to the regimentation of mind; it destroys the individuality of man. But man is not a mere animal to be content with eating and procreating. He has an urge w hich goes beyond that, which cannot be met merely by the material things.

In our system individual liberty and social solidarity were both ensured. The individual was freed from the shackles of economic bondage, because he was assured of a profession from his very birth. Even in the West, thinkers have begun pondering on these lines. This system ensures a clear way to rise to God-hood, devoid of the worry for worldly needs. Thus it was that among all the castes, saints of the highest order were born. This is a wonderful democracy on the spiritual basis. All are one on that basis."

Guruji was the very embodiment of all the qualities that he preached for the good of society. We hardly come across a person who devoted every moment of his life and every iota of his energy for the fulfillment of the great vision of a resurgent Bharat. The highest glory of the country was the only goal before him. A strong and well-organised Hindu society was the sure means for achieving this. Creating a network of Swayamsevaks in every nook and corner of the country who are imbued with this patriotic fervour, disciplined and dedicated, imbued with personal and national character, ever ready and willing to surrender themselves at the alter of the nation, was sacred task for which Guruji devoted his entire life.

Like Shankaracharya and Vivekanand, he travelled from one end of the country to the other preaching this gospel of Hindu unity and national glory. No other leader had criss-crossed the country as many times as Guruji. He was an eternal traveller, a pilgrim always on the move.

As Vivekanand has visualised, the queen of his adoration was Bharat Mata. The mantra on his lips was "Victory to the Mother". True to his commitment, Guruji passed away with the same mantra on his lips. Naturally his life is a burning flame of inspiration for anyone who has a desire to serve the country. To know Guruji is to know the soul of India, and to follow him is to make one's life sadhana, rooted in patriotism.

(The writer, a veteran RSS Pracharak and ideologue is Director, Bharateeya Vichar Kendra and President, Vivekananda Kendra, Kanyakumari, Kerala.)

5

Our Gurujee: As I saw Him

Justice Dr. M. Rama Jois

THE comparison made in a popular subhashita to the effect that "Ekahschandraha tamo hanti na cha tara ganancha" only one, the moon destroys darkness but not myriads of stars" applies aptly to Sri Madhav Sadashiv Golwalkar, popularly known to the nation as Guruji, who had been the 'Sarsanghchalak' of the mighty organisation the Rashtriya Swayamsevak Sangh (the RSS) for three decades and three years. I have had the opportunity of knowing him intimately on account of my becoming a Swayamsevak from my high school days in the year 1944 in Shimoga. At the outset, I may say with all humility and sincerity that he was a divine personality and one among the greatest sons of Bharat Mata, born in the 20th century. He was incarnation of 'Dharma' and "Rashtra Dharma" whose contribution to the nation building is everlasting.

I was very fortunate in coming into the contact with the RSS in 1944. I began to participate in the daily *Shakha* named after one of the greatest heroes of the nation in 16th century namely Chhatrapati Shivaji. By attending and participating in the daily programme of the *Shakha* by singing patriotic songs, listening to stories of patriots and *Bauddhiks* on our nationalism and cultural values, I secured good *samskara* in patriotism, character and discipline. After a few years thereafter I became acquainted with Sri Guruji by attending his baithaks and hearing his bauddhiks and public speeches. I was greatly inspired by his speeches and magnetic personality. He was a moving encyclopaedia as he had acquired profound knowledge in various branches by 1940. By attending the programmes of the RSS and the guidance I received from the leaders of the RSS including Guruji, my character was moulded and my attitude towards the nation was shaped. Guruji took over as Sarsanghchalak of the RSS in the year 1940 and continued in that exalted position for 33 years. It is a matter of history how the RSS had spread to all parts of the country. The RSS grew into a mighty voluntary organisation and the strongest nationalist steel frame both in Bharat and abroad under the dynamic leadership of Guruji.

But for the founding of the RSS by Dr. Hedgewar and the successful leadership of Guruji in making it the biggest nationalist force in the country, I shudder to think what would have happened to our nation at the hands of anti-national forces. I was further extremely fortunate as Guruji stayed in my newly-constructed house in 1972 at Bangalore during his penultimate visit to Bangalore, which remains ever green in the memory of myself and members of my family. I also had the benefit of meeting and hearing Guruji during 1951 and 1952 when I attended the 1st and 2nd year OTC at Tumkur and Bangalore and the 3rd year OTC at Nagpur during the year 1958. In the nature of things, I cannot claim to know about him in a large measure and further it is also not possible to write all that I know about him. However, it is my desire to quote a few reminiscences about him.

At some point of time after he came into contact with the founder of the RSS Dr. Hedgewar, he was desirous of becoming a Sanyasi and join Ramakrishna Muth as he was greatly inspired by Swami Akhandananda. But the magnetic and powerful personality of Doctorji made Guruji give up that idea and work for the nation-building activity of the RSS. Guruji himself used to say how it happened. He used to say that he met Doctorji and told him that he had decided to become a sanyasi and in reply Dr. Hedgewar told him that he never thought that Guruji was so selfish. Guruji was taken aback by that remarks. Then Guruji told him that "I am not taking to family life, I want to become a sanyasi giving up all worldly desires and still you call me selfish, which is not justified". Doctorji reiterated and said "Yes you are selfish because you are thinking of '*moksha*' to yourself and not to the nation". This one remark by Doctorji changed the desire and attitude of Guruji and he decided to devote his entire life to the nation. Regarding this incident Guruji used to say that from the aforesaid one remark of Doctorji, "I realised the extraordinary greatness and personality of Doctorji who as otherwise looked to be an ordinary person". After this incident Guruji devoted and dedicated his entire life, remaining a bachelor, to the cause of nation-building activities of RSS.

In order to inculcate the feeling of patriotism, Guruji had said, "One's mother, however not good-looking, illiterate or otherwise deficient is the dearest person on earth to him. That is our attitude towards Bharat Mata." This advice greatly inspired the Swayamsevaks in particular and citizens in general to develop a sense of deep love and affection for Bharat Mata.

Shri Guruji was hurt and suffered acute pain about the division of the country and strongly criticised the Partition. A prominent leader who did not see any thing objectionable in the Partition said, "there is no reason to be perturbed by partition as Hindus and Muslims are brothers and it was natural and not unusual that brothers partition their property." To this Guruji said, "Yes there is nothing special about partitioning the property by brothers; but we never regarded or considered Bharat as property. We adored and worshipped her as our Mother and called her 'Bharat Mata' and brothers do not partition their mother. Therefore, the Partition was a sin". There was no answer to this. However, it was too late as the Partition was fait accompli.

It was a great misfortune of our nation that distardly

assassination of Mahatma Gandhi took place and thereafter an attempt was made by the then rulers to finish the rapidly growing nationalist force by levelling heinous charges against the RSS. The organisation was banned and Guruji was arrested by the central government. This was probably the most heinous act of the then Government under the leadership of Jawaharlal Nehru who had taken a vow to finish the RSS. I can say that this period was the most painful period which I have undergone during my lifetime. On account of such onslaught, any other organisation would have perished and would have become a matter of history. But Guruji remained undaunted and provided indomitable and courageous leadership remaining unperturbed during this darkest period in the life of the Sangh. Subsequently, the ban was withdrawn but only after a powerful satyagraha was held throughout the Country in 1949 during which satyagraha I too had to suffer imprisonment in Central Jail, Bangalore.

Before and after the ban was imposed, a large number of Swayamsevaks were subjected to hardship and cruelty by those who were inimical towards the RSS. After the ban was lifted, Guruji went on a whirlwind tour throughout the country. Millions of people greeted him everywhere and listened to his powerful speeches. I still remember the mammoth public meeting held at Bangalore. Then, at a press conference Guruji was asked as to what revenge Sangh was going to take against those who inflicted injury on them.

Shri Guruji asked who are all those who inflicted injury on us. After all, they are our own. As you are aware sometimes it so happens that our teeth bite our own tongue, but in retaliation we don't break our teeth. That is our attitude towards those who caused trouble to us? Such was the magnanimity and quality of statesmanship of Guruji.

During his whole life he spent every iota of his energy and every moment of his life only in the service to the nation. He had toured the entire country for more than 50 times. Once he had come to Shimoga. The world famous, attractive

Jog Falls is situated just 60 miles away from Shimoga. It was suggested by local Sangh Adhikaris to Guruji as to whether a trip could be arranged for him to see the magnificient Jog Falls. Guruji curtly replied "I have no time for any pleasure trips during this life." The proposal was dropped.

Sometime in 1960, an organisation called "Hindi Raksha Samiti" was formed in Punjab by protagonists of Hindi and they started a movement against the imposition of study of Punjabi. Guruji called the persons concerned and gave them a bit of his mind. He said, "Your movement is a great threat to National Unity. Punjabi is as much a national language as Hindi is. Those who are staying in Punjab are under a duty to learn Punjabi in addition to Hindi. This is a national necessity and essential for National unity". The sponsorers of the movement realised their folly and the movement died down.

During the leadership of Guruji, RSS activities spread into several countries abroad to which a sizeable section of the Hindus had migrated for employment or business. Guruji addressed them: "It is natural that you have deep love towards Bharat, but this should not in any way stand in the way of your unadulterated loyalty to the country where you have decided to stay and earn your livelihood. You must strive for the progress and development of that country and should maintain cordial relationship with the original inhabitants." This advice is being followed by all the Hindus staying in various countries of the world. If this universal outlook is followed by all the persons concerned, there will be no cause for dispute or intolerance among the people belonging to different countries staying in any country.

Once Guruji was asked, as the RSS is organising only Hindus, does it not prove the allegation that the RSS is against Muslims. Guruji replied, "This is nothing but a false propaganda indulged in by a few who are against Hindu Sangathan for collateral reasons. Even if a single Muslim was not available in Bharat, the Sangh was bound to take up the work of Hindu Sangathan for the reason notwithstanding noble principles and cultural values evolved in Bharat, Hindu society is divided on the basis of four varnas, various castes, sub-castes and untouchability. This is the problem of Hindus only and it has to be solved by them only. Therefore, Hindu *Sangathan* is a national necessity, which is based on common cultural values. It is a positive ideal and it is not against any community.

It is unfortunate that either on account of not understanding this aspect or deliberately with ulterior electoral motive, enmity is sought to be created between Hindus and Muslims and Christians. Therefore, earlier the truthful answer given by Guruji is understood by the minorities, it is good for both the majority and minority and there will be no reason for any dispute and conflict among them as our Constitution confers fundamental right to equality on all.

Shri Guruji always gave utmost importance to national character and interest. Once a leader of an opposition party who had gone abroad, severely criticised Jawaharlal Nehru. Guruji took exception to this. He said, 'Whatever may be the differences here, when one goes abroad it is not proper to criticise Nehru there, as he was our Prime Minister and it would be inconsistent with the national character required of every citizen of Bharat.

A Swayamsevak in Karnataka fell in love with a Christian girl. He was in a dilemma whether he should marry her or not because of different religion. He met Guruji when he was here. He told his problem to Guruji who replied, "When both of you love each other, religion should be no bar to marry. Even after the marriage you follow your religion and go to temple, and let your wife go to church. The children born out of this wedlock will have the liberty of opting to the religion of their choice." They followed the advice of Guruji and lived happily. Such was the liberal attitude of Guruji.

During the year 1958, when I had been to the 3rd year OTC at Nagpur, Guruji advised how an ideal Swayamsevak should conduct himself in his life. As it is of utmost importance and relevance today, the same is set out hereafter: For every Swayamsevak Bharat Mata is the common deity to be worshipped and the Sangh prarthana is the common '*mantra*' to be recited which binds all of them together including the people of this country. In every sphere of activity, namely in the family, in any profession, occupation, trade or business or in politics or in social activities, the conduct of a Swayamsevak should be ideal. In the course of his speeches or actions, he shall always remember that he is a Swayamsevak of this great organisation and that he shall do nothing that is derogatory or bring a bad name to this great organisation or cause any injury to national interest. In sum, he should always behave in a manner worthy of being a swayamsevak. He should always remember the prayer "*Susheelam jagdyena namunrambhavet*" (Oh God confer on me such good character by seeing which others should respect me)" which is part of Sangha Prarthana.

(The writer is former Chief Justice of Punjab & Haryana High Court.)

6

Re-incarnation Of Swami Vivekananda

S. Gurumurthy

INDIA, Maharishi Aurobindo said, is not just a geographic piece. It is *Parashakti* concealed in physical landscape. It would require more than a mere reason and intellect to understand the consciousness that is India. A seeker who endeavours to explore the consciousness of India, has to transcend the limits of reason. He has to travel into mystic and metaphysical domains to capture her deeper and mysterious inner personality. This is the substance of Maharishi Aurobindo's understanding of India. The course of her history too cannot be grasped without such understanding of this mystic dimension of her personality. Her survival - when all her sister civilizations had been reduced to archival materials by armies driven by religious fanaticism that marched across the face of the earth - and her re-emergence are not explainable except by the mystic element in the Indian civilisation, which seems to guarantee a kind of durability and continuity to the Indian civilisation, something that destiny seems to have denied to others.

Even the way the freedom movement of India evolved too cannot be captured purely in rational terms. It needs penetrative contemplation to see the drive of mystic India behind physical and manifested India in powering the freedom movement. The Indian people, let down by its divided traditional military and intellectual leadership and fatigued for nearly a century, suddenly woke up and worked themselves to kinetic effect and rose up to win freedom in the 20th century. That is, the masses of India, substituting for their traditional leaders, rose up and agitated to free India. How did this happen? Was it just an accident of history or the reassertion of the Soul of India?

The rise of the Indian people to assert their nationalism was not an accident of history. There were mystic powers working to drive India's freedom. There was, of course, a direct and perceivable link between Sri Ramakrishna Paramhamṣa and Swami Vivekananda, who re-articulated the idea of this ancient nation in the modern world. But, there was a mystic and unseen link between the spiritual penance and mission of Sri Ramakrishna-Vivekananda in the 19th century and the intense wave of nationalism that swept across India in the 20th century. It is this subtle link - not fully comprehended by Indian intellectuals - that triggered massive and exponential growth of nationalist activities that eventually led to freedom. A rational or superficial study of Sri Ramakrishna, without factoring this mystic phenomenon, would hardly link him to the nationalist movement to free India while a deeper contemplation would make it difficult to de-link his disciple and rebellious Hindu monk, Swami Vivekananda, from the nationalist spirit that constituted the soul of the freedom movement. While the spiritual penance of Sri Ramakrishna constituted the secret reservoir of energy for the nationalist drive of Swami Vivekananda, the explosive ideas of Swami Vivekananda became the inspiration for hundreds and thousands of nationalist initiatives all over India.

Perceived from this domain of mystic India, one of the silent, but most powerful, initiatives in the cause of this ancient nation, that was subtly but not explicitly linked to Ramakrishna-Vivekananda spiritual-nationalist tradition was the emergence of the Rashtriya Swayamsevak Sangh [RSS]. It is undeniable that the ideology of the RSS is clearly and explicitly traceable to the gigantic nationalist ideas and thoughts that emanated from Swami Vivekananda. But apart from this ideological inspiration, that there was a live and direct spiritual link between the Ramakrishna-Vivekananda spiritual nationalist penance and the evolution of the RSS, is least noticed in Indian intellectual discourse. The bridge that constituted this direct spiritual link between Sri Ramakrishna-Vivekananda tradition and the RSS, was Shri Guruji Golwalkar, the second Sarsanghachalak of the RSS who shaped the intellectual and spiritual foundations of the RSS. But this subtle, least known, link between the kinetic RSS and spiritually potent Sri Ramakrishna order is not within comprehension of rational India, which does not recognise mystic aspects of existence.

The spiritual vision to rebuild the ancient nation in India, which had slipped into centuries of drift, re-emerged in the advent of Sri Ramakrishna Paramhamsa. Sri Ramakrishna was among the greatest of the saints of India who lived and demonstrated that all faiths are ultimately harmonisable. But the condition for harmony is mutual and true respect among the different faiths. The mutual respect of different and even differing faiths towards one another is the essence of Sanatana Dharma, the timeless Indian wisdom for all times and its unique contribution for the entire humankind. The absence of true, mutual respect of faiths leads to civilisational, cultural and religious clashes. But the mutual respect has to be rooted in the faiths themselves, not to be left to the option of the faithful. This is the essence of Sanatana Dharma. As Swami Vivekananda said Sri Ramakrishna Paramhamsa took *avatara* to save Sanatana Dharma which, decades later, Maharishi Aurobindo defined as the nationalism of the Indian nation. Sri Ramakrishna was the answer to the urge of the times in the 19th century that called for consolidating the scattered spiritual forces of India. Sri Ramakrishna, the potential energy, turned kinetic in form through Swami Vivekananda to prepare the ancient nation to battle for freedom to pursue its mission. Sri Ramakrishna spoke of Sanatana Dharma, but not of the Indian nation.

But, Swami Vivekananda, who constituted the expression of the soul of Sri Ramakrishna emphasised and mandated the worship of the nation, the Hindu nation, as the only God for the next 50 years, for Sanatana Dharma to re-emerge. Maharishi Aurobindo's conception that Sanatana Dharma and India are one and the same and they cannot be severed and one cannot survive without the other explains that when Sri Ramakrishna spoke of Sanatana Dharma he actually spoke of India and when Vivekananda spoke of India he actually spoke of Sanatana Dharma. Sanatana Dharma constituted the potential of which India was the kinetic effect; if Sanatana Dharma was the contemplative thought, India was its action-platform. So if Sri Ramakrishna's work constituted the contemplation, Swami Vivekananda's work was the resultant action based on the contemplation. When Swami Vivekananda gave Indians the mission to rebuild India and to position India as the spiritual guide to the world - the *Jagat Guru* - he was saying what Sri Ramakrishna had left unsaid for his chosen disciple to say. But Sri Ramakrishna did give a clue to what he had contemplated and spiritually directed his disciple Swami Vivekananda to expound. He told his disciples: "While other religions which are also true will come and go it is Sanatana Dharma which will ultimately prevail" [*Gospel of Sri Ramakrishna,* 20-10-1884]. So taking cue from his Master, Swami Vivekananda prescribed this mission to rebuild India to save the world from intolerance and violence promoted by exclusive faiths, by reinstating, reliving and protecting Sanatana Dharma, which was central to Sri Ramakrishna's experience. Swamiji also made this mission of India clear in his spectacular address to the World Parliament of Religions.

But this expansive mission that Swami Vivekananda called upon this nation to undertake was not to be exclusive task of the Ramakrishna Order. It would appear from his address at Madras how Swami Vivekananda wanted the Hindu society to be organised, namely through man-making training for youth. The instrument that was chosen by destiny to concretise the mission of Swami Vivekananda on the field and to spiritualise and consolidate the patriotic forces of India was the Rashtriya Swayamsevak Sangh. The mystic and spiritual link between this clarion call of Swami Vivekananda and the RSS was Shri Guruji as Shri Madhav Sadashiv Golwalkar was first known to his students in Benaras Hindu University. Before destiny willed him to carry on, on the ground, the mission unveiled by Swami Vivekananda in his lecture titled *My Plan of Campaign* at Madras through the RSS, he had been initiated into the spiritual stream of Ramakrishna Mission by Swami Akhandananda, a direct disciple of Sri Ramakrishna. Given his deep spiritual leaning, had Shri Guruji been born in early part of the 19th century, he would perhaps have become a direct disciple of Sri Ramakrishna Paramhamsa and also perhaps a monk in the Ramakrishna Order. Had he been born in the later part of the 19th century he would have become a companion-disciple of Swami Vivekananda. But, he was born in the 20th century when the need of the times had changed from consolidation of spiritual forces to the kinetic task of rebuilding the ancient nation - the Hindu India. This called for more intense physical activity on the ground than a monastic order could engage in. So the potential energy of Sri Ramakrishna transformed into kinetic energy in Swami Vivekananda who began urging particularly the youth of India to undertake work of nation-building. The mandate of Swami Vivekananda became the agenda for the forces fighting for India's freedom. The freedom movement that took shape in diverse ways - from revolutionary dimensions of Maharishi Aurobindo to the extremist politics of Balgangadhar Tilak to the moderate campaign of Mahatma Gandhi - was undeniably influenced by Swami Vivekananda's idea of worship of Bharatmata, the Motherland. Whether it was Gandhi or Tilak, Nehru or Rajaji, all were one in acknowledging that Swami Vivekananda had laid the moral and intellectual basis for Indian freedom movement. Thus the movement for Indian freedom was only apparently political but its real foundation was rooted in the spiritual dimensions implicit in Sanatana Dharma.

While those who fought for freedom only thought how to win freedom, one of the freedom fighters, Dr Keshav Baliram Hedgewar, was deeply disturbed by another issue and that was how India lost its freedom. He diagnosed that lack of unity, even strategic unity, among the Hindus was the reason why we lost freedom. He wanted to address this lacuna in the national character of Hindus which made conquest of India by foreign and colonial forces possible. He intensely contemplated for a remedy for this structural weakness of the Hindu society. The result was that Dr Hedgewar founded the RSS to repair and remove this distortion in the national psyche. He set as mission of the RSS man-making and nation-building, which Swami Vivekananda had mandated for India and its global mission. Shri Guruji came in contact with Dr Hedgewar a little more than a decade after Dr Hedgewar had founded the RSS. Thus Shri Guruji met Dr Hedgewar not as an impressionable child or as a boy, but as a grown-up man and as the initiated disciple of the Ramakrishna Order. Shri Guruji soon began experiencing Dr Hedgewar as a spiritualist in intense action, a *karma yogi*. So he decided to dedicate himself to the mission that Dr Hedgewar wanted to hand over to Shri Guruji, namely, the mission of RSS. Just as a young and rebellious Narendra, who came in contact with Sri Ramakrishna, spiritually transmigrated into Vivekananda, a saint, the touch of Dr Hedgewar transformed Shri Guruji, the other way, from a saint-in-the-making into a servant and worshipper of Mother India.

Thus Shri Guruji subsumed his high personal spiritual stature and abandoned his penance for personal spiritual advancement, which would have led him to sainthood, to undertake the more and perhaps the most arduous dimension of Swami Vivekananda's agenda, namely man-making and nation-building through the RSS. This decision of Shri Guruji might have in effect denied him of his rightful place among the great saints of India. Renunciates give up normal life, name and fame, but they are eternally elevated to rank among the revered saints. But Shri Guruji consciously and gladly dedicated his saint-hood and turned himself into a social scavenger to rid the Hindu society of the evils that it had accumulated over centuries. So apart from renouncing fame, which would have accrued to him as saint, he willingly accepted, as gift for the nation-building he committed himself to, the dirt with which his uninitiated detractors smeared him. He knew that a nation that was undermined by invasions and colonialism and a nation that had a message for harmony of faiths and cultures of the world cannot rise to give that message to the world without experiencing excruciating pain for its transformation and undergoing great sacrifices.

He unreservedly accepted Dr Hedgewar's diagnosis that a nation is only as great as its ordinary people are and not as great as its great men are. So he accepted with determination the onerous challenge of man-making and character-building work among ordinary Hindus for re-establishing Hindu Rashtra with a non-conflicting and assimilating agenda. He was firm in his convictions that all who were born in India are Hindus by culture, irrespective of whatever faith and worship practices they followed as suited to their spiritual needs. He saw no conflict between worship practices of different faiths and cultural nationalism of this ancient nation. This, he believed, is the real assimilation and integration. This is precisely the assimilative concept in which the Western countries commend to themselves and practice today for assimilating and integrating the minorities into the mainstream culture and identity of the respective nation. But it was precisely for this noble assimilative thought and concept of cultural nationalism based on it - which Shri Guruji articulated perhaps ahead of times - that the Indian establishment led by powerful men like Pandit Nehru undermined, even delegitimised Shri Guruji and his work. But Shri Guruji stood by his conviction, which was good for all times and not by convenience of times. In this sense, he substantially moved away, from contemporaneity to see and work on the future of not just his motherland but also the whole world. Now, the whole world, whether it is the West or the Rest, seems to be inclined to accept his view that minorities should be assimilated into the mainstream of a nation for unity and integrity of nations.

Shri Guruji was thus both a spiritualist and a nationalist visionary who considered atomised spiritualism only an individual's selfish advancement when Sanatana Dharma was under pressure, unless it was practised for promoting and preserving Sanatana Dharma for the collective good of the society. Shri Guruji thus renounced personal spiritual pursuits and saint-hood, which would have made him reverent and famous. Thus, abandoning his spiritual pursuits he turned into an ordinary servant of Mother India. He, a saint, dwarfed himself into a mason for nation-building through mighty effort of RSS. Now it is the rising India and its global influence, which is the result of the organisation's work, which will stand high, not even the name of the organisation, nor the names of millions who were inspired by Shri Guruji, the architect and mason of the temple of Mother India, himself. All of them, including Shri Guruji, will remain anonymous unless future history, fairly written, chooses to record their great work. If history did its job fairly, it would do credit to it as a truthful discipline, but that would not make any difference to Shri Guruji who commanded his colleagues not to make any memorial for him. This is real renunciation, real sainthood. When great leaders like Rajaji and Jayaprakash Narayan paid tributes to Shri Guruji they particularly referred to him and revered him as a saint. Yes, Shri Guruji was a saint but he was not just a saint in the sense of one who pursued *moksha* for himself. He was a saint who renounced his sainthood also in the mission of re-establishing Sanatana Dharma, which Maharishi Aurobindo defined as the soul and the very idea of Indian Nationalism. The motto of his life was: *Rashtraya swaha; Idam namaha.*

(The writer, a professional Chartered Accountant, is a reputed intellectual.)

7

Untouchability and Conversion – the Twin problems

Historical Role Of Sri Guruji

K. Suryanarayan Rao

THE pioneers of Hindu Renaissance like Maharshi Dayananda Saraswati and Swami Vivekananda had struggled a lot to bring an awareness about the perversions and divisions crept into the Hindu society and their rectification. They had given a call to free the Hindu society from the pernicious practice of untouchability. Swami Vivekananda had warned that no Hindu should be allowed to go out to any other religion. He had gone to the extent of telling, "Every person going out of the Hindu fold is not only one number less to the Hindu society, but one enemy the more." Swamiji had desired that every person who has been converted must be brought back into the Hindu fold.

Dr. Keshav Baliram Hedgewar founded the Rashtriya Swayamsevak Sangh (RSS) to organise the Hindu society getting rid of all its defects. He trained the Swayamsevaks to recognize every countryman of ours as a Hindu, without making any distinction on the basis of region, language, class or caste. When Mahatma Gandhiji and Dr. Ambedkar visited the RSS camps in thirties they were pleased to experience total equality and integrity with complete absence of untouchability or any discrimination amongst the Swayamsevaks. Whereas outside, the Hindus in general were victims of the age-old evil custom. Even after independence this obnoxious practice of untouchability has persisted inspite of a law enacted making the practice of untouchability punishable. In this situation the Christian and Muslim hawks got an excellent opportunity to feed upon the deprived and discriminated sections.

Shri Guruji Golwalkar, the second Sarsanghchalak of RSS made a thorough and an in-depth study of this problem. By and large the Hindus are religious. A certain amount of religious sentiment is associated with this practice of untouchability. The guidance of dharmagurus and acharyas who are traditionally revered by the common Hindu will be very much useful in tackling this matter. Such authorities of Hindu way of life and religion should be involved in this uphill task, was the analysis of Shri Guruji. He inspired and promoted Vishwa Hindu Parishad in 1964, which had the objective of bringing together all heads of the religious institutions of various samprodayas, sects and castes of Hindu society. A common forum was provided for them to think and act as one Hindu family.

The first national conference of VHP was held in Prayag-Triveni Sangam- in 1966. Nearly 50,000 delegates including hundreds of Dharmacharyas, Jagadgurus, Mahamandeleshwars participated in the conference from all parts of the country and all sections of Hindu society. Shri Guruji thought that this was the most opportune moment to bring before the vast assembly the problem of converts and discuss about it. After a few persons spoke about the subject a resolution was put before the assembly that there should be a provision to take back, into the Hindu fold, those persons who have crossed over to other religions like Christianity or Islam, and remove the religious taboo on them in this regard. While all the delegates welcomed the resolution with great enthusiasm, the then Jagadguru Shankaracharya of Puri's Govardhana Peetha, vehemently opposed stating that there is no provision in our Shastras for accepting the converts back. Once a person relinquishes his or her mother religion, he or she becomes a 'bhrashta' and deserves to be boycotted. None can go against the

Shastras! This was the prevailing orthodox way of thinking. There was a big disappointment all around.

Shri Guruji personally met the Shankaracharya and discussed the matter in detail. He explained to the Acharya about the dangers the Hindu society and the country has to face if this same attitude towards the converts continues. This was at the root of partition, the Kashmir problem, the continuous depletion of Hindu population and territory, the enormous growth of anti-national activities and the enemies of our country and culture making use of these gullible converts as their tools. The revered Jagadguru realised the depth of the problem. But he had already made a strong speech opposing the resolution that it would be against the Shastras-the written books of authority. How to go back from his pronouncement from the seal of a Jagadguru? This was the big question!

Again Shri Guruji putforth his point of view and had a frank talk with the Acharya. The poverty and ignorance of these deprived and discriminated people have been exploited to the full and they have been made the victims of allurements and threats. Exceptions if at all are only a few. The Acharya ultimately agreed and how to proceed further was also discussed. It was decided that the Jagadguru himself should speak making this point clear to the conference.

The next morning when the revered Shankaracharya rose to address, the audience were inquisitive about what the Acharya is going to speak once again. But the Jagadguru gave a very pleasant surprise! He explained that conversions have taken place by fraudulent methods exploiting the poor and ignorant conditions of the victims. They have been forcibly taken away. It is just like a robber stealthily robs money and keeps the same with himself. Actually it does not belong to him. It belongs to someone else. In the same way the converted Christians and Muslims of our country all belong to the Hindu Society. These Hindus have been robbed and taken away stealthily. These so-called converts are Hindus originally. As it is not wrong to take back one's own stolen money, it will not be wrong to take our own Hindus back into the Hindu fold. We have to welcome them with open arms to their mother religion. There was a great applause and excitement amongst the audience, bringing enthusiasm and joy all around. The resolution was passed unanimously. Shri Pejawar Swami Jagadguru Madhwacharya of Udupi declared-Na Hindu patito bhavet (No Hindu will ever fall and become bhrashta). All the dharmacharyas blessed and came forward to preside over the taking back ceremonies. A significant name paravartan (Home coming) was given to this procedure. The religious blot over the converts was wiped out by the highest authorities of Hindu Dharma themselves. This was a victory for the perseverant and sagacious efforts of Shri Guruji Golwalkar, opening a new chapter in the Hindu history.

The Karnataka VHP provincial conference was held at Udupi in December 1969. It had an amazing response with more than 15,000 delegates from 1200 places in the state with an equal number of visiting participants beyond all expectations. The conference was graced and blessed by about 40 heads of major religious denominations like Shaiva, Vaishanava, Lingayat, Jain, Bodha and Sikh sampradayas and about a hundred other Sadhus. Shri Guruji was totally involved in this conference also. He felt that it was the right moment to get the approval and blessings of the dharmacharyas for practicing equality amongst all Hindus without any discrimination of touchability or untouchability in their social and religious affairs. Prior to the conference itself, Shri Guruji had appealed to all the dharmacharyas to give a directive to the Hindu society in this regard.

The Jagadgurus, Mahamandaleshwars, Acharyas and Munis had signed a statement to the effect that "In pursuance of the objective of Vishwa Hindu Parishad to integrate the whole of Hindu society, the entire Hindu society should be consolidated with the spirit of indivisible oneness and that there should be no disintegration in it because of the tendencies and sentiments like touchability and untouchability, the Hindus all over the world should maintain the spirit of unity and equality in their mutual intercourse."

After the inaugural session, this was the first subject taken up for discussion. This was presided over by Shri R.Bharanaiah, a learned IAS (retd) and sitting member of the Public Service Commission of the state, himself born in a so called untouchable caste. After a few persons spoke about the problem of untouchability and the signed directive of the dharamgurus was read out to the assembly, the president Sri R. Bharanaiah moved a resolution that "In keeping with considered directions of the revered dharmagurus and Acharyas, this conference appeals to the Hindus to abandon any discriminatory feeling of high and low, touchable and untouchable and conduct all their religious and social affairs on the basis of one single common Hindu brotherhood irrespective of caste, creed, birth, etc."

As soon as the president completed reading the resolution, the entire assembly burst into cheers and claps in acclamation of the resolution. All the Dharmagurus seated on the dais heartily blessed the same. Indeed this was a moment of history worthy to be carved in letters of gold. It was a moment of victory of the true spirit of Dharma over a pernicious custom. It was a moment which proved once again that the Hindu society is a dynamic race nourished with the nectar of immortality.

The entire assembly felt that it was passing through-indeed created-a great moment of history. Shri Guruji, the chief architect of this unique moment was naturally extremely happy. He desired that there should be an expression of gratitude to the Dharmagurus for having brought this remarkable moment. Shri Guruji instructed the secretary to go up the dais and offer compliments to the dharmacharyas with gratitude. Accordingly the secretary spoke about the worthy role of the Dharmagurus in this historic decision. Immediately full throated shouts of "victory" to our dharmagurus "long live Hindu unity" rent the skies. Even

Sri Guruji also participated in this jaikar and clapped which he did not do usually. The Pejawar Swamiji declared- Hindvah sahodarah sarve (all Hindus are brothers and sisters erasing the disgraceful blot of untouchability in the Hindu society). A sentimental hurdle in the way of consolidation of Hindus was successfully removed. It was established that religion or our Shastras have nothing to do with this pernicious custom and social evil prevailing for a long time. The discerning and judicious effort of Shri Guruji Golwalkar was victorious once again. This was one of the happiest moments in Shri Guruji's life.

Sri R. Bharanaiah had adjusted his busy schedule of official tour, so that he could be present on the first day to preside over the session when this particular subject was to be discussed and immediately leave Udupi for his next destination. But the proceedings of the session and the overwhelming support the issue received from all sections including the orthodox made him change his mind and he requested the secretary to permit him to stay till the conference conclude the next day evening.

In the concluding session Sri Guruji gave a stinging call "now that our Dharmagurus themselves have directed us to give up untouchability, it is the bounden duty of everyone of us to obey the directive in our own lives. We have to look upon every son of this soil, every adherent of our dharma and samskriti as our own brother and never inquire to what caste he or she belongs. It is only when we emphasize the unifying factors and ignore the difference that we can bring about lasting cohesion and harmony. I am telling this from my own experience in the organisation- Rashtriya Swayamsevak Sangh. By practicing the above golden rule in Sangh we find no trace of any dissension because of caste or sect or language or any other score."

In his final benedictory message Pujya Pejawar Swamiji announced his dedication to the service of the lowly, the downtrodden and outcast. In the end the full recitation of Vande Matram sent the audience into silent raptures. One by one the dignitaries on dais started dispersing. Shri Gurji was standing below the dias near the steps and bidding farewell personally to everyone of them. All having dispersed, Shri Bharanaiah remained alone on the dias, immersed in emotions. He was reminded that the session was over. As he came down and saw Shri Guruji waiting, with joyous tears gushing from his eyes he firmly embraced Shri Guruji. There was silence all around for a few seconds. Then Shri Bharanaiah exclaimed in a voice choking with emotion, "Oh! How good of you that at least you have come to our rescue and taken up this mission for our sake"! Shri Guruji softly remarked, "What of me, the whole society is with you and has taken up the cause." The ecstasy of joy and gratitude for an act which had wahed off the blot of injustice and humiliation of centuries had, as it were, found an expression in the tears of Shri Bharanaiah.

Just a month later, on the Makara Sankraman day (14.1.1970), Shri Guruji gave a down to earth and timely guidance to the workers, through the following letter to the secretary, the present writer:

My dear Suryanarayan Raoji,

The Karnatak provincial conference of the Vishwa Hindu Parishad is over. It was a grand affair beyond even the most extravagant expectations of the conveners and workers. Naturally its success has roused great expectations in the minds of all. But I think it will not be reasonable to suppose that all things will change for the better immediately as if by magic. Hard persistent work is called for. Indeed the conference may be rightly considered to be a clarion call to untiring efforts for the all round betterment and consolidation of the Hindu people. The success of the conference should not make us complacent.

To take an example: The resolution on untouchability - blessed by all our *Acharyas* and *Dharmagurus, Mathadhipatis* and other holy men of all our sects - cannot be translated into actual life by mere pious expressions. Centuries old prejudices do not disappear by words or wishful thinking. Hard work, right propaganda has to be undertaken from town to town, village to village, house to house and people have to be educated to accept and practice what has been resolved, not merely as a concession to the pressure of modern times but as an abiding principle and way of life, in an humble spirit of atonement for past mistakes. A change of heart, a moral and emotional change in attitudes and behaviour has to be brought about. Working for the economic and political betterment of those who had been relegated to the background and bringing them up to stand shoulder to shoulder with all the rest of our people is a Herculean task. But this in itself is not enough for such 'equality' may not be brought about without shedding the feeling of separateness. What we should desire and strive for is not merely economic and political 'equality'-we want a real change a complete integration. This change is beyond power of politics of governmental plans. It is impossible to achieve it by the clever manipulations of political parties dealing in patch work in the name of integration. Strenuous work springing from the heart and manifesting itself - in day to day behaviour work on a spiritual, moral and social plane is called for and all participants in the conference, as well as all who had extended sympathy and support must come forward to put their shoulders to the wheel and with one mighty stroke shatter to pieces the age long pernicious prejudices.

Another important task is educating our people in the principle and practice of dharma in both aspects- the general and all comprehensive one; and the norms of the particular sect one may have been born into or later accepted. This education has to begin with ourselves, for no one wanting to educate others can do so effectively without first educating himself and putting into practice what he has learnt and what he wants to teach. Burning faith and absolute devotion, purity of character, of words, feelings and deeds alone can confer on one the authority to teach others. And so we have to cultivate assiduously these great qualities.

We have to carry this education to the remotest corners of our country, to those for whom Dharma has been reduced to a mere bundle of crude superstitious rites, to those who never had the opportunity to learn and live Dharma - in far off villages in the hills and in the dense forests. We must expect hardships, troubles and tribulations in this work and often we may feel that it has been a thankless task. But without expecting immediate results or miracles to happen, we must face the hard facts and with infinite patience plod on -to success in the true spirit of a *karmayogi.*

Many workers appear to take a delight in blaming others for all ills .Some may put the blame on the political perversities, others on the aggressive activities of the Christians or Muslims and such other faiths. Let our workers keep their minds free from such tendencies and work for our people and Dharma in the right spirit, lend a helping hand to all our brethren who need help and strive to relieve distress wherever we see it. In this service no distinction should be made between man and man. We have to serve all be he a Christian or a Muslim or a human being of any other persuasion for calamities, distress and misfortunes make no such distinction but afflict all alike. And in serving to relieve the sufferings of man let it not be in a spirit of condescence or mere compassion but as devoted worship of the Lord aboding the heart of all beings, in the true spirit of our Dharma of surrendering our all in the humble service of Him who is Father, Mother, Brother, Friend and everything to us all.

And may our actions succeed in bringing out the glory and effulgence of our Sanatana - Eternal Dharma.

M.S. Golwalkar

Makar Sankraman
Shaka 1891
14-01-1970

(The writer, a former Sewa Pramukh of RSS, was then the Secretary of Udupi Conference.)

8

Gurujee And Misguided Muslims

Rakesh Sinha

THE advent of Islam in India was not only an addition of a new religion in the Hindu civilisation but also the beginning of ceaseless social and religious confrontations. It repudiated age-old convention of religious freedom. Aggressors were conscious of inclusive nature of Hindu civilisation, Assimilative character of Hindu cultural environment was, in the eyes of Muslim elites a serious threat to Muslim way of life and called for 'constant vigilance and effort' to thwart it. (Madan 1997: 112)

Shri Guruji points out, "Many persons came to this country from various parts of the world. They have chosen to stay here. They have adapted themselves to the life here, the ideology and philosophy here. Some have made their own contribution towards enriching this mainstream. The Muslims unfortunately, stayed apart." (Guruji: 1974:48)

Thus a trail of two civilisations continued for more than thousand years. While one had the state power, organised force with a mission and a zeal to expand Islam, another had "highly developed civilisation, religious traditions which were radically different' (Madan 1997: 145) extremely disorganised polity and divided social structure. There is no parallel of the heroic tales of the people who resisted religious onslaught from generations to generation and despite all the criminal and barbaric acts committed by the

Muslim invaders, Hindu civilisation stood the test of time. Numbers of Hindus, who surrendered to Islam or forcibly converted, were far less than number of people killed by the aggressors. Sikh gurus faced persecutions to save the indigenous culture and traditions.

Shri Guruji draws a line between Muslim aggressors and the converts. Aggressors belonged to different race; nationality, civilisation and culture while the converted Muslims have commonality with Hindus. They have common ancestors, common culture and history. Guruji follows more comprehensive criteria to define a Hindu. He says, "We are not so mean as to say that with a mere change in the method of worship an individual ceases to be a son of the soil. We have no objection to God being called by any name whatever... he can not be a Hindu at all who is intolerant of other faiths. (G 2000 : 125)

How can a body of converts claim separate culture or disassociate with their ancestors and delink themselves with the history and trajectory of the national life? Guruji feels that Indian Muslims have been trying to compartmentalise all aspects of their life whether it may be language, culture, uniforms and festivals or national heroes. He says, "Why should they (Muslims) behave as they are doing? As a matter of fact, in no other country in the world, where Islam has spread, the earlier dress, the language, the way of living etc., of those countries have changed. In Iran, Turkey and other countries their original dress, language, view of life etc., have remained the same. But in our country everything, even thinking also, is changed. (Guruji, 1974:46)

Cultural Bond

Shri Guruji begins with his theory that people of the land, irrespective of their religious beliefs, belong to the same cultural and ancestral origin and says, "Muslims must realise that we are all one people and it is the same blood that courses in our veins. They are not Arabs or Turks or Mongols. They are only Hindu converts...the problem can and must be solved by Indian Muslims owning the country and its ancient culture as theirs. Indian history did not begin with Mohammed Ghazni" (G:1974:43-44)

Shri Guruji's proposition is absolutely free from any ambiguity. He says that no race, community or nation can claim to be the custodian of all wisdom and discard rest of the humanity. Creative wisdom is not confined to some people. He says, "No people on the face of this earth are entirely without some abiding virtues, nor will they be endowed with all the necessary noble qualities...there are indeed very pious people worthy of emulation in all countries." (G 2000:346) K.S. Durrany wrote,

> *"The RSS does not preach that Hinduism is the only religion in the world. The concept of finality and paramountcy of a single shade of divine revelation has always been alien to Hinduism and it appears that the RSS wants to retain that religious diversity with a sense of cultural unity throughout the length and breadth of the country." (Durrany : 86)*

Guruji believes that philosophical and spiritual diversities need to be protected and encouraged. Cultural assimilation does not mean negation or rejection of freedom of religion. It does not "mean that anyone should give up his way of worship. We can never advocate this, or even think of it. We believe that one single way of worship is not suitable for the whole of humanity." (Jeelany; 48) His submission is that Hindu way of life is based on this very concept. It is originally inbuilt in the Hindu civilisation. So any sermon on secularism to Hindus is like using candle in daylight. Prof. Moazziz Ali Begh underpins Guruji's argument stating that, "I have found average Hindu ethically far more elevated than an average Muslim. A Hindu is definitely more humble and mild, and a Muslim (barring the truly God loving people) is definitely more arrogant and aggressive." (1992 : 85) Guruji further elaborates the difference between tolerance and respect as follows - "The word 'tolerance' which is often used to express this idea (Truth is one, sages call it variously) is very meek, it is just another word for sufferance. It implies an element of ego, which just tolerates other viewpoints without any love or respect for them. But our training has been one of respecting and even accepting other faiths and viewpoints as so many paths to reach the same Truth." (G : 2000:38) The Muslim mind does not accept this. As one of them writes,

> "Positive respect breeds nothing but stagnancy... two diametrically opposed viewpoints can tolerate each other, but they can not be expected to respect each other." (Maulana Akhlaq Ahmed Qasimi, secularism : mazhabi rawadari (secularism: Religious Tolerance) (Urdu daily Al Jamiyat, Delhi July 30, 1969)

This clearly shows Islamic mind is not prepared to rehearse its basic framework of religious philosophy.

Nehru's following bunch of self-introspective questions to Muslims is virtually repudiation of their attitude, mindset and philosophy of life and vindicates Guruji. Nehru spoke only a few months after the independence before the educated Muslim audience of the Aligarh Muslim University (AMU), which was considered a breeding ground for Two Nation Theory (Pro-Pakistanis) during the colonial period. He observed,

> *"I have said that I am proud of our inheritance and our ancestors who gave an intellectual and cultural pre-eminence to India. How do you feel about this past? Do you feel that you are also sharers in it and inheritors of it and, therefore, proud of something that belongs to you as much as to me? Or do you feel alien to it and pass it by without understanding it or feeling that strange thrill which comes from the realisation*

that we are the trustees and inheritors of this vast treasure... You are Muslims and I am a Hindu but that does not take away from us that cultural inheritance that is yours as well as mine." (Convocation address at the AMU, 24 January 1948).

Shri Guruji was a practising ideologue. He views that philosophy of cultural nationalism does not deny space to pluralism in social and religious life. In fact religion does not find pivotal position in the concept of cultural nationalism. Thus he withdraws the role of religion in the formulation of nationality. He also does not find any direct relationship between secularism and nationalism. It is a mistaken idea to co-relate them. Sociology of religion reflects nature of the society and its civilisational roots. Nationalism is based on mental allegiance of the people to their nation, it is not plausible that the change in religious composition would affect nationalist spirit. Nationality does not change with the change in religion in India. (G IX : 45)

Shun sense of religious superiority

Shri Guruji uninhibitedly argues, "My feeling is that the nature abhors excessive uniformity. It is too early to say what these uniformities will do to Western civilisation in times to come. Apart from the here and the now we must look back into distant past and also look forward into the remote future... we in this country have millennia of experience. We have the tested way of life. And our experience is that variety and unity can go together." He believes that there has not yet been any honest efforts to either remove their misgivings or to assimilate them. He wisely believes that hope for assimilation cannot be generated either by appeasing them or reviling their sentiment. One should not be artificial while interacting with them at any plane. Pleasantly responding to Id's greeting by a Muslim he stated that, "All sacred religious festivals have one common objective to remind people about devotion to God." (G VIII: 157). "His social philosophy can be summed up as progressive harmonisation between religion and Sanatan Dharma or eternal culture of Bharat. Here there is no place for religious egoism or sense of superiority. Locked and aggressive Muslim mind could not shake his firm belief and confidence in his own ideological moorings of religious freedom. His dialogue with a Kashmiri Sufi Nazir Ahmed in Aligarh presents a contrast between the Hindu and Muslim perceptions of achieving harmony and peace. Ahmed suggested him that 'the threat of godlessness and communism was overtaking all of us and we who believe in God should get together to meet the threat'. Showing his complete approval with his proposition Guruji tried to unravel his mind. Guruji said, "I perfectly agree with you but the difficulty is that we have, as it were, broken the image of God, and each one has got his own piece. So what is to be done? You think of God in one particular way, the Christians think in another, Buddhism says there is no God, there is, only Nirvana; the Jain will say it is nothing; then so many will say we worship God in the form of Rama, Krishna, Shiva etc. How to ask these people to believe in one common God? Have you any recipe for this?" Now this Kashmiri man known to be Sufi, which I take to be thinker and God-minded man, you will be surprised at his answer. He said, *why not all of you come to Islam.* (Emphasis added) Guruji was amazed by the answer because Sufis are known as liberal rather than fundamentalist. Then Guruji argued, "Don't you think that people will say, why not join Christianity? Suppose, I, devotee as I am to my religion, say why not become a Hindu. It comes to the same thing and the problem will never end." Ahmed wanted to know whether Guruji had solution to this vexed question. Here Guruji showed his finest philosophical aptitude when he argued,

> "*There is no substantial philosophy which does not belong to the Hindus or to the Muslims. Call it Advaita or whatever you like. It says that there is one single existence, which is truth, which is bliss. It is the Creator, Sustainer and Destroyer.*

All our conceptions of God are only limited conception of that ultimate reality, so that the rock bottom of ultimate reality will join us together. It does not belong to any one religion. Everyone can accept it on this account. Religion is only way of worship. This is not such a way; it is a philosophy. It is the philosophical understanding of the world. It can be taken to be the rock bottom." (Jeelany: 46)

Shri Guruji advised Ahmed that as a Sufi he should accept it. His proposition is, in fact, a question before the Muslims of India whether they are prepared to respect the vision and wisdom of the Mother country which provided them opportunity to live, prosper, govern despite their antipathy to whatever belonged to Hindu civilisation before and after their advent to Indian soil.

Shri Guruji's ideological conviction is in a complete countenance with the Vedic philosophy, "Truth is One, Sages call it variously" {*Ekam Sat, Viprah bahudha wadanti*), He describes it as a 'Himalayan vision' (G 2000:38). At another place he says that he does not consider anybody whether Muslim or Christian as alien if one demonstrates his unqualified loyalty for the Bharat. (Banka: Vol. II : 142)

Expectedly, the Muslim thinkers and theologians take such proposition as all religions are equal and deserve respect as an insult of Islam. As Shaz says that considering Islam at par with Hinduism is a 'mischievous idea'. (Shaz : 69) Another Muslim mind makes the thing more clear. Kettani wrote, "The process of assimilation is particularly effective when the Muslim community has no special schools for its children and does not have adequate number of mosques for its adults... Muslims should continue to believe that Islam is the only true religion and that all other religions, as stated in the Holy Quran will he rejected by the Creator. Believing that all religions are equally valid is the first sign of religious assimilation." (Kettani.: 10-11)

Role of British colonialism

Muslims are not to be solely blamed for their alienation from Hindus and the indigenous culture. The process of their integration with the national life, which was in vogue, however intermittently, says Guruji was disrupted by the British colonialism by applying divide and rule. (G IX: 47) After independence this process has been blocked by vote hungry politicians. He also blames 'extremely narrow minded religious leaders' for creating schism and not viewing the problem of integration from the 'whole national concept in their mind.' (Jeelany, 46-47). He genuinely feels that the responsibility to create inter communal harmony lies on both Hindus and Muslims and adds that there is an odd which discourages such constructive approach, "our leaders are prone to put blame on Hindus and absolve the Muslims. This has given the minority community, that is the Muslims, encouragement to continue to indulge in their own communal activities." (Jeelany : 47)

Shri Guruji does not use the term Hindu as a classical religious concept. His idea is similar to B.C. Pal who points out that Hindu Culture is the very soul and essence of what we now understand as nationalism. He too does not equate Hinduism with a religious concept. (Pal: p81) It is a mistaken idea that Hinduism is parallel to Islam. Heinrich Von Stietencom rightly says, "Why is Hinduism so difficult to define? It is because we always try to see it as one "religion". Our problems would vanish if we took "Hinduism" to denote a socio-cultural unit or civilisation which contains a plurality of distinct religions." (G2001 : 38) He says, "Hinduism is a civilisation formed and enriched by a group of religions which developed a particularly liberal way of co-existence and interactions between themselves." (Ibid : 40)

Hindu Rashtra and Muslims

Shri Guruji's prescription that India is a Hindu Rashtra becomes confounded when it is superficially perceived from the western philosophical and terminological parameters. Its semblance to theocratic nation can then be superficially created. Guruji says that the fear that Hindu Rashtra "will imperil the existence of other religious groups arises by applying Semitic yardstick to it and imagining that the concept of Hindu Rashtra is analogous to that of the Semitic states notorious for their religious bigotry and persecutions." (G 2000:160)

He firmly rejects the communal state and says non communal state has always been a feature of Indian culture.

He defines the non-communal state as follow, "If the state does not meddle into religious issues then the state would be called non-communal. Even if a Muslim would be the Prime Minister of India then too the state would be non-communal. If he would try to metamorphose the culture of the country then he would be democratically defeated because his action would be against the interests of the people." (G IX: 68) Thus he argues that exclusive Hindu state that denies citizenship to minorities or treats them unequally is "a phantasm created by overstrained nerves and too lively an imagination, deserving only to be ignored as not worthy of consideration."

Unlike the western model of secularism, he does not take into account numerical value of any religious community. He believes there is one people in a nation with diverse approaches of their lives. There is no religious pre-condition for patriotism or nationality.

Partition

During colonial period, the RSS maintained that unity of anti-imperialist struggle should not be disrupted on the basis of respective ideologies of contemporary social, cultural, caste, religious and political organisations on the one hand and personal ambitions, caste or community's interests on the other. Despite its serious ideological differences with the Congress, particularly on minority issue, the RSS, in the given circumstances and limitations, unflinchingly supported the Congress programmes. Most remarkably, it has not raised any issue or led campaign, which could weaken the national movement. The Muslim attitude to the national movement was one of self-exclusion and divisive. In 1905 at Benaras session of the Congress the number of Muslim delegates fell to 17 out of total delegates of 756. (Rajput : 18)

Shri Guruji draws a parallel between their role in the medieval and modern period of Indian history. He sensibly says, "The Muslim desire, growing ever since they stepped on this land some twelve Hundred years ago, to convert and enslave the entire country could not bear fruit, in spite of their political domination for several centuries. In the coming of the British they found an opportunity to fulfil their desire. They played their card shrewdly and ultimately succeeded in browbeating our leadership into panicky surrender before their sinful demand of Partition." (G2000 178-179).

Shri Guruji says that had the Congress leadership taken the right and rational approach, things would have been different. When the Muslim question came before them they showed the lack of conviction, clarity and confidence. They were not prepared to contemplate alternative method. Cultural nationalism propounded and successfully practised by Lokmanya B.G. Tilak and his contemporaries was rejected by them. Guruji says the remedy of the Muslim separatism and non-cooperation lay in the firmness of the Congress leadership.

Shri Guruji says, 'There was a very rational and patriotic way of approach. That was to tell them frankly: "Dear friends, the days of old Moghul Badshahi have passed. Now both of us will have to live ultimately as brothers here, as co-sharers in this national life. After all you also belong to the same race as we, to the same blood as ours, but converted to Islam at the point of sword by those Moghul, Turk and other foreign races. Now, there is no point in continuing to associate yourself mentally with those foreign aggressors and trying to follow in their footsteps. Forget all such separatist memories; merge yourself in the life of this soil. Hereafter try to respect and follow the examples of the great sons of this land who fought for the freedom and honour of the motherland and our culture." (G2000:142)

There has been misgiving created by secularists that the RSS had also advocated inferior position to Muslims in Hindu dominated India. How this allegation is baseless is obvious from Guruji's position on this issue, "What would happen of non Hindus (Muslims) in independent India? Would they be treated as second rank citizens? Undoubtedly these questions emanate from the inner self. The extremist organisation would say 'yes' to the second question since non Hindus (clearly Muslims) have committed heinous crimes against the Hindus in the past. It has created ill feelings among the Hindus against them (Muslims). Even now they are demanding separate and privileged status against the interests of the nation. They are virtually behaving like enemy of the nation! Irrespective of their such hostile and intemperate behaviour for which they deserve to be condemned, the Hindu Nation in accordance with its liberal temperament and tradition is bound to forgive them if they are prepared to fulfil minimum expectation not to be dishonest to the nation and refrain from creating hurdles in its progress (which he then meant freedom Movement)."

Shri Guruji persistently campaigned against the communal politics of the Muslim League. In his speech on 12 August 1946 he attacked 'the forces trying to poison the atmosphere by raising communal issues.' (Indurkar 65). Jinnha's sole object was "to destroy Indian nationalism by undermining the faith in India as Motherland on which it is founded." (Tara Singh: 152) His slogan and programme of 'Direct Action' in August 1946 changed the social psychology of the country. Guruji equated Direct Action with direct aggression. (G2000: 178) The Tribune wrote, "The happenings in Calcutta are reminiscent of the happenings of the days of Mahmud Ghazanavi and Muhammad Ghori and those of Nadir Shah." The city of Calcutta was turned into 'bloody slaughterhouse'.* Guruji pointed out, 'The relationship between the Hindus and Muslims was never so bitter and estranged as in those years of 1946 and 1947. Millions of families were uprooted from their ancestral homes; provinces after provinces turned crimson by the flow of the rivers of blood; and death, destruction and disgrace, scarced the faces of crores of innocent human beings. Even the normal social intercourse which had existed between the two was shattered during that period." (2000:148)

Shri Guruji traces the seeds of the partition in the Congress' policy of appeasement. The leadership lacked confidence and courage to 'face Muslim intransigencies squarely, from the standpoint of undiluted nationalism' (G 2000; 143). Jaykar too endorsed Guruji when he writes, "we have no Benjamin Franklin who could tell the Muslims we will not allow you to secede and if you wish to fight, we shall meet you on our own ground.' From the very beginning the process of giving concessions went on and on and a year ago the appeasement took the form of concessions surrendered at the sight of violence." Guruji observes that if there was any basis for the formation and perpetuation of Pakistan it is hatred for Hindus. He says, "Naked fact remains that an aggressive Muslim state has been carved out of our Motherland." (G : 2000:178) He describes even the division of countries like Germany, Korea, Vietnam on the basis of any particular contentious idea or event as most unfortunate. (Guruji IX : 45) He strongly pleads the unification of the Pakistan with India. Its existence perpetually inspires the Muslims for anti-national activities and separatist mentality and gives them ample strength for such activities." The reason behind communal riots has been that Indian Muslims could not identify themselves with people and culture. There is a need to change their psychology. (8:69) Partition had not resolved the Muslim problem at all. (Guruji VIII: 43) The feeling should be created in Muslim consciousness that the concept of two nationalities was a sinful concept, that the partition was a grave mistake. (Guruji IX: 44) The logical conclusion and correct resolution is, says Guruji, unification of both the parts of the historically one nation, Bharat. The only way, he believes, is the change of heart. (Guruji IX: 46) This may seem impractical but one day it would be a reality. He further says that the unification would not mean slavery of one or another set of people but 'equal responsibility in carrying on country's administration and business and sharing one another's sentiments in the hour of joy and sorrow.' (Guruji IX : 46-47)

The self-introspective and poignant debate in the Constituent Assembly of India demonstrated that the Congress leadership was largely disillusioned with their own tryst with minorities during the freedom movement. Neither Guruji was a member of the Assembly nor the RSS had any direct or indirect organisational or ideological communication with the Congress. Yet after the partition, the language, ideology, sociological intentions and nationalist objectives of the RSS largely reflected in the debates of the Constituent Assembly. Dr Hedgewar's vision was inexorably creating impact on the people of all layers. This was not a sudden overture but re-emergence of the seeds of cultural nationalism ingrained in the sub-consciousness of every Hindu. However, this opportunity was destroyed by the tragic assassination of Mahatma Gandhi by Nathu Ram Godse.

Indian Muslims conscientiously continued their practice of cow slaughter. Their obsession with it unravels their uncompromising and non-accommodative mentality for the last hundreds of years. For them there is more pleasure than benefit when they slaughter cows, which have been respected as mother and worshipped also. Guruji conclusively observes that cow slaughter was 'a sort of a way of spitting the Hindus in the old days', and wonders on its continuation even after independence. (Jeelany: 46) He further says, "Whenever the Muslims slaughtered cows to insult Hindu feelings, the Hindus were told that it was the religious right of Muslims and that, being tolerant to other religions, they should not object it. Although there is not a word of sanction in Quran for cow slaughter." (G 2000:144)

The Congress had never stood firmly against Muslim demand to perform freely cow slaughter in the public gaze as their 'cultural' and 'traditional' right and community's sentiment. Whosoever did not support and advocate this proposition or campaigned to protect cows faced the music of being ridiculed as anti-Muslim or communal Hindu.

Two Nation Mentality

The country's politics and socio-religious reality vindicates Guruji's prescription. The Indian polity has been facing challenges from within: whether secular judiciary of Islamic court; whether secular education in Madarsa; whether competition-based admission in educational institutions and jobs whether the Vande Mataram as a national song for all Indians. These are the same old questions with similar arguments once used by the Muslim League and now being replayed by the 'Muslim India'. The Muslim vote bank tactically and shrewdly has been used to affect the secular politics of the country. It has been increasingly revolving round the decrees of Mosques rather than the spirit of the Indian constitution.

Says Guruji, "the Indian Muslims have yet to converge into Indian culture and its people. The problem would cease to exist once they will feel and speak that this is their motherland and the people are their own people. It is a matter to entrench such desirable changes in their psychology." (Samadhan:60)

When he uses the term danger of 'internal subversion' he also means the Muslims' defiance of the state. Guruji has been vindicated by events, which took place after his death. In 1985, the Supreme Court favoured the formulation and implementation of the Uniform Civil Code in the Shah Bano case. It evoked protest among the Muslims. Minister of State for environment in Rajiv Gandhi government Z.R. Ansari proved that the separatism was a creed with the Indian Muslims. He lambasted the SC on December 20, 1985 for trying to interpret the Muslim Personal Law. Speaking in the Lok Sabha he ridiculed Chief Justice Y.V. Chandrachud and said that the Chief Justice was incompetent to interpret the Islamic law. Another Muslim member Saifuddin Soz said that the Muslim felt terribly insecure because of the presence of article 44 in the Constitution, which speaks of the UCC.

Indirect Aggression

After independence, Muslims have replaced their old strategy of direct action, says Guruji, by indirect aggression. He means infiltration in border districts of Assam, Bengal, Bihar and other parts of the country to turn them into Muslim majority areas so that they would "automatically fall into the lap of Pakistan in course of time." (G2000:179) His farsighted warning was as usual ignored by the state thinking it as an anti-Muslim propaganda. After his death, the problem became more acute. He had warned, "It would be suicidal on our part to dismiss their plan of realising the dream of Jinnah as mere wishful thinking. And so did we, at one time, dismiss Jinnah's demand for Pakistan as 'fantastic'." (G2000: 180)

Vande Mataram

The one indicator of change in the Muslim mind after independence could be their attitude towards the national song Vande Mataram. Surendra Nath Baneerjee compared this song with those of Garibaldi and Mazzini:

"Bankimchandra Chatterjee could hardly have anticipated the part it was destined to play in the Swadeshi Movement... Dante, when he sang the Italian unity, had no conception of the practical use to which his song would be put by Mazini and Garibaldi, or the part it would play in the political evolution of the Italian population. (quoted by Bandopadhyay: 221)

Similarly Sri Aurovindo said, "the Mantra (Vande Mataram) had been given and in a single day a whole people had been converted to the religion of patriotism. The Mother had revealed herself. Once that vision comes to the people, there can be no rest, no peace, no further slumber till the temple has been made ready, the image installed and the sacrifice offered. A great nation which has had that vision can never again be placed under the feet of the conqueror." (Bandopadhyay: 221). Both of them called it a song of patriotism. It has nothing to do with one or other religion. Bankim takes the metaphors and examples from the historical journey of the nation since times immemorial. The fact is that the Muslims detest this song even after India's independence. Guruji remarked that it was just a repetition of unpatriotic attitude and ingratitude of the Muslims. (G2000 : 263-264).

Shri Guruji rejects the Muslim's claim for Urdu and believes that their advocacy is not concerned with their love for a language but it is aimed at consolidating their political role in the country. He says that it cannot be a religious language of the Muslims. Holy Quran is in Arabic. If at all there is a 'religious language' for Muslims, it is Arabic. There is hardly any difference in the Muslim psyche before and after independence. In the pre-independence days, the issue of Urdu was projected as a part and parcel of Muslim identity. For instance the Muslim League of the Orissa province raised in addition to other grievances, the arrangements for the teaching of Urdu where the people speaking Urdu are almost negligible.

Shri Guruji is not opposed to Urdu or any other language. Variety of languages, dialects and scripts, says he, is a beauty of our national and cultural life. All of them contribute in our cultural progress. He only cautions against the use of a language as a weapon to construct a nationality.

Change of Heart

Shri Guruji raised a fundamental question regarding the post-partition Muslim mind when he asked, "Is it true that all pro Pakistani elements have gone away to Pakistan? It was the Muslims in Hindu majority provinces led by UP who provided the spearhead for the movement for Pakistan right from the beginning. And they have remained solidly here even after partition. In fact, the Muslims of Punjab, Bengal, Sind and NWFP which went over to Pakistan had totally rejected Muslim League in 1937 elections." (G2000:177)

Sardar Patel debunked the Muslims claim of fraternity with Hindus and their demand for privileges and protection on the pretext of their status as minority community. Patel, like Guruji, perceived it as a symptom of the same old disease. He on the floor of the Constituent Assembly warned the Muslims, "if the process that was adopted, which resulted in the separation of the country, is to be repeated then I say:

Those who want that kind of thing have a place in Pakistan not here (Applause). Here we are building a nation and we are laying the foundations of One nation, and those who choose to divide again and sow the seeds of disruption will have no place, no quarter, here, and I must say that plainly enough." (Emphasis added)

Shri Guruji reiterated his advise to the Indian Muslims to identify themselves with culture and people of this country. He said, "It is obvious that Indian history does not begin with Mohammad Ghazani." (Guruji 9:107). The same sentiment was expressed on the floor of the Assembly. Patel said, "My friends you must change your attitude, adapt yourself to the changed conditions. And don't pretend to say 'Oh, our affection is very great for you'. We have seen your affection. Why talk of it? Let us forget the affection. Let us face the realities. Ask yourself whether you really want to stand here and co-operate with us or want again to play disruptive tactics. Therefore, when 1 appeal to you, I appeal to you to have a change in your heart, not a change in the tongue, because that won't pay here.. Why go on saying, "Oh, Muslims were not heard;" Further like Guruji he reminded the nation, "You have got what you wanted. You have got a separate state and remember, you are the people who were responsible for it, and not those who remain in Pakistan. You led the agitation. You got it. What is that you want now? I don't understand. In the majority

Hindu provinces you, the minorities, you led the agitation. You got the partition and now again you tell me and ask me, to say, for the purpose of securing the affection of the younger brother that I must agree to the same thing again, to divide the country again in the divided part. For God's sake, understand that we have also got some sense." (Emphasis added) (28 August 1947, CAD*, Vol. V, pp 271-272)

Shri Guruji does not find any substantial change in the Muslim mind and says that the perpetuation of the same old demands and politics would be like recycling the history without any lesson from it.

Shri Guruji's faith in the cultural nationalism remained unshaken at the hour of the greatest tragedy of the country. He was not a populist or the man blown by the incidents and circumstances. He always had long-term vision. He and the RSS acted accordingly. At this juncture of history when the demand for exchange of population was supported by a large number of people, Guruji did not stand for such demand. He did not consider it as a proper (judicious) solution. (Guruji VIII: 41) He believed that the cultural foundation of the country would one day overpower religion-based separatism. He rightly says, "no body is happy with the partition of the country" (Guruji: 9:41). The existence of Pakistan in itself is a factor for some anti-national feelings and actions among the Indian Muslims.

Concept of Minority

The biggest absurdity of Indian secularism is legitimacy to the concept of minority. The classification of the people on the basis of mode of worship and its application in the principle of governance militates against our own historical experiences. Guruji says, 'History bears testimony to the fact that Bharat, the cradle land of religious generosity has always welcomed and assured all religious groups a free, honourable and secure life (G2000: 321) He further argues that in India there is 'no question of majority and minority.' (Guruji: 1986:12) His submission has again and again been attacked by the secularists (Red-Green club) as anti Muslim tirade. For decades both Guruji and his critics ceaselessly made their respective proposition. And the Indian judiciary finally endorsed Guruji. The Supreme Court of India in a landmark judgement on August 10, 2005 said that the National Commission for Minority (NCM) "should suggest ways and means to help create social conditions where the list of notified minorities is gradually reduced and done away altogether." Moreover three-member bench of the Court consisting of Justice R.C. Lahoti, Justice D.M. Dharmadhikari and Justice P.K. Balasubramanyam gave their equally important observation, "The objective of a democratic society ought to be to eliminate majority and minority..."

Shri Guruji's perception and articulation had many votaries in the Constituent Assembly. Dr. H.C. Mookerjee, vice chairman of the Assembly and Christian by faith on May 25, 1947, raised two fundamental questions before the Assembly, 'the first is, are we really honest when we say that we are seeking to establish a secular state? And the second is, whether we intend to have one nation? If our idea is to have a secular state it follows inevitably that we can not afford to recognise minorities based upon religion. (CA Debates, Vol. VIII, p 298)

Shri Guruji rightly pointed out that "while bringing about integration with the nation in its practical life, destruction of distinct ways of worship is not aimed at, only putting an end to undesirable tendencies of exclusiveness and intolerance is aimed at." (G 2000:168)

Concept of Mother-India

Shri Guruji treats the nationality above religious and all other identities and consistent with Indian tradition he elevates the nation as a Mother and above all Goddess to be worshipped. The concept of Motherland is a common point of assimilation of Muslims with the culture. It is the supreme religion. However, it is not idolatory in a religious sense or merely ritual to worship the symbol of the Mother-India but it is identification with the nation. Such dedication is not meant to create any totalitarian state or expansionist mission. It establishes an organic link between the people and the land and its culture and history. He defines the nation as "a practical and physical manifestation of the culture and a set of values, samskars, inherited by the people inhabiting in a geographical boundary." (Guruji: 1997:21) He further underlines the importance of the motherland in the Hindu tradition. He observes, "In our concept of nationality some elements have been emphasised. Abounding reverence for the Motherland is placed at the top. Then comes in order the respect for our history, which of course does not mean of a few centuries but entire gamut of Hindu civilisation. Its natural corollary is regard for our ancestors. (Guruji IX:105)

The emotional cry of *Bharat Mata ki Jai* is absent among the Muslims. The Muslims' position has not changed even after the partition. For them the land of birth does not make any deeper-sense, "boundary of a nation merely reflects administrative arrangement" and "does not enjoy permanent sanctity." (Radiance, 2-8 October 2005)

"They call themselves as "Sheiks" and "Syeds". Sheiks and Syeds are certain clans in Arabia. How then did these people come to feel that they are their ascendents? That is because they have cut off all their ancestral moorings of this land and mentally merged themselves with aggressors. They still think that they have come here only to conquer and establish their kingdoms" (G 2000:128)

Shri Guruji observes that the reclaiming back to home all those people who were converted by other religions is legitimate, morally and historically justified. The concept of reconversion is the latest addition to the creed of Hinduism and credit goes to Swami Dayananda for it. Guruji says: "it used to be said that a person who has left the Hindu *dharma once,* is gone for ever. But this cannot be. He has to be brought home again. If somebody trips to take away our own people, it is our first duty to be careful that hereafter nothing of that kind will happen and if it does, we must take every step to reclaim him and bring him home.'

Indianisation

The secularism adopted by the Congress as a creed of the nation is not only 'because it was moral, relevant and appropriate' (Chandoke: 41) but the fact is that the tradition of the land and temperament of the Hindus adhere to the concept of equal respect for religions and philosophies. However, politics prevented the assimilation of Muslims, which should have been a natural course of history. This historical tradition of evolution is defined as Indianisation. Guruji says it does not mean converting other religionists into Hindus. He unambiguously and succinctly defined the concept as follow:

> *"Let us realise and believe that we are all children of this soil coming from the same stock, that our great forefathers were one, and that our aspirations are also one. This is all, believe, the meaning of 'Indiannisation'. (G2000:495)*
>
> *The opposition to theory connotation and concept is astonishing. He says, "It seems that this sacred country, immortal nation is a victim of some curse otherwise instead of showing repugnance to this very word it would have been welcomed and appreciated." (Guruji VII: 356)*

The problem arises because Indian Muslims show affinity with aggressors and identify with them. Guruji makes a distinction between aggressors and Indian Muslims, "the aggressors were foreigners and have nothing in common with the Muslims here. Let our Muslims here say that they are of this land and the past aggressors and their aggressions are not part of their heritagc," (G2000: 493) He is not demeaning Muslims but it is a demand for cultural regeneration of Muslims.

Indianisation means owning India's past beyond religious history and profile. Guruji presents Indonesian model before the Indian Muslims. Indonesia where majority professes Islam and controls society and politics have Hindu names (like Sukama, Kartikeya). They worship Ganesh and Saraswati, read with reverence Ramayana. However the Indian Muslims adopt Arabian instead of Indianised names. He says, "After all Indonesia is a big Muslim country. Yet Muslims have not been cut off from the tradition, culture and language. They have adopted names, like Sukarna, Ratnadevi. Does it mean they cease to be Muslims?" But in India the first thing for a convert is to adopt the Arabic name. This is substantiated by the following example. In Perayur in Mudarai district (Tamilnadu) some villagers embraced Islam in 1984 and 1994. Mathu Karuppiah became Saddam Hussain in 1984.

Indianisation is not at all dilution of one's faith. It is a creation of motivating force for cultural unity and loyalty to the Motherland. To consider it as superimposition of Hinduism on Muslims shows lamentable lack of understanding the cultural assimilation and its consequences in Indian history. Guruji says, "I have no quarrel with any class, community or sect wanting to maintain its identity so long as that identity does not detract from its patriotic feeling." His views on the personal law substantiate his claim.

Personal law

He assertively presents the essence of our socio-cultural paradigm, "I think uniformity is the death knell of nations. Nature abhors uniformity. I am all for the protection of various ways of life. However all the variety must supplement the unity of the nation and not range itself against it". Guruji's views on Muslim Personal Law may be surprising for those who do not try to understand his paradigm or his philosophy in terms of endurance of civilisational progress, evolution and who hold myopic view on minority problem. When Guruji was asked, "does he not think that the common civil code is necessary for promoting the feeling of nationalism" he gave a straight answer in a very unambiguous term "I don't". He was aware of the superficial debate on this issue. He did not forget to add, "this may surprise you or many others. But this is my opinion. I must speak the truth as I see it". Merely presence of various customs and traditional laws does not pose any danger as long the men practicing them consider their root in the soil of their birth, own its culture and paradigm.

Mutual Goodwill & Respect

Shri Guruji's objective is to restore an atmosphere of mutual goodwill and respect between Hindus and Muslims. He says, "Harmonious pattern of mutual goodwill and respect is precondition for cultural nationalism. (G 2000:39). Muslims are secure in India if they earn the goodwill of Hindus whose philosophy of life is based on secularism. It is pertinent to quote G.B. Pant's reply to Ismail Khan, a League member, October 1937:

"The security of their interests will depend on the extent to which they continue to retain the confidence of general mass of the people, and the attitude of the general mass towards them will be determined by their attitude towards the large vast mass of the people in the country... No artificial guarantee can secure for them what their real conduct and their practical behaviour will deprive them of."

Shri Guruji says "it is only a strong and resurgent Hindu Rashtra that can stand guarantee to the free and prosperous life of the so-called minorities here, sharing equal opportunities as the proud children of the Motherland." (G2000:161) The goodwill theory of Guruji found support in the Constituent Assembly.

V.V. John, who happened to be a Christian, prefered the protection of human rights rather than minority rights. According to him leaders of minority communities practice 'selective secularism' and demand from Hindus what they themselves do not practice. (Quoted by Madan, 1997:255)

When Guruji was asked by a Muslim about his attitude towards Muslims, he aptly responded, "we are the children of the same forefathers and must always bear this in mind.

Follow your religion honestly, but in the national context we all have to be one. There can be no claiming of rights and privileges at the cost of the nation." At the same time he says that the majority can also not be a privileged community. He further says, "We do not say to anybody that because we are Hindus, we alone are entitled to this and that. Not at all." (Jeelany:44) He out rightly denounces the feeling of Muslims to reinforce the separate identity and warns "there can not be a state within a state...when people look at things from the point of view of political aggrandisement, dangerous difficulties crop up. But once this aggrandisement is left out, our country becomes one and we can meet the challenge of the whole world."(ibid)

Shri Guruji unequivocally stated, "so far as the work of the country is concerned, I do not distinguish between Hindus and Muslims." (G2000: 489) Muslims should be given their due share but their demand for special rights and privileges go against the principles of secularism. (G2000:89) His vision on Muslim problem is philosophically sound and pragmatically consistent with our history. The political culture and the Muslim politics together is a challenge to secular democracy. The sociology and politics of Indian Muslims is based not on idealism once shown by the Congress or cultural tradition of the country but is based on 'India does not consist of One but two peoples'. That's why Guruji says, "the Muslims look upon partition only as a springboard of further aggression." (Spotlights, p 45)

Post independent India has been facing a challenge of old habits of minorityism. So Guruji rightly raises the question "Do the Muslims accept India as Bharat Mata? and "How many of them shout '*Bharat Mata ki Jay*'?" Still the Indian Muslim psyche has to come to terms to these core questions raised by Shri Guruji decades back. His philosophy is a call for Indianisation and assimilation, evolution and progress of national outlook.

(Biographer of R.S.S. founder and an erudite academician, Rakesh Sinha is a prolific writer on socio-political problems.)

References:

1. Also see Qureshi, Ishtiaq Hussain, 'The Muslim Community of Indo Pakistan Subcontinent' 1962, (610-1947), p. 103
2. Dr. Durrany, KS, associated with Indian Institute of Islamic Studies.
3. Guruji to Muhammed Rafi, March 3, 1970.
4. Memoirs of Shri Madhavrao Mule
5. In Burma publishing of Quran needs official permission they are forbidden from performing hajj. (Kettani: 142) in Canada Islam is not recognised on equal footing with Christianity. (Kettani: 207)
6. Rashtra Mimansa, Foreword, p 24 (* August 23, 1946)
7. M.R. Jaykar to Sapru, 21 May 1947, Sapru papers, S-I, NMML, New Delhi
8. Qamuruddin Khan, spokesman of the AMU wrote in *Light* of Lahore, "Pakistan's presence in the neighbourhood would embolden the Muslims... The Indian Muslims should maintain close relations with Pakistan..." (Dixit:100)
9. With Editors of national dailies in Delhi on 11 June 1970.
10. Indian Express 21 December 1985 Ansari Attacks Supreme Court
11. Indian Express 23 December 1985
12. According to 1991 census Muslim presence in the border areas of eastern states increased substantially. In 1991 Muslims presence was: Up: 20.47%, Bihar: 21%, West Bengal 47.14%, Assam 37.15%. For details see Religious Demography of India by A.P. Joshi, M.D. Srinivas and J.K. Bajaj, Centre for Policy Studies, Chennai-2003.
13. Indian Express, August 11, 2005
14. Indian Express, August 11, 2005
15. The Indian Express, January 22, 2001.
16. Motherland 23 August, 1972

9

Gurujee And Christian Missionaries

Shripati Shastri

INDIA is an ancient nation and during the course of its mighty long history, numerous religious beliefs were propounded and numerous religious practises were evolved. Hinduism is the name of a confederation of all these religious beliefs, it is not one religion in the sense that Islam and Christianity are understood to be. Certainly Guruji's connotation of the word Hindu is national not religious. He was fully familiar with the nature and character of the Hindu people and their attitude concerning religion.

Hindus are proud to have in their midst any number of faiths, beliefs, sects and religions. They do not only just tolerate but also appreciate their existence. A Hindu does not visualise God as a Hindu God, a Christian God or a Muslim God. To a Hindu, God is God - pure and simple. He also does not distinguish ideas of God as true or false adopting one particular idea as the standard for the human race. Therefore, people professing various religions abound in this country and Hindus take pride in it. Guruji believed not only in universal toleration but accepted all religions as true. He was proud that he belonged to a nation which has, during different stages of history, sheltered the persecuted and refugees of all religions and of all nations of the earth.

If any of our countrymen wanted to practise a particular religious faith and if there was no scope for it, Guruji would have felt that the country has grown poorer for it. It was not true that Guruji was against any religion. It was equally untrue that he was against Christianity.

To Guruji there is much to admire in Christianity - the life story of Jesus Christ, sayings of the prophets, educative parables and moral ideas represented therein. But despite all this he was unable to reconcile himself with the practices of orthodox Christianity and the Church. So when Christianity challenged Hinduism, he would draw a sharp distinction bctween Christian sectarianism and dogmatism and the Spritit and Teachings of Christ. It is a line that seperates Christ from Christians. The Holy Bible and Jesus Christ were held in high reverence by him but the activities carried on by the Churches in His name were looked upon with suspicion. Infact no pious Hindu had anything against Christian religion as such. Mahatma Gandhi did say that the Hindus won't even think in their dreams to eliminate the Christians. If they wanted that they would have very easily finished them, when they landed on this country. If the Christian church besides,

> *"educating, doing medical services and doing such humanitarian and compassioned works, use these services to convert the people. I will certainly ask them to leave this place (country)"*[1]

Neither the RSS (Rashtriya Swayamsnak Sangh) nor any other Hindu Organisation had anything against Christian brethren or against Christian faith but certainly against all de-Hinduisation. But never did our forefathers anticipate that the religions that were greeted with a cordial welcome would one day throw a mortal challenge to the unity, integrity and happiness of this country.

The challenge of the Christian Church

A challenge was hurled at the Hindu people when the highest church authorities exhorted their followers to plant the Cross in the Asian continent in the Third Christian millennium. The church dreamt of reaping "a rich harvest of souls in Asia," Remove the tapestry of language. It simply meant to convert and Christianise the country,

The Christian Church has a long self-proclaimed policy of conversion. The history of Christianity is an unbroken record of atrocities against Hindus in its quest for new recruits to their gospel. Foreign missionaries and even the Pope had come to promote the cause of Catholicism, which meant the conversion of the Hindus. The Christian Missionaries stick to their basic dogma of One True God and the Saviour which Hindus should accept or be made to accept whereas Guruji had embarked upon a holy mission in defence of the Hindu Dharma and the Hindu people.

The Church has discovered that Hinduism is full of faults. The fiction of a degenerated India and debased Hiduism seems to be the life-blood of the Christian Church and they have no intention of parting with it. They have never made any secret of their conviction and also have never lost any opportunity to proclaim openly that they are the only true religion and as such superior to others. In fact they derive their right to convert precisely from this religious conviction that they are commanded by their Prophets to save the souls of others who have been the victims of other false religions. That is why they honestly believe that means of conversion fair or foul does not matter. It also explains why they do not hesitate to denigrate Hindu gods and goddesses in the filthiest of language.

The bloody history of the Church in America, Africa and Asia is an open-book and is well known. In Bharat, the Goa inquisition was probably the worst. It involved the torture and murder of thousands of Hindus and the destruction of many Hindu temples over a period of several decades. It is the Indian version of the genocide of Native Americans. The Christian Church is not prepared to disown their ugly past so that a process of reconciliation could be initiated. Nay, the arch murderers are glorified as saints! How can the Hindu be persuaded to embrace the most inveterate enemy and thus endanger his own existence?

It is a mortal challenge. It seeks to destroy the natural right of the Hindu people to live with their religion, culture and civilisation. It aims at the destruction of the religious diversity flourishing in this country.

Shri Guruji's concept of religious integration

Unity of the country is an article of faith with Guruji. The Hindu concept of unity of integration is harmony, certainly not uniformity. A man can be a Hindu by nationality and at the same time be a Sanatani or an Arya Samaji, a Muslim or a Christian a Sikh or Buddhist. In Guruji's Hinduism there is room enough for Jessus, as there is for Mohammed, Zoraster and Moses. He would have been shocked if anybody had suggested anything less than equal right to Muslim or Christians. He considered it as un-Hindu to discriminate between any two persons just on the basis of religious faith. He put it thus - The non-Hindu who lives here has a Rashtra Dharma (National responsibility) a Samaja-Dharma (duty to ancestors) and only in his Vyakti-Dharma (Personal Faith) he can choose any path which satisfies his spiritual urge. Even after fulfilling all those various duties in social life, anybody says that he has studied Quran or the Bible and that way of worship strikes a sympathetic chord in his heart, he is welcome to follow it.

To a question 'do you approve religious toleration in respect of Islam and Christianity', Guruji replied that he not only tolerated them but respected them. To him Indian Christians were none other than the Christianised section of the Hindu Society - nothing more, nothing less.

If and when they maintain that they are Christian first and Indian next, the Christian Missionaries come in conflict with their loyalty to the nation. The Christians living in non-Christian countries including India are torn between these two loyalties. Their Political loyalties and social outlook are all shaped by it more than by anything else.

Common Emotion and common Ancestors

Shri Guruji was emphatic that thc Christians should also share the 'common emotion' with the rest of the countryman towards the nation. What is that 'Common emotion', that common basis on which all can come together? Guruji maintained that in the first place a feeling of burning devotion to the land which from times immemorial has been regarded as the sacred motherland. In the second place the feeling of fellowship, of common fraternity born out of the realisation that we are the children of that one great common mother. And in the third place, an intense awareness of a common current of national life, born out of a common culture and heritage, common history and traditions, of common ideals and aspirations. This trinity of values or. in a word Hindu nationalism. formed the bedrock of our national edifice.

There are so many people in the Hindu Dharma who do not believe in the Divine Incarnation of Rama and Krishna. But they believe that they are great personalities, worthy of emulation. So what does it matter if Christians do not believe that God incarnated himself. Why should they not consider such personalities as their national heroes?

According to our ways of religious belief and philosophy a Muslim or a Christian is as good as a Hindu. It is not the Hindu alone who will reach the ultimate Godhood. Everyone has the right to follow his path according to his own persuasion. Guruji further said on one occasion:

> *"Let me give you the instance of the previous Shankaracharya of the Shringeri Math, His Holiness Shri Chandrasekhara Bharati Swamiji. An American approached him to be converted to Hinduism. Swamiji asked him the reason. The American replied that he was not satisfied with Christianity, that it left his spiritual longing unquenched.' The Acharya asked him: 'Have you honestly practised Christianity? Try it first. If it*

does not satisfy you, then come to me'. That is our attitude. Ours is a non-proselytising Dharma. In almost all cases, proselytisation is motivated by political or some such gain. We reject it."(2)

A Confession by the Mission

The institution of Indian Christians Mission, FOIM. published A collection of Papers from church people wherein a frank confession was made on this behalf. They confess:-

"However, due to historical and socio-political factors, the call to conversion and baptism has been problematic in the Indian context. We Christians ourselves must bear a part of the responsibility for this. The Christian attack on the indegenous religions of India from a position of colonial power was understandably seen by many as a threat to their identity and even their very existence. The continued impression that Christianity is a foreign religion in India also has much to do with the colonial legacy and also the reluctance of Christians to look positively on the tradition and culture of India".(3)

Shri Guruji maintained that the Christians must realise that we are one people and it is the same blood that courses through our veins. The Indian Christians are not Italians, French, Dutch or the English. They are only Indian converts. The Hindu suspects the Christian because his loyalty to the nation, national heritage and ancestors has come under cloud.

The main reason why there is Hindu-Christian tension in India is that the Indian Christian is yet to identify himself fully with India, its people and culture. Let the Indian Christian feel and say that this is his own country and all these are his people and the problem will cease to exist. It is a matter of changing his psychology. The problem can be solved by the Indian Christian just by owning this country and its ancient culture. After all, Indian history did not begin with Vasco-de-Gama.

For A Harmonious National Life

Guruji was not prepared to accept the mere accident of birth as adequate to earn the nationhood of the country without any reference to their mental attitude and mind-set. In expounding his concept of nationalism Guruji preferred to accept ground realities unlike the modern day secularist who preferred convenient illusions.

It is not true that Guruji was intolerant of any religion. It is equally untrue that he was hostile to the Christian missionaries in India. The criterion he prescribed for promoting a harmonious national life was both patriotic and practical. The prescription he offered had room for all minorities on condition of their whole-hearted submission to the supreme value of the nation in their lives. The Hindus complain that the:

> *Christians consider themselves "as agents of international movement for the spread of Christianity and refuse to offer their first loyalty to the land of their birth and behave as the true children of the heritage and culture of their ancestors. They therefore remain as hostiles and will have to be treated as such".*(4)

The Church is not tired of claiming that they are only helping the poor destitutes, the deprived, the needy and the unattended. If the Christians had been benefactors why should such stalwarts of Indian Nationalism as Vivekananda and Gandhiji feel outraged at the Missionary machinations. In fact their vilification of Hinduism is so excessive that it will leave most tolerant of the Hindus distressed. Without mincing words Gandhiji confessed that 'It pained him to have to say that the Christian Missionaries as a body, with honourable exceptions, have actively supported a system which had impoverished, enervated and demoralised a people considered to be among the gentlest and most civilised on earth.'

Shri Guruji had put his finger on this humanitarian mask of the missionaries:

> *"So far as the Christians are concerned, to a superficial observer they appear not only quite harmless but as the very embodiment of sympathy and love for humanity. Their speeches abound in words like 'service' and 'human salvation' as though they are specially deputed by the Almighty to uplift humanity! Everywhere they run schools, colleges. hospitals and orphanges. The people of our country, simple and innocent as they are, are taken in by all these things. But what, is the real and ulterior motive of Christians in pouring crores of rupees in all these activities?"*(5)

During the course of his conversation with the editor of the *Illustrated Weekly*, Guruji made a candid observation:

> *"We have nothing against the Christians except their methods of gaining converts. When they give medicine to the sick or bread to hungry, they should not exploit the situation by propagating their religion to those people".*(6)

A Pillar of strenghth to the British

Early British conquests had resulted in the firmer establishment of Pax-Britanica. Security of the empire haunted the rulers. The Christian Church was a source of hope and strength. In the words of Lord Halifax., the secretary of state:

> *"Every additional Christian is an additional bond of union with the Country and an additional source of strength to the empire".*(7)

In order to provide stability to the empire the British rulers undertook various measures. According to Guruji:

> *"First and the foremost method was to multiply the number of their co-religionists whose support to the British rule would be uninterrupted. Since*

the British were Christians, Christianisation of the Hindus gradually became a state enterprise. Quite a few did succumb to their inducements. But by and large, the British experience was that the ordinary folk did not abandon the Faith of their ancestors".[8]

Inspite of the Christianisation campaign carried on by thousands of Christian Missionaries in the tribal belts for more than 150 years, backed up by their own political ascendancy and by endless flow of money the experience was bitter. At every step the shoe was pinching. Guruji reccollected:

"....... thousands of Missionaries and crores of Rupees were poured in. Officials for local administration were appointed in view of their utility towards conversion and on the recommendation of the missionaries. Preachers of other religious Faiths working in the same area were just driven out. A few Arya Samaji activists who ventured to set foot in the same belt could not be seen again alive. They were just murdered. Similar fate including manhandling, abduction, and murder befell the Sangh workers who had managed to step in that area. The law of the land had chosen to maintain a stony silence towards these happenings......."[9]

Conversion - Not Voluntary

The Christians of India are converts or descendents of converts whose conversion had been secured during some period of history by force or fraud. Nobody objects to any voluntary change of faith promoted by spiritual motives. e.g. Pandita Ramabai, Rev. Tilak in Maharashtra, Brahmabandhav Upadhyaya in Bengal and Manilal Parekh in Gujarat. But conversion by persuasion is a rarity. Voluntary change of faith born out of spiritual motive does not diminish their love for the country's cultural heritage. But how are the villages converted enmass in no time. Is there a spiritual motive at play here? Voluntary change of faith is preceded by great psychological revolution: nobody abandoned Hinduism that way.

Most of the conversions are due to threats, allurements, financial stringency, deception and persecution. The less said the better about the role the sword played. It is an ugly record. Guruji often reminded the people about the hidden agenda of the Church where in conversion aims at subversion. He recalled:

> *"Are we not aware of the atrocious history of the Christian missionaries, in our own country, of how they carried sword and fire in Goa and elsewhere?*
>
> *There is the story of "saint" Xavier who used to experience the highest joy of his life when he used to see the new converts trampling upon their former gods and goddesses razing their temples to the ground and insulting their own parents and elders who had remained Hindus".*(10)

Shri Guruji does not want our countrymen to forget how hundreds of ancient and sacred Hindu temples including the famous one at Shabarimalai were desecrated and their idols broken by the Christian vandals and how the Memorial Tablet on thc Vivekananda Rock at Kanyakumari was smashed by the same Christian fanatics not very long ago. Said he;

> *"Such are the men who came to us to preach that Christianity would shower peace and milk of human kindness on humanity."*(11)

Shri Guruji would sometimes remark the oft-repeated saying;

"There was but one true Christian and he died on the cross."

That is why they honestly believe that means of conversion

fair or foul does not matter. It also explains why they do not hesitate to denigrate Hindu gods and goddesses in the filthiest of language.

It is a mortal challenge. It seeks to destroy the natural right of the Hindu people to live with their religion, culture and civilisation. It aims at the destruction of the religious diversity flourishing in this country.

Politics of Conversion

Indeed in the whole of the Christian-Hindu strained relationship there has been no greater cause of friction than the Christian campaign of coversion. What is conversion? When the one who is in an advantageous position seeks to force his conception of God and the Universe on the other who is in a vulnerable position, when the one strikes at that which is deepest and precious in the heart of the other, he invites resistance. A missionary brings pain and misery when he kidnaps a member of the family in the name of Christ and conversion. To the question: "Would you prevent missionraries coming to India in order to baptise?" Mahatma Gandhi was ruthless in his reply and is reported to have said that 'if he had the power to legislate, he would certainly stop all the proselytising. In Hindu-households, the advent of a missionary had meant to Gandhiji 'the disruption of the family, coming in the wake of change of dress, manners, language, food and drink'.

There is something unhealthy in the whole Missionary idea. To go to a people like the Hindus, a race of high culture and a long tradition of philosophical, ethical, and religious systems ante-dating Christianity and to go avowedly to save its people from damnation is certainly something grotesque! Humanitarian and philanthropic works are only excuses to enable themeselves to go near their victims and strike at the simple and trusting hearts. What Gandhiji wanted to stop viz. Conversion, has been held by the Christian Missionaries as their basic right.

Conversion is not only sanctioned and glorified by their

theologies but is also practised by their followers with earnestness. The Christians, like others, have got a right to have their own belief systems. But what right do they have to thrust them upon others? Quite a few missionaries not only justified but also recommended this crime of conversion as a basic "human right". A human right cannot be an exclusive right of a Christian but can reasonably be claimed by the Mussalman or for that matter by a Hindu also. It is not and cannot be one way traffic. It takes the form of a game of numbers. Can this promote national harmony?

What ails the North East

The creation of 'Nagaland' is a glaring example in point. That open rebellion launched in the Naga Hills was all engineered by the Christian missionaries, was accepted even by Pandit Nehru. The Nagas used foreign arms against Indian army and even our planes were shot down. The rebel leader of this gangsterism fled the country and he was given asylum by a noted Christian Missionary - Michael Scott who abetted him in making various statements damaging our reputation. They started 'peace talks' and the 'peace mission' included this gentleman called Michael Scott. The dream was to convert Nagaland into an independent state ridden and dominated by the Christian. Today when a Christian Naga comes to Shillong he says 'I am going to India' as if he is a non-Indian and Nagaland is not India. The troubles during the agitation for a separate Jharkhand, desecration of Hindu temples in Kerala including the Shabarimalai, the trouble engineered at the Vivekananda Rock memorial at Kanyakumari, the troubles of Nilakkal in Kerala, the pitched battles which the rebel Mizo fought with the Indian Army and the terrorist gangs roaming in the North-east killing and demanding ransom, are all gifts of the Christian Church.

The Church was quick to recognize that separate state could be carved out by means of number. The high sounding principle of self-determination incorporated in our polity was exploited with deadliest effect. It only whetted the appetite of the head-hunters. Shri Guruji did not mince words when he said:

> *"Such is the role of the Christian gentlemen residing in our land today, out to demolish not only the religious and social fabric of our life but also to establish political domination in various pockets and if possible all over the land. Such has been, in fact their role wherever they have stepped, - all under the alluring garb of bringing peace and brotherhood to mankind under the angelic wings of Jesus Christ".*[12]

Shri Guruji considered the missionaries' overtures to teach religion to our people is like forcibly feeding the one who is already overfed.

It is this aspect of Christianity that has today come into conflict with Nationalism and has created a strong suspicion in the minds of the national societies. That explains why conversion of a man to Christianity is not just a change in the form of worship but also a change in the priority of loyalties. That again explains why Christians are looked upon by many as a potential fifth column. Dr. J.C. Kumarappa himself a Christian and a veteran Gandhian economist has hit the nail on the head when he said: 'The western nations have four Arms - the infantry, the navy, the airforce and the Church' Guruji did not hesitate to describe conversion as nothing short of aggression on Hindu society.

Return of the Converts

Meanwhile it needs to be stressed that the question of return of those Hindus converted to Christianity back into the Hindu fold falls into an entirely different category. For long Hindus had developed a suicidal habit of declaring these converts as "outcastes" and the Hindu house had only 'exits' and no 'entrance'. They did not take back converts willing to return to the ancestral faith. But of late, Hindus have become alive to the dangers inherent in this one way traffic and have dccided to throw open the gates of

Hinduism to the lost tribes. If Christianity claims conversion as its basic right, it must give the same right to the Hindus so that they could claim their lost brethren back. It is a homecoming not only to their original faith but also to the whole gamut of their social and cultural milieu. Dr. Rajendra Prasad wrote in his book 'India Divided' that 'If Hindus' on their side also start converting non-Hindus to their faith, it is no business of the non-Hindus, specially if they are themselves engaged in the work of conversion, to object.'

Conversion one way traffic

It is a question most puzzling how is it that this process of conversion has always been a one way traffic all along? And this process has gone on unabated for hundreds of years? And again it has not stopped even after the country became independent? The toll it has taken is terrible.

An epic struggle had been launched by our people to free the country from *British* bondage. But besides freeing the country from the political serfdom, the leaders of our country did not think of freeing our brothers and sisters who had been kept under the religious subjugation of the Church. Though there were certain attempts in that direction, they were meagre and scattered. Unfortunately this trend did not develop into a vibrant national movement of freeing our kith and kin from the shackles of religious slavery. During the course of his conversation with the Maulvis of Coimbatore and in response to the complaint that the Hindus themselves are taking to converting *Muslims and Christians* nowadays, Guruji remarked.

> *"It is not conversion into Hinduism. It is only giving all opportunity for those who had been made to change the faith by force of circumstances in the past to return to their ancestral faith. Is it not a fact that only a handful Muslims and Christians came to our country from outside? All the rest have only changed their faith for well known reasons. Returning to one's ancestral faith*

is not conversion at all. It is merely home-coming".[13]

At a time when the movement for Home-coming had not yet acquired any momentum Mahatma Gandhi camc out with greatcr emphasis in its favour. "In my opinion", said Gandhji, "they are not examples of real conversion. If a person through fear, compulsion, starvation, or for material gain or consideration goes over to another faith, it is a misnomer to call it conversion. Most cases of mass conversion of which we have heard so much during the past two years have been to my mind false coin. I would therefore unhesitatingly readmit to the Hindu fold all such repentant without much ado." Asked whether he favoured receiving the converts back Swami Vivekananda said "Certainly they can and ought to be taken."[14]

One wonders why Christian proselytisation should lead to an excess of love with western countries. The converts were given not only a psychological affinity with the western countries but were weaned away from national society. The language, the script, the dress, other modes of life, the fasts and the festivals, the names and nomenclature all undergo a change. The demands of the Goan Cathloics to adopt Roman script for Konkani in place of Devnagri is the reflection of this attitude.

Conversion - Unconstitutional, illegal

The Church claims that the constitution has conferred on them a right to propagate which is as goud as a right to convert. Neither the Hindu Society nor the law of the land accepts that the right to propagate means right to convert. The Suprcme Court is unequivocal on this behalf. It is strange that the Christian Missionaries are even to this day carrying on a relentless battle to secure the legal right to convert unrestricted". When Madhya Pradesh and Orissa Governments enacted "Freedom of Religion Act", in 1968 seeking to control certain objectionable practices of conversion, the missionaries challenged them in courts of law. When they lost in the High Courts, they appealed to the Supreme Court. The Supreme Court upheld both the Acts as constitutional and turned down the argument of the missionaries that the 'right to propagate one's religion' enshrined in the constitution implied the right to convert. In recent years there have been many attempts to prevent conversions through legislation. A number of states have passed anti-conversion bills. A private member introduced the bill in Parliament to oppose conversion. The first "Freedom of Religion Act was introduced in 1967". The Supreme Court Ruling 1977 said that 'there is no fundamental right to convert any person to one's own religion'. The second and third Freedom of Religion Act 1968 and 1978 and a few other similar Bills were introduced in the legislature. Why such a spate of bills to prevent conversions? It is eloquent in itself. It is crystal clear that the right to convert is illegal and unconstitutinal.

Church and Secularism

Moreover it should be noted that the act of conversion to Christianity violates a basic feature of our Constitution i.e. of secularism. For Secularism has been times without number defined as Sarva Dharma Sama Bhava (attitude of equality towards all faiths). The Christian Church has never made secret of their conviction that theirs is the only true religion and as such superior to others. Conversion is the corollary of this conviction. Can there be any doubt that this kind of religious conversion militates against the basic tenet of secularism enshrined in our Constitution?

The Christian Church will not hesitate to approve that secularist ideal. The gullible Hindu dances in delight at the response evoked by his theories of secularism. A Christian missionary talks in the loudest language about secularism because it helps his conversion and denationalisation activities. But can he hoodwink all? Is he ready to accord equal respect to other religions and display his belief in Sarva Dharma

Sama Bhav? He throws his hands up, and says, *"my religious faith does not permit it"*.

According to the Church all others are "heathens" to be "saved" from "damnation" by making them believe in that "One word of that one God". All the good and great among the holy Christians, otherwise admirable, are, when it comes to the question of Church, all closed minds.

Church and Foreign Funding

It should be noted that the uninterrupted inflow of huge foreign funds to various Church agencies is confirmed by the Union Home Ministry. It is at the root of all conversion activities based on inducement. It becomcs the patriotic duty of everyone who has the integrity of our nation at heart to plug all such surreptitious channels of funding. The annual Home Ministry Report indicates that over 80% of the voluntary organisations receiving foreign aid are infact Christian organisutions engaged in Christian religious work either directly through propogation or indirectly through social service.

The top five purposes for which huge funds are pumped into India, as per Home Ministry Report are: Health Care, Family Care, Care of orphans, Help to poor, construction and extension of schools and colleges. It is interesting to note that the funds are utilised where majority population is Hindu and a large chunk has been going to the southern states.

Foreign Missionaries

India is infested with a large number of these uninvited guests, the Michael Scots and the Father Ferars. One need hardly emphasise public attitude towards them. They have come to India to 'save' the 'heathens' from 'damnation.' We are to believe that they have come on a mission of mercy.

Let a missionary try to convert a single Muslim in any Islamic country, he is sure to be lynched and murdered immediately by the Muslim mobs even before the state apparatus could confiscate visas and issue orders of expulsion.

Could he recruit a convert in any Communist counrty without being caught as an 'imperialist agent' and sent to a labour camp? Are not certain missionaries languishing in prisons in certain Southeast Asian countries on the charge of 'subversion'? Even Buddhist Burma has barred their entry. One does not want India to be marred with ugly events. Every child knows what reception awaits Christian Missionaries in Bangladesh. Remember how Pakistan dealt with Christians during recent past and how its blasphemy laws operate. It is time they should not take India for granted and should return home. Christian church in India requires to be deinternationalised.' In fact Guruji was glad that there was move to make the Indian Churches autonomous and independent of Rome.

The Harijan and the Girijan

The tribals and the Dalits (the so called Untouchables) were looked upon by the church as 'green pastures' for conversion. Theories were propounded and arguments discovered to show how the above two are alien to the Hindu fraternity. They deliberately used the expression Adivasi for the tribals which meant that they are the orginal inhabitants of India before the entry of Aryans into India. The Church was bent upon establishing the tribals as a separate racial entity. Because of the geographical isolation enjoyed by the tribals, they were able to preserve their socio-religious identity, faith and practices without being assimilated. So ran the missionary argument.

Shri Guruji rang the alarm bell. While with friends in Punjab, he warned:

> *"We have to take special care of tribals and those who live in the hilly areas. If we persist in our attitude of indifference towords them then foreign Christian missionaries will succeed in converting them to Christianity and making them enemies of our motherland."*[15]

The Church is extremely intolerant of the Hindus working among the tribal population whom they consider their natural exclusive 'Prey'. If it is entirely a matter of serving the neglected sections, the Hindu response should not have caused irritation to them. It is the fear of a merachant losing a monopoly market.

Shri Guruji rejected all the missionary theories that sought to render tribal people alien to the Hindu society and positively maintained that they were an integral part of the Hindu social structure. "Vanavasi" he called them as distinct from the 'Nagarvasi'. Some called them Girijan. He pointed out how stubbornly the Vanavasis were clinging themselves to their traditions and customs and further reminded that these were the people. i,e, the forest dwellers who lent a helping hand to the patriotic endeavours of Rana Pratap and Chhatrapati Shivaji. Vanavasi Kalyan Ashram (Tribal Welfare Movement) was the instrument he forged to bring the tribal back to the main stream and uplift them.

It was maintained by the Church that the Dalits were embracing Christianity to get rid of the stigma of untouchability and acquire the status of equality. Pushed to the wall the Dalits are asserting a sense of dignity and self-respect by conversions, the Missionary boasted. The Dalits had been touched by the loving service of the missionaries who treated them as equals, he claimed.

Shri Guruji dealt with the problem of untouchability in his own style which was unique as well as effective. There was a Hindu awakening concerning the plight of the Dalits due to the herculean efforts he displayed. Mammoth gathering of Hindu representatives and religious heads assembled at Prayag in 1969 and elsewhere subsequently made the historic declaration that untouchabiltiy is no part of Hindu Dharma and pronounced a new Mantra *'Na Hindu Patito Bhavet'* - a Hindu is never polluted signifying the birth of a new Smriti.

The Church is found arguing and agitating to stress that

the benefits available to Hindu Harijans be extended to the Christian Harijans also. Christianity was offered as a wayout to the Hindu Harijans but once they are Christianised, the old basis with its old stigma is reborrowed. It is a confession that the Hindu Harijans converted to Christianity are not benefitted, their economic condition not improved, social segregation not stopped and in brief, the change of religion is not a change for better. The Christian church cannot give equality they promise at the time of enticement.

A movement for reclamation and Hindu Consolidation which included Dalits and the tribals is underway. The wave is catching up. With the Hindu tolerance and secularism are inborn. He considers it as un-Hindu to discriminate two persons just on the basis of religious faith. It is simple commonsense that no minority can be safe by constantly irritating its neighbouring majority. Wisdom lies in the Christian Church cultivating the goodwill of the Hindu. That is the greatest guarantor of the long range interests of the Christians themselves. Remember what H.C. Mookherjee. one of the prominent leaders of the Indian Christian Community said,

> *"We have to demonstrate by every word we utter and by every act we perform that the professing of a different religious faith has not trended in the very least to make us less Indian in our own outlook than our non-Christian brethren that we are prepared to play our part and to shoulder our share of the responsibility in every kind of work undertaken for the benefit of our country as a whole."*

Shri Guruji wanted India to be a land of many religious faiths, as in the past, all equally honoured and respected. but with one national outlook.

(The writer is retired professor and Head of History Department, Pune University and a senior RSS activist and ideologue.)

References

1) **The Harijan** 07.02.193 1

2) **Spotlights** (A collection of Shri Guruji's views oŋ a wide variety of topies) Bangalore 1974, pp 51.52.

3) **Mission and Conversion**. Ed. Joseph and Mattam, pp. 07.

4) **Bunch of Thoughts**, pp 186

5) **Ibid**. pp 179.

6) **Spotlights**, pp 56,

7) **Neogy Commission Report**, Part 21, pp 14-15

8) **Guruji Samagra** Vol. 4, pp 195 (from original Hindi). A series of 12 Vol. Covering complete works of Guruji. Surichi Prakashan, New Delhi-55 Pub. 2005.

9) **Ibid.**

10) **Bunch of Thoughts**, pp 185-186.

11) **Ibid**, pp 186

12) **Ibid**, pp l85

13) **Spotlights**, pp 118-119

14) Arun Shourie, **Missionaries in India** pp 44

15) **Spotlights**, pp 147 -

10

Shri Gurujee And Communism

Dr. Satish Mittal

(English rendering by Shri R. S. Goyal)

SHRI Madhavrao Sadashivrao Golwalkar belongs to the genre of ancient saints and intellectuals. He would certainly have been conferred upon one of the highest decorations of the Greatest spiritual leaders of the twentieth century, had there been provision for such a title. He was offered the pivotal position of Shankaracharya which he thankfully declined owing to his preoccupation with RSS. Swami Amitabh, the head of Ramakrishna Mission, addressed him in 1949 as 'Prince among patriots' of Rashtriya Swayamsevak Sangh. He was among the most affable and inspirational dignitaries of 20th Century. He was, in essence, a spiritual inspired soul who made unique contribution in the field of country's socio-cultural upliftment and national resurgence.

Shri Gurujee had undertaken an extensive study of many philosophical treatises while he was in Kashi. Later on he came in direct contact of Rashtriya Swayamsevak Sangh and left an indelible imprint on Dr Keshavrao Baliram Hedgewar, the founder of R.S.S.

It was, therefore, a befitting honour for him when he was handed over the reins of RSS by Dr Hedgewar prior to his death. Guruji adorned the prestigious position of the head of Rashtriya Swayamsevak Sangh on June 20th, 1940 and remained at its helm till his death in 1973 circa.

Shri Guruji's vision of life

Shri Guruji's view is that our chief problem lies in lack of clear-cut vision. According to him human society is manifestation of God where each individual is important. No one is high or low. He should make sacred offering of worldly assets in the service of God. Guruji lays stress on the need of being frugal in consumption and keeping the wants within limits and control.

India vis-a-vis different societies

The main aim of each and every social group has been the ultimate welfare of the humanity. Gurujee ascribes the nomenclature of Materialism (जड़वाद), Religionism (सम्प्रदायवाद) and Spiritualism (आत्मवाद) to these tendencies. Materialism bases the formation of human society on the basis of economic progress. Seeking and searching for physical pleasures is the chief concern of man. It gives rise to economic and political systems which in turn lead to mental discontentment and culminates in feudal skirmishes. Man does not find material comforts fully satiysfying and after sometime realises that life has become wretched and miserable.

Thus, in desperation, he forms a separate group on the basis of his religious beliefs and adopts different means of worship. In the third stage of exalted spiritualism, the man searches altogether new avenues capable of providing him with a perennial source of happiness.

Shri Guruji is of the firm belief that all aspects of life have been dealt with thoroughly by the Indian philosophers. There has been an elaborate consideration in India on subjects ranging from mundane materialistic thoughts to ultimate Universal Truth. The role of individual, social and universal aspects in its total hues in life cycle has been deliberated upon. The Hindu view and approach has taken into full consideration and ensured that the individual, besides availing himself of worldly comforts, also enjoys spiritual freedom. In a nutshell, right equilibrium has been created among individual, national and universal interests. This exalted position has been found to be a sound solution to conflicting claims as also a means of attaining eternal bliss.

Social perspective

Shri Guruji states that social philosophy has been studied intensively in India. He avers that Indian society achieved greater heights of evolution through unity in multiple diversity. He emphasised that equilibrium should be maintained without overlooking the individual talent. On this count he boldly declares that our society stands for co-operation among nations and not for their disintegration. All members of the community cannot be elevated to the optimum level and we cannot afford to set up a single universal model by doing away with individual traits. On the contrary, it is our avowed aim to create an integrated society which allows full play of individual talents and aspirations in conformity with human good and goal.

He wanted political power and economic power to be maintained as separate entities. He maintained that amalgamation of the two entities could be crucially harmful. He stated that there should not be concentration of these two powers in one single individual or group of individuals. It will harm peace and harmony in the society. He wanted that these two should be under proper and adequate control. He was a great votary of decentralised political system. Political authority and economic power must be guided by Dharma (not bigotry). People should realise that society alone is the true expression of the Creator of all of us.

Shri Guruji had unflinching faith in basic unity of our country. It is in the interest of individual to infer that his wisdom, prowess and wealth should be in conformity with the supreme social well-being. So the economic disparities as also its exploitation for selfish political gains and its undue importance help only in keeping the people in turmoil and is thus detrimental to the progress of the country. He believed that equitable distribution of country's wealth and keeping strict vigil on dubious business practices would prove beneficial in creating cordial atmosphere in the society.

Shri Guruji was a votary of decentralisation of government agencies. He favoured representative form of government right from local to the central level under one unitary form of government. He considered rural areas as fulcrum of the centre and advocated setting up of mandal, janapad and provincial units under a strong centre. He was a protagonist of Panchayat Raj system and approved of decentralised system of governance.

Guruji has also expressed views on contemporary world affairs time and again. He was against the principle of maximum good of the maximum number of people as propounded by Utilitarians. Instead, he pleaded for the spirit of Sabka Sukh (universal good) as supreme need of the hour. He was averse to 'national consciousness' being overshadowed by cosmopolitanism. He feels League of Nations, United Nations and other World forums should function as co-ordinating agencies between National aspirations and International exigencies. Solution to international conflicts lay in spiritualism and not in materialism. Emphasis on basic human unity alone can save the situation.

National Perspective

The Cardinal thought running through most of his speeches has been national consciousness. He has time and again referred to the disintegration of Hindu society. He has tried to trace the causes of its pitiable and dilapidated state and concluded that the chief factors responsible for it are—absence of unity, rise of provincialism, absence of national pride and blind aping of western thoughts. This gave an impetus to provincialism, casteism and separatist tendencies. He attributes stagnation and inactivity as the major factors responsible for India remaining under foreign domination for such a long time. This changed our attitude towards national life. He holds lack of strong feeling of nationalism and loss of identity as the major causes. So he stresses on the need of strengthening solidarity and unity in the society and country.

Nonetheless, he considers Indian history not as of disgraceful surrender but of continuous heoric struggle. A small territory of India could have been under Muslim rule or might have been under British domination, but Indians have always been fighting for their freedom. He feels that defeatism crept into our national life due to social dissensions, lack of unity and mutual hostility that existed at several levels.

The crux of his speeches was national awakening in Hindu society. He emphasised the need for imparting wholesome traits pertaining to day to day affairs. He prepared Rashtriya Swayamsevak Sangh to play a pivotal role in fostering these traits and inculcating inner strength in society.

Shri Guruji insisted upon strengthening national character. He declared that India could regain national glory and its due place in the committee of nations when our society would forge strong bonds of heritage, culture, community, integrity and national out-look. All these factors are dependent upon the evolution of national character and consciousness. Side by side he gives full consideration to personal character also since both are of paramount importance for enhancing national prestige. Gurujee considers character and culture as the twin wheels of nation's march towards pinnacle of glory.

Shri Guruji and Marxism

Shri Guruji undertook an extensive study of Western philosophy and thought besides Indian philosophy, culture, religion and literature. He studied very minutely Marx, Marxism and its practical aspects. He severely criticised Marxism with all its facets in his speeches, writings and news conferences while he was on tours. He has presented its critique and comparative study vis-a-vis Indian history, culture and literature. In plain language it amounts to his rejection of Marxism, especially its materialistic feature and emphasis on economic history, class struggle, violent revolt and the so-called rise of the proletariat. He criticised Russia and China vehemently and warned that Marxism would prove to be very dangerous for India and exposed the dangers accompanying these ideologies.

Socialism - Product of Reaction

Shri Guruji held the belief that Western socio-political upheavals erupted as a result of reaction. They captured power and encouraged feudalism. The feudal lords amassed wealth by making use of scientific discoveries. It brought about Industrial Revolution. French revolution trumpeted vague slogans of liberty, fraternity and equality. It was the direct result of reaction against Feudalism. Similarly Socialism was born as a result of reaction against government's misuse of power and pelf.

Decline, not Development

Shri Guruju stated that Communism and Feudalism proved to be the cause of nations' downfall. While addressing a meeting in Jodhpur about man's progress from humble beginning to great heights he said: "In my view Communism does not spell boom, but doom. Man is being pushed backwards. A casual perusal of human progress makes this observation crystal clear. In the initial stage man is concerned about his physical needs only. Afterwards he evolves. On mental level, man finds himself torn between many pursuits. He sharpens his mental faculties and crossing the physical and mental barriers, attains solace in spiritualism. There is a very beautiful account of such phenomena in our Upnishads.

Shri Guruji forcefully criticised material progress made by Communism and the resultant prosperity. He has aptly termed it as 'the great fall'. He stated that it has given rise to a system where selfish tendencies prevail. It is an utter downfall. It is human abyss. Man pursues a life style which does not behove mankind and is only found in the kingdom of wretched creatures.

Shri Gurujee doubted the intentions of those who eulogised Communism and its philosophy and acclaimed it as a sign of advancement. He pointed out that there was the least sign of amity in Marxists system. Karl Marx, the founder of Marxism had once stated that his doctrine of Communism did not prohibit religion and God but his followers discardid both. The very term 'Progressive Communism' is fallacious. Guruji's assertion is that Marxism is wholly based on materialistic foundations. Their main source of inspiration is physical charms. Their main doctrine is Materialism.

Illusive Materialism

Shri Guruji called Marxism an unadulterated Materialism, purely a hoax and Russia its foster mother. He brushed aside a man's query in Trivandrum whether he believed in Dialectical Materialism. His prompt reply was that the doctrine had already been thrown to the winds. Albeit Karl Marx never professed that he was a crude materialist in 'The Philosophical and Economic Manuscript' as far back as in 1844. Guruji stated that when the war was on, the churches in Soviet Russia had to be revived and renovated to inspire people to fight to defend their 'fatherland'.

State and Anarchy in Society

Shri Guruji does not subscribe to Karl Marx's thinking that state is the instrument of exploitation nor Prince Kroptkin's views on anarchism, nor does he find Marx's concept of "Whithering away of State" practical and his idea of a social set up devoid of state control as viable and practical. Both of these are Utopian and fanciful dream. He simply asked how could human society remain free and independent without checks and balances exercised by the state. How could the people be safe under jungle Raj.

What should then be the way out? Marx's views as expressed in the context of Kroptin were discarded by Guruji. He did not endorse the dictatorship of the Proletariat either, even in the transitional period. He could not digest that human beings would be well off in the absence of state control. There is absolutely no refernece to this aspect in Communism. Guruji believed that Communist doctrine will collapse like whithering leaves losing contact with the tree. Of course, Indian philosophers too visualised the stateless society. But Gurujee reminded that Indian philosophers could fancy a state where Dharma and not government might be the order of the day. He quoted a verse from Shanti Parva of *Srimad Bhagawat.*

न राज्यं न च राजासीन्न दंडो न च दांडिकाः ।
धार्मणैव प्रजाः सर्वाः रक्षन्तिस्म परस्परम् ।।

i.e. There will be no state, no king, no seat of government, no room for punishment and it could only be possible when the society is guided by Dharma. Such a society, consisting of well contented and mutually self disciplined souls will need no extraneous controls.

Dharma - A true perspective

Shri Guruji does not approve of Marx's views on Dharma and conceptualises it in broadest dimensions. To him Dharma connotes a system which allows an individual to blossom here in this world. This keeps society well-knit in a single thread of plenty and boundless prosperity. Gurujee maintains that there should be substnatial check of Dharma on governance. To him Dharma is the basis of life. Man should subscribe to Dharma regulated state and Dharma controlled consumption. Non-compliance, on the contrary, turns a man into devil and such a person bereft of innate virtues will prove to be a cause of catastrophe to himself and the whole society.

The Hindu scriptures, make a mention of four-fold features leading to human salvation. Founding a society on the pillars of Dharma guided existence. Dharma governed consumption and worldly enjoyments and detatched existence help attain salvation or eternal bliss.

Class-struggle

The main stay of Marxist Communism is class-struggle. They see in it success of Communism and death knell of

Capitalism. But Gurujee does not approve of mutual hatred as a means of achieving success. Communism often breeds bitterness between different sections of society, causes ill-will and prompts the people to take up cudgels for class struggle. Marx has analysed history on the basis of this bitterness and hatred. One of their leaders boasted that the success of their ideology lay in the inherent animosity - "Intense hatred is the basis of our success". Prompt came the reply from Gurujee, "Intense love is the basis of our success." To him landmarks of national resurgence are brotherhood, co-operation, co-ordination and positive contribution instead of class-struggle. Gurujee feels that the concept of class struggle is a ploy to divide our society. According to Gurujee the concept of 'Haves' and 'Haves not', is neither a permanent feature nor is it congenial for the creation of classless society.

Dictatorship of the Proletariat

Karl Marx dreamt of the rise of the dictatorship of Proletariat in the transitional period for the establishment of statelss society. This dictatorship was in vogue in Russia and continues in China with no hold bars. 1917 saw a bloody revolution in Russia and facilitated the so-called one party government which in fact was an unbridled crude regime of a single individual—Lenin and then Stalin. Khruschev talked of collective leadership which people hoped could usher in democratic rule. But Gurujee reminds that Khruschev was left high and dry as everybody for sook him. People soon realised that he was a cut above Stalin and for that a cleverer one. Mao, of China, also professed "Let hundred flowers bloom" but ninetynine of them were literally crushed under the boots and Mao alone blossomed. The Communists brook no dissent from within. How could they co-exist with others?

Shri Guruji recalled that many unethical and cruel methods were employed to capture and sustain power in Russia and China. The long history of these countries bear testimony to this fact. They unhesitatingly massacred their own countrymen for capturing power. Still these countries brag and make tall claims that they are progressive. Both these countries have attempted to bring other countries under their thumb. Gurujee compares them to demons as depicted in the sixteenth chapter of Srimad Bhagawat Gita.

Shri Guruji adminsters stern warning to Indian masses that, in the light of this bloody history of Marxism, they should not fall a prey to devilish tendencies and be lured by slogans being blared loudly in the name of Socialism and Communism.

Violent Revolution

Shri Gurujee is an avowed critic of the theory of violent revolution of Communism. According to him the very call of revolution is nothing but senselessness. Elsewhere Gurujee has stated that Communists raise much hue and cry shouting slogans like Inquilab Zindabad. We should ask ourselves - what do we need - perpetual Revolution or Peace? Blowing trumpets for continuous revolution sends signals for lawlessness and armed disorder. 'Inquilab Zindabad' as such is not a propitious proposition.

Ugly face of Communism

Shri Gurujee's view is that the long history of Communism is nothing but a series of revolts, expansion and use of force. Special trait of Communism is expansionism. Communist China showed least remorse on brutal massacre of 96 lakh of its citizens - not caricatures, but men of flesh and blood - in the name of Communism. Gurujee had forewarned in public address way back in 1956 regarding Chinese incursons into Indian territory. He foresaw China's evil designs on Tibet, Burma, Indonesia and Nepal. He also mocked at the principles of 'Panchsheel' as mere ploy. He concurred with Kriplani's remark that Panchsheel was born out of the sin of rape of Tibet. Khrushchev and Vorshilov, the two leading leaders of Russia did not condemn it and did not call China an invader. Not to speak of Chinese aggression, they did not even have the courage to point out that China had tresspassed.

Shri Gurujee accused Indian Government of inaction and weakness on Chinese illegal occupation of Tibet and criticised Pt. Nehru who called the territory grabbed by China as belonging to the Chinese. Even Britishers did not accept the Chinese claim and kept their forces posted there. He ridiculed Indian response, especialy Nehru's comment that not a blade of grass grows there.

Chinese attack on India in 1962 compelled Gurujee to make a scathing statement that China had stabbed us in the back and it was nothing short of aggression and that India had failed miserably in assessing China and it's evil designs. He called China's unconditional ceasefire as a deceitful strategy. He made clear China's underhand tactics as a well thought out and contrived ploys. The Communists not only attack their neighbours, grab their territory, but also employ unethical methods of forcing people to embrace Communism, incite them to revolt against their own country and declare them 'liberated' by invading them in the guise of the so-called 'liberating Army'. Thus, they capture territories and strengthen Communism. Communists adopted this very policy in China and nationalist Chiang-Kei-Shek had to fled his own homeland.

Communism in India

Rashtriya Swayamsevak Sangh had always entertained serious doubts about the efficacy of Marxist doctrine in Indian context. RSS and Communism share 1925 as the year of their genesis. The former has roots in India while the latter had its roots abroad. Dr Hedgewar's era did not have much to say about Communism because the movement remained disguised most of the time. By 1930 they intruded in the Congress and made firm inroads. Dr Hedgewar was well aware of variance in the principles and practices of Communists. To cite an example, once Shri Ram Bhau Ruikar, a noted labour leader of Nagpur approached Dr Hedgewar to invite him to hear an eminent communist leader of England. The entry to the lecture was by ticket worth Rs. 5/-. It was quite a big amount those days. Dr. Hedgewar told him and jokingly: "I am not rich enough to spare five rupees for this lecture. After all I am a poor capitalist whereas you are a rich Socialist".

Shri Gurujee was well conversant with Communists' congenital opposition to Rashtriya Swayamsevak Sangh. He was also aware of their dubious role in freedom movement of India. Gurujee knew that communists were at the back of ban imposed on RSS and atrocities inflicted on Swayamsevaks in the aftermath of Gandhiji's assasination. Calcutta's leading newspaper, Swadheenta, known for its Communist leanings, played a dirty role. Bombay's Blitz weekly too indulged in RSS bashing. Communists in Assam threatened to kill seven swayamsevaks who they thought had a role in Gandhi's assassination. On 24th September Gurujee, through a letter, informed Pt Nehru and Sardar Patel about it reiterating that RSS alone could check the menace of Communism in the country.

Shri Gurujee termed Communists of different hues as fifth columnists. They favoured splitting India into small fragments. They were inducing our people to pass on secrets to our enemies so that they could fulfil their object of domination. Specific role was being assigned to people to carry out their intents. Some power hungry Communists were adopting sugar coated means to coverup their insidious activities. They keep their secrets close to their chest and carry out their tactics. Every citizen who loves his country will easily see through their sinister designs.

Shri Gurujee was skeptical about Communists role at the time of Chinese aggression on India in 1962. They showed preference for Mao to Manu. Their game plan was simple yet intriguing. They surreptitiously gained entry into Congress, in administration and Defence establishments. It proved to be harmful and could be more shocking in future. Their well thought out plan was to capture power in India by ousting Congress in one go and shattering the establishment from within and sending fear signals throughout the country.

Not Communism but Hindu Nationalism

Shri Gurujee warned not to be swayed by sweet slogans of democratic socialism. He reminded that Socialism is not a product of this soil. It is not in our blood and tradition. Its thought is alien to our people. It was deterimental to building character and fostering love and affection in our lives. Gurujee declared that Communism could at best be called an incomplete and faulty economic philosophy.

Shri Gurujee knew that Russia was a total failure in economic field. Russia could not provide two square meals to its own people though she confiscated personal proeprty, put all industries under state control and forced co-operative farming. Farm produce fell short. Russia was importing food grains from Canada, USA and other countries.

The term democratic socialism is a mere publicity stunt since both are totally contradictory concepts. Where there is individual freedom, Communism cannot flourish.

Shri Gurujee discards Socialism in absolute terms and prefers nationalism instead. To him socialism gets a good hold where democratic principles are thrown overboard and Nationalism and spirit of renunciation are discounted. Russia too realised this, though very late. Russian revolution showed signs of progress in the initial stages, some gains were also made but they were at the expense of national initiatives. The mass liquidation, slave camps, communes, forced labour, brain washing and dictatorship reduced the individuals to an existence of penury and slavery. Heavy industries were converted into army camps. People's morale could be boosted only by arousing national consciousness during the Second World War. They were reminded of their past national heroes - Catherine the Great and Peter the Great. Gurujee strived for nationalism. national character, moral discipline, diligent discharge of social obligations and spirit of sacrifice to help build an invincible nation. Inculcation of national commitment in totality gains inspiration from the glorious past and prepares us for future action.

Shri Gurujee calls Nationalism as a very fine trait of Hindu society and calls it an age old commitment. It has deep roots in our various customs and traditions. Joys and sorrows, ideas and ideals usages are intermingled with love and affection. Gurujee firmly believed that India has only one Dharma (distinct from way of worship) and one culture, bubbling with national aspirations. According to him the ideal model for Indian society can only be Hindu Rashtra and not Communism.

Shri Gurujee's ideology regarding Hindu Rashtra is neither sectarian nor contradictory. He believes in the age old Hindu-Vedic heritage as true precursor to India's mainstream. Any one who bears allegiance towards India and accepts her value-system is a true son of the soil.

Dr R.C. Majumdar, an eminent Historian of world fame, said in Calcutta in 1960 that Dr Hedgewar had intended inculcation of spirit of nationalism as the mainstay of his organisation. He had fearlessly suggested that Hindu alone could be called true national. A large number of people feel ashamed to own and admit this fact, though they hold it genuinely right from the core of their heart. These persons should feel elated and proud to embrace the truth that wherever people talk about India's glrious past and great ancient culture, they are in fact eulogising Hindu history, Hindu civilisation and Hindu culture. And this is the truth, nothing but the truth.

(The author, Dr. Satish Mittal, is Retired Professor and Head of The History Department, Kurukshetra University. Dr. Mittal is an authoritiy on Modern Indian History and has over two dozen books to his credit. He is a frequent contributor to national and international journals on related topics.

The Translator, Shri R.S.Goyal, is retired Lecturer and academician)

References:

1. Shree Gurujee : Vyakti Aur Karya (N.H. Palkar, Nagpur)
2. Shree Gurujee Vichar Darshan-I (Nagpur)
3. Shree Gurujee Samagra Darshan-7 (Nagpur)
4. Shree Gurujee Samagra Darshan-5 (Nagpur)
5. Rashtrabhakti Le Hridaya Mein (Gurujee's public speech, December 27, 1970, Patna)
6. Shree Gurujee Samagra Darshan-2 (Nagpur)
7. Swatantrata Ke Pashchat Samaj Sangathan Ki Kyon Avashyakta Hai (Jahnvi, August-September, 1973, New Delhi)
8. Shree Gurujee Samagra Darshan-4 (Nagpur)
9. Panchjanya (Deepavali Special, November 15, 1983, New Delhi)
10. Maharashtra Mein Patrakaro Ke Saath Vartalap (February 2, 1960)
11. Smritikan (Jabalpur)
12. Dr. Hedgewar Charitra

11

Undercurrents In Sangh Journey

Prof. Devendra Swaroop

WHEN on Vijaya Dashmi (Dussehra), 1925, Dr. Keshav Rao Baliram Hedgewar started a new volunteer organisation with about half a dozen young men, no one could imagine that this organisation without any formal name, constitution, or literature would continue beyond 20th century and grow into mighty organisation destined to undertake various activities, and hundreds of its units will develop into the most effective public service institutions in their respective spheres. Few believed that the organisation which no newspaper knew till 1943 would enjoy the reputation of one of the premier organisations in all spheres of national activities. The latest proof is the 3600 page document of 3 volumes collected by a professor of Delhi University, Parthasarathi Gupta under the Indian Historical Research Project 'Towards Freedom'. He admits that in spite of close scrutiny of hundreds of documents based on leftist ideology, no reference to Sangh could be traced out. Though, by 1940, the seeds of Sangh had been sown all over India, except Assam and Orissa. The Communist movement had been launched five years before the RSS came into existence. Even the, 'omniscient, ubiquitous, omnipotent' British Government was in complete darkness about Sangh upto 1942. The Sangh files maintained in the National Archives at Delhi reveal that it was in 1942, the CP and Berar (modern M.P. and Vidarbha) governments got scared of the activities of

Sangh-becoming popular and collected information about RSS activities from every district. The Central government acted on the basis of this development and opened the first RSS file.

Those days Sangh-activities were limited to its daily 'Shakhas'. In some open fields, shishu-bal-kishore-tarun (Children, adolescents and youths) would gather in front of the Bhagwa-Dhwaj (Saffron flag) pitched before them in the playground. They played indigenous games, laughed and enjoyed, sang in chorus and sometimes quietly discussed some topics of national interest, and concluded with the prayer, loaded with patriotic fervour. Last came the salute and unfurling of the flag before 'disperse'. On one or two annual occasions, they had a route march in full uniform, gave public demonstration of drill and gymnastics accompanied by the Sangh-band. This form continued till 1947. There was no printed literature except a small life sketch of its founder Dr. Hedgewar. No photos, no papers, no party building, no activity except the daily 'shakhas'. They had kept themselves aloof from all agitational movements or publicity;

(O saviours of Hindu Nation! Relinquish the petty ambition of personal publicity in newspapers and felicitation.)

Prasiddhi parangmukhtaa (shunning publicity) was the fundamental tenet of a swayamsevak.

Naturally, people, looking at the Sangh activities from a distance took it as a semi-military organisation based on ekchalakanuvartitva (blind followers of a single fuehrer). But no outsider could comprehend the intense resolve of its activists to spread RSS in every nook and corner of Bharat, working with full vigour day and night. If questioned, there was only one answer - 'Our sole aim is to organise the Hindu society'. What for? "Organisation for the sake of organisation." Once, somebody asked Dr Hedgewar what he would do when his organisation process would be all complete. He wittingly replied that he would assemble them all and ask them to go to sleep. Evidently this was an evasive reply; no body could guess about his entire plan. Even Savarkar, disgusted by this ambivalent attitude of Sangh, once remarked, "When a Swayamsevak would die, an epitaph on his samadhi would reveal that he was born, attended Sangh Shakha and died without doing anything whatsoever for the country."

This was the image Sangh had built for itself upto 1947, when the country was partitioned and Bharat attained Freedom. The critics of Sangh got an opportunity to blame that it had done nothing to avert this catastrophe, yet all were impressed by the valour and exceptional bravery of Sangh workers during the traumatic and painful exodus of Hindus from Pakistan. It is a glorious chapter of intense patriotism, courage and sacrifice. Naturally, Sangh became very popular and its organisation spread to the remotest corner of Bharat. Even Mahatma Gandhi and Sardar Patel admired Swayamsevaks for their idealism, simplicity and freedom from the scourge of casteism. Unfortunately in some circles this caused jealousy and apprehensions about their ambition for political power. In the vitiated atmosphere, the murder of Mahatma Gandhi at the hands of an extremist provided a handy opportunity to the opponents of Sangh, which was banned and thousands of Swayamsevaks, including Shri Gurujee the Sarsanghchalak, were arrested and interned. It was impossible to carry on 'Shakhas' and absolutely no one came forward to plead for their cause and against this uncalled for injustice to Sangh.

But this helplessness proved to be a blessing in disguise. The power of concerted action earned through the network of organisation built so far began to discover new avenues of expression and articulation. To prove its innocence about Gandhiji's murder or complicity in the conspiracy thereof, Sangh built up peoples' fronts like Janadhikar Samiti and Akhil Bharatiya Vidyarthi Parishad. In the sphere of publicity and mass contact the first indigenous news agency 'Hindusthan Samachar' was founded. A greater surprise came with the publication of several weeklies in different Indian languages on Gandhi Jayanti, October 2, 1948 by this organisation of so-called thoughtless people. Underground pamphlets and newsletters came out in large numbers.

An extensive all India Satyagrah in which about 80 thousand Swayamsevaks courted arrest was a historical event of an organisation planning and struggling to seek justice and fair play. In spite of all propaganda or manipulations of witnesses the government failed to prove the complicity of Sangh in any way in the murder of Gandhi Ji. The case in the Red Fort proved to be a baseless allegation and the ban on RSS was lifted on 12 July, 1949.

On the Horns of a Dilemma

If the Shakha-centred organisation upto 1947, can be called the first phase of Sangh, the period of 1947-49 should be regarded the very crucial second phase of metamorphosis into an institution with the support of the masses and will equipped with publicity potentials. After the lifting of the ban, started the Third phase. The question that agitated the Swayamsevaks during partition and its aftermath was never aired publicly to ensure the resettlement of the displaced person and lifting of the unjustified ban imposed on RSS. Sarsanghchalak Shri Guruji M.S. Golwalkar replied to these questions in his five lecture series at Nagpur during October 18-22, 1949, later incorporated at p. 106-142 in the 'Samagra Sahitya'.

As an introduction to the lecture series, Shri Guruji said:

The workers meetings far and wide have brought to light many questions and doubts agitating Swayamsevaks minds. It also showed considerable differences of opinion and assessment of the complicated problems confronting the country.

Some Swayamsevaks even frankly pointed that they were at the end of the blind alley. Some even suggested to put the Sangh system of working on shelf now (p.110). Another

Swayamsevak questioned our wisdom in keeping away from political power, which is the only way to solve big national problems.

Others recommended taking up rural cleanliness, health and hygiene, as mass-service. But what is more important - cleaning village-paths or cleaning hearts? (p.120). Still others wanted to try other methods and modes for the upliftment of the country. This is not new. It was suggested 5-6 years before also (Was he hinting the British plans of transfer of power and the Muslim League's vivid and violent preparations for the enforcement of partition?)

After Nagpur, in two conferences of Pracharaks (wholetime workers) at Jaunpur and Sitapur, the same subject was dealt with by Guruji. This was published as 'Dhyeya Darshan' by Rashtra Dharma Prakashan in Dec. 1949; republished by Suruchi Prakashan in 1997 as Dhyeya Drishti with the introduction by Shri Guruji that the lecture-series was a result of some new suggestions by some illustrious admirers of Sangh. This series was repeated at Anand Parvat, Delhi conference also just before the ban. (Dhyeya Drishti p.6). The book 'Brotherhood in Saffron by Walter Anderson and Shridhar Damle writes, on the basis of interview with Yashwant Rao Kelkar that in 1947, in a conference in Bombay, Guruji had hinted to the grave turmoil and differences of opinions amongst prominent workers (p.56 and note 152p.70). During the ban the dilemma grew deeper. Consequently in the lecture series. Guruji once again repeated the questions raised and his elucidation's thereof:

The basic question is why we have got into a dilemma in spite of our success in building up such a wide and powerful organisation.

There must be some mistake or lacuna. Why have we been treated so roughly by our own countrymen for whose benefit and welfare we have been arduously toiling with Herculean efforts so far? (Dhyeya Drishti p.7)

"Some Swayamsevaks have also thought that there was

something basically wrong in our working. Now there is no foreigner to provoke us to rise against. The British have gone; the Muslims have settled down in their newly acquired homeland. Where is the need for Sangh now? One reaction was that we had suffered at the hands of people in power, so we should also catapult ourselves to political power. Thus politics began to predominate every thought and discussion." (ibidp.8)

"This also leads to the introspection as to how can we make our country prosperous, if we keep aloof from politics. We have been working for 24 years with a vow to make our Hindu nation independent. But the British, while making exit, have rendered millions of refugees hapless and helpless in their own motherland and, which may further be vivisected, if we keep blinking and gazing at the sky like this. The country and our people habitating this sacred land will go down deep into the dustbin of history with only stories of ancient glory. One worker also expressed his apprehension that, devoid of an active programme, our organisation will break down under its own weight."(ibidp.9). The same question was asked about our economic programme or role during elections. (p.10).

There was an expression of great remorse why we had not propagated our views while we were making efforts and sacrifices for so many years. Was there something wrong with our concepts and ideology? Was it not now incumbent upon us to publicise our views widely in the society? (ibid, p.20)

Introspection

In 1960, in a meeting at Indore Shri Guruji dealt with the suggestions of replacing the terms 'Hindu, Hindustan, Hindu society, Hindu nation by Bharat, Bharatiya etc. which may not offend others. (khand 4, p.24/Samagra Sahitya/ Sh.Guruji).

This introspection in Sangh started reflecting itself in the printed media also. During 1949, through Organiser weekly,

Balraj Madhok and editor K.R. Malkani made a powerful case for taking to active politics. The first whole timer and Dr.Hedgewar's lifelong companion Shri Dada Rao Parmarth also lent his support to this view. Bala Sahib Deoras, the general secretary and according to Shri Guruji Dr. Hedgewar's alter-ego who held the post of Sarsanghchalak for 21 years after Guruji, wrote an article under the title. 'The Next Step for Sangh'. He advocated and hinted at the decision of Sangh to let its Swayamsevak's enter into all sorts of public activities. The article aroused wide discussions for and against. Vasant Rao Oke, Delhi Prant Pracharak and the first Sangh pioneer in North India also emerged as a staunch advocate of this view. Guruji had firm conviction that the main role of Sangh was to build a cadre of patriots equipped with sterling qualities of head and heart and an impeccable character. This was possible through the daily Shakha. It would not be fruitful without the organisation attaining sizeable numbers and quality for the Swayamsevaks to start participating in all sorts of activities with the aim of national reconstruction. According to him, freedom from the British had not changed the circumstances much. He elucidated in his lecture-series at Nagpur.

"The attainment of Freedom is circumstantial incident. The protection of independence and security of the national prestige and prosperity is a question of perennial importance. For that the nation should be ever vigilant and ever ready for action. For this we should remove our short-comings, obliterate our deficiencies and build up a powerful disciplined organisation covering all areas and all sections of the population irrespective of caste, creed and gender (S.S. p.117-118).

"I feel it inappropriate to prematurely take to various social service and national reconstruction activities including politics without the organisation achieving the required standard. On one hand public expectations have greatly enhanced, on the other there has been a substantial dilution in idealism, efforts and sacrifices. In such a situation, it is futile to attempt and claim satisfactory achievements in other fields. (ibid, p.125).

The foregoing discussion makes it abundantly clear that even at the time of partition and attainment of freedom, the prominent RSS workers were agitated that they could do nothing to prevent the vivisection of their motherland and the Independence was attained without them. They were eager to play a leading role in the reconstruction of their country and for that they had begun to feel that a change ought to have been made in the methodology of RSS before Independence. A section endorsed the idea of participating in the national reconstruction through head long jump, whereas very senior Maharashtra RSS leaders like Appa Phendse and Madhu Deval preferred to undertake social reconstruction work. That is why Shri Guruji insisted that all other spheres of national or social activities could be successfully taken up only after achieving a requisite standard in the organisation, for which untiring efforts should be made in every part of the country and every section of the society.

But what was the goal? What was the action plan and method of working? These questions perplexed the minds of many devoted workers. In Guruji's own words, "Many feel that the assigned goal or the requisite standard has been entagled in a vicious circle attempting to build up a minimum practical standard before initiating the various projects by embarking upon the particular fields or attaining standard through incessant improvements in the execution of responsibilities accepted (ibid p.121). The allied question can also be about the time needed to reach the requisite standard and whether it is possible to sit with eyes closed in the face of all the vicissitudes of national travails? (ibid p.120-121)

Even if we agree to build up a mighty well-knit disciplined organisation with all the unimpeachable qualities of head and heart and character for embarking upon national reconstruction, is it imminent to stick to the same process of Man making in the present environment which was envisaged and practiced by Dr. Hedgewar in 1925 and subsequently polished and given finishing touches in Sindhi Conference in February, 1939. Those who were caught in a dilemma wanted a change. But, Guruji's contention was that there was no alternative to the Sangh method of character-building, qualities-inculcation, willingly accepted discipline and well-knit unity of the entire country. The way was very long, but there was no short cut. Could any change in the Sangh-methodology produce better results in reforming the drawbacks and evils of the society and inculcate sterling qualities in the individual and the society as a whole? (ibidp.110). There was a counter-question from some people- How far Sangh Swayamsevaks were free from the evil influences in the society. (ibidp.110).

Shri Guruji was an intellectual giant. He had the gift of a very powerful expression also. All respected his scholarly qualities, clear headedness, Selflessness, Transparent noble character, Renunciation and dedication to Dr. Hedgewar and his plan of action for national-upliftment. It was incumbent upon the Swayamsevaks persistently trained in ekchalakanuvartritva (obedience and loyalty to one leader) to follow his guidance, because Dr. Hedgewar himself had chosen Shri Guruji as his successor. Thus most of the workers surrendered their doubts and started to work with the same old Shakha-centred methodology under the spiritual light and leadership of Shri Guruji. Only a few senior swayamsevaks like Vasant Rao Oke articulated their opposition to this thought and later even revolted.

But some fundamental questions arise whose answers are necessary for the sake of history. Every living organisation must critically review its long history of rise and falls and crucial turns to understand its basic tenets and inspiration. This makes them more dedicated towards its ideology. The workers get a clearer comprehension of the principles, better vision of the aims and objects and their devotion to the institution gets deepened. Nobody can keep his institutional inspiration and energy intact merely on the sentimental attachment to some individual. That is why Dr. Hedgewar, adopted the Bhagwa Dhwaj (Saffron Flag) as its Guru or source of inspiration instead of traditional faith or hero-worship as it was the symbol of our nation's glory. Shri Guruji also being a very open minded intellectual, liked swayamsevaks to introspect and critically examine their actions and behaviour in the prevailing situation and circumstances. Addressing the pracharaks of U.P. zone, he emphasized;

"Difference of opinion is natural in human beings. We do not preach blind-faith, we want a thorough churning of the mind and deep-thinking before accepting an ideology and making it a life-long aim." (Dhyeya-drishti p.8).

"It is natural to react to the thoughts propagated. I do not regard those who review and retrospect as way lost or way-out. I have respect for them. It is better to work after considerable thought about the pros and cons than to be merely carried away on the wave." (ibidp.10).

Shri Guruji, felt that the agitated feeling and commōtion in workers minds was caused by the vacuum created by the ban imposed on Sangh and its activities, which included Shakhas-morning, noon, evening, night; meetings of gats (locality groups), shakhas pathaks (platoons) or at bigger levels of districts, zones, states and All India level, all hectic and one after another in quick succession occupying body, mind and conversations. Sometimes they will muse over the numbers of participants, thereafter planning about the increase in number, 'quality, discipline and co-ordination-techniques etc etc. Another aspect had been personal contacts with absentees, taking care of those ill or those in difficulty ('their difficulties are our opportunities' attitude) and above all how the huge Hindu Society could be organised as a united integrated whole systematically leading a perfectly harmonized corporate life. The Swayamsevaks, young and old, new-comers and experts, had no time to think about anything else-not even about their families or themselves in the pursuit of that goal. This total devotion and dedication became a sheet anchor against all doubts and depressions. The sudden stoppage full and ruthless, broke that armoured cover and created a dent and released all the pent-up energies in the form of questions, doubts and perturbations. (ibid p.6-7).

"I have nothing to feel sorry or say anything against the natural introspection's and even heated discussion. On the other hand I would have been disappointed if we had been quiet and inert because RSS is not an organisation of thought-less idiots running heretically helter skeltor without rhyme, reason, logic or foresight."(ibidp.11).

It is indeed, imperative to understand that there is a conviction behind every task. And every task has some basic principles and ultimate objectives to carry on ardently the efforts in any movement. What is the core principle of the Sangh? What is the inspiration? One must always remember the essence of his activities. If he forgets it, he becomes inert. And his faith turns into a blind, mechanical activity.

Against this background, one has to go back to the genesis of the Sangh. Why was it founded? What was its objective? To comprehend this, one will have to go deep into the pages of its history. But Sangh had all along avoided formalities, declarations and publicity. Hence, there is no literature available to throw light on this.

Understanding Dr. Hedgewar

One has, therefore, to delve deep into the life and activities of its founder Dr. Hedgewar. The booklet "Sangh Vriksha ke Beej: Dr. Hedgewar" published in 1988 (Delhi) describes how he was disillusioned and disappointed by the political activities and social movements of the time, the agitations, movements, agreements, parleys and attempts at unification of vested communities. He relinquished his prominent role and position amongst the leaders, in spite of being a very successful organiser of movements aimed at the emancipation of the country from the foreign yoke and founded a novel organisation of young adolescent boys and concentrated upon moulding their character and personalities and inculcate an unimpeachable discipline and steel like muscles and staunch determination. But did he want to make this process of moulding men of steel a perennial affair? Or he aimed at attaining his objective "Yachi dehi, Yachi dola" with his own eyes during his lifetime? Had he visualized Sangh to disintegrate after the attainment of freedom just as Gandhiji visualized about Congress?

But the generation which Dr. Hedgewar had moulded has now passed away or has become quite old. The branches and fronts have spread widely in every direction, many of them even bigger than the original Banyan tree. Many workers of these institutions have not directly come from Sangh process but their faith and confidence in Sangh is firm and unquestionable. The Sangh-image in the public mind is that of the multi-storeyed building with strong foundations with multi-farious social activities of importance for the nation.

Let us now come to Dr. Hedgewar. What is the source of his life history? One small book, published on June 21, 1940, immediately after his demise, initially in Marathi and later on in other languages. The latest edition, recently published reveals the writer as his closest colleague Uma Kant Keshav Apte alias Baba Sahib Apte. In 1949, after the ban was lifted, two memoirs entitled 'Hamara Adarsh' and 'Smriti Kan' were published. These were from the pen of the senior most people of the organisation. It was in 1960 that Late N.H. Palkar presented the concise life history of Dr. Hedgewar. The Special No. of 'Yuga Dharma' (Hindi) in 1962, which includes articles about Doctor Ji by such Veterans as P.B. (alias Bhaiya Ji) Dani does throw more light beyond Palkar's Biography of Dr. Hedgewar.

Born on Varsha Pratipada (Hindu New Year Day), 1889 in a poor Nagpur Brahmin family, this extra-ordinary energetic boy started his patriotic and revolutionary activities against the British even at the age of eight. As a matric student at Neelcity High School, he was rusticated for organising the singing of 'Vande Mataram' instead of 'God Save the King' on the arrival of the English Inspector of Schools. Somehow he passed his matriculation examination held by Rashtriya Shiksha Parishad of Bengal, and got admission into the National Medical College of Calcutta. As a medico from 1910-1916, he came in intimate contact with the secret revolutionary movement and organisations of Bengal, headed by Nalini Kishore Guha, Trailokya Nath Chakrovarty, Ram Lal Vajpayee and others. The biographies of these great champions of armed revolt mention Hedgewar (Secret Name 'Cocaine') with great respect and regarded his hostel room, a safe, reliable, refuge for revolutionaries.

On his return to Nagpur in early 1916, he spurned all proposals of marriage or lucrative appointments as doctor in government and private hospitals, home and abroad. In spite of all financial privations, he worked along with Bhan Kabres with all his time, energy and resources at his command to make preparations for a decisive mortal and extensive strike at the citadels of British Imperialist power. For that, from every nook and corner of the country, from every section of the population, dare-devil youths ready to lay down their lives at the altar of Freedom for the Motherland had to be organised. This is the period of his life which is shrouded in deep mystery.

Whatever has been revealed is that he had made frantic efforts for a simultaneous rebellion around all British Cantonements with the help of indigenous and imported arms and ammunition during the First World War. But the strategy of a grand coup miserably failed because of the gradual emaciation of the society at large. By and by even the topmost powerful leaders like Arvind, Lala Lajpat Rai and Lokmanya Tilak also had begun to feel the futility of armed revolution in the society. Dr. Hedgewar studied deeply the limitations, weaknesses and drawbacks of armed struggles. These had to be organised under a leader of skill and vision with utmost secrecy. The steps taken for raising finances, the secret of the conspiracies resulted in a cruel and thorough repression by the imperialist power. The inspirations of the revolutionaries mainly came out of a deep hatred towards the foreigner and his rule, not out of mellowed patriotism with an enlightened national reconstruction vision. As such Dr. Hedgewar withdrew from the revolutionary path and cast his lot with the Congress under the leadership of Lokmanya Tilak. Ultimately he resigned himself to follow the Gandhian path after the death of Tilak on August 1, 1920 and after the refusal of Arvind to come back to politics from his newly chosen path of spiritualism.

During the Nagpur Session of the Congress in 1920, he was the Commander of the Volunteer Corps. Those days, there was a controversy raging in Congress -Dominion State or Full freedom? But the public was carried away by Gandhiji's promise of 'Independence in One year and 'Khilafat Movement'. Dr. Hedgewar also courted arrest. In the jail, he saw a wide gulf between Hindu and Muslim psyche. The Hindus looked upon India as Bharat Mata and were prepared to sacrifice and die for Her sake while the Muslims supported world Pan Islamism and the rule of the Khalifat over Turkey. Although numerically in an advantageous position, the Hindus were disorganized, weak and conciliatory whereas the Muslim leadership was assertive and perceptibly aggressive.

With the end of 'Khilafat', Muslims withdrew form the struggle for independence and the movement fizzled out. Gandhiji withdrew it on the plea of violence at Chauri-Chaura. There was depression everywhere. In such an atmosphere of despondency, Muslims attacked, looted converted and disgraced Hindus everywhere. The Leaders of the majority like Madan Mohan Malviya, Lala Lajpat Rai, Dr. Munjey, Swami Shraddhanand were very much worried. Hindu Mahasabha was revived at Varanasi in 1923. Nagpur also felt the heat of communal clashes. Gandhiji was very much distressed at the cowardice of the Hindus and aggressiveness of the Muslims.

He wrote in 'Young India' of May 29, 1924 that Hindus invariably are the sufferers because they are generally cowards and Muslims are goondas. I am not so much enraged with the Muslims as I am ashamed of the pusillanimity of the Hindus. At Saharanpur, they looted the Hindus, murdered them, raped their women. Who is to blame? The impotent Hindus.....I would prefer violence to cowardly withdrawal. During 1924, Lala Lajpat Rai wrote a series of inspiring articles in Tribune. Those days the Congress was not scared of the use of the word Hindu.

Dr. Hedgewar's Analysis

What grieved Dr. Hedgewar deeply was that the Hindus had lost self-confidence and were disorganized. That is why even for the struggle for Independence they frantically sought the co-operation of the Muslims and make unilateral efforts for unity. After a deep study of the situation, Dr. Hedgewar came to the conclusions that -

(a) Because of thousand of years of intimate relationship, Hindus regard the country as their revered Mother. Hence, they are spontaneously fired with an ambition to achieve her freedom.

(b) Because of world-relationship, the Muslim is motivated by Pan-Islamism instead of patriotism like Hindus.

(c) The Hindus, therefore shall have to wield the responsibility of the attainment of India's freedom and be prepared to make all sorts of sacrifices.

(d) Under a long subjugation, Hindu has lost self-confidence and he frantically seeks co-operation and unity from others, particularly Muslims. The remedy lies in making the Hindu society well organised and disciplined.

(e) Their cadre has to be made of mainly young energetic youth instead of the conciliatory elderly people.

(f) The success of both the sporadic revolutionary movements as well as of non-violent Satyagraha movements initiated by Gandhiji is doubtful. Only a countrywide, disciplined, thoroughly trained organisation built up with alacrity and sacrifices which at the right time, can emancipate the motherland from the foreign yoke and carry on the national task of total reconstruction resolutely on the right lines.

Dr. Hedgewar's concept of the Sangh is revealed to great depths by Appa ji joshi, his confidant and comrade in arms in his earliest plans to liberate the nation from the British. He writes that when the Doctor was a in prison during 1920-22 Non-co-operation movement alongwith other Congress leaders, the only subject of his discussions, confidential exchange of views and secret plans used to be how to build up an extremely powerful organisation and make all preparations in advance to strike like lightning at the enemy at the right time.

Appa ji reveals that Dr. Hedgewar presented his plans before several of his intimate friends and trustworthy leaders of the freedom struggle. After his release from the jail, he made extensive tours to take his companions and followers into confidence and solicited their co-operation in building up such a powerful organisation. "When these people did not show much interest, I ventured to advise Doctor ji to start such an organisation on his own, without depending on the co-operation of such uninspired self proclaimed leaders. They may also join, once the strength of your organisation manifests itself sufficiently." (Tarun Bharat, 1970-see Panchjanya, January 22, 1978).

Dr. Hedgewar discussed Non-Cooperation Movement with his companions in prison, during 1920-22 and his plans of building powerful organisation so as to strike at the foreign ruler at the right time to achieve freedom. He also made extensive tours after his release to convince his companions and followers about the need for such an organisation but he did not get encouraging response from them.

It was in this background, that RSS was founded with the objectives of national liberation. For this, he adopted a technique to build up a highly disciplined force of freedom fighters imbued with an unflinching dedication, iron-will, stout hearts and vast and varied capacities. Such bands of workers would also possess rare courage and spirit of sacrifice for the emancipation of the motherland from the foreign-yoke and would be given thorough training to work in close co-ordination to achieve the objectives of the chalked out plans and strategies. They should be bound together with noble ideals, lofty goals and feelings of fraternity. They should be prepared to forego all the comforts and ambitions of life with the sole purpose of building their nation, a thoroughly organised society. They should display immense zeal and enthusiasm to devote their maximum time and energy to achieve the time-bound targets.

For this, Dr. Hedgewar adopted the 'daily-meet' tradition of Maharashtra Vyayamshalas (gymnasiums), uniform, drill and band, like the Indian Army, mode of Salutation from the Scout Movement, the secret vow like the revolutionary Anusheelan Party, the Lathi-training technique from local Akharas, to integrate in the Sangh-Shakha programmes of physical training gradually. His focus was on the target and the preparedness needed to hit the Bull's Eye. With perfect poise and self-confidence, in the daily meets, he sought to channelise the emotions of the Swayamsevaks to uphold the glory and grandeur of the ancient Bharatiya traditions of which Saffron flag was found to be a symbol of great significance. In the Pratigya, the words 'Hindu Rashtra Kee Swatantrata, were purposefully included to strengthen the resolve for complete Freedom.

The Prarthana together with 'Bharat Mata Ki Jai' at the end kindled intense patriotism and the resolve to achieve Freedom took the shape of volcanic eruption. The inclusion of Shivaji's Coronation Anniversary amongst the six major All-India Sangh-Festivals added solidarity and solemnity to the resolve. The Supreme test of a Swayamsevak's dedication to the organisation was that he should develop the requisite organizational skills adequately and devote sufficient time for Sangh-activities to be able to become a whole-time worker.

The greatest concern of Dr. Hedgewar was that no chance should be given to the British government to strangle and scuttle the infant organisation before it gains strength for achieving full and complete freedom. For this he showed uncanniness and avoided any publicity so that the rulers might not become alarmed. He averred that the only aim of Sangh was to organise the Hindu society. The query 'why such an organisation?' was tacitly answered: "Organisation for organisation's sake!" because organisation was a pre-requisite for any society. Moreover, he took special precautions that there should be no propaganda in newspapers about their programmes. The workers should be enthusiastically motivated and involved in making their 'shakhas' gather more and more numbers. The method of increasing the number of such 'shakhas' was under well-planned 'Vistaar Yojna' (extension programmes). The publicity craze was to be shunned. For this he very prudently established the cult of 'Prasiddhi Parangmukhta' (aversion to publicity) in Sangh. The idea behind this was two fold. On one hand the instinct of superiority born out of egoism amongst workers was to be curbed and on the other hand to hoodwink the British rulers from sensing revolt against the empire and to protect the organisation from repression. This is abundantly clear from his letters. The news of the arrival of Vasant Rao Oke in Delhi in November, 1936 for initiating Sangh activities was published in a newspaper. Dr. Hedgewar promptly wrote to him:

"Your arrival in Delhi and embarking upon Sangh-work has been published in a newspaper. Whosoever may be responsible for the lapse, this is nor proper and appropriate in the interest of the organisation. Such a publicity brings about many obstacles for the organisation." (Dr. Hedgewar: Patra Roop Vyaktitva, 1989, Indore:p.74). The newspapers from Maharashtra were more prone to publicity-drive. On 10-12-1936, he informed Kashinath Rao Limaye of Sangli that the report of the Vijayadashami festival celebrations were much more detailed than what the Sangh desired which, according to its accepted policy, preferred its mention as a normal daily news-item. We do not mean that the information should be blacked out but it should not be unnecessarily highlighted. (Sangh Nirmata Ke Aapt Vachan/ B.N. Varhadpande, Nagpur, 1989). In 1932, the Central Provinces Government issued a circular prohibiting government servants from attending RSS shakhas. Doctor's strategy of nullifying the effect of that circular was to ignore it altogether as he wrote to Baba Saheb (Uma Kant Keshav) Apte; "This circular need not be given the least importance and the issue should not be raised in the papers or elsewhere."(ibid.p.27).

However, even while pretending to keep aloof from the struggle for Independence, all the workers of Sangh were impatient to achieve the freedom of the nation. Doctor ji attended the 1928 session of the Congress at Calcutta. There he discussed the Sangh strategy with his old revolutionary colleagues. He was highly impressed by the organizing capacity of Subhash Chandra Bose as the Commander of the Volunteer Corps. He was also inspired by his resolution of Complete Freedom. He discussed his Sangh-plan with him. That is why, as soon as the World War II broke out, his old revolutionary friend Trailokya Nath Chakrabarty came to Nagpur and asked him to make full preparation for the armed revolt because the much awaited opportunity had arrived.

Doctor ji adopted the medium of intimate personal-contact for the propagation of Sangh, instead of publicity through newspapers. His motto was:

Ek deep se jale doosra;

Aise aganit hoven.

(Let one lamp ignite another to build a galaxy of lights)

Inspiring the Young

Initially, Doctorji through his daily meet at the 'Mohite Bara' Sangh-shakha, charmed and created magnetic impact on the small batch of impressionable youths, trained them and taught them the methodology and technique of building a disciplined organisation and presented before them his own example for inculcating the requisite qualities. A self effacing personality though he was, he sowed the seed of organisation and infused spirit of idealism in the hearts of young aspirants. Thus Doctor ji can be regarded as an organiser of superb qualities and skills. He took great pains in chiselling the character of each one of his followers. He burnt himself like a silent lamp and thereafter kindled others with the missionary fire. These thoroughly trained missionaries were deputed to other suitable places. Initially, the number of 'shakhas' multiplied in Nagpur itself. Thereafter the organisation was extended to Vidarbha and thence to Maharashtra. In North India the first RSS Branch was inaugurated in 1930 by Bhaiya ji Dani at Hindu Vishwa Vidyalaya, Benaras, as he took admission there for higher studies. After 1936, chief organisers were sent to the various provinces of North India. Calcutta and Madras received Sangh emissaries in 1939. Thus, by 1940 most of the important towns in every province of the country were connected with Sangh-shakhas so that during the All India representative Sangh Shiksha Varga (Training Camp) at Nagpur in 1940, Doctor ji could happily comment that he was viewing a miniature Hindu Rashtra.

However, Doctor ji had to withdraw himself from all public activities to get completely engrossed in his activity of spreading the network of shakhas as early as possible in every nook and corner of the country. Like a skilled sculptor, he was lost in chiselling and moulding the sensitive young generation into a rock like fine structure of well-disciplined and dedicated patriots ever ready to lay down their lives at the back and call of Bharat Mata. Working under very trying circumstances and facing heavy odds. He strived hard and literally with the sweat of his brow worked so that the target of organisation could be achieved well in time to strike at the right opportunity. In line with his technique of inspiring intense enthusiasm in the hearts of his youthful band of workers he used to remind them that Sangh was not out to celebrate its 'jubilees'. We are wedded to our goal of achieving our aim *'Yaachi deha, Yachi dola.'* (with this very body with these very eyes).

With the same hope, Bose sent the first Sarkaryavah Balaji Huddar and Dr. Ram Samjhagiri on a mission to Doctor ji at Deolali near Nasik, where the latter was recuperating after illness. Even on June 20, a day before Doctor Ji's sad demise, Subhash Babu called on him to discuss his plans but this could not be possible due to his critical state.

Doctor ji kept himself fully informed about all the movements of the struggle for Independence, in spite of his all-out pre-occupation with the work of Sangh. When the Congress adopted the Declaration of Complete Independence at its Lahore session in 1930, Doctor ji felt overwhelmed and he at once issued a circular to all RSS branches that they should naturally celebrate and welcome the decision of the All India National Congress for declaring their aim as Complete Independence. We should cooperate with every institution striving for that aim'.(ibid p.5-6).

The truth is that without making any public declarations every Sangh worker was convinced that he was steadfastly working for the liberation of his Motherland, Bharat Mata from the abominable foreign yoke.

All the same, sometimes some of them grew impatient and felt and even vocally urged during discussions to take recourse to some more drastic and revolutionary measures to expedite the achievement of their goal. Bala Saheb Deoras reported that it was in such a vein that after Bhagat Singh and his other companions were hanged, some Swayamsevaks were so agitated that they resolved to learn bomb making. They even conveyed this resolution to Dr. Hedgewar through

Bala Saheb. Doctor ji spent several nights to dissuade such zealots. He did not want the organization's strength to be dissipated in fissiparous plans which were bound to fail in premature confrontations with the mighty British Empire. He emphasized the necessity to exercise all their time and energy to make the organisation all encompassing. He wanted Sangh to cautiously avoid getting involved in spontaneous local agitation's. Instead, he was drawing elaborate plans to reserve the entire might like Brahmastra (supreme weapon) to be used at the most appropriate time. That is why when the entire freedom-movement was seized with Gandhi ji's Namak-Satyagrah (Salt-agitation) in 1930, and many Swayamsevaks were impatient to participate, Doctor ji himself courted arrest under the aegis of the Jungle Satyagrah along with some very enthusiastic workers like Dada Rao Parmarth. In the prison he established intimate contacts with other Satyagrahis. He had an extensive tour after his release and strengthened those ties by associating them with Shakha-Vistar (extension of Sangh-branches).

A letter from Shri Guruji written to Dr. Sadagopal, a B.H.U. colleague reveals how dedicatedly the Sangh-workers were striving to build up their strength. This letter was written before Guruji left for the Sargachhi Ashram of Swami Vivekanand's Gurus Bhai Swami Akhandanand and as a result of his growing contact with Dr. Hedgewar and acceptance of Sangh-responsibilities consequent upon his return to Nagpur in 1934.

"The world political situation is changing every moment. No body can foretell when all of a sudden the appropriate opportunity will come when we may have to jump into the fray. If we do not rise to the occasion and successfully avail of it, it may turn out to be a case of Now-or-Never. We may have to wait infinitely for a second chance with uncertainty and despondency. Hence instead of depending upon fate for such an opportunity, we should be thoroughly prepared to avail of it as fortune favours. We should not give a chance to posterity to blame us, as we do now to blame our ancestor's unpreparedness and losing the opportunity offered by World War-I in 1914. We should ensure well knit powerful Sangh-branches everywhere in the country, so that at the right moment, we are able to give a decisive fatal blow to the enemy to attain the freedom of our motherland."" (Patra Roop Shri Guruji/Nagpur/1983/p/388).

The Goal

Thus Doctor ji had planned the working of RSS and evolved a staunch revolutionary technique under the garb of an apparently innocuous social movement to avoid being detected by the British government's eye and for this, he camouflaged and completely kept the organisation aloof from the contemporary mass-movements. But sometimes, during unguarded moments Doctor ji echoed his surging patriotic sentiments, but such slips were rare. A stray rejoinder to a critic blaming Sangh for apathetic reaction reveals:

"Often Sangh is charged with apathy and criminal indifference to the struggle for independence going on with sacrifices of all freedom-loving patriots. But it should not be forgotten that there can be no life of self-respect without being deeply concerned with the attainment of independence. But for this purpose the existing shows of superficial political gimmicks are too insignificant to demand our participation." (Hamare Doctor ji/Nagpur/1943 p.66).

To the Hindu Mahasabha leader who tried to rope in RSS in 1938-39 Bhagya Nagar (Hyderabad) Satyagrah, Dr. Hedgewar clearly refused to dissipate the energies of Sangh in any contemporary movement. As directed by him, 'Savdhan Weekly' of Nagpur published his statement in its issue of May, 1939.

"In the growing tempo of Bhagya Nagar movement, G.G. Adhikari revels so gleefully that he forgets that the nation has still to achieve its independence. As such till that final victory in that crucial battle of life, all movements like

Bhagya Nagar Satyagrah are of only a subsidiary importance. An organisation working for invincible ever-ready national power cannot afford to divert its determined march towards its goal of perennial importance." (Dr. Hedgewar Charitra/ N.H Palkar/1962/p.370).

Dark clouds of the impending storm of World War II had already risen up above the horizon and started hovering over the sky. But the strength of Sangh organisation was lagging far behind the scheduled target. In his address to the trainees in 1939, while giving vent to his deep anguish, he exhorted:

"We have been working incessantly for the last fourteen years, which cannot be brushed aside as an insignificant period. We should deeply introspect whether we have been able to reach even anywhere near our goal...of course, we have never declared that we would attain independence in two days or two months...all the same, we also do not envisage a preparation for generations or centuries producing no result. Our effort is to attain our objective within our lifetime. But, if our efforts and preparations are akin to the examinee who only burns the mid-night oil when the final papers have their 'date-sheets' announced, then surely we cannot come out with distinctions and flying colours." (Hamare Doctor ji/Nagpur/1940/New Edition 1988/Indore/ p.136-140).

He elucidated the background of Sangh concept:

"Understand it fully that Sangh is neither a gymnasium, nor a club; nor a military school...We have vowed to concretise our vision with in our lifetime: Sangh does not want to celebrate its jubilees like other educational institutions and carry on running it as an Alma-mater for generations after generations.(ibid).

"Sangh should be understood as an extraordinary medium of the Divine Power. Like all great men, it fulfils its mission in the short life. We can expedite the march towards our goal only with the all-out active participation of every Swayamsevak. We are determined to attain our objective "Yachi-deha, Yachi dola" (with this body and with these eyes we want to participate in the victory-parade)' (Hamare Doctor ji/Nagpur/1943 Edition/p.131).

The European sky was by now overcast with dense clouds, ready to burst any moment. The D-day had arrived, for which Doctor ji had turned his blood literally into water to prepare the organisation. Doctor ji was worried whether Sangh was prepared for the fray...To test he ordered Pune-Sanghchalak, Vinayak Rao, to assemble at the Shivaji Mandir Shakha-place all the volunteer force of the city within two hours, "This was the first test of an 'Emergency Call". (Dr. Hedgewar Charitra/Palkar/p.374).

The clouds of the II World War ultimately erupted in September 1939. The crucial opportunity had arrived and was at door. But Dr. Hedgewar had lost his health completely. And, Sangh had gathered momentum only symbolically as an All India organisation. It comprised mainly of children and adolescents. Doctor Hedgewar's mental struggle and worry is described by former Sarkaryavah, H.V. Kulkarni in the following words:

After the World War II broke out, Dr. Ji one day summoned me at night... In spite of his induced sleep, Doctor ji in a state of great worry, apprehended that we might lose another golden chance to fight and win the battle of freedom. It was incumbent upon us to have gathered a formidable strength before the war. I had foreseen the event. But if in this disorganized country of innumerable subdivisions there could have been developed one Hedgewar in every village, the Hindu nation could have had some hope of achieving its long-aspired freedom. But God seems to have willed otherwise."

His voice was lost in a heart-touching emotion submerged in an outburst of tears. (Yug Dharma/Dr. Hedgewar Smriti Visheshank/April, 1962/p.76).

Doctor ji was lost in this helpless despondency, when his old colleague of the revolutionary Anushilan Party, Trailokya Nath Chakrabarty, all of a sudden, stood before him. In a few measured words he solicited co-operation from the Dr. Hedgewar of revolutionary days. While departing, Chakrabarty asked him to keep at least some of the selected swayamsevaks ready to take part in the revolt to be planned. If once the bugle was blown by this band, from everywhere in the country, countless fighters will join the army of liberation (ibid/p.392-303).

A storm raged in the heart of Doctor ji. His physical strength was failing him. On the ardent persuasion of his senior colleagues on Jan. 31, 1940, he was taken to the health-resort of Rajgiri in Bihar. But even that pleasant and peaceful atmosphere could not calm down the fury of the storm that raged in Doctor ji's heart. One day during the trance after dinner, he was heard babbling:

See, see! The opportunity of 1940 is also slipping out of our hands! We have been able to do nothing at all. We are under the damned British yoke but we shall win our freedom sure and certain! (ibid p.398)

Lost in these thoughts full of anxiety and deep anguish, Doctor ji returned to Nagpur along with Appa ji Joshi on March 9, 1940. During his stay there upto March 16, he posed a question to the Swayamsevaks as to how many dedicated patriots were needed for the fierce fight for freedom. Pondering over the various replies, he once again came to Rajgiri and therefrom wrote a letter to the workers at Nagpur to muster by 1942 at least 1 % Swayamsevaks in full uniform among the rural population of the Province and 3% in the cities. (ibid p.401) Evidently Doctor ji was referring to Vidarbha, where RSS had by then reached even in the nooks and corners of the rural area. He could not expect such a target anywhere else in the rest of India. Shri Guruji's biographer, Shri C.P. Bhishiker also traces the origin of this letter in the contemporary Praurh Shivir (Elders

Conference) held at Chandrapur. (Bhishiker/Navyug Pravartak Shri Guruji/Lucknwo/p.46).

The above target also makes it abundantly clear that Doctor ji foresaw 1942 as the crucial year for the struggle for freedom. His prophecy proved correct as it was in 1942 that Gandhiji launched his 'Quit India' movement and Netaji Subhash Bose reached Japan from Germany and assumed the supreme command of the INA for entering India through the North East. Would Dr. Ji live upto the extremely crucial year of 1942? He came to Nagpur on April 20, 1940 and upto May 14, attended the OTC (Officers Training Camp) at Pune. Thereafter he returned to Nagpur, where 1400 Swayamsevaks from all over the country were participating the unique III year (Final) training camp, representative camp of the entire Akhand Bharat. The biographer Palkar writes that the bed-ridden Doctor ji murmured a few sentences now and then to the trainees who visited him. This manifested the storm that raged in his heart on the realisation that the World War had set in yet the RSS freedom-fighters had lost another opportunity. (p.423/Doctor Hedgewar Charitra/Palkar)

He was kept at Baba Saheb Ghatate's bungalow near the Training Ground. Just two days before his eventual death, information was received that Netaji Subhash Bose was coming to see him. Netaji came but he could not have even a word with the dying revolutionary organiser. The latter, in a state of almost coma, could only weep bitterly. Next morning he breathed his last. The biography published soon after shows the intensely afflicted state of mind of the Swayamsevaks of the day. The epilogue is in the form of a Marathi-poem full of heart-rending pathos which depicts Dr Hedgewar requesting the God of Death to postpone his demise so that he might see the Independence of Mother India and solemnly promising to present himself willingly thereafter. This was the sentiment that made the valiant weep.

Shri Gurujee - The Successor

Doctor ji passed into an eternal sleep after handing over his charge to his colleagues led by his nominated successor Shri Guruji (M.S. Golwalkar). The latter put their life and soul into the efforts to attain the target indicated by Doctor ji. The outcome was that youths in thousands left the sancturies of their homes to become Pracharaks (whole time missionary workers) and strewed themselves all over the land to raise exuberant shakhas sprouting with budding patriots flowering into hardy valiant disciplined freedom fighters. Every province organised 'Instructor and officers' Training Camps (ITC's and OTC's) of 15 days and a month duration respectively. The number of the daily attendance rose immensely. The result was that the institution that was absolutely neglected as insignificant by the government till 1940, became an eyesore to the British Intelligence Deptt in 1942. So much so that when uniforms and drills were banned for all volunteer organisations in 1940, RSS had not been included in the list at all. But on Oct. 19, 1942, the Chief Secretary of the C.P. and Berar Provinces, which included all districts of the present Vidarbha, Mahakoshal and Chattisgarh, issued a circular to the collectors and district magistrates to provide the history and the strength of RSS in their respective areas. In the Central government order in which semi-military activities were banned, Khaksars and RSS were particularly included amongst these organisations. The provinces were asked to keep a watchful eye on the activities of the RSS.

The CID report of Shri Guruji's lecture in the 1942 Sangh Shiksha Varg (OTC) mentions it as a very sharp and comprehensive tirade against the British Govt. Ultimately, the 1942, Quit India movement was launched. The government arrested all leading congressmen during the night before they could take even a step and the Indian National Congress itself was banned. It assumed an underground and a violent turn totally incompatible with the avowed commitment to Satya and Ahimsa (truth and non-violence). The widespread disturbances were led by the youthful socialist leaders like Jaya Prakash Narayan, Acharya Narendra Deva, Achchyut Patwardhan and Ram Manohar Lohia and in some areas by the enthusiastic Forward Block founded by Subhash Bose. After the attack on Soviet Russia by Hitler, the Communist Party of India came forward to render all help to the British-war efforts and to oppose tooth and nail the struggle for Independence of India.

What was going on in the undercurrents in Sangh is worthy of cautious note. The occasion for which the founder and Sarsanghchalak Dr. Hedgewar had issued specific unambiguous order to all Swayamsevaks to get prepared tooth and nail had arrived with a bang. But it is also a fact that Sangh did not jump into the fray. Why? We have no records whatsoever to enlighten what was the discussion that took place among the Sangh senior hierarchy in the discussion that took place to decide the policy and line of action except the Prapatra (Circular letter) sent by Shri Guruji on 26.4.1943 to all provincial Chief organisers. This letter stipulated that in view of the government order, prohibiting military dress, parades and weapon-practices, all programmes pertaining to their use have been excluded from the Sangh training and daily activities. Accordingly, instead of Khaki uniform, military type helmet, crossbelt etc. white shirt, khaki short and black cap was adopted as Sangh uniform and the military department and the offices of Senapati and Sar-senapati were also abolished. Sh Martand Jog holding Sarsenapati rank since the Sangh-inception by Dr. Hedgewar resigned. But it needs deep investigations to know how and why Sangh kept itself away form the 1942 movement and who took the decision to change Sangh uniform and programme in accordance with the British government order and how this decision was arrived at and after what sort of internal discussions of its pros and cons.

It seems necessary to find out the individual views of the senior close associates of Doctor ji like Dada Rao Paramarth, Appa ji joshi, Bala Saheb Deoras and others. But the tradition of Sangh not to make public or speak out or write down the differences of opinion makes it difficult to ascertain the same. There is a small reference to the issue in Martand Rao Jog's auto-biography 'Smriteen Chee Chaahata Pane' (Nagpur/1978/p.135).

In 1960, in the conference of Sangh-Pracharaks at Indore, Shri Guruji confessed that there was an animated discussion and controversy on this issue. There had been earlier in 1930-31 a mass-movement. Several people had approached Doctor ji even then. This delegation did insist that the movement had the potentiality to win the country's freedom and Sangh should not lag behind in its participation. During 1942 also many people were deeply agitated. On this occasion also Sangh activities continued as before without directly participating in the national struggle.

The dilemma, however continued in many Swayamsevak's minds. Not only outsiders, but also many active workers contended that Sangh was an institution of escapists and their views were meaningless, purposeless. They had felt even disappointed. (Samagra Darshan/part4/p.39-40).

In this very collection of speeches, Guruji at one place referred to the time-bound target determined by Doctor ji and his expectation about the period which could be enough for achieving our objective:

"Doctor ji had anticipated the attainment of the requisite strength of the organisation within 15 years. He fixed a target for the number then and gave 3 years for its completion. He stipulated the number of full uniform Swayamsevaks as 1% of the rural population and 3 % from the urban towns and cities. He had in a way expressed about active whole-time workers. And, why did he fix the time-limit as 3 years? I feel that he was a prophet who could foresee the coming events. If we could carry on our efforts according to his expectations and guidance, the future of the country in 1942 movement could have been moulded in an entirely different shape. But people do not understand how to accomplish time-bound programmes." (ibid p.42-43).

Shri Gurujee's Analysis

Thus according to Shri Guruji, Sangh-strength in 1942 was too insufficient in comparison with the requirement for attempting a successful national coup-d'etat.

Shri Guruji's views in the decision of Sangh's non-participation in the 1942 movement are revealed also in Dattopanat B. Thendgdi's words:

Because of the 1942 movement, many Swayamsevaks including some Pracharaks were terribly agitated. All of them questioned themselves about the purpose of the accumulated organised strength of Sangh, if it remained inactive in such a state of national emergency. Those days I was a pracharak at Calicut. Mangalore being very near, I was asked to see Shri Guruji there on behalf of all workers and acquaint him about the views of most of the workers. Accordingly, I went to Mangalore and saw Shri Guruji and reported to him. On the basis of his interviews, Shri Thengdi enumerates six reasons for Sangh's non participation in the Quit India movement. The chief among them are the Congress mistakes and the blatant insufficiency of Sangh strength. (Navyug Pravartak Shri Guruji/C.P. Bhishikar/ Lucknow 1999/p/59-61)

Shri Thengdi was the only survivor now testifying to the prolonged talk with Shri Gurji. But Quest, an English journal from Pune published fifteen years ago an article by Vasant Rao Mirsikar, a Political Science professor at Pune University, who had gone as a pracharak, under the inspiration of Bala Saheb Deoras, from Nagpur to Karnataka in 1942. This may even be regarded as an echo of Bala Saheb's own views. According to Bhishikar's accounts also several senior Sangh activists like Bala Saheb were eager to jump into the fray at the moment. But Guruji differed in the assessment of the situation.

Fortunately, a voluminious file in the National Archives carries all the accumulated detailed information about Sangh during the period and just preceding it. It reveals that the British Govt. Through its C.I.D. and provincial intelligence got ample information about Sangh, which led it to the following conclusions:

The ultimate objective of RSS is complete Independence of India.

Sangh is not an organisation of henchmen of any political party. Both Congressmen and Hindu Sabhaites in fairly large numbers support it.

Sangh does not want to be a target of British repressive measures in any way before achieving ample strength to retaliate.

To avoid premature confrontation, Sangh adopts suitable diversions, but secretly it is making all-out preparations for the final battle.

One top most official has reported even so much so that Sangh is ultimately going to present grave danger for the empire and hence should be nipped in the- bud.

If our district-administrators impose restrictions regarding uniform or military programmes etc., Sangh with their well-planned policy will stick to the orders to the letter.

The Sangh chief M.S. Golwalkar is a very prudent and foresighted leader. When he does not want a confrontation why should we unnecessarily invite trouble? Of course, a careful watch must be kept on him.

This file contains names of many swayamsevaks who were arrested for participating or attempting to do so in the 1942 August movement at many places. At a place named Chimur Aashti, even a parallel government was formed.

There is no doubt that the question has been storming the thoughts of many workers even later on as to what Dr. Hedgewar would have done if he had been alive. Could he have with his innovative instinct devised some novel way of using the strength of his organisation even if it was not upto the mark? Why a leader of superior-wisdom and unconditional dedication like Shri Guruji knowing in full the mind of his predecessor could not discern any alternative? Here it becomes essential to comprehend deeply the difference between the character and thinking of these two super-human leaders of extraordinary caliber.

Dr. Hedgewar was a product of freedom-movement. The furious throb of freedom pulsated his every vein. He never boasted of a super-intelligence and avoided all philosophical or logical discussions. He was a son of the soil inseparably connected with the mass movements and many active public-workers. He had a sound practical intuition and instinct. He easily found new alternative quickly learning from experiences of trials and errors. He was a real Karamayogi (man of action). He had founded Sangh as a medium for the struggle for freedom. He had invented an absolutely novel technique of organisation with that very objective in view. He had fostered the organisation with his blood.

Shri Guruji was basically a spiritual being of superlative wisdom and intelligence. He had developed a deep-laid renunciation very early in his life. His long letters from Madras during 1929 manifest the same spiritual turbulence and flights of other worldly imaginations. During the same period, he even thought of going to the Himalayas. Even after his contact with Doctor ji in 1934, he was vacillating between spirituality and nationalism. In 1936 he entered the Sargachhi Ashram of Swami Akhandanand for salvation.

His entry into Sangh was not through the normal Shakha tradition but from above because of the personal contact of Doctor ji. It was a sort of Parkaya-Pravesh (soul's entry into another body). He accepted Sangh intellectually. But he completely surrendered to Doctor ji, immersed himself wholly in Sangh and put his heart and soul in carrying out the responsibility assigned to him by Dr. Ji. He proved himself marvelously effective interpreter of Sangh concept, philosophy and technique in all the three languages-English, Marathi and Hindi. He nursed Doctor ji dedicatedly during the latter's last days. His experience about public life outside Sangh was almost negligible.

He provided Sangh with high level philosophy through his public lectures. But, probably he lacked the practical intuition of Doctor ji which finds alternative ways in intricated terrain's. That is why he could not provide the leadership in 1942, which probably Doctor ji's extraordinarily constructive intuition could have given. But his idealism, scholarly education, dedicatedly renounced life and extraordinarily impressive personality helped all workers to tide over the blame of escapism in the opportunity of Struggle for Freedom and kept on their efforts for building greater and sufficient strength for the final battle.

They had full confidence that ultimately it would be their Herculean efforts which would usher-in the dawn of independence. Upto 1947, the chief inspiration of all Sangh workers was the attainment of the freedom of the Motherland. But in 1947, Independence came along with Partition.

Soon after assuming the office of the Sarsanghchalak Bala Saheb Deoras, in his interview with an old worker and journalist D.V Gokhale, confessed that Sangh had not foreseen the premature Independence impregnated with the abominable partition. We were caught unawares! Had the tragedy of Partition not occurred Sangh would have had to face the terrible challenge of 'what now'. Serious question would have accrued regarding the propriety of the Sangh-technique in the changed circumstances.

But for sometime all such questions were swept away and all the strength of Sangh was engaged in fighting for life in the storm and massacre that burst out like a bolt from the blue with Partition and in fighting against the uncalled for unjust ban involving Sangh in Mahatma Gandhi's murder without any rhyme or reason ending with the victorious movement to get the ban lifted on July 12, 1949.

This logically brought about a churning of retrospection and introspection regarding the policy and technique of the organisation including the above mentioned undercurrents that have escaped the common eye in the long journey replete with amazing vicissitudes.

(The writer, a voracious reader, well-informed Columnist and persuasive intellectual, is a distinguished Historian.)

12

A Rainbow Across The Horizon

Atul Rawat

ONCE someone asked Sri Guruji why he was not using the great power that was available to him (in the form of the energy of millions of swayamsevaks) for the purpose of constructive work? Sri Guruji asked him what did he mean by the term constructive work? He answered that he was referring to constructing roads, sanitation works, providing medical and educational services to the needy etc. Sri Guruji explained to him that developing disciplined persons of high character was a more fundamental work. Then he told him with his characteristic wit and smile that the persons with undisciplined mind were a danger even if they were in a happy mood. He further told him that giving *samskaras* (discipline is but only a part of it) to the mind (*mana*) and intellect (*buddhi*) were the most primary of all the national priorities. Then Sri Guruji asked him if he would not call this work as a constructive work? In this brief and simple answer he had disclosed his lifelong methodology, which he had inherited from Dr. Hedgewar.

This methodology has been internalized in the Sangh Parivar where everyone believes that the Sangh engages itself only in a process of producing men with right *samskaras* and character. These men in turn take upon themselves to engage in constructive works. This methodology has been so much successful that some of the organizations that Gurujee's followers created are the largest organizations in their fields in India. The leaders who created these organizations and are running them had all come out of the RSS process that was envisioned by Dr. Hedgewar and provided with a very sound philosophical foundation and strong organised human force by Shri Gurujee.

There have been many attempted nomenclatures to describe the RSS, host of its affiliates and their somewhat less understood but more maligned ties. These attempts have resulted in creation of interesting perceptions or even stereotypes that describe this modern manifestation of the core of the eternal Hindu values in various ways. They range from "Brotherhood in Saffron" (Walter Andersen, an American observer) to "the Hydra-Headed Organization" (a stereotype created by the communist-Islamic fundamentalist unholy alliance). On the other hand the name "Sangh Parivar" caught the imagination of many and the term became very popular with the Indian journalists in particular.

Some important insiders wish their "Parivar" to be described as "a great Banyan tree" where in due course of time the roots hanging from branches become trunks supporting the whole tree. Probably, this is the best metaphor to describe the "Sangh Parivar". Counting the offshoots of the RSS is as difficult as counting the branches of a large banyan tree. What may add to the confusion of an outsider is the fact that many of the offspring are now having their own offshoots. The Vishwa Hindu Parishad (VHP) or the World Council of the Hindus is an RSS affiliate, but has its own offspring in the form of the Bajrang Dal and the Durga Vahini. Even these "third generation members of the Sangh Parivar" as they are sometimes called are really very large organizations and their membership runs in millions. Sheshadri very rightly mentions that there is no place for a totalitarian set up. He further writes, "the Sangh does not seek to play the role of a central authority controlling and directing the activities of those various fields." He compares the relationship with that of mother and her children in the sense that the children may take up various professions but yet they carry the imprint of mother's training in their conduct and norms of life. The swayamsevaks similarly may join any of the organizations on the basis of their interest and convictions but they usually carry the *samskaras* imparted in the Sangh to these organizations. That indeed makes a very strong bond between the Sangh and that particular organization on the one hand and among the various organizations of the Sangh brotherhood on the other. On this subject Sheshadri further writes:

And each of the organizations that they have built such as the VHP, BMS, ABVP, BKS, BJP, Vidya Bharati, and others is completely autonomous with its own independent set up and mode of functioning. But all of them together feel themselves as part of a wider family sharing common national goals and aspirations, and bound by fraternal ties. (ibid. p.396).

In most of the organizations of the "Sangh Parivar" the whole-timers and some old-timers of the RSS usually provide a core group. The general membership comes from all walks of life and all shades of opinion. Non-Hindus are also members of these organizations. The Sangh Parivar has given rise to some really unique and very large organizations and it is proposed to describe some of them here to highlight their distinctive Character and contribution.

The Akhil Bharatiya Vidyarthi Parishad

The Akhil Bharatiya Vidyarthi Parishad (ABVP) meaning the all India council of students is today the largest voluntary organization of the college going students in India. It was born just after the independence of India from the foreign yoke. The independence had brought in its wake the mammoth challenges of reconstruction of this eternal nation. The genius of the country had rusted through almost seven and a half centuries of foreign rule. It was imperative, therefore, that the society re-organized itself in all its fields, each member doing his bit in his own field. As the re-organization and reconstruction of each field would ultimately result into national reconstruction, the founding members of the ABVP chose the field of imparting the right *samskaras* to the students. Their main objective was to canalize the Indian students' energies in the task of national reconstruction rather than taking part in any political activities. The initiative came from a group of students and teachers who drew their inspiration from the RSS. Its growth process was slow and sporadic in the first few years but it picked up after Prof. Yeshwantrao Kelkar, a lecturer in Mumbai (formerly Bombay), became its main organizer in 1958. He was the real architect and builder of the ABVP. He passionately tried to build up this organization till his death in 1987. It was his hard work and single-minded devotion that the ABVP could become the largest organization of the students.

Perhaps no social organization has its members changing so quickly and regularly as an organization of the college going students. That is because like all the other charms of life, the college life is also very short. A student is in college for three to five years usually. In such a situation it is difficult to maintain the stability in the organization. After all at least almost twenty percent members pass out every year. Yet the uniqueness of the ABVP lies in the fact that it has emerged as a stable organization of floating population of students. Partly, it has overcome the problem by inducting teachers in the organization. It is merely the manifestation of the idea that the teachers are lifelong learners. It has gained strength day by day. In all probability, the ABVP is the only example of its type throughout the world. Ever since its inception teachers have been deeply involved in building up the organization and they comprise the permanent component of the membership.

What distinguishes the ABVP from other organizations is the fact that it is a full-fledged and regular non-political students' organization, which has evolved it's distinct philosophy and role. It organizes multifarious activities to fulfil its objective of national reconstruction. So far as ABVP's contribution to the national life is concerned, it can be said that apart from organizing a lot of constructive and meaningful activities it has helped to solve the problems facing students and education.

The ABVP has successfully led the students, in different parts of the country, in their struggles and agitations for their rightful demands and against corrupt and inefficient authorities. They have more than once played historical role in various issues of national importance. During the early 1970s they were elected to a few students unions all over the country. When Indira Gandhi imposed Emergency and curtailed all civil liberties and even the fundamental rights, the ABVP was deeply involved with other Sangh parivar outfits in fighting the draconian Emergency. The Student Action Committees became the nerve centers of the resistance to the Congress regime both during and prior to the Emergency. The ABVP leadership provided the core group for these Student Action Committees. The Gujarat Nav Nirman Andolan and the Chhatra Yuva Sangharsha Samiti in Bihar were two very important movements that left lasting imprints on the history of that eventful decade. The Samiti soon became active in other states as well. The ABVP provided the backbone to these movements. Even the Socialist leaders like J P Narayan supported them.

During more recent times the ABVP has undertaken the struggle for Indianisation of education and saving it from the Communist conspiracies and hijacking. It is an important ingredient in the Shiksha Bachao Andolan, which had to be started due to the UPA Government's attempts to take the education away from the Indian ideals and ethos. Other Sangh Parivar organizations are also part of the movement to save education. Presently the issue of denationalization of education is on a very high priority of the ABVP as is clear from the following extract from its resolution of 2005. The resolution says:

Present educational system in the country is far away from Indian Culture, Philosophy and contemplation due to major role of the gang of three foster sons of Macauley, Marx and Madarsa in its making and dispensation on education in independent India. We do not find the person cultured and patriotic even after taking higher education. Due to the lack of self-confidence and sufficient training in the present educational system we find there is a hoard of unemployed youth in independent India. The decisions taken by the Ministry of Human Resource Development clearly indicate that the newly elected Government at the center has sworn to continue the tradition of Denationalization of Education. Whatever changes were introduced democratically in the national curriculum by the National Council for Educational Research & Training (NCERT) during recent few years have been dubbed as "saffronisation", which allegation has been dismissed by the Supreme Court by upholding the introduced changes.

Agitations and satyagrahas have been the most democratic means and methods of opposing the establishment in India. The ABVP has constantly engaged itself in such activities. Some of the more important agitations that the ABVP launched are listed below. It includes the mention of the ABVP participation in the university administration and major national conventions and seminars as organized by this organization.

In 1975, over 10,000 ABVP activists offered Satyagraha against imposition of the Emergency in order to uphold democratic values.

In October 1983, over 1000 students offered Satyagraha at Guwahati against infiltration.

More than 10,000 students from all over the country, undeterred by the threats from terrorists, took part in the 'Save Kashmir' March on September 11, 1990.

A massive protest demonstration against transfer of Teen Bigha area of West Bengal to Bangladesh was organized at that very place on 26th January, 1992.

ABVP activists have been fighting the anti-national, violent Naxalites in Andhra Pradesh, even at the cost of their lives, but keeping the nationalist flag aloft on the campuses.

The ABVP also has much more positive contributions to the national life which have no parallel in the student world today. In the states of Maharashtra, Karnataka, Madhya Pradesh and Rajasthan the ABVP organizes exhibitions of working models by polytechnic students providing a forum for the students and the industrialists to interact with each other, understand the mutual needs and provide mutual help and support.

The ABVP's record in the National emergencies is worthy to be noticed. It's participation and selfless devotion in the various State Civil Defense Committees and Students' Leadership Programs received appreciation and recognition from the officials and the people alike. It may be noted here that the medical students of the BHU were among the first to reach Bhopal after the Bhopal Gas Tragedy to serve the victims. Similarly, the ABVP activists were at the forefront when the earthquake devastated Marathwada.

The ABVP has played an important role in highlighting and solving larger problems of the country. The thoughts and ideals of the ABVP on educational change can prove as valuable assets for any educational ministry or department. Be it the issue of terrorism in Kashmir or of infiltration of foreigners into Assam and border states, or the issue of reservation and Mandal recommendations or the gigantic task of integrating north-eastern citizens with those of the other parts of the country or the problem of unemployment and economic reconstruction of the country or the fight against social inequalities or the calamity of earthquake in Marathwada, the ABVP has never been found wanting both on the plains of thinking and action. The ABVP today has cadre of socially committed workers, which is capable of undertaking any challenging task.

The Vidya Bharati

Every time the wave of the cultural renaissance has touched the Indian land and its inhabitants, it has begun with upsurge of knowledge and its dissemination among the masses. It was as much true for the Pauranic Renaissance, as it was true for the upsurge of Bhakti during the medieval times. Similarly, the great upsurge of the Indian assertion of cultural nationalism spearheaded by the Sangh Parivar during the last century also had education as a major focus of its activities from the very beginning. Even otherwise the question of education of the children is a very central question in the methodology of "man-making" as professed and practiced by the RSS. Sri Guruji himself laid the foundation of a very unique school - The Srimad Bhagwat Geeta Vidyalaya at Kurukshetra in Haryana in 1946. The school has been serving the nation since then and has had many a laurels to its credit as a unique institution imparting the Indian values based knowledge to its students.

It was the younger brother of Bala Sahib Deoras, the redoubtable Bhau Rao Deoras who along with Nana -ji Deshmukh (who was to later on found the Deendayal research Institute and the Chitrakoot Gramodaya Vishwavidyalaya) and Krishna Chandra Gandhi took up the cause of the education of children in an organized manner and as a mission. The first Saraswati Shishu Mandir began to function in 1952. It was started at Gorakhpur in a building rented at a monthly rent of five rupees. After due consideration, the name Saraswati Shishu Mandir or the temple of the Mother-Goddess Saraswati-the deity of knowledge was chosen to highlight the departure from the Western emphasis in Indian education. Today the name has come to be associated with the nationalist education. Most of the schools run by the Vidya Bharati are either named as Saraswati Shishu Mandir or Saraswati Bal Mandir. Some other names are also in use. But all the names convey the idea of Indian-ness.

Thanks to the zeal, dedication and hard work of the

founding fathers, such schools began to be established at other places also. Slowly, state level committees began to come-up in other states also as the number of schools began to increase all over the country. Punjab and Chandigarh had a Sarvhitkari Shiksha Samiti while Haryana had Hindu Shiksha Samiti. The emergence of all India body had to wait till 1977 when the Vidya Bharati was established with its headquarters in Delhi. All state level committees were affiliated to the Vidya Bharati: Akhil Bharatiya Shiksha Sansthan. The Vidya Bharati is a registered society and has around seventy state committees affiliated to it.

Almost three decades after its establishment, the Vidya Bharati has come a long distance. With 26000 schools affiliated to it, the Vidya Bharati is the largest educational NGO in the whole world. There are around three million students who are being imparted the finest education with the Indian value system and the best of the Hindu *Samskaras* with it. There are more than 125,000 teachers who are engaged in imparting this education to the Indian students.

The Vidya Bharati is always conscious of its national and social responsibilities. Even if the various state governments or other state agencies are not able to utilize the findings of commissions and committees, the Vidya Bharati is alert to them. The Kothari Education Commission had recommended that within a radius of eight to ten kilometers there should be a complex of schools of various levels. The idea was that this would end the isolation of the schools in far-flung areas of the country and this group of schools would serve as a viable unit. The Vidya Bharati accepted this recommendation and developed 3200 such complexes all over the country, which it termed as *Sankulas*. The Vidya Bharati, today has its own educational research institute called Bharatiya Shiksha Shodh Sansthan. Established in Lucknow and working since 1980, it has all the required infrastructure including laboratories and a well equipped library.

There may be differences of opinion even on vital issues

with the Government of India, yet the Vidya Bharati contributes to the national programs of the Government. The contribution of the Vidya Bharati to the "Education for all" scheme has been termed as remarkable even by some critics. The universalisation of the primary education is a common dream of every Indian and that is why the Vidya Bharati contributes to it in a whole-hearted manner.

Some of the aims and methods of the Vidya Bharati include (but are not limited to) evolving an integrated system of education in conformity with the aims of Indian Culture and its ideals of life and to meet this aim it establishes educational institutions at various levels and in different areas for the physical, mental, moral and spiritual development of the child and to help, organize, promote and guide such institutions. Besides that the Vidya Bharati also affiliates various educational institutions and organizations that are already functioning on such lines and co-ordinates and helps in their working. The Vidya Bharati provides financial assistance in the form of loans, donations, grants, scholarships etc. to schools, hostels, literary and other institutions as well as competent and deserving students. It arranges for the preparation, printing and publication of circulars, magazines and books related to the above areas and establishes liaison with such organizations and their managements. One of the very unique areas where the Vidya Bharati contributes, unlike the so called public schools, is in establishing laboratories and scientific organizations for developing among students scientific temper, research inclination and awareness about achievements of science and to the extent possible make appropriate arrangements for the development of schools and other organizations already engaged in such activities.

One of the larger aims of the founding fathers of the Vidya Bharati was to develop a national system of education which may mould the posterity into such a youthful generation as is fully saturated with the feelings of Hindutva and patriotism, having completely attained all-round physical, mental, intellectual and spiritual development, capable of facing modern challenges successfully and dedicating their life for the service and upliftment of the Indians living in backward and remote tribal areas and the dwellers of the slums in the cities so that these down-trodden brethren of ours may get rid of economic exploitation, social humiliation and injustice and usher in a new era of mutual equity, cultural integrity and economic prosperity.

Believing that majority of Indians still lives in villages and easily fall under the category of deprived, the Vidya Bharati has given special priority to these sections whether they live in villages or in slums, in cities or in deep forests or on the mountains. There are ten thousand schools functioning in villages, 583 in underprivileged localities and around 1300 in tribal areas. In many of the areas the Vidya Bharati was the first to reach to open a school. They did it even before the Government agencies. Presently their emphasis is on the border regions of the country and other disturbed areas like Bastar, Telangana and Jharkhand.

Separate projects with special emphasis have been started for the Northeast, which had been exploited by the foreign Christian missionaries. There are around 182 tribes living in deep forests and other far-flung areas. During the British rule the Christian missionaries were able to impose the Roman script on their languages. The Vidya Bharati has now offered them the Devnagari script which is much more appropriate for writing these languages. The major success story of the Vidya Bharati in that region is the residential school at Halflong. Started in 1983, this school has successfully established a gurukul type hostel. Almost similar is the story of the school at Ratanpur in Jharkhand. The Vidya Bharati is presently running about 150 residential schools all over the country. They are quite evenly spread so that each state has at least more than one model residential school. Another area of special emphasis is the Chhota Nagpur where the Vidya Bharati is running around 150 schools for the tribal people.

The Vidya Bharati arranges for the proper training of teachers engaged in the fulfilment of its aims. It also produces training material to make their teaching work more effective and to provide protection, promotion and financial assistance to persons already engaged in the above two activities. The Adarsh Vidya Mandir Post Graduate Teacher Training College Jaipur conducts full time training of the teachers of Vidya Bharati schools. It arranges for the exchange, analysis, discussion etc. of the innovations and experiences in the field of education.

Evolution of an alternative model of school education that is more in tune with Indian culture and ethos has been a major achievement of the Vidya Bharati. It has been able to provide additional educational facilities in backward/ rural and tribal areas at a level that no other NGO or any private initiative has succeeded.

Vishva Hindu Parishad

The main purpose of the RSS from the outset has been to organize the Hindus. In due course of time it was felt that the unity of the Hindus was impossible until a similar unity was achieved among various spiritual leaders and denominations. Historically, the Hindu has always believed in possibility of salvation through more than one means. That gave rise to many *Panthas* (religions). Now in due course of time this phenomenon took the form of disunity, and thus became a major weakness, especially when dealing with the state sponsored anti-Hindu form of secularism. Underlining this need of unity among various Hindu sects and *Panthas,* Shri Shiva Shankar Apte the first Secretary-General of the VHP wrote in a letter for inviting prominent Hindu leaders, Dharmacharyas, thinkers for the first Convention at Bombay in August, 1964:

It is proposed to call a convention of representatives of all sects, faiths and religions, which have arisen, in this land. All those whether born here in this country or abroad who regard India as the fountain source of their faiths, religions, culture and philosophy and worship her as the Motherland and the Holy land, are intended to be invited to this Vishva Hindu Parishad. Jains, Buddhists, Sikhs, Vaishnavas, Veer Shaivas -Lingayats and all denominations falling under the generic term Hindus are being approached with a request to come together in this first convention of its type....

Free and politically united as we are now, it should be our ambition to mitigate the differences, recognize the unity behind the diversities and bring in a harmonious understanding, national integration and an order in the life of the whole society in accordance with the genius and spirit of our ancient and noble heritage.

Undoubtedly, the cow protection is a very dear cause for every Hindu but the need for unity among various Hindu religions was a much more pressing need. Revered Swami Chinmayananda, who was also the host of the meeting, wrote in his *Tapovana Prasad.*

Very vaguely it comes to me that it is time we convened a World Hindu Council either at Delhi or Calcutta inviting delegates from all over the world to meet and discuss and discover the difficulties and needs for the maintenance and growth of the Hindu culture. In this Council we shall try to hammer out the plans and programs to hold our spiritual family of Hindu religion together.

The then Sarsanghchalak of the RSS, Sri Guruji had himself entrusted the responsibility of creating this front to S S Apte. A meeting was held at Sandipani Sadhanalaya, Mumbai, on the occasion of Sri Krishna Janmashtami on 29th-30th of August 1964. It was decided at this meeting that the name of the proposed organization would be Vishwa Hindu Parishad and that a world convention of Hindus would be held at Prayag (Allahabad) during Kumbha

Mela of 1966 to launch the VHP, which was to be a non-political organization. The following aims and objectives were set before the Parishad.

1. To consolidate and strengthen the Hindu Society.
2. To protect, promote and propagate Hindu values of life, the ethical and the spiritual in the context of modern times
3. To keep in touch with all the Hindus living abroad, and to organize and help them in all possible ways in protecting their Hindutva.

Besides Sri Guruji, prominent Hindus from all walks of life including politics were present in the meeting. Many Congressmen also participated. The philosopher President of the Republic Dr. Sarvapalli Radhakrishanan sent his message of greetings.

Master Tara Singh, the Akali leaders, who was present in the meeting emphasized the need of rejuvenating the Hindu Dharma, saying:

Protection of Dharma is our Dharma. Khalsa Panth was born for that purpose. Never have I left Hinduism. Guru Govind Singh has produced a lot of Gurumukhi literature based on Vedas, Puranas and the like. Are we to leave all that? In fact Hindus and Sikhs are not two separate communities.

Besides the President himself, their Holinesses the Shankaracharyas of Kamakoti and Sharda Peethas supported the move wholeheartedly. Shri K M Munshi offered to sponsor the convention on the platform of his great institution - Bharatiya Vidya Bhavan. Rashtra Sant Tukadoji not only gave his blessings and guidance but offered all what he could muster at his disposal. Shri Chandrashekhar Shastri who had recently ascended the holy Peetha of Shri Sankaracharya of Puri blessed the VHP. Dr. Sampurnananda and H.H. Kushok Bakula supported and wanted to participate personally.

Shri Apte contacted many Hindu organizations of foreign countries through correspondence leading to the spread of the Parishad abroad in the subsequent years. After 1300 years of the last great Hindu Emperor Harshvardhana (648 AD) the first ever world Hindu Conference in the history of India was held at Thirtharaj Prayag on the holy occasion of Kumbha Mela on 22nd 23rd and 24th January 1966. Around 25,000 Hindu Delegates participated in this conference from twenty-two countries of the world.

The Second World Hindu Conference was held on 25th, 26th and 27th January 1979 at Prayag. It was inaugurated by His Holiness Shri Dalai Lama, the great religious leader of Buddhists and was presided over by Shri Bhagawat Singh, Maharana of Mewar. More than a lakh of representatives from India and abroad attended this Second World Hindu Conference.

The first twenty years of the VHP were a period of formation and consolidation. The infamous Meenakshipuram (Tamilnadu) conversion scandal became as much a turning point, as much it was outrageous. There was an Islamic mass conversion of about 800 Dalit Hindus and the Islamic zealots were boasting of readiness of around one hundred thousand Dalit Hindus to fall into their trap. The Hindu organizations, particularly the Sangh Parivar, took swift and effective action. They formed Hindu Ottrumai Maiyam or Centre for Hindu Unity. The HOM took upon itself to stop any further conversions and bring back the Dalits into the Hindu fold.

The VHP after the success in warding off the threat in the South began to prepare for the biggest mass movement that the country has ever seen. This was to liberate the Sri Ram Janmabhoomi. The foreign Islamic invader Babar had demolished the Sri Ram Janmabhoomi temple in 1528 AD and had constructed the so-called Babri mosque in its place. The Hindus had never given up their claim on that place and there had been at least seventy-six liberation attempts. The VHP launched the seventy-seventh liberation struggle. In the late 1980s, the Bharatiya Janata Party (BJP) brought the temple issue to the center stage of national politics. The issue reached its zenith when on 6 December 1992 the large Hindu crowds assembled there on the call of the VHP demolished the old and dilapidated structure.

The Ram temple issue, conversions and a uniform civil code are some of the priorities for the VHP. It has been demanding legislation from Parliament authorizing the temple construction. The VHP says India has historically been a Hindu nation, in culture, heritage and history. Foreign invaders brought Islam into India and imposed and coerced it upon millions of Hindus (corroborated by many historic acts of temple destruction, pogroms and mass conversions); Christian missionaries brought in Christianity when the Portuguese, French and the British colonized the land. It is a fact that Christian missionaries often denigrated and demonized the Hindu religion to coerce native peoples into converting them. While working to convert Christians, tribal peoples (native Hindus) and Muslims back to Hinduism, the VHP states that all Muslims and Christians were Hindus in the first place, and that all citizens of India are naturally Hindus. The VHP demands are broadly as follows:

- Creation of Ram temple at Ram Janmabhoomi
- End of forcible conversions by Christian missionaries and Islamic institutions.
- Ban on cow slaughter.
- Declaration of India as a Hindu Rashtra, literally Hindu Nation.
- Tougher anti-terror laws and tougher penalties for terrorists.
- Implementation of a Uniform Civil Code.
- Revocation of Article 370 of the Indian Constitution.
- Eradication of casteism from Hindu society.

Power hungry politicians have always been spreading casteism to subserve their electoral purposes. This erodes the sense of Hindu unity and the society is fragmented. The reservations were made for Scheduled Castes and Scheduled Tribes with good intentions but now politicians have developed vested interests. The cunning diplomacy of the British, which has fostered casteism, has taken all the more ugly turn in independent India.

According to the Sangh Parivar the only effective remedy for this malady of casteism is Hindu consciousness and a sense of pride in Hinduism. The Dharmacharyas have proclaimed that there is no scriptural basis for this practice. On the other side, the VHP workers tried to remove this feeling of untouchability by proclaiming the oneness of Hindu society by personal contact, conduct and work.

Dharmacharyas have a great influence on the minds of the people. Dharmacharyas belonging to various cults and modes of worship have come together on one platform and have been exhorting people to rise above the differences of caste, creed and cult in the cause of Dharma and Hindu unity. Acharyas, who were confined to Sadhanas for liberation from the transitory and unreal world, are standing by unitedly for the social and national cause. They stood behind the cause of Shri Ram Janmabhumi and gave a lead to mass awakening. This is good sign for the future of the Hindus.

During the British period and subsequently also many Hindus left for foreign lands for livelihood and earning wealth in those countries. However, they were so scattered that they were not organized as Hindus". In the midst of the mundane plenty of the West they are constantly anxious that their Hindu identity should not be lost. They are anxious that their new generations, brought up in an altogether different atmosphere, should not forget that they are Hindus. In response to this urge the VHP must do some thing. Realizing this, the VHP undertook to organize the Hindu brethren abroad and render such services as they require in between protecting and promoting their Dharma, culture and traditions. A glance at the successful conferences of the Parishad recently held in America or Europe or South East Asia would give an idea about the fruitful efforts in this connection. For decades and decades we are being told that the Hindu society is incapable of uniting and many have come to believe this propaganda. But the mass programs under taken by the VHP under the dynamic and dedicated leadership of Ashok Singhal, a front ranking RSS pracharak and Gurujee's blue eyed boy , have proved them wrong.

The Bharatiya Mazdoor Sangh

The dusk of the nineteenth and the dawn of the twentieth century saw an unprecedented upsurge in the labor movement in Europe. The year 1919 saw the birth of the International Labor Organization (ILO). Soon the trade union movement began to be organized in India also. Lala Lajpat Rai organized the first such union and it was named All India Trade Union Congress (AITUC). Trade unionists of almost all political opinions were represented in it. This organization was split in 1947 and a new organization named Indian National Trade Union Congress (INTUC) was born. The socialists further split the INTUC the very next year and organized the Hind Mazdoor Panchayat. The Indian Federation of Labor (IFL) was also organized around the same time. Later the Hind Mazdoor Panchayat and the IFL merged to form the Hind Mazdoor Sabha (HMS). All these labour organizations have continued to break and merge. Some RSS workers under the leadership of the now legendary Dattopant Thengadi who was inspired by Gurujee and enjoyed his full confidence went into this field and organized the Bharatiya Mazdoor Sangh (BMS) in 1955. Today the BMS is the largest trade union organization in India. It effectively checked the tendency of splitting and till this date there has never been any break up in the BMS.

Before the rise of the BMS the labor field was dominated by political unionism. The recognized Central Labor Organizations were the wings of different political parties or groups. This often made workers the pawns in the power-game of different parties. Some conscientious workers were awaiting the advent of a nationalist leadership, based upon genuine trade unionism. The RSS workers who went into the trade union movement naturally provided such leadership. The founding fathers of the BMS believed the trade union to be an organization of the workers, for the workers, and by the workers. They were not only opposed to the concept of political unionism but also refused to accept the Marxian logic of the economic motives being the only determining factors. They termed it as "bread and butter unionism".

The founding fathers of the BMS were votaries of *Rashtra niti* and *Lok niti*. They had full confidence in the ability of our national genius to evolve new social systems and philosophical formulae. They were determined to steer clear of both Capitalism as well as Communism. They were opposed to the crude materialism of West and felt that in the absence of Bharatiya spiritual values, it was impossible to evolve any healthy social structure free from internal dissensions and strife. They had implicit faith in the scientific character and ultimate victory of Bharatiya social order based upon the tenets of integral humanism. They rejected the Class Concept. They stood neither for class-conflict nor for class-collaboration. The class concept - which they believed was a fiction - would ultimately result in the disintegration of the nation. They however, refused to identify national interests with those of the privileged few in the economic, political or any other department of national life as the criterion for determining the level of national life. The criterion for determining the level of national prosperity was, according to them, the living condition of the financially weakest constituent of the nation. To improve the lot of the underdog they would resort to the process of collective bargaining, as far as possible, and to agitate, wherever necessary. Exploitation, injustice and inequality must be put to an end. The ratio between the minimum and the maximum income in the land should be 1:10. For industrial workers, they demanded security of service, need based minimum wage, wage differentials on the basis of job-evaluation, right to bonus as deferred wage, full neutralization of price-rise so as to ensure the real wage, massive industrial housing programs, and integrated social security and welfare schemes.

The factors that set apart an organization as a dynamic, vibrant, outstanding and well-knit force is reflected in how it blends its goals for growth with the myriad needs of its most precious asset - its members and officers, that lends strength to its success ratings. The uniqueness of their ideas did not end there. They sought protection and promotion of workers' interests within the framework of national interests, since they were convinced that there was no incompatibility between the two. Most important of all their ideological position was that they considered society as the third - and more important party to all industrial relations. According to them the consumers' interests are the nearest economic equivalent to national interest.

'The RSS methodology of working on the pattern of a family, naturally entered into the culture of the new organization also. It shows care and concern for the well being of every member in its family. They carried with them a philosophy that prides itself in the welfare of all. BMS is unique among labor organizations that conscientiously cares. Every member in the BMS family has a deep sense of belonging and a pride unmatched, mainly because BMS reaches out to him or her humanely. Little wonder, BMS romped home with a clear majority during the membership verification in 1989 conducted by the Government of India. Without the least opportunity to look back since then it is rising steadily and till now is undisputedly the largest in the country with the confidence of around 76.39 Lakhs (7.639 Millions) workers in it.

The nationalist and patriotic credentials of the BMS were to be tested very soon after its birth. Keeping the Indian leadership engaged in the ruse of *Hindi-Chini Bhai Bhai*, the Chinese launched a full-scale border war against India. At the time of such grim national crisis the Communists played an extremely anti-national role. A major section of the Communists and their leaders like Basavaponnaiah declared that India was the aggressor and had occupied the Chinese territory. They also declared that the Chinese were coming to liberate India. The labor unions affiliated to the Communists decided to support the Chinese attackers. They began to sabotage the Indian defense effort. The water transportation union in the Northeast, which was affiliated to the Communists, served notice for strike. The transport of food and other required material to the army fighting an unequal war was sought to be hampered. It was a testing time for the BMS, which naturally decided to fully support the war effort. The BMS withdrew all agitations that its unions were heading. Similarly, it also put off all the pending demands for the time being. It called upon the workers to give top priority to all the production work, particularly the defense production and for assisting in all defense efforts, BMS also saw to it that the anti-national communal, Trojan horses could do no mischief. It made special efforts in strategically important industries like transport, power generation, transmission and defense production. Even after the Chinese aggression was over the BMS continued to focus on these sectors and in the defense production sector it was able to attain a premier position where it started Bharatiya Prati Raksha Mazdoor Sangh. After the 1962 incident the Communists could never dare to act in a similar anti national manner. Similarly, during the Pakistan war, BMS unions suspended their demands and engaged themselves in repairing runways and donating blood for army men.

At the time of other national calamities also the BMS has never been found wanting in taking initiative just as the workers of other RSS organizations during the era of terrorism in Punjab. The Hindu-Sikh relations were never allowed to be strained by the Sangh workers even though the terrorists had attacked the Shakha also. At several places the BMS organized peace marches and unity conferences. Instead of "workers of the world, unite", the BMS believes in "workers, unite the world". The emphasis of the call is much more positive and the BMS does not believe in class struggle. Its emphasis is on duty rather on the rights. There have been instances where the BMS workers have actually helped the management in troubled times instead of taking advantage of the crisis. Such help by the BMS ensured profits for the Rajasthan Road Transport Corporation, which was going in red for many years due to trade union activities and corruption. It was because of that profit, that the employees could get ten percent bonus-all due to an overall improvement in the financial condition of the corporation.

The BMS has extended the concept of family in the industrial relations also. They consider the interest of the consumers as an essential factor in any agreement between the union and the management. It motivates the workers to perform their duties honestly and also with the assertion of their rights. They believe in *"Desh ke hit mein karenge kaam, kaam ke lenge poore daam"*. (Work we shall in the interest of the nation and also charge full compensation.) Dr. R.B. Patil, a professor of Industrial Relations has noted:

> In some industrial centers, the number of unions affiliated to BMS is far more than the unions affiliated to any other organization. BMS affiliated unions are more positive, reasonable and accommodative. They are interested in the survival of the organization and do not make unreasonable demands. They are more democratic in internal functioning. (Sheshadri, 177).

True to its RSS roots, the BMS from its very inception has believed in non-political trade unionism, something unthinkable for the other trade unions, particularly the Communist trade unions, as all of them are born from various political parties. Initially they ridiculed the very idea of non-political trade unionism. But interestingly, it was the World Federation of Trade Unions-a confederation of the Communist trade unions from all over the world including the Communist world of those days- which endorsed the BMS position in the XII World Trade Union Congress, held in Moscow in 1990. It said: "WFTU bases itself on combative and democratic trade unionism that is genuinely independent of employers, governments, political parties, and religious institutions." (Sheshadri, 178).

During the All India Conference at Dhanbad in 1994, BMS had given the clarion call to all its Karyakartas to be prepared to face the THIRD WORLD WAR AND SECOND WAR OF ECONOMIC INDEPENDENCE unleashed by the developed countries against the developing countries. The emissaries of the developed countries are the multinational companies who look up to India as an ideal market to sell their outdated consumer products & technologies with a view to syphon out the profits to their respective countries. In fact there is concerted effort to even change the tastes and outlook of the average Indian through satellite and junk food channels to suit them. One might recall that the Indians were addicted to tea and coffee by the then British rulers by distributing them free of cost during 1940s. Today, not surprisingly, India is the largest consumer of both the beverages. Now in this decade the soft drinks and potato chips rule the roost. BMS has made it adequately clear that every country that has to develop has to adopt and adapt methods, which suit it, both culturally and economically. Today India needs modernisation and not blind westernisation. BMS publications *Hindu Economics* by Shri M.G. Bokare and *Third Way* by Shri Dattopant Thengdi are eye-openers to the planners of the nation in this direction. Practising SWADESHI is the only remedy to counter this onslaught.

Vanavasi Kalyan Ashram

Vanavasi simply means a forest-dweller. But the use of this term has a complex and long history behind it. The Indian civilization from the beginning has been a Knowledge based civilization. The tradition of Knowledge had already begun when the man was still living in the forests. That is why some of the finest books that the Hindu civilization has given to the humanity were written in the forests. Some are even called *Aranyakas* or the forest books. Since the greatest sages used to live in the forests, living there had no stigma attached to it. On the contrary, it was considered worthy of respect. That is why when the Muslims attacked the Hindu villages and cities, the tormented and the defeated Hindu rulers and armies took shelter in the forests. Many of them could never return to their kingdoms and became one with the forest life and culture. Though tragic, this has been a very significant theme in the medieval freedom struggle of India.

It is significant here to understand that During the Hindu period no social or cultural stigma was ever attached to the life in the forests. But when the foreign rule was established and the *Mlechchhas* termed these Forest dwellers as tribal people, their status was lowered for the first time. They either did not realize or simply chose to ignore that they were dealing with the Kshatriyas, who were forced to abandon their Kingdoms. In reality it was more useful for the missionaries and the officers of the British Government in India to declare them to be the descendents of Shudras and *Antyajas*, who used to live outside the villages and cities due to the necessities of their jobs. On the other hand the Indian tradition linked the ancestry of the vanavaṣis or the forest dwellers to the Kshatriyas, like the Pandavas. Bhima had married Hidimba and Lord Krishna himself had married Rukmani. That is why Barbarika, the grandson of Bhima and son of Ghatotkatchha is still worshipped by the so-called high caste Hindus as the Shyam Baba Khatuwale. Similarly, the right to first worship the Lord Jagannath's new wooden idol every twelve years belongs to the Shabar people, who are vanvasis. Almost every religious tradition among the Hindus has such a component. If Lord Jagannath is a form of Lord Krishna, and thus belongs to Vaishnav tradition, the Shaivism is also full of such traditions. A Santhal named Baiju is supposed to have established the Baijnath Dham, one of the twelve great Jyotirlingas.

The marriage connections with the forest dwellers have continued till the Mughal times as we find the examples of such marriages. Dalpat Shah married Durgawati, the great medieval freedom fighter. The British establishment scholars and missionaries also chose not to ask or answer the question why these so called tribes lived deep in the forests? If they were the descendents of the Shudras and *Antyajas*, they should have been living near their livelihood in rural and urban settlements rather than in deep forests.

Soon after independence, the workers of the RSS took up the challenge of the Christian missionaries who were seeking to take an undue advantage of the poverty of the Vanavasis and convert them into Christianity. That this poverty was a byproduct of the British rule, was never told while an imaginary exploitation by Hindus was always emphasized. Initially even the leftist intellectuals were apprehensive of the missionaries as they considered them to be the agents of the Western imperialism. Only later did they realize that abusing Hindus was much more politically beneficial.

However, the biggest challenge that the foreign missionaries posed, was their activities of conversion, most of which were through either force or allurement of material benefits or even outright deception. The change of religion through such conversions has never been a spiritual exercise for anyone. For the converted it was usually a matter as mundane as keeping the body and soul together and that is why the term "rice Christian" came into being. For the Christian missionary it has always been financial and political gains-meaning patronage from the British in past and now it has come to mean funds from the foreign lands. Besides that, the normal gains of the vote bank politics in the present day political context also play an important role. For the patronizing secular politician it is a matter of consolidated votes and so a political matter. In short the conversion to Christianity, was almost never a spiritual affair.

These factors naturally undermine the nationalist loyalties of the converted Indians. How much de-Indianisation the conversions may lead to, can be seen from this example. The Christian missionaries active in the Jashpur Nagar area were against the freedom struggle purely due to the communal reasons. They believed it to be against the Christians, as the British were Christians. So much so that just after the independence, they provoked the people to show black flags to Pt. Ravishanker Shukla, who was the first Chief Minister of the CP & Berar state of which the area was a part. The great Congress leader was shocked. He understood the necessity of nationalist work among the vanvasis and discussed the matter with Thakkar Bappa, the legendry Gandhian tribal leader. It was in this background that Thakkar Bappa asked an old RSS worker Ramakant Keshav Deshpande, better known as Bala Sahib Deshpande who was practicing as an advocate in Nagpur to come and join his Backward Class Development Scheme. Deshpande was one of the initial swayamsevaks initiated by Dr. Hedgewar himself. Gurujee himself inspired Deshpande to take up the work as a kin to RSS work. The change that came in the Jashpur Nagar area was soon visible. He established one hundred primary and eight middle schools in Jashpur Nagar where he had started his work and that too within the very first year of his work. After the death of Thakkar Bappa Bala Sahib Deshpande established the Vanavasi Kalyan Ashram (VKA) in the year 1952 at an obscure, remote place Jashpur, in the then Madhya Pradesh. Now it is in Chhattisgarh state. The VKA was started with merely nine students. Sh. Moru Bhaiyya Ketkar also joined it from the very beginning. Another person who helped the VKA from the very beginning was the King of Jashpur, Maharaja Vijay Bhooshan Singh Deo. Later Shri Bhimsen Chopra and Krishna Rao Sapre also joined. During the next half a century the work grew silently but effectively. One of the initial patriotic works in which the VKA helped expose the Christian missionaries was providing ground level data to the Bhawani Shankar Niyogi commission. By the 1960s the VKA work had begun to take a definite shape. It was understood early that all the self-respect depends upon respect for the tradition and Dharma. That is why the VKA emphasized on creation of *Ramayana mandalis* and *Bhajan mandalis*. The distribution of copies of the *Ramayana* was taken up as a movement. A large number of temples devoted to Lord Hanuman were also constructed. Some very important sage of the time including Ramabhikshukaji, Swarupanandji, and Prabhudattaji Brahmachari joined in these movements.

A silent revolution had begun in the vanavasi areas in India. It was not before 1963 that the VKA had a house of its own. In that year Sri Guruji and a vanavasi sage called Gahiraguruji inaugurated a new building for the VKA. The 1960s and the early 1970s saw the emergence of a hospital, a girls' hostel and expansion of the work in the new areas of Bihar, Orissa and some regions of central India. The imposition of the Emergency on India by Indira Gandhi led to confiscation of the VKA properties and jailing of the main leaders. The work however, grew at a fast pace after the lifting of the Emergency. The VKA became an all India organization and the first all India convention was held in 1981 in New Delhi. It was truly an all India meet as the representatives from all the states of India were present in the convention. The work also began to diversify soon. The year 1985 saw the first all India convention of women associated with the VKA. One of the most famous projects of the VKA i.e. the Eklavya Sports Project to organize the vanavasi youth through sports began in 1987. Meanwhile special efforts were undertaken in 1993 to promote and protect the rights of the vanavasis. The oldest projects of Dharmajagaran not only continued but were given additional emphasis. Bala Sahib Deshpande continued to guide the organization till his death in 1995.Since then the VKA is headed and guided by Shri Jagadevram Oraon. During the last five and a half decades of its existence the VKA has become the largest single NGO engaged in mission work.

The VKA has now expanded its activities in each and every state of our country. It has earned the proud distinction of operating the highest number of missionary projects (12078 as on 1-3-2006) conducted by any organization in our country. Out of a total of 347 vanavasi districts, the VKA currently operates in 283 districts, covering 9219 places and with dependable, active contacts established in over 39396 villages. In addition, the VKA also operates in all major cities and in many other non-adivasi districts. It proposes to reach each of the remaining vanavasi districts in the next few years. A remarkable feature of this organization is that nearly 45% of their full-time workers come from the vanavasi areas (440 out of 1041). Their remarkable methodology of grooming local leadership is bound to have a snow-balling effect in fulfilling all their ambitious expansion proposals.

The VKA operates in all the missionary areas i.e. Health, Education, social organization, economic development as well as carrying out numerous casual or need-based programs. Since nationalism is the foundation of their mission, the VKA leaders and workers use an Indian vocabulary. Thus, mission is Seva, and a tribal is a Vanvasi and so on. Their major in-puts are in the field of education, development of sports, re-establishing and strengthening the blurred cultural links and weaning the vanavasis away from the evil influence of foreign missionaries, anti-social, and anti-national forces, etc. The impact of the selfless, untiring, all encompassing activities and programs is now becoming manifest in all the places where the VKA operates. The burgeoning demand for opening VKA seva projects, the growing self-reliance of the Vanavasis and financial support from all over the country are indications of favorable impact of the Vanvasi Kalyan Ashram.

The Vivekananda Kendra

Sri Ramakrishna Paramhansa had counselled his great disciple Swami Vivekananda to work for a larger cause than mere personal realization of God. Swami Vivekananda set out as a wandering monk in search of his mission. His search finally led him to the other side of the globe. Just before he embarked upon his voyage to the United States of America, Swamiji went to the very tip of the peninsula of this ancient land called Bharat. This was as if a great son of the Mother India went to touch the feet of the Mother Eternal to seek her blessings before embarking upon what turned out to be the greatest mission not only of his own life, but probably the greatest mission beyond the seven seas, that any Hindu had undertaken during the last many centuries. This is where the Divine Mother, in Her eternal youthful form, seemed to stand in penance. And this is precisely the place the young monk chose for contemplation of the great future of his people. Taking the blessings of the Mother Divine, he swam across to the mighty rock (that now bears his name) as if to have the darshan of the Mother after touching Her feet.

Swami Vivekananda sat on the rock for three days - on 25th, 26th and 27th December 1892 - meditating on India's past, present and future. Sitting on this rock, he discovered the mission, which he unfolded afterwards. He had a vision of rejuvenated India. To explain this vision in the very words of Swamiji: "...One vision I see clear as life before me, that the ancient Mother has awakened once more, sitting on Her throne rejuvenated, more glorious than ever. Proclaim Her to all the world with the voice of peace and benediction." It was here that Swamiji hit upon the plan to shake the Hindu society from its slumber. This vision of Swami Vivekananda was no different from the vision of our ancient sages. In reality he was the modern representative of that ancient lineage of the great sages who are the soul of the greatness of the Mother Divine. When Dr. Hedgewar began the RSS, he started a process by which this eternal vision of the glory of the Mother India began to be converted into action. Vivekananda Rock Memorial stands not only as a witness to that action but also reminds us of our national commitment to realise that vision.

No wonder, decades later when some people were planting a cross on this rock, it did not go unnoticed and finally attracted the attention of the RSS leaders and workers. The place had sanctity of a place of pilgrimage as it had a great potential to inspire to carry on Swamiji's work. Inspired by Shri Gurujee, Sri Eknath Ranade, the then General Secretary of RSS, conceived of a memorial, with the participation of millions of people, to symbolize the glorious mission of India as clearly seen by Swami Vivekananda sitting on the rock decades earlier.

As the Vivekananda Rock Memorial was taking shape,

Eknath Ranade also envisaged a mission that would manifest the idea of "man making and nation-building". The result was the conception and formation of the Vivekananda Kendra as a spiritual and service oriented mission, which reflected Swami Vivekananda's vision of glorious India. The Vivekananda Kendra is an eternal call for those youth who aspire to dedicate their life to serve the nation. It aims at national reconstruction through 'Man Making.' To mould dedicated workers, the Kendra adopts a methodology unique to it by organizing 'Yoga varga' (class), 'Bal-samskar varga', 'Swadhyaya varga' and training camps.

What started as a small stream in 1972, is now a mighty flow. The Kendra has now over 200 dedicated workers, and 205 branch centers spread over 18 States of India to rebuild the nation and serve all strata of the society. To achieve this, Whole-time Workers and the local workers of the Kendra, undertake various service activities like Rural Development, Education in interior tribal and rural areas, Organizing Youth and Women, Development of Natural Resources, and Publications based on the life and Message of Swami Vivekananda. The Kendra has evolved a system of screening selected workers and training them as Whole-time workers with dedication and skill to undertake the great task of National regeneration. The whole-time workers are of three categories. *Jivanavrati* or life workers are the young men and women who join Kendra for life; *Sevavrati* are the ones who join Kendra for specific period of time and *Vanaprasthi* are the ones who join Kendra after their retirement. The Kendra urges all those who aspire to serve the nation to join in this task of national reconstruction. Swami Vivekananda pin-pointed lack of proper education among the masses as the root cause of the malaise in the Society. Kendra has, therefore taken up Education as one of its main service activities. Kendra is running many residential and day-scholar schools in Arunachal Pradesh. It also runs schools in Assam, Andamans, Karnatak and Tamil Nadu. In all 20000 children receive education in the Vivekananda Kendra schools. Besides, the Kendra runs scores of Balwadis and centres imparting pre-primary education to the budding children.

Swami Vivekananda said that a new India would emerge through the awakening of the neglected rural masses. Keeping this in view, Vivekananda Kendra started activities combining service with a cultural thrust in the districts of Kanyakumari, Tirunelveli, Tootukudi, Virudhunagar and Ramanathapuram in Tamil Nadu, Tiruvananthapuram district in Kerala, Chandil in Singhbhum district of Bihar, Tinsukia and Karabi Anglong districts in Assam.

To generate social awareness and cultural renaissance, various programmes like nursery schools with nutrition programmes, youth camps, rural libraries, medicare, cultural classes and competitions, Balasamskar varga and Shiva Poojas and Deepa Poojas for women are being undertaken.

There is indiscriminate exploitation of natural resources. The need of the hour is to conserve and judiciously use our existing resources and also to discover alternate resources. Realising the gravity of the situation, Kendra has also joined in this quest for alternate resources of energy under the name NARDEP. Under this, use of solar powered devices, biogas and other non-conventional resources are being popularised.

The Vivekananda Kendra and NARDEP won the 10,000 pound second prize in the Food Award. The Vivekanand Kendra has been awarded the Ashden Award - an international prize . The award is for making the use of biogas technology yet more appealing to farmers by devising innovative ways of turning the slurry into effective organic fertiliser. VK-Nardep have made a series of advances in biogas designs which generate gas for cooking and have developed effective ways of using the slurry as a powerful fertiliser using a combination of new and traditional techniques.

Vivekananda Kendra took up Medicare which is one of the essential needs of the people but scarcely available in

Northeastern part of country. While running the mobile medical centres, the Kendra realised the need of an hospital. The Kendra founded Vivekananda Kendra Medical and research foundation to manage and run a well-equipped hospital to meet the needs of the people of Northeast, which is being set up at Numaligarh, Assam. The VKMRF also has a plan to set up a hospital at Pullong in Arunachal. Both the hospitals will not only have facilities for patients, but also will function as a referral hospital. The hospitals will have facilities for the other systems of medicines viz. Ayurveda, Yoga therapy, and local medical systems. A research wing to carry out research in all traditional medical systems will also form part of the hospitals.

Since the grand inauguration of the Vivekananda Rock Memorial on 2nd September, 1970 by the then Rashtrapati, V.V. Giri, incessant streams of people from remotest corners of the country and abroad reach the haloed spot situated at the confluence of three great oceans.

The Memorial stands as a light house of hope and confidence for the entire humanity symbolizing the spirit of RSS which also stands for Ready for Selfless Service.

Vasudhaivaktumbakam

That the Hindus were never a sea-faring people and they never ventured out of India, were pet themes for some of the British scholars and their Indian followers. But these anti-India elements were always answered by the impartial scholarship. It is now well established that waves of Indians continued to go abroad at different points of time in the history. Even if the Aryan migration out of India may be a point of debate, the going of the Gypsies from India and later the establishment of the Shailendra empire in the South-East Asia are some of the examples of the Indians going abroad during the historical times. The British also sent Indians abroad in very inhumane conditions. They were called "Girmitiya" laborers, the term being corrupt form of the English word 'agreement' under which they were taken abroad. This was in reality a new system of slavery, which it had replaced due to the recent ban on slavery. But the latest wave of emigration began during the 1960s when a large number of Indians went to the West. Some RSS swayamsevaks were also a part of this wave. They naturally carried with them the samskaras they had imbibed in the Shakha. They also carried with them the great concepts like "*Swadesho Bhuvanatrayam*" (the whole world is my own native land) and "*Udaracharitanamtu Vasudhaivakutumbakam*" (the whole world is a single family for the liberal minded), their mind was shaped by the ideal "*Aa no Bhadra kratavo Yantu Vishwatah*" (Let the noble thoughts flow to us from all sides) and their ideal was "*Krinvanto Vishwamaryam*" (We shall make the world noble minded). Imposing the Hindu culture on others has never been the ideal for any Hindu. All are welcome in it as Hindu is an all-inclusive faith. That is why a clash between the Hindutva and nationality of the adopted country never emerged even if opportunities might have come up in that direction. Sri Guruji had accordingly advised the swayamsevaks settled abroad, thus:

The first thing that our brothers abroad have to bear in mind is that earning and amassing money should not be their sole aim. Some portion of their earning should be kept apart for promoting the welfare and enlightening their local compatriots on the great principles of values of Hindutva. They should also set up personal examples before them through their behavior and living, and demonstrate that they hail from a land of a great and hoary culture. (Sri Guruji quoted by Sheshadri).

The story of the first Shakha outside the sacred land of India is equally interesting. It was in the midst of high sea when two swayamsevaks, unknown to each other but travelling on the same ship to Kenya, came to the deck in a turbulent evening and realized that they were more than mere fellow travellers on the same ship. They embraced each other and recited together the Sangh prayer. That was the first time when the "*Namaste Sada Vatsale Matribhoome*" was sung outside India. It was in September 1946 and on the Makar Sankranti day of the very next year the Bharatiya Swayamsevak Sangh was started in Kenya.

Presently the Hindus are living in sizeable numbers in around 120 countries of the world. The swayamsevaks and their next generations have started their own organizations in many of the countries. These organizations are totally independent in all their activities and are governed by the rules and regulations of the countries in which they operate. They usually have their memberships as well as their services open to people of the host society as well. The core group is provided by some old swayamsevaks. The philosophic basics were determined by the above quoted words of Sri Guruji.

The idea has been internalized even by the next generation of the swayamsevaks who settled in these countries. They believe that Hindutva does not teach extra-territorial loyalties, very much unlike many other religions. That is why the youth of the generation of the Hindus born abroad usually identifies itself as the Hindu nationals of the countries where they were born like American Hindus or British Hindus or South African Hindus etc. Their countries command their loyalties, though they may have special affection for India as their ancestral land. Their organizations run projects and programs for the benefit of their local communities also, even though their Indian projects get more publicity. Bharatiya Swayamsevak Sangh, an organization affiliated to The Hindu Council has partnered with a community organization NDEKA - (Ndakaini Dam Environmental Conservation Association) to plant trees around Ndakaini dam, which is the source of Nairobi's drinking water. Empty areas surrounding the dam will have indigenous trees planted for its safety, aesthetics and sustainability. The commissioning event was held on 25th September 2005 at Ndakaini, which is at the border of Thika and Maragua Districts. Nurturing the trees planted is Total's key role in this undertaking. 30,000 indigenous trees have been planted around the dam.

This is just one of the many success stories that can be narrated regarding the missionary zeal with which the Swayamsevaks have organized themselves under many banners all over the world. It is not possible to recount their heroism in this small monograph. That is why only some representative examples are being described in the following section.

The Hindu Swayamsevak Sangh was registered as a charity, which is the same as a charitable organization in India. The main aim of this organization is to advance the Hindu religion and to educate the public in the Hindu ideals and way of life. It is based in Leicester. The organization had set up a project arm in 1991 known as Sewa International (UK). The purpose of the project arm was to help aged, sick, poor and distressed persons. A major relief work that this organization had undertaken was the help that it gave during the Gujrat Earthquake in 2001.

The anti-Hindu lobby was very jealous of the relief work and began to disseminate negative propaganda against the organization. It spread serious concerns about the Hindu organizations. Following concerns expressed over the administration and expenditure of the appeal, an Inquiry was opened on 4 October 2002. The purpose of the Inquiry was to establish whether the funds raised had been properly applied in accordance with the terms of the appeal. The results of the official inquiry exposed the intentions of the anti-Hindu lobbyists in the UK. The inquiry found that the Sewa International launched the appeal in January 2001 following the earthquake in Gujarat. Primary accounting records supplied by the Charity show that £2,330,000 was banked in the name of the appeal. The HSS was able to produce satisfactory evidence that all the funds raised as a result of the appeal had been sent to an established Indian non-governmental organization known as Sewa Bharati. This organization would utilize the funds towards the rebuilding of six villages in Gujarat. The organization also produced a detailed breakdown of the application of funds by Sewa International (UK) in India. The funds were utilised towards the following projects:

- £1,062,000 for the reconstruction of six villages
- £123,352 for schools project 1
- £1,282,352 for schools project 2
- £118,887 for other projects

The investigation showed that all of the money, US$4.3 million, could be accounted for and that the charges brought by some Indians in the UK that money was being misdirected to radical Hindus, was unfounded. The report states, "The Commission is satisfied that the trustees have taken sufficient steps to ensure funds have been applied in accordance with the appeal."

India Development and Relief Fund is a tax-exempt organization under the U.S. Internal revenue Code Section 501 (c)(3). It aims to support the grassroots and non-government organizations (NGOs) involved in serving the most disadvantaged, impoverished, illiterate, poor and needy people.

Dr. Vinod Prakash, a World Bank economist from 1971-81, founded IDRF in 1978. He received his Ph.D. from MIT. Dr. Prakash, in founding the IDRF, crusaded the non-resident Indians to actively find solution to the problems of poverty, illiteracy, malnutrition and natural disasters facing the Indian masses. As a selfless social worker and a visionary, Dr. Prakash has dedicated his life to the IDRF cause. IDRF, since its modest beginnings, has grown as a non-profit, tax-exempt organization managed entirely by a group of motivated volunteers. IDRF has so far distributed over $800,000 to grassroots and charitable organizations in India. A major concern among the Hindus and their friendly organizations abroad has been that can they be assured that their hard earned money will be properly used for the purpose for which it is intended? This is a very genuine question and the IDRF provides the most satisfactory answer due to its wonderful track record of having very minimal overhead expenses and sending the maximum amount to the intended target NGOs. The IDRF claims that "This is precisely an inherent strength of IDRF and the source of its steady growth. We attach utmost importance to the NGOs' accountability and integrity. We select NGOs with proven track records only. Furthermore, IDRF's President, Dr. Vinod Prakash, has been living in USA for more than 30 years and has been visiting India almost every year. Since his retirement from the World Bank in 1988, he has been volunteering virtually all his time for IDRF."

Friends of India Society International (FISI), founded in January, 1976 strives to bring Indians living abroad onto a common platform to preserve democratic processes, economic interests, human rights and civil liberties of Indians living in and outside India. FISI tries to project a positive image of India and people of Indian origin by educating the media and the general public about the inherent message of Indian culture and civilization; establish and foster close cultural and personal links between Indians abroad, their adopted homeland and India; promote the interests of India and of Indians living abroad; provide an international forum for participation in matters of vital world concerns - especially human rights; provide inputs to the lawmakers of adopted country about India and Indians. FISI now has over 86 chapters all over the world.

The Emergency was a nightmare in the history of independent India.

It was during this period some of the activists of Indian origin living abroad, actually concerned about the demise of democracy in their motherland started the Friends of india Society International (FISI) with chapters in almost all countries where expatriate Indians resided. The news that was censored by the dynastic regime was printed for circulation through "Satyavani", Voice of Truth.

Today, 20 years later, the threat to freedom and liberty does not come so much from a flat of a capricious ruler of Delhi, but from the TERRORIST GUNS, whose bullets are supplied by a terrorist state Pakistan - across the Radcliff line. 300,000 Hindus have lost their basic human rights and are completely cleansed out of their ancestral land in Kashmir. The large minority of Hindu population in Bangladesh are being reduced to destitutes and forced to convert or migrate to neighbouring West Bengal state thru communal terrorism of another fundamentalist state called Bangladesh. All this is well documented by Ms. Taslima Nasreen.

These are but some of the concerns of Friends of India Society. 20 years back "Satyavani" was like a lamp in an enveloping darkness of tyranny. Today, the Friends of India Society International News will be like a transmission wire that connects various energy stations. The power generated and distributed may enlighten all of us to achieve the higher goal of seeing India strong. If the price of liberty is eternal vigilance, FISI is proud to be part of that vigilance. There are at present millions of Indians, as well as, people of Indian origin living in more than a hundred countries outside India. They are thus a truly worldwide community. An estimated 1.25 million people of Indian origin live in the United States alone.

(Shri Atul Rawat, a D.U. and J.N.U. product and winner of Ful bright Scholarship (U.S.A.) in History, is currently in the vanguard of Shiksha Bachao Andolan, under the convenership of renowned educationist Shri Deena Nath Batra.)

13

Dharma Rajya and Rajya Dharma

Deen Dayal Upadhyaya

IN our country, the state was produced as per the social contract theory. Formerly there was no king. Mahabharata describes that in Kritayuga, there was no state or king. Society was sustained and protected mutually by practising *Dharma*.*

Later on, interruption and disorganisation came into existence. Greed and anger dominated. *Dharma* was on the decline and the rule of "might is right" prevailed. The *Rishis* were perturbed over the developments. They all went to Brahma to seek counsel. Brahma gave them a treatise on "Law and the Functions of the State", which he had himself written. At the same time he asked Manu to become the first king. Manu declined saying that a king will have to punish other persons, put them in jail and so on; he was not prepared to commit all these sins. Thereupon Brahma said, "Your actions in the capacity of a king will not constitute sin, as long as they are aimed at securing conditions under which the society can live peacefully and according to *Dharma.* This will be your duty, your *Dharma.* Not only that, but you will also have a share of the *Karma* of your subjects, whereby you will gain *Dharma* considerably if your subjects maintain conduct according to *Dharma*".

---

* न राज्यं न च राजासीत् न च दण्डो न दाण्डिकः ।
धार्मेणैवप्रजाः सर्वाः रक्षन्ति स्म परस्परम् ।।

Although it is not explicitly stated here, I believe that if the society under any king committed sin, a part of that too must automatically go to the account of the king. It is not proper if only good things are shared by the king and not the bad ones; both must be shared in the same proportion. Thus the state came into existence as a contract. *This contract theory can be applied to the state, but not to the nation.* In the West, it was exactly opposite. Society as a nation, according to them, was a contract, but the king claimed divine right and proclaimed himself the sole representative of God. This is wrong. In our country, the king may have been first recognised in antiquity but the society as a nation is considered self-born. The state is only an institution.

An Individual is a Plural Entity

Similarly other institutions, like the state, are created from time to lime as the need is felt. Every individual is a limb of one or more of these institutions. A person is a member of his family as well as his community, he may also be a member of some association of his fellow professionals, if he pursues a profession. Above all, he is a member of the nation and society. If we consider even the larger sphere, he is a member of the whole mankind, and then the entire universe. Truly speaking, an individual is not merely a single entity, but a plural entity. He is a part of not just one, but a member of many institutions. He lives a variety of lives. The most important aspect is that, despite this multiple-personalily, he can and should behave in a way which does not bring different aspects of his life into mutual conflict but which is mutually sustaining, complementary and unifying. This quality is inherent in man.

A person who uses this quality properly becomes happy. On the other hand, one who does not do so reaps unhappiness. Such a person will not have balanced development in life. As an illustration - a man is son of his mother, husband of his wife, brother of his sister and father of his son. A single individual is a father and is also a son. He is a brother and also a husband. He has to maintain all these relations with intelligence, understanding and tact. Where a person fails to do so, there is conflict. If he sides with one party, the other feels wronged. The conflicts between his wife and his sister, his wife and mother, result from his inability to behave properly. Thereupon some of his relations are strained. He is pained because his duties towards his mother and towards his wife clash. When he can resolve this conflict, and fulfil all his obligations properly, it can be said that his development will be integrated.

Society and Individual Not Conflicting

We do not accept the view that there is any permanent inevitable conflict among the multi-dimensional personality of an individual, and different institutions of the society. If a conflict does exist, it is a sign of decadence, perversion and not of nature or culture. The error in western thinking lies in the fact that some people there believe that human progress is a result of this fundamental conflict. Therefore they consider the conflict between the individual and the state as a natural occurrence, and on the same basis they also theorise on the class conflict.

Classes do exist in a society. Here too, there were castes, but we had never accepted conflict between one caste and another as a fundamental concept underlying it. The four Varnas, according to our conception, are thought of as analogous to the different limbs of *Virat-Purusha*. It was suggested that the Brahmins were created from the head of the *Virat-Purusha,* the Kshatriyas from his hands, the Vaishyas from his abdomen and the Sudras from his legs. If we analyse this concept we are faced with the question whether there can arise any conflict among the head, arms, stomach and legs of the same *Virat-Purusha*. If conflict is fundamental, the body cannot be maintained. There cannot be any conflict in the different parts of the same body. On the contrary, "one man" prevails. These limbs are not only complementary to one another, but even further, there is individuality, unity. There is a complete identity of interest, identity of belonging. (The origin of the caste system was on the above basis.) If this idea is not kept alive, the castes, instead of being complementary, can produce conflict. But then this is a distortion. It is not a systematic arrangement. Rather there is a lack of any plan, any arrangement. This is indeed the present condition of our society.

This process of deterioration can set in the various institutions of a society, due to a variety of reasons. If the soul of the society weakens, then all the different limbs of the society will grow feeble and ineffective. Any particular institution may be rendered useless or even harmful. Besides, the need and the usefulness of any particular institution may change with time, place and circumstances. While examining the present state of an institution, at the same time, we ought to think of what it should be like. Mutually complementarity and a sense of unity alone can be the standard of proper conduct. Family, Community, Trade Union, Gram Panchayat, Janapada, State and such other institutions are various limbs of the nation and even of mankind. They are interdependent, mutually complementary. There should be a sense of unity through all of them. For this very reason, there should be a tendency towards mutual accommodation in them, instead of conflict or opposition.

The State is Not Above All

The state is one of the several institutions, an important one, but it is not above all others (सर्वोपरि). One of the major reasons for the problems of the present-day world is that almost everyone thinks of the state to be synonymous with the society. At least in practice, they consider the state as the sole representative of the society. Other institutions have declined in their effectiveness while the state has become dominant to such an extent that all the powers are gradually being centralised in the state.

We had not considered the state to be the sole representative of the nation. Our national life continued uninterruptedly even after the state went in the hands of foreigners. The Persian nation came to an end with their loss of independence. In our country, there were foreign rule now and then in various parts of the country. At some time the Pathans seized the throne of Delhi, and then the Turks, the Mughals, and the British too established their rule. Despite all this, our national life went on, because the state was not its centre. If we had considered state as the centre, we would have been finished as a nation long time ago. In some tales for children it is described that an evil spirit resided in some parrot and to kill the evil spirit one had to kill that parrot. Those nations whose life centred in the state were finished with the end of the state. On the other hand, where state was not believed central to its life, the nation survived inspite of the transfer of political power.

We Remained Indifferent Towards State

This had its bad effects also. The late Dr. Ambedkar had said that our Gram Panchayats were so strong that we neglected the throne of Delhi. We did not remain alert as regards the state, as much as we ought to have done, thinking that nation's life did not depend on the state. We forgot that, though it may not be central, the state is definitely an important institution serving some needs of the nation like a limb of the body. It is possible to pluck a hair without much harm, but along with the hair, if some skin is also removed, and a little further, if the head too is cut off, then there will be great loss for the body. Therefore the body must be protected. Although the various limbs of the body are not absolutely indispensable yet each of them serves an important purpose. From the same standpoint, state, too, should have been deemed important in the life of a nation. There were persons who had paid attention to this aspect. It was for this reason that the great teacher of Shivaji, Samarth Ramdas Swami, directed him to establish his kingdom. *Dharma* wields its own power, *Dharma* is important in life. Shri Ramdas would as well have preached to Shivaji to become a mendicant and spread *Dharma* following his own example. But on the contrary, he inspired Shivaji to extend his rule, because state too is an important institution of the society. However, to consider something important is different from saying that it is supreme (loksZifj). The state is not supreme. The question arises, then, that if the state is not of fundamental importance, what is it that is absolutely important. Let us consider this question.

Dharma Sustains the Society

We shall have to examine the reasons why the state was established. No one will dispute that the state must have some specific aim, some ideal. Then this aim or ideal must be considered of highest importance rather than the state which is created to fulfil this ideal. As a watchman is not deemed greater than the treasure he is supposed to protect, so is the case with the treasurer. The state is brought into existence to protect the nation, and to produce and maintain conditions in which the ideals of the nation can be translated into reality. The ideals of the nation constitute *Chiti,* which is analogous to the soul of an individual. It requires some effort to comprehend *Chiti.* The laws that help manifest and maintain *Chiti* of a Nation are termed *Dharma* of that nation. Hence it is this *'Dharma'* that is supreme. *Dharma* is the repository of the nation's soul. If *Dharma* is destroyed, the nation perishes. Anyone who abandons *Dharma,* betrays the nation.

Dharma is not confined to temples or mosques. Worship of God is only a part of *Dharma. Dharma* is much wider. In the past, temples have served as effective medium to educate people in their *Dharma.* However, just as schools themselves do not constitute knowledge, so also temples do not constitute *Dharma.* A child may attend school regularly and yet may remain uneducated. So also, it is possible that a person may visit temple or mosque without break and yet he may not know his *Dharma.* To attend temple or mosque constitutes a part of religion, sect, creed, but not necessarily *Dharma.* Many misconceptions have originated from faulty English translations, and the one most harmful of them is due to the confusion of *Dharma* with religion.

Dharma and Religion are Different

On the one hand we used the word religion as synonymous with *Dharma* and on the other hand increasing ignorance, neglect of our society and *Dharma* and greater acceptance of European life became the outstanding features of our education. As a result, all the characteristics of a narrow religion, especially as practised in the West, were attributed automatically to the concept of *Dharma* also. Since in the West, injustice, atrocities, were perpetrated, bitter conflicts and battles were fought in the name of religion, all these were *en-bloc* listed on the debit side of *Dharma* also. We felt that in the name of *Dharma* also battles were fought. However, battles of religion and battles for *Dharma* are two different things. Religion means a creed, or a sect; it does not mean *Dharma.* *Dharma* is a very wide concept. It is concerned with all aspects of life. It sustains the society. Even further, it sustains the whole world. That which sustains is *Dharma.*

Principles of Dharma are Eternal and Universal

The fundamental principles of *Dharma* are eternal and universal. Yet, their implementation may differ according to time, place and circumstances. It is a fact that a human being requires food for maintaining his body. However, what a particular person should eat, in how much quantity, at what intervals, all these are decided according to circumstances. It is possible at times that even fasting is advisable. If a typhoid patient is given normal food, the consequences may be disastrous. For such a person, keeping away from food is necessary. Similarly, the principles of *Dharma* have to be adapted to changing times and place.

Rules Constituted on Philosophical Basis are Dharmic

Some rules are temporary and others are valid for longer periods. There are some rules regulating our conduct at meeting. One of the rules is that I speak and you listen to with attention. If in contravention of this rule, we start conversing with one another or addressing the gathering at the same time, then there will be a disorder; our work will not progress; the meeting will not be sustained. It can be said that we have not observed our *Dharma*. Thus it is our *Dharma* that we observe the rules by which the meeting proceeds smoothly. But this rule is applicable only as long as the meeting lasts. If the meeting is over and you do not speak even after reaching home, a different problem will crop up. Your family might have to call in a doctor. It is essential to observe the rules of the home if you reach there. The complete treatise on the rules in general, and their philosophical basis constitute what we mean by *Dharma*. These rules cannot be arbitrary. They should be such as to sustain and further the existence and progress of the entity which they serve. At the same time they should be in agreement with and supplementary to the larger framework of *Dharma* of which they form a part. For instance, when we form a registered society, we have the right to frame the rules and regulations, but these cannot be contradictory to the constitution of the society. The constitution itself cannot violate the Societies Registration Act. The Act has to be within the provision of the Constitution of the country. In other words, the Constitution of the country is a fundamental document which governs the formulation of all acts in the country. In Germany the Constitution is known as the "Basic Law".

Is the Constitution too, not subject to some principles of more fundamental nature? Or is it a product of any arbitrary decisions of the Constituent Assembly? On serious consideration, it will be clear that even the Constitution has to follow certain basic principles of Nature. Constitution is for sustaining the nation. If instead it is instrumental in its deterioration then it must be pronounced improper. It must be amended. The amendment is also not solely dependent on majority opinion. Nowadays the majority is much talked of. Is the majority capable of doing anything and everything? Is the action of the majority always just and proper? No. In the west, the king used to be the sovereign. Thereafter when royalty was deprived of its so-called divine rights, sovereignty was proclaimed to be with the people. Here, in our country neither the kings, nor the people, nor the parliament have had absolute sovereignty. Parliament cannot legislate arbitrarily.

It is said about the British Parliament that it is sovereign and can do anything. They say that "British Parliament can do everything except making a woman a man and *vice versa*". But is it possible for the Parliament to legislate that every Englishman must walk on his head? It is not possible. Can they pass an act that everyone in England must present himself before the local authority once everyday? They cannot. England has no written constitution. They have high regards for their tradition. But their traditions too have undergone change. What is the basis for making changes in their traditions? Whichever tradition proved an obstacle in the progress of England, was discarded. Those which were helpful in the progress were consolidated.

The traditions are respected everywhere, just as in England. We have a written constitution, but even this written constitution cannot go contrary to the traditions of this country. In as much as it does go contrary to our traditions, it is not fulfilling *Dharma.* That constitution which sustains the nation is in tune with *Dharma. Dharma* sustains the nation. Hence we have always given primary importance to *Dharma,* which is considered sovereign. All other entities, institutions or authorities derive their power from *Dharma* and are subordinate to it.

Fundamental Error of Our Constitution

If we examine our Constitution from the point of view of the growth of the nation, we find that our Constitution needs amendment. We are one nation, one society. That is why we did not entertain any special rights on the basis of language, province, caste, religion, etc., but gave everyone equal citizenship. There are separate States. Yet there is no separate citizenship of State and of Union. We are all citizens of Bharat. By the same token, we have denied the right to secede to individual State. Not only that, the power to demarcate the boundaries of States and to choose their names is vested in the Parliament, and not in the Assemblies. This is as it should be in tune with the nationalism and tradition of Bharat. However, despite all this, we made our Constitution *Federal,* whereby what we have adopted in practice, we have rejected in principle. In a federation, the constituent units have their own sovereignty. They voluntarily relinquish their sovereignty to the federation by an agreement. It may be that they surrender all their rights and thereby the Centre acquires sovereignty. But these powers are given to the Union. It has no power of its own. Thus the federal constitution considers the individual States as fundamental powers, and the Centre as merely a federation of States. This is contrary to the truth. It runs counter to the unity and indivisibility of Bharat. There is no recognition of the idea of Bharatmata, our sacred motherland, as enshrined in the hearts of our people. According to the first para of the Constitution "India that is Bharat will be a Federation of States", *i.e.* Bihar Mata, Banga Mata, Punjab Mata, Kannada Mata, Tamil Mata, all are put together to make Bharatmata. This is ridiculous. We have thought of the provinces as limbs of Bharatmata and not as individual mothers. Therefore our Constitution should be Unitary instead of Federal

Unitary State

A Unitary State does not mean concentration of all powers in the Centre, just as the head of the family does not have all the powers with him even though all the transactions are carried out in his name. Others also share the executive powers. In our body also, does the soul possess all powers? Thus a Unitary State does not mean a highly autocratic centre nor does it entail the elimination of provinces. The provinces will have various executive powers. Even the various entities below the provincial level, such as the Janapadas, will also have suitable powers. The Panchayats too should have powers. Traditionally, the Panchayats had a very important position. Nobody could dissolve Panchayats. (Today, however, our Constitution does not have any place for these Panchayats). There are no powers to these Panchayats in their own right. They exist at the mercy of the states only as delegated authorities. It is necessary that their powers be considered fundamental. In this way, the decentralization of power will be accomplished. The authority will be distributed to the lowest level, and will be fully decentralized. At the same time all those entities of power will be centred around the Unitary State. This arrangement will embody *Dharma.*

Entire Mankind Included in the Concept of Dharma

If we carry this concept of *Dharma* even further, not only the State and the Nation, but the nature of the entire Mankind will have to be considered. In other words, the constitution of a nation cannot be contrary to the natural laws. There are a number of norms of behaviour which are not found in any statute book, yet they do exist. At times they are even stronger and more binding than any statutory law. The precept that one should respect one's parents is not written in any law. The present day governments which are turning out variety of laws, day in and day out, have not passed a law to this effect. Still, people respect their parents. Those who do not, are criticized. If tomorrow there arises a discussion, even in a court, it will be generally accepted that as long as a person does not attain majority, he should accept his parent's decisions.

Dharma: Standard for Deciding Propriety

Thus the fundamental law of human nature is the standard for deciding the propriety of behaviour in various situations. We have termed these very laws as 'Dharma'. The nearest equivalent English term for *Dharma* can be "Innate law", which, however, does not express the full meaning of *Dharma.* Since *'Dharma'* is supreme, our ideal of the State has been "*Dharma Rajya*". The king is supposed to protect *Dharma.* In olden times at the coronation ceremony the king used to recite three times - "There is no authority which can punish me". (Similar claim was made by kings in the western countries, *i.e.,* it was said, "King can do no wrong", and hence there too, nobody could punish the king). Upon this, the *Purohit* used to strike the king on his back with a staff saying, "No, you are subject to the rule of *Dharma.* You are not sovereign." The king used to run around the sacred fire and the *Purohit* would follow him striking him with the staff. Thus after completing three rounds, the ceremony would come to an end. Thereby the king was unambiguously told that he was not an unpunishable sovereign. *Dharma* was above him. That is, even he was subject to *Dharma.*

Can the people do whatever they please? It may be contended that democracy means just that. The people can do what they please. But in our country, even if people wish, they are not free to act contrary to *Dharma.* Once a priest was asked: "If God is omnipotent, can he act contrary to *Dharma*! If He cannot. He is not omnipotent." This was a dilemma. Can God practise *adharma* or is He not omnipotent? Actually God cannot act contrary to *Dharma.* If he does, then he is not omnipotent. *Adharma* is a characteristic of weakness, not of strength. If fire, instead of emitting heat, dies out, it is no longer strong. Strength lies not in unrestrained behaviour, but in well-regulated action. Therefore, God who is omnipotent is also self-regulated and consequently fully in tune with *Dharma.* God descends in human body to destroy *adharma* and re-establish *Dharma,* not to act on passing whims and fancies. Hence even God who can do every thing cannot act contrary to *Dharma.* But, at the risk of being misunderstood, one can say that *Dharma* is even greater than God. The universe is sustained because He acts according to *Dharma.* The king was supposed to be a symbol of Vishnu, in as much as he was the chief protector of *Dharma Rajya.*

Dharma Rajya not a Theocratic State

Dharma Rajya does not mean a theocratic State. Let us be very clear on this point. Where a particular sect and its prophet or *guru* rule supreme, that is a theocratic State. All the rights are enjoyed by the followers of this particular sect.

Others either cannot live in that country or at best enjoy a slave-like, secondary-citizen's status. Holy Roman Empire had this basis. The same concept was existing behind "Khilafat". The Muslim kings world over used to rule in the name of Khalifa. After the First World War, this came to an end. Now efforts are afoot to revive it. Pakistan is the most recent theocratic State. They call themselves an Islamic State. There, apart from Muslims, all the rest are second-class citizens. Apart from this difference there is no other sign of Islam in Pakistan's administration. The *Quran. Masjid, Roza. Id. Namaz* etc., are the same both in Bharat as well as in Pakistan. There is no need to tie-up state and religion. By such a tie-up, there is no increase in an individual's capacity to worship God. The only result is that the State deviates from its duty. This does not happen in a *Dharma Rajya.* Rather there is freedom to worship according to one's own religion. In a theocratic State one religion has all the rights and advantages, and there are direct or indirect restrictions on all other religions. *Dharma Rajya* accepts the importance of religion for peace, happiness and progress of an individual. Therefore the State has the responsibility to maintain an atmosphere in which every individual can follow the religion of his choice and live in peace. The freedom to follow one's own religion necessarily requires tolerance for other religions. We know that every kind of freedom has its inherent limits. I have the freedom to swing my hand, but as soon as there is a conflict between my hand and someone else's nose, my freedom has to be restricted. I have no freedom to swing my hand so as to hit another person's nose. Where other person's freedom is likely to be encroached upon, my freedom ends. The freedom of both parties has to be ensured. Similarly, every religion has the freedom to exist. But this freedom extends only as far as it does not encroach upon the religion of others. If such encroachment is carried on, it will have to be condemned as misuse of freedom and will have to be ended. Such limitations will be required in all aspects of life. *Dharma Rajya* ensures religious freedom, and is not a theocratic State.

Secular State ?

Nowadays the word "Secular State" is being used as opposed to a theocratic state. The adoption of this word is a mere imitation of the western thought-pattern. We had no need to import it. We called it a secular state to contrast it with Pakistan. There is some misunderstanding arising out of this. Religion was equated with *Dharma,* and then secular state was meant to be a state without *Dharma.* Some said, ours is a निधर्मी state (without *Dharma),* whereas others trying to find a better sounding word called it धर्मनिरपेक्ष (indifferent to *Dharma)* State. But all these words are fundamentally erroneous. For, a state can neither be without *Dharma* nor can it be indifferent to *Dharma,* just as fire cannot be without heat. If fire loses heat, it does not remain fire any longer. State which exists fundamentally to maintain *Dharma,* to maintain law and order, can neither be निधर्मी nor धर्मनिरपेक्ष. If it is निधर्मी, it will be a lawless state, and where there is lawlessness, where is the question of the existence of any state? In other words, the concepts of धर्मनिरपेक्षता, (attitude of indifference towards *Dharma)* and state are self-contradictory. State can only be a धर्मराज्य (rule of *Dharma),* and nothing else. Any other definition will go against the very *raison d'etre* of the state.

State : Absolutely Powerful ?

In a *Dharma Rajya,* the state is not absolutely powerful. It is subject to *Dharma.* We have always vested sovereignty in *Dharma.* Presently there has arisen a controversy. Whether the Parliament is sovereign or the Supreme Court, and whether the Legislature is higher or the Judiciary. This is like a quarrel as to whether left hand is more important or right hand? Both are the limbs of the state, the Legislature as well as Judiciary. Both have distinct functions to perform. In their individual sphere each is supreme. To consider either one above the other would be a mistake. Yet the legislators say, "We are higher". On the other hand, members of the Judiciary assert that they have a higher authority, since they interpret the laws which the Legislature makes. The Legislature claims to have given powers to the Judiciary. If necessary, Legislature can change the Constitution. Hence it claims sovereignty. Now since powers are bestowed by the Constitution, they are talking of amendments to the Constitution. But I believe that even if by a majority the Constitution is amended, it will be against *Dharma.* In reality, both the Legislature and the Judiciary are on an equal plane. Neither the Legislature is higher nor the Judiciary. *Dharma* is higher than both. The Legislature will have to act according to *Dharma* and the Judiciary too will have to act according to *Dharma. Dharma* will specify limits of both. The Legislature, the Judiciary or the people, none of these is supreme.

Some will say "Why! People are sovereign. They elect". But even the people are not sovereign because people too have no right to act against *Dharma.* If an elected government allows people to go against *Dharma* and does not punish, then that government is in reality a government of thieves. Even the *general* Will cannot go against *Dharma.* Imagine what will be the situation if, by some manoeuvring, thieves gain a majority in the government and send one from their ranks as the head of executive. What will be the duty of the minority, if the majority is of thieves and elects a thief to rule? The duty clearly will be to remove the representative elected by the majority.

During the Second World War when Hitler attacked France, the French army could not stall the onward march of Nazi troops. The then Prime Minister of France, Marshall Petain, decided to surrender. The French public supported the decision, but De Gaulle escaped to London where he declared that he did not accept the surrender. France is independent and will remain so. From London, he formed a Government of France in exile and eventually liberated France. Now if the majority rule is to be considered supreme, then De Gaulle's action will have to be condemned. He had no right to fight in the name of independence. De Gaulle derived his right from the fact that the French nation was above the majority public opinion. The national *Dharma* is above all. Independence is *Dharma* of every nation. It is the duty of every citizen to preserve independence, and to strive for regaining it, when it is lost. Even in our country a majority had not risen against the Britishers; only a few had. Some revolutionaries sprang up, some brave people stood and fought. The Lokmanya declared: "Freedom is *my* Birthright". He did not declare this birthright with the support of a majority or a referendum of the people. Nowadays people advocate that the merger of Goa should be decided by referendum, that there should be a plebiscite in Kashmir etc., etc. This is wrong, National unity is our *Dharma.* A decision concerning this cannot be made by plebiscite. This type of a decision has already been taken by the nature. Elections and majority can decide as to who will form the government. The truth cannot be decided by the majority. What the government will do, will be decided by *Dharma.*

Challenge to the Majority

We all know that in the USA, where Americans swear by democracy, Lincoln did not accept wrong public opinion on the question of the abolition of slavery. When the Southern states declared their intention to secede, Lincoln stood firm and told them: "You have no right to secede even in a democracy". He fought against this and did not allow them to secede. Nor did he tolerate slavery. He did not show readiness for a compromise whereby there might continue partial slavery to accommodate Southern states. He did not favour the policy of compromise. He categorically declared that the system of slavery was against tradition, the *Dharma,* the principles which were at the basis of American nation. Therefore the system of slavery had to be abolished. When the Southerners decided to secede, he told them "You cannot secede." On this point there was a civil war and Lincoln did not compromise with *adharma.*

Here in our country the situation in this regard is very much like the old Hindu marriages where a married couple could not divorce even if both the parties wished. The principle was that their behaviour should be regulated not by their sweet will but by *Dharma*. The same is the ease with the nation. If the four million people of Kashmir say that they want to secede, if the people of Goa say - they want to secede - some say they want the Portuguese to return - all this is against *Dharma*. Of the 45 million people of India, even if 449,999,999 opt for something which is against *Dharma*, this does not become truth. On the other hand, even if one person stands for something which is according to *Dharma*, that constitutes truth because truth resides with *Dharma*. It is the duty of this one person that he tread the path of truth and change people. It is from this basis that a person derives the right to proceed according to *Dharma*.

Real Definition of Democracy

Let us understand very clearly that *Dharma* is not necessarily with the majority or with the people. *Dharma* is eternal. Therefore, it is not enough to say, while defining democracy, that it is the government of the people. It has to be a government for the good of the people. What constitutes the good of the people? It is *Dharma* alone which can decide. Therefore, democratic government *Jana Rajya*, must also be rooted in *Dharma i.e.* a *Dharma Rajya*. In the definition of Democracy *viz.* "government of the people, by the people and for the people", 'of' stands for independence, 'by' stands for democracy, and 'for' indicates *Dharma*.

Therefore the true democracy is only where there is freedom as well as *Dharma*. धर्मराज्य encompasses all these concepts.

(One of the foremost builders of erstwhile Bharatiya-Jan-Sangh, late Shri Deen Dayal Upadhyaya was not only an outstanding R.S.S. pracharak and Gurujee's most trusted lieutenant but also an acknowledged socio-political Philosopher. The present article has been excerpted from Shri Upadhyaya's magnum-opus - Integral Humanism - for obvious reasons and relevance.)

14

Western Model Has Failed: We Have The Better Alternative

D.B. Thengdi

IN their sub-conscious minds Hindus have always felt that human misery anywhere constitutes a threat to human happiness everywhere. We in this country have instinctively realised that 'the cultural wealth to which we are natural heirs belongs to the whole humanity, that it is India's obligation to offer to others the benefits of her unique culture and "to accept from others their best'.

Indians: Temperamentally Internationalists

We have never been isolationists. Even in the recent past Bharat has sent abroad its saints, scholars, soldiers, scientists, technocrats, artists, artisans, professionals, traders, industrialists, and labourers who have been working conscientiously with the same end in view, - as our unofficial cultural ambassadors. Temperamentally, we are internationalists. For us, there is no incompatibility between nationalism and internationalism. In the onward march of human consciousness, nationalism is a bridge between tribalism and humanism which, in its turn, is a long step ahead in the direction of universalism.

Presumption of Intellectuals

Our intellectuals are enamoured of Westernism. For them,

everything Western is standard, everything Hindu sub-standard. For them, Shakespeare is not a Kalidas of Great Britain, nor Napoleon a Samudragupta of Europe, but Sardar Patel is Bismarck of India. 'Geeta' must be a great book, because Emerson said so.

Who is singing glory of the golden period of Hindu history under the Guptas, or under the Shailendra empire in South-East Asia which Stood as a powerful bulwark against Chinese expansion for seven centuries? These are all idle gossips, - cock-and-bull stories. It was the Europeans and not the Hindus who reached American shores first. All talk about the advance .of Hindu sciences in the past must be non-sensical; how can sciences flourish on the eastern side of Ural? History was standing still till the inauguration of European Renaissance. Sanskrit is a dead language, Latin the source of all knowledge. The Western Theories regarding Aryan race, - the original inhabitants of India, and chronological order of Indian history, may be purely hypothetical; but none can challenge their veracity, since they are proclaimed by western scholars. It is fantastic to claim that the insight furnished by Patanjali is superior to the combined wisdom of Freud, Jung and Adler.

It is inconceivable that as a social philosopher Samartha Ramdas was far ahead of his European contemporaries, such as, Hobbes, Locke, Descartes, Liebnitz and Spinoza. For all maladies, remedies can be provided only by the West. For solutions of our socio-economic or political problems, our intellectuals rush to seek help from western theories. They have nothing to learn from their own culture; they can no longer depend upon the brilliance of their own intellect.

They may accept that Marx as well as Adam Smith, J.S. Mill, Ricardo and Malthus have become outdated. They may be skeptic about the relevance of Alfred Marshall, Wickell, Gunnar Myrdal and Keynes to the present day conditions. But they will stubbornly refuse to conduct independent thinking in the light of their own national requirements. Instead, they will feel homely with the five stages of

Economic Growth enunciated by Prof. Rostow and get busy in discussing whether we have reached his third 'take-off stage' so as to pass over to his fourth "drive to maturity" leading to the stage of 'High Mass-Consumption'.

"The Letter Killeth..."

"If you want to talk with me", said Voltaire, "define your terms". For any meaningful dialogue, this is essential, particularly when the topic under discussion is technical and the people are in the habit of using words in a rather loose sense. For correct thinking it is necessary to free oneself from tyranny of popular words which are often used in a loose manner. The havoc played by wrong translation of the term 'religion' into Indian languages as 'Dharma' is a glaring example of this fact. 'Communism' is translated as 'Samya-Vada', though there is no 'commune' in 'Samya-vada' and no 'samya' in 'Communism'. The translations of the terms 'Astik' and 'Nastik' as 'theist' and 'atheist' are also in the same category; these Sanskrit terms denote believer or non-believer in the Shrutis and Smritis,-they are not connected with belief or non-belief in God. The erroneous translation of the words 'maya' and 'mithya' as 'illusion' is yet another familiar example of this type. In course of time we are bound to realise that the translation of 'Hindutwa' as 'Hinduism' would render great disservice to the cause of 'Hindutwa' the correct English equivalent of which is 'Hinduness'.

The word 'secular' as being used in India today is yet another instance. 'Secular' means "something concerned with the affairs of this world, worldly, not sacred, not monastic, not ecclesiastical, temporal, profane, lay." The Encyclopaedia of Social Sciences states: "Secularism in the philosophical sphere may be interpreted as revolt against theological and eventually against metaphysical absolutes and universals. In the political sphere, it came to mean that a temporal ruler was entitled to exercise power in his own right." In other words it conveys a principle enunciated by Jesus: 'Give to God what is God's and to Caesar what is Caesar's.' Thus, what Pandit Nehru wanted to convey through the use of the term 'secular' was something different from what is generally understood by that term all over the world. The nearest equivalent of the Nehruvian concept of 'secular State' would probably be 'non-denominational State', though I am mentioning this word for want of any other more exact term. "The letter Killeth", remarked Jesus, and any public debate on technical subject is bound to result in confusion worst confounded, if the main terms used therein are not precisely defined.

Can we define 'Modernisation'?

'Modern' means 'of the present and recent times' or 'characteristic of present or recent time'. To non-European countries, therefore, 'Modernisation' should simply mean 'equipment to solve the problems and meet the challenges of modern times, with a view to ensure all-round progress in future.' And now, what is 'Westernisation'? Broadly, it means 'making oriental people or country to adopt ideas, ideals, institutions, systems, structures, living standards and values of life, of the West.'

Western or Eastern !

Can any one specify whether the following items are Western or Eastern?

1. The well-known theorem of Pythagorus who was described by King Clement of Alexandria as "the pupil of a Brahmin (Boudhayan)".
2. The atomic theory of the West which was anticipated thousands of years ago by परमाणुवाद of Kanaad (कणाद).
3. Dialecticism of Hegel and Marx,-which was flirst envisaged and systematised by Kapil Muni (कपिल मुनि).
4. The fact that it is the Earth which moves round the Sun, and not the Sun around the Earth,-which was proved by Copernicus, and, more than one thousand years before Copernicus, by Arya Bhatta.
5. 'Materialism of Democratus, - of which the first ever Sutra was written by Brihaspati (बृहस्पति) centuries back (असतो सत् अतायत) (out of non-existence emerged existence).

6. Scientific concepts of Space and Time explained by Einstein and enunciated first by Vedanta Philosophers.
7. The scientific definition of 'Matter' given for the first time to modern science by Heisenberg and to Hindus by Patanjali (पतंजलि).
8. The Relativity of Time and Space, the unity of the universe, a Space-Time Continuum, etc. established in ancient times by Vedic thinkers and proved in this century by Einstein.
9. The process of scientific philosophical thinking initiated by Parameshti (परमेष्ठि) of Nasadiya (नासदीय) and climaxed by Einstein.

As H.G. Chernyshevsky observed, "the principles explained and proved by the present day sciences were already found and taken to be true by the Greek philosophers,-and much earlier-by the Indian thinkers."

All Knowledge Universal

True the advance of the West in this direction commenced after the European Renaissance, and during this entire intervening period we could not register normal rate of progress for the simple reason that we were throughout engaged in the life-and-death struggle on a national plane; but it is an indisputable fact that Hindu Sciences and Hindu Arts had migrated to Greece, via Arabia and Persia, before the European Renaissance, which was preceded by the Dark Age of Europe. Newton once remarked, "If I have been able to see further than others, it was because I stood on the shoulders of giants." During Renaissance, entire intelligentsia of Europe stood on the shoulders of Hindu giants. It is, therefore, unrealistic to describe any knowledge as 'Western' or 'Eastern'; it is all universal.

Nor would it be realistic to describe the difference between the East and the West as that between belief and disbelief or theism and atheism, - though it is true that the West is predominently materialistic. The theists in Bharat have no quarrel with the atheists of the West because the

God the latter condemn is different from the God the former worship. Theirs is a Personal God, ours impersonal, without any name or form.

On the contrary, after the declaration by materialist philosophy that consciousness is the highest development of matter, and particularly with the advance of modern science, the line of demarcation between the material and the non-material is becoming thinner and thinner, and is now almost vanishing. "The New Soviet Psychic Discoveries" by Henry Gris and William Dick also indicates the same fact. Instincts, impulses, urges, intelligence, sentiments, emotions, - even intuitions,-all these are essentially 'human'; they cannot be branded as 'Western' or 'Eastern'.

Cultures - Different

Though human mind everywhere is essentially the same, it would be unrealistic to deny the fact that different societies have gone in the past through different situations and different historical courses of events, and these latter have left deep impact on collective mind of every society. Geography and History are main factors responsible for such differentiation. For example, regarding India, Vincent Smith says, "India, circled as she is by seas and mountains, is indisputably a geographical unit and as such rightly designated by one name. The type of civilization too has many features which differentiate it from all other regions of the world; while they are common to whole country in a degree sufficient to justify its treatment as a unit in the history of the social, religious and intellectual development of mankind."

The word 'culture' denotes a trend of impressions on the mind of a society which is peculiar to its own, and which, again, is the cumulative effect of its passion, emotion, thought, speech and action throughout its history. This trend of impressions cannot be the same in case of socities, say in Arabian deserts and Gangetic plains, in Germany which is a camp in the open field and Italy or isolated Great Britain, in young America or ancient India.

Special Characteristics

The modern West also has certain special characteristics of its own. For example, being predominantly materialistic, it has evolved a value system with consumerism as its pivot and permissiveness its natural corollary. Being still under the influence of Newtonian science, the West clings to the myth that mind is only a super-structure on matter, which is basic. Socio-economic structure is, therefore, basic, deserving our exclusive attention. The religion, culture, ethics, literature, arts, etc., all these constitute mere superstructure which will automatically undergo appropriate corresponding changes, once the socio-economic order is altered suitably. Mind need not be specially attended to, 'samskars' are a superfluity. The exclusive concern of all the modern Western thought-system is the appropriate socio-economic transformation; they have no time to indulge in the subject of psychological transformation which will, they are convinced, take care of itself after the inauguration of new social order.

Homocentricism is yet another special characteristic of the West. Humanism is no doubt preferable to self-centred individualism. Protagoras declared, "Man is the measure of everything". Marx observed, "Man is the root of mankind". Homocentricism is expressed in the realistic manner when character in Maxim Gorky's play 'The Lower Deptho' declares: "All Things are part of man; all Things are for man". "Man-that is the truth". Exploitation of man by a man cannot be tolerated; but exploitation of non-human beings by human beings can even be encouraged. Recently, we formulated universal charter of human rights; but non-human beings are entitled to no rights. They say that 'culture' is what we are and 'civilization' what we have.

Western Humanism-Not Adequately Humane

Because of its characteristic values of life, even humanism of the West could not be adequately humane. Firstly, it has been anti-God and homocentric. And, secondly, it could not generate an environment conducive to the growth of human harmony. Mr. John Kleinig has rightly remarked: "Unless there is love, care and concern for others as individuals, in addition to the recognition of rights, there remains a moral lack in international relationships. There is something morally inadequate in doing something for another because it is the other's due. Actions motivated simply by the rights of others remain anonymous or impersonal, whereas if motivated by love, care or concern for the other, their focus is on the other's particularity. Only relations of the latter kind are morally adequate. They are person-specific, whereas rights are species-specific." Exclusive emphasis on 'rights' is one of the peculiar characteristics of the Western value-system.

The Fragmentary Approach

Again, the thinking of the West has always been compartmentalised, its approach fragmentary. (It was only during the second world war that Western scientists began to appreciate the utility of inter-disciplinary approach). They fail to understand inter-relatedness and inter-dependence of all phenomena. In this globally interconnected world - physical, biological, psychological, social, political, economic, cultural or environmental phenomena are all inter-dependent. Problems confronting mankind are many and varied; but these are all different facets of a single crisis. Indiscriminate addiction to "growth" without first defining the growth concept with reference to and in the light of other varieties of growth, has rendered all Western schools of economics unrealistic and irrelevant. These economists must have received a jolt when Schumacker illustrated the value-dependence of economics by comparing two economic systems embodying entirely different values and goals. One is the Western materialist system, in which the "Standard of living" is measured by the amount of annual consumption and which therefore tries to achieve the maximum consumption along with an optimal patttern of production. The other is a system of Buddhist (Indian) economics, based on the notions of "right livelihood" and the "Middle Path", in which the object is to achieve a maximum of human well-being with an optimal pattern of consumption. While the West could conceive of the indices of different material factors, will it be able to think of indices of human happiness and other social or psychological factors?

Gurudev Tagore, who once remarked that "it is idle mendicancy to discard our own and beg for the foreign", while, at the same time "it is the abjectness of poverty to dwarf ourselves by rejecting the foreign", condemned India's imitation of the West. Imitation, he says, is "like dressing our skeleton with another man's skin, giving rise to eternal feuds between the skin and the bones at every moment." This would be impracticable as well as intolerable.

The moment one expresses such views one is condemned by the interested parties as a status-quoist. It is not realised that most of our social reformers were staunch patriots - not at all inclined to get Westernised. There can be progressivism without aping the West. These are two different processes, though sometimes slightly overlapping.

When the term 'Westernism' is used, what is meant is Western cultures and Western paradigm. And when we talk of 'Modernisation' with, or without, Westernisation, we are in fact raising a question whether Western paradigm should be accepted as a universal model of progress and development.

History might pattern itself on the past, but is there any reason that it should pattern itself on the Western past? Even for the purposes of a more wholesome science, would it not be best to set no limits to the social and Sociological imaginations?

The Relevance

As Dr Radhakrishnan put it, "The aim of India has been to realise the one amongst the many, not by effacing the differences, but by retaining the differences and uniting them all. To perceive the one amongst the many, to forge unity in variety, has been its-fundamental purpose."

Being accustomed to visualising unity in the midst of

diversity, Hindus are adept in adapting new ideas and structures from any quarter, and assimilating them in their body politic. They had realised that continual self-renewal is the price of glorious survival. In the light of the unchanging Universal Laws, they had, till before eleven centuries, an ever-changing social order. Through different Smritis composed by moral leaders, old order changed from time to time, yielding place to the new, through a process of synthesis. Their catholicity ensured peaceful co-existence of different systems. Even Valentine Chirol said that Hinduism always remained singularly fluid and that it "lends itself to the most divergent schools of thought, sometimes verging on pure theism and sometimes drifting into absolute atheism, but more often resolving themselves into universal pantheism". This characteristic inspired Max Mueller to say, "If I were asked under what sky the human mind has most fully developed its choicest gifts, most fully pondered on the greatest problems of life and has found solutions of some of them, which deserve the attention of even those who have studied Plato and Kant, 1 should point to India. If I were to ask myself from what literature we, in Europe, may draw corrective which is most wanted in order to make our life more perfect; more universal, in fact, truely human, again I should point to India".

In the past, we have always enriched and strengthened our cultural identity and national personality, by adapting and assimilating whatever good was found in foreign cultures, structures and systems. But every time, it was a process of assimilation.

In India, the Macaulian campaign succeeded in selling to Hindu intellectuals the idea of 'white-man's-burden', in creating inferiority complex in their minds, and in convincing them that the European civilization is the only standard, ideal civilization. Every society or people in the world, we were told, has necessarily and inevitably to pass through the same stages of evolution which are characteristic of European history. Every Indian situation must be gauged by

European standards, - there is no escape from this. For, we were told, Western paradigm is the universal model of progress and development.

Growing Scepticism

Now, whether western paradigm can help Westerners in achieving their cherished goals, is itself doubtful. There is growing scepticism in the West about the efficacy of its paradigm. The dazzling advance of science and technology, they are now realising, is not exactly an unmixed blessing. The rape of nature, with no consideration for either ecological factors or the fate of the future generations, is already becoming a boomerang. The technological development, unaccompanied by commensurate cultural elevation is likely, they apprehend, to lead mankind to its total annihilation.

They have no doubt taken due cognisance of all the maladies their societies are suffering from. The chronic and degenerative "diseases of civilisation", such as, heart-disease, blood-pressure, cancer, STD, etc; severe depression, schizophrenia and other psychiatric disorders; rise in violent crimes, suicides, accidents, alcoholism, and drug addiction; rapid depletion of energy and natural resources, such as, coal, petroleum, natural gas, metals, forests, fish-reserves, oxygen, ozone, etc; a severe degradation of the natural environment affecting not only humans but also plants, animals, ecological systems and global climate, resulting in 'a nebulous veil of air-pollution' encircling the entire planet; high rate of inflation, massive unemployment and maldistribution of wealth; stock piling of tens of thousands of nuclear weapons, costing the world over one billion dollars a day.

Wrong Values

Everything in the West is only in an experimental stage, and not yet tested by time. We rushed to appreciate and applaud their values of life based upon materialism, consumerism (if not exactly hedonism), homo-centricism, and unalloyed individualism. Now it is being realised that these are precisely the values that are responsible for disintegration and disorganisation of individual, family and social life in the United States which is full of large crowds of solitary, self-alienated individuals. Their systems are showing signs of decay and decline." The failure of the Western parliamentary democracy is obvious. Alexander Solzhenitsyn has rightly remarked that 'the Western democracies to-day are in a state of political crisis and spiritual confusion'.

In our country, Mahatma Gandhi, Shri Guruji, Acharya Vinobaji, Lok Nayak Jayaprakashji and other great thinkers have already expressed their skepticism about this Western system. It is difficult' to point out where and in which manner Socialism has succeeded in the West. As C.E.M Joad observed, Socialism is a hat that has lost its shape because everyone wears it. Even in the cradle of Western parliamentary democracy and trade unionism, Socialism has already lost its glamour and grip on public mind. Again, according to Scientific Socialists, Socialism is irrelevant in case of third world countries since economic abundance is an essential pre-requisite for Socialism. In 'The German Ideology' Marx wrote that the high "development of productive forces is absolutely necessary as a practical premise" (for Socialism). And in a country with the highest economic abundance, i.e. the United States, the total number of Socialists does not exceed 10,000 to-day.

Communism, which presented itself as the better alternative, has also failed miserably though the house that has taken a century and a half to come up, will take some more time to demolish itself completely.

A Search

A few, but saner elements in the West are already in search of a new path, a new value-system, a new culture, a new paradigm. The goal or objective that has failed the West, cannot be helpful to the East.

We must conceive of our model of progress and development, in the light of our own culture, our past traditions, present requirements, and aspirations for the future. We should study in depth the Western paradigm, and benefit from it wherever possible, but not accept it as our model for future.

In India, it is heartening to note that the foreign inspired attempts to delink modern science from culture are being opposed by some of the eminent scientists. Raja Ramanna exposed the hollowness of the argument, that to speak of a synthesis between science and spiritualism is nothing but obscurantism and revivalism, in a paper read in a Seminar organised by Bharatiya Vichar Kendra in co-operation with other institutions at Trivandrum. Shri K.I. Vasu of the Indian Institute of science at Bangalore, made an important announcement. He spelt out the philosophy of the 'Swadeshi Science Movement' launched by him. In his concluding paragraph he says: "In this venture, there is an urgent need to re-orient the national priorities in scientific research, development and education. This calls for a national science and technology policy and national science and technology plan. The essential element of such a policy and plan wood be truly Swadeshi in spirit and fully Swadeshi in execution. Only such a Swadeshi Science Movement can make our Nationhood fulfilled, our ruralism protected, our culture preserved and the whole world served."

Similarly Claude Alvares and Dharampal have been striving hard to initiate the Swadeshi Technological Movement, though they have not named it thus so far. Claude Alvares believes that every culture has its own paradigm and model of progress and that development of technology should be suited to the character of such paradigm and model.

By God's grace, to us are available all the factors that go to make any country great - the human, the material and the intellectual resources. We are second to none in all these matters. What is lacking is the requisite national will, leading to national unity, not the lack of potentialities, but the lack of will and unity.

Shri Guruji on New Order

Stressing this point Shri Guruji said, "Once the life-stream of Unity begins to flow freely in all the veins of our body-politic, the various limbs of our national life will automatically begin to function actively and harmoniously for the welfare of the Nation as a whole. Such a living and growing society will preserve out of its multitude of old systems and patterns, whatever is essential and conducive to its progressive march, throw off those as have outlived their utility and evolve new systems in their place. No one need shed tears at the passing of the old orders, nor shirk to welcome the new order of things. That is the nature of all living and growing organisms."

In 'The Sacred Thread', J.L. Brockington conveys the same view when he observes, "Tradition (for Hindus) is not always just what it seems, but has constantly been undergoing reinterpretation to accommodate new understandings and changed circumstances. Innovation is not the enemy of tradition but that by which it maintains its relevance. Hinduism does not reject the old in favour of the new, but blends the two, expressing new dilemmas in traditional language and accommodating fresh insights to established viewpoints. The ability to adapt itself to changing circumstances has been a mark of Hinduism throughout its history, and the unifying factor bringing together its many diverse threads lies in their common history within this unique weaving together of tradition, and innovation. Hinduism is ever the same, yet different."

The awakening of the national will is essential not only for accomplishing the task of national reconstruction but even for fulfilment of the global mission of the Hindu nation as envisaged by Shri Guruji. After his demise, the world situation has been fast deteriorating. There is a growing awareness among western intellectuals that 'We find ourselves in a state of profound, world-wide, complex, multi dimensional crisis whose facts touch every aspect of our lives-our health and livelihood, the quality of our environment and our social relationships, our economy, technology and politics. It is a crisis of intellectual, moral and spiritual dimensions; a crisis of a scale and urgency unprecedented in recorded human history. For the first time we have to face the very real threat of extinction of the human race and of all life on this planet.'

Capra, one of the eminent modern thinkers, believes that the Westerners so far favoured rational knowledge over intuitive wisdom, science over religion, competition over co-operation, exploitation of natural resources over conservation,.........and that these factors, among others, have led to a profound cultural imbalance which lies at the very root of our current crisis,-an imbalance in our thoughts and feelings, our values and attitudes, and our social and political structures. "The Current crisis," he says, "is a transition from sensate culture. As individuals, as a society, as a civilisation, and as a planetary ecosystem, we are reaching the turning point."

Western Paradigm Inadequate

Can the Western paradigm help the perplexed humanity at this "turning point"? The learned author says, "What we need, then, is a new "paradigm" - a new vision of reality; a fundamental change in our thoughts, perceptions and values".

There is a view that India is facing today all types of problems that are confronting the humanity, but of all the countries India alone has the ability to overcome these difficulties because of her inherent aptitude to visualise unity in the midst of diversity. Consequently, India alone can show a new and the right path to the distressed world. That is the conviction of Arnold Toynbee.

Sir John Woodroffe is confident that cultural ideas of the Hindus will pass over into the West, the spirit of their ancient culture will persist, whatever happens in future to the race which evolved them. Where can India "gain strength to save Herself, except from Her own cultural inheritance? The universal assertion and adoption by all peoples of the noble and essential principles of Her spiritual civilisation would lead to world-peace."

Sri Aurobindo who had clearly visualised the nature of the impending world crisis declared confidently: ".......she (India) can, if she will, give a new and decisive turn to the problems over which all mankind is labouring and stumbling, for the, clue to their solutions is there in her ancient knowledge".

(The author, late Shri D.B. Thengdi, a front-ranking life-long RSS Pracharak and close confidant of Shri Gurujee, was a rare blend of accomplished organizer and original thinker. As founder of the Bharatiya Mazdoor Sangh, Thengdi has left an indelible mark on the labour movement in independent India by propounding a nationalist labour philosophy as opposed to the well entrenched but out-dated Marxist labour policy based on the concept of class-conflict.)

15

Aryan Invasion Theory: The Myth Exploded

Prof. Shivaji Singh

FOR building a castle in the clouds you need not know the rules of architecture. The truth of this popular saying is amply demonstrated by the manner in which the so-called Aryan Invasion Theory (AIT) was propounded in Europe by mid-19th century. No distinction was made between a 'theory' and a 'hypothesis'. There are two well-known methods of theory-building, the inductive and the hypothetico-deductive. In this case, none of the two procedures were followed. A mental model was taken for a theory and unstructured linguistic data was used to substantiate it! Epistemologically-speaking, therefore, the AIT cannot be called a theory at all. It is no wonder, then, that the AIT propagated several false notions. The concept of an 'Aryan race' and the arrival of Vedic language and culture in India from somewhere outside were the two most dangerous ideas loaded on this bogie of false notions.

Earlier, in 18th century, when several European stalwarts were convinced that India was the cradle of entire human civilization and a scholar of eminence like Voltaire had openly declared that "everything has come down to us (the Europeans) from the banks of the Ganges, astronomy, astrology, metempsychosis, etc." (Voltaire, quoted in Poliakov 1974 : 185), no theory of an 'Indian Aryan Invasion on Europe' was ever contemplated! Is this paradox, in itself, not enough to prove that considerations other than scholarly were behind the AIT?

The circumstances and motives that led to the propagation of this theory are now well-known. L. Poliakov (1974) traces its roots to the acute ante-Semitic feelings of 18th century Europeans who were eager to distinguish their Christian heritage from that of the Jews. He appears to be correct so far as Europe is concerned for it ultimately precipitated there the holocaust brought about by Nazi Germany. In India, on the other hand, the main driving forces behind the propagation and perpetuation of this theory have ever been the policies of 'Divide and Rule' and 'Divide and Convert'.

As the castles in the clouds are blown away by winds the AIT has now been demolished on the basis of solid evidence. The irony of fate, however, is that it has already proved to be a great disaster to Indian society and polity, and its adverse effects are still continuing. The worst aspect of the overall situation is that its supporters are changing their strategies with every new discovery that goes against their stand. They have been renaming and reformulating the AIT again and again, but they are not prepared to accept the fact that the very basis of their theory is wrong. Oliver Wendell Holmes, Jr., has at a place (Collected Legal Papers) given a noble hint: "To have doubted one's own first principles is the mark of a civilized man". Only God knows when this noble hint will strike the minds of the supporters of the AIT!

The present paper has three sections. The first of these shows how the absence of any literary and archaeological evidence to support the AIT ultimately forced its proponents to rename and reformulate it as the AMT (Aryan Migration Theory). The second section demonstrates that the AMT is equally untenable for it too is contradicted by archaeological, genetic, and other recent findings. In the third and the final section of the paper I propose to prove the Vedic-Harappan identity. The paper ends with a new and significant argument: If the Vedic and Sarsvati-Sindhu (Harappan) cultures are part and parcel of one and the same cultural tradition.[1]

I

The death and resurrection of a theory: reformulation of AIT as AMT

For over a century and a half, scholars of Indian history have remained under the spell of the Aryan Invasion Theory. The spell has broken now but its hangover still continues. It was indeed a period of spell, a bewitched state, for otherwise it is difficult to understand why during such a long span of time scholars, who normally maintain a distinction between a theory and a fact, not only overlooked this important epistemological difference but even accepted this theory as a Gospel Truth that cannot be doubted or challenged. The theory perpetuated the notion that the authors of the Vedic culture were not indigenous to South Asia but had arrived here from somewhere outside as invaders in about 1500 BC. While the place of their original habitat continued to be debated, the image of the Vedic Aryans as a culturally backward but physically vigorous and bellicose people soon found general acceptance. By the time the Indus Valley civilization, now known as the Harappan or Indus-Sarasvati Civilization, was discovered, the image of the 'barbarous invading Aryans' had turned into an article of faith and, therefore, it was readily accepted that these very invading people destroyed this earliest civilization of South Asia. It was said that they were nomadic pastoralists not doing even agriculture but, being extremely warlike and possessing horses and horse-drawn chariots, that provided them superior maneuverability in battles, they succeeded in destroying the Harappan cities and in forcing their inhabitants, the Dravidians, to move to the south. This notion of a culturally backward, nomadic and tribal Vedic Aryans has persisted till now and contradicted only recently.

The AIT stands rejected today. A theory based on wrong assumptions is bound to collapse ultimately and this is what happened to the AIT. It was based on two basic assumptions: the one, that the Harappan Civilization came to an abrupt end in about 1500 BC, and the other, that the dating of the **Rig-Veda** to circa 1200 BC, as casually estimated by Max Muller, was correct. Both these assumptions have been proved to be wrong. Surprising is not that the theory has collapsed, surprising is the fact that the historians accepted this linguistic theory without verifying it independently. Historians normally base their conclusions on literary and archaeological evidence, but none of these two basic sources of history has ever provided any support to the AIT.

Literature does not oblige the supporters of the AIT

The literature has completely refused to oblige the supporters of the AIT. Neither the Vedic literature, the literature of the presumed invaders, nor the ancient Tamil texts, the literature of the presumed invaded people, refer to any Aryan invasion.

However, the supporters of the AIT have ever been looking for reminiscences, even though vague, of north-western foreign localities and tribes in the *Rigveda* so that they could evidence the sojourn of the Rigvedic Aryas in those areas on their way to India. But, they have never succeeded. Long ago, in 1891, Alfred Hillebrandt had proposed the identification of the Rigvedic river Sarasvati with the river Arghandab (Avestan Harakhvaiti) flowing through Archosia. He had also tried to equate the Rigvedic social groups named Panis, Paravatas, and Brshayas with Iranian and Afghani tribes called Parnians, Paroyetai, and Barsaentes respectively. These identifications have since been rejected by eminent Vedicists as pure conjectures. It was rather a surprise to the scholarly community, therefore, when a few years ago Irfan Habib and Faiz Habib (1992) once again tried to place the Rigvedic Sarasvati in Archosia identifying it with Helmand this time instead of Arghandab. But, as I have shown elsewhere (Singh 1997-98a:140), the Helmand is Avestan Haetumant and, so, had this river been known to the *Rigveda,* it would have been known as Setumant, not as Sarasvati. Moreover, the *Rigveda* (10.75.5) clearly situates the Sarasvati between the Yamuna and the

Sutlej. Hence it cannot be identified with any river outside India.

To my knowledge, the latest attempt to find literary evidence in support of the AIT was made by Michael Witzel in 1995. He referred to a couplet of the *Baudhdyana* ***Sraut-Sutra*** (18.44) which, according to him, was a "direct statement" of the arrival of the Aryans in India. The couplet runs as follows:

"Pran ayuh pravabraja tasyaite kuru-panchalah kasi-videha ityetad ayavam.

Pratyan *amavasus-tasyaite gandharayas-parsavo-arattd ityetad* ***dmdvasyam."***

The meaning of this couplet is quite clear: Ayu went eastward. His (people) are **Kuru-Panchaalas** (and) Kasi-**Videhas.** They are (called) **Ayava. Amavasu** (went) westward. His (people) are **Gandhari, Parsu,** (and) **Aratta.** They are (called) **Amavasya.** The statement is obviously being made at a place somewhere in the Sarasvati valley area. There are two persons named Ayu and **Amavasu.** Ayu is said to have gone in the eastern direction while **Amavasu** in the western direction. The people living in the two regions are named and said to be their people. They are classified as **Ayava** and Amavasya, that is, peoples belonging to Ayu and **Amavasu** respectively.

But, Witzel (1995:320-21) tries to twist the meaning of these lines to suit his purpose. He takes only Ayu as a proper name and translates ama+vasu as "stayed at home" and, thereby, interprets the two categories of people, **Ayava** and **Amavasya,** as migrants and non-migrants! He is totally unjustified in not taking **Amavasu** as a proper name. **Amavasu,** he must know, is a well-known Figure in Sanskrit literature whom several *Puranas* consider to be the son of **Pururava** and Urvasi.

Moreover, in not taking **Amavasu** as a proper name, he has committed a grammatical mistake of leaving the second line of the couplet devoid of any subject. In fact, Witzel has done a great harm to his reputation by knowingly playing on words to suit his purpose since every Sanskritist, who has come across this translation of Witzel, has rejected it. Thus, the so-called "direct statement" of the Aryan arrival in India turned out to be a hoax. Koenraad Elst (1999:165) aptly remarks: "The fact that a world-class specialist has to content himself with a late text like the **Baudhayana** Shrauta **Sutra,** and that he has to twist its meaning this much in order to get an invasionist story out of it, suggests that harvesting invasionist information in the oldest literature is very difficult indeed."

Archaeology provides positive evidence against the AIT

The supporters of the AIT are disappointed by archaeology too, for it has never provided any evidence to substantiate their theory. At one time, however, a hope was generated in them when, at the fag end of his career in India, Mortimer Wheeler claimed to have at last found a clinching evidence of Aryan destruction of Harappan cities. He had heard that Indra, the chief god of the **Aryas** in the *Vedas,* has been designated as *Purandara,* i.e., a 'destroyer of cities'. So, on the basis of a few skeletons reported earlier to have been found scattered in disorderly manner at Mohenjo-Daro, he jumped to the conclusion: "It may be no mere chance that at a late period at Mohenjo-Daro men, women and children appear to have been massacred there. On circumstantial evidence, Indra stands accused" (Wheeler 1947:82). The evidence was later thoroughly examined by G.F. Dales. He found that Wheeler had totally misread the archaeological evidence for neither those skeletons belonged to one and the same stratigraphical context nor were they proof of any massacre. Most of the skeletons positively indicated that the persons were actually drowned in severe and sudden flood in river Indus. Out of the 37 skeletons found, only 2 or 3 bore cut-marks and those too were found to have been healed up showing that these few individuals also were not killed in any massacre. So he wrote a paper entitled 'The Mythical Massacre at Mohenjo-Daro' (Dales 1964:36-43) and exploded the myth of the Aryan destruction of Harappan cities. K.M. Srivastava (1984:441) quashes Wheeler's judgments: "Indra, therefore, stands completely exonerated." Thus, the only archaeological evidence ever produced in support of the AIT was found to be false.

The archaeological excavations done during the last three decades have revealed an unbroken sequence of Indus-**Sarasvati** cultural tradition. There is neither any break nor any major or minor upheaval to justify any invasion whatsoever from about 7000 BC to around 600 BC (Possehl 1996:9). The conclusion is clear: the archaeological evidence goes positively against the AIT.

The AIT reformulated and renamed as the AMT

Finding no support from either literature or archaeology, the proponents of the AIT were forced to revise their stand. They reformulated and renamed their theory as the Aryan Migration Theory (AMT). According to this revised version of their theory, the Aryans did not invade India but they did arrive here from outside. They came here as migrants in small batches at different points of time spread over a long duration. The absence of the archaeological evidence was explained away thus: since such a gradual trickling in of the Aryans was not a cataclysmic event, it could not be reflected in the archaeological record. What an explanation! The people arrive, change the language of half the subcontinent and the culture of the entire subcontinent, but leave no trace of their arrival!

Asko Parpola is perhaps the foremost among those scholars who were quick to realize that the AIT cannot be maintained in absence of literary and archaeological evidence. Unlike Wheeler, he has first-hand knowledge of Vedic literature and he knows well that Indra had destroyed his enemy Sambara's *purs* (strongholds or forts) in a mountainous region, not in a plain like that of the Indus. So he was looking for archaeological evidence of some sort of forts in a hilly area en route the presumed Aryan march to India where he could locate Indra's battles with Sambara. His desire appeared to be amply fulfilled when a team of Russian archaeologist led by Victor I. Sarianidi brought to light the remains of a Bronze Age civilization in the Bactria-Margiana region. Bactria is the alluvial basin of the Amu Darya (Oxus river) in northern Afghanistan and Margiana is the oasis in the deltaic area of the Murghab river in adjacent southern Turkmenistan. The region is hilly and the excavations had exposed remains of forts at some of its sites. This was enough for Parpola, and he jumped to the conclusion that it was this very region where Indra's battles with Sambara, described in the Rigveda, took place. So he wrote a lengthy paper (Parpola 1988) using the words "coming of the Aryans to India" in place of Aryan Invasion on India, and thus transformed the AIT into the AMT.

BMAC (Bactria Margiana Archaeological Complex) is the name given to this Bronze Age civilization by Sarianidi, the principal excavator of its sites. This is the designation used by most of the scholars. Henri-Paul Francfort, however, prefers to call it the Oxus Civilization. Parpola finds it convenient to use both these designations reserving the name Oxus Civilization for its early and BMAC for its later phases taking the assumed arrival of Aryan-speaking people in the region from the northern steppes as the line of demarcation between the two. According to Parpola BMAC represents the culture of the Rigvedic Dasas then living in Bactria and Margiana region. They were forced from behind by the Aryas coming from the northern steppes to migrate further towards southeast. The migration brought the Dasas followed by the Aryas to India. Parpola has been constantly developing his version of the AMT and in a recent paper (Parpola 2002:240-47), he has envisaged four waves of what he calls 'the BMAC Aryans' arriving in Central Asia from the northern steppes one after the other and subsequently moving on further to southern and southeastern regions from there. He distinguishes these successive waves as Pre-Proto-Iranian **Dasas,** 'Atharvedic' Proto-Indo-Aryans, Rigvedic Proto-Indo-Aryans and Proto-Iranians.

Through his continuous reformulations, Parpola has not

only replaced the idea of Aryan invasion by Aryan arrival, he has also introduced another noteworthy shift in the earlier paradigm. While in the AIT the enemies of the Vedic **Aryas** like the **Dasas,** Dasyus and **Panis** were taken to be non-Indo-European-speaking aboriginals of India, in the AMT they too are considered to be outsiders and Indo-Aryan-speakers, albeit speaking a dialect somewhat different from the one used by the Vedic **Aryas.** There is another change introduced evidently for face-saving. As the concept of 'Aryan race' has been discredited, the reformulations designate the Aryans as a 'language-culture group' but, for all practical purposes, use this designation in the racial sense. As the supporters of the AMT do not agree with each other on several significant points, we have several versions of the theory current simultaneously. However, despite all its various reformulations, occasional shifts in stand and claimed sophistication, the AMT has not been able to justify its validity.

II

The AMT is found to be equally untenable

The AMT too is breathing its last for no tangible evidence has been produced to justify its validity. Neither the historian nor the archaeologist is in a position to accept it, for all available literary and archaeological data, far from supporting it, actually speak against it. And, above all, recent anthropological, biological and genetic findings have contradicted it. The supporters of the AMT are formulating and reformulating it again and again and often changing their stand but not succeeding, for by the time they meet one challenge, two are posed before them. To illustrate their efforts and failure, let me refer to two greatest proponents of the AMT, namely, Asko Parpola and Bernard Sergent.

Proponents of the AMT fail to establish it

Parpola has made Herculean efforts for gathering archaeological and literary evidence to support his version of the AMT. We have reviewed and demonstrated the untenability of his views elsewhere (Singh 2004). In fact, his style of argumentation is suggestive but never concrete and inferences often misleading and fallacious. Let us take up just two examples to illustrate the way he argues. He connects the ceremonial structure with three concentric circular walls found at the BMAC site of Dashly-3 in southern Bactria with Indian *tripur,* associated with the Asuras in post-Vedic literature. He claims that a reference to *tripur* is found in the *Satapatha Brahmana* (6.3.3.24-25). The passages of the text referred to simply prescribe the drawing of three circular lines around the ritual fire to protect it from odds. This prescription has absolutely nothing to do with the Asuras. Moreover, if these three lines represent a *tripur,* it is an evidence of a *tripur* being made by followers of the Vedic religion, not the Asuras that Parpola wants us to believe! Another example: On a few BMAC seals a goddess is depicted with a peculiar animal. Parpola takes the animal to be a lion and concludes that the worship of Durga was prevalent among the Dasas of Bactria and Margiana. He interprets the name Durga as 'the protectress of the stronghold *(durga)*'. Now, first of all, the animal with the goddess on these BMAC seals is a mythical animal, not a lion, and so identifying this Bactrian goddess with Durga on the basis of that animal itself is wrong. Then, Durga is so named because she is *Durgamya* or Durgama, that is, difficult to be approached. Even today the famous seats of her worship are found located in places that are inaccessible or difficult to be reached despite modern improvements in transportation. **Durga** is basically a deity of lonely and difficult-to-be-reached areas, not a deity of forts. It is another matter that the word *durga* for forts too has the same sense of inap-proachability. To be sure, Parpola's advocacy of the AMT is full of such clear cases of special pleading and tunnel thinking in which 'willing' rather than 'thinking' dominates the entire exercise.

Bernard Sergent is another great supporter of the AMT. He is admittedly a well-known archaeologist and physical anthropologist. He has written an important book (Sergent 1997) marshalling various pieces of evidence in support of his version of the AMT that differs from that of Parpola on several points. His book is in French, still unavailable in English. My knowledge of his arguments depends on the exhaustive examination of the book done by Koenraad Elst (1999:238-320). Without going into the details, I would like to quote from the concluding remarks of Elst: "Bernard Sergent has written a book of incomparable erudition to narrate the genesis of the "composite culture" of Hinduism from what to him are the separate sources of Harappan, Dravidian, Indo-European and Austra-Asiatic elements. As part of this effort, he has tried to pinpoint the arrival of the Indo-Aryans in India, and this attempt has become the heroic failure of his book. Even in his two fields of expertise, he has not succeeded in finding decisive evidence for the Aryan invasion [read the AMT]: in archaeology, he has not shown where a Bactrian or otherwise foreign culture crossed the Indus into India (indeed, the one entry he identifies as the Indo-Aryan invasion doesn't get farther than Pirak in Baluchistan); and in physical anthropology, he has not been able to identify an immigration wave coinciding with the supposed Aryanization of northwestern India" (Elst 1999:320). This, then, is the present status of the AMT which seeks to perpetuate an alien origin of the Vedic culture in India!

Some hard facts that rule out the possibility of any Aryan invasion/migration

Once we stop speculating and come to hard facts, all versions of the AIT and AMT start evaporating. We may refer here to some of them. Consider just one such fact from archaeology. As is well known, the Harappans used copper extensively, but they used bronze also which they produced by alloying copper with tin to harden the metal. While copper was readily available to them in abundance, tin was considered to be a precious commodity as it had to be procured from Khorasan and the areas between Bukhara and Samarkand (Chakrabarti 1979:70; Asthana 1993:276-

78). After the decline of the Harappans, tin-based bronze objects are not found in India for more than a millennium. No tin-based bronzes are reported from Copper Hoards and Painted Grey Ware assemblages, and Ahar and Kayatha complexes also do not have them (Agrawal 1971; 1974). It is evident that the earlier contacts with the areas of Baluchistan and northern Afghanistan, from where tin was obtained, were severed. Referring to the AMT, J.M. Kenoyer (1995:230) puts the point-blank question: "why were the migrants not supplying one of the most important raw materials for bronze production, i.e., tin?"

Now, take up a fact from biological anthropology. After a detailed examination of biological adaptations and affinities in the Indus-Sarasvati area, a team of towering scholars in the field, namely, Hemphill, Lukacs and Kennedy has found only two biological discontinuities: the one between 6000 and 4500 BC and the other between 800 and 200 BC (Hemphill *et al* 1991). This shows that in the intervening period between 4500 and 800 BC, the biological make-up of the people living in the area remained fairly constant. "In such a situation", B.B. Lal (1997:287) rightly wonders, "how can one envisage the entry of hoards and hoards of Vedic Aryans who are supposed to belong to an alien, non-Harappan biological group, around the middle of the second millennium BC?"

Next, look at a fact from genetics which is just one finding from a series of several others that are proving to be the last nails in the coffin of the AIT/AMT. In a study of deep common ancestry of Indian and western-Eurasian lineages based on mitochondrial DNA tests, T. Kivisild and his team of scientists have found that the western Eurasian strain, which is present over 70 percent in the populations of European countries like Germany, is found to be merely 5.2 per cent in the gene-pools of both north as well as south India. They remark: "The supposed Aryan invasion of India 3000-4000 years before present therefore did not make a major splash in the Indian gene-pool. This is especially counter-indicated by the presence of equal, though very low, frequencies of the western Eurasian mt-DNA types in both southern and northern India" (Kivisild *et al* 1999:1334).

And, finally note a fact about the Rigvedic horse. P.K. Manansala (2000) is of the opinion that the Indian indigenous horses with only 17 pairs of ribs constitute a variety different from that of the Iranian, Central Asian and European horses that have 18 pairs of ribs. That, this difference between Indian and northwestern horses existed in the Rigvedic times too, is demonstrated by him on the testimony of the *Rgveda* (1.162.18) which informs: "The axe penetrates the thirty-four ribs of the swift horse; the beloved of the gods, (the immolators) cut up (the horse) with skill, so that the limbs may be imperforated, and recapitulating joint by joint" (Wilson's translation). I have scrutinized the translation of the original verse occurring in context of a horse sacrifice. There is absolutely no ambiguity about the number of ribs *(vankrih)* of the horse involved in the sacrifice, which is clearly stated to be thirty-four *(chatuhtrinsat)*. If Manansala's observations about the anatomical and taxonomical distinctions between the Indian and northwestern horses is correct, this is certainly a very significant piece of evidence. Since, had the Aryans arrived in India on horse back or in horse-drawn chariots, as the AMT presumes, they would have never used inferior indigenous horses in their most important sacrifice.

These are a few hard facts, and there are many more equally solid, that have led the informed historians of today to reject the AMT too outright.

III

The Vedic and Harappan cultures represent a single cultural tradition

The Vedic and Harappan cultures are not different from each other. This is not to say that their relationship can be expressed by the equation 'A is the same as B'. The two cultures are not identical in that sense. The data at hand shows that the Harappan or the Indus-Sarasvati Civilization is an aspect or a spacio-temporal phase of a much earlier, more extensive and more durable Vedic Culture. There is another significant distinction between the two. The considerations that define the Harappan and Vedic cultures are not exactly the same. It is basically the rise, intensification and collapse of an urban process that defines the Harappan Culture. As against this, it is the emergence, spread and dominance of an ideology, based on a kind of sacrificial ritual and concomitant social psychology that constitutes the hallmark of the Vedic Culture. Significant is also the fact that the ideological process survived the collapse of the urban process. Thus, notionally they represent two distinct processes, urban and ideological, but as we shall see, despite this perceived functional difference, they are part and parcel of one and the same cultural tradition.

The discussions on Vedic-Harappan identity are based on three basic parities, geographical, chronological and cultural, between the Rigvedic and the Harappan cultures. It may be noted that here too, as usual, the term 'Harappan' stands for Early-to-Mature Harappan excluding its phase called the Late Harappan that started with its decline in about 1900 BC. Let us discuss these parities between the two cultures briefly.

Rigvedic and Harappan geographical horizons coincide

The geographical parity between the Rigvedic and Harappan cultures is confirmed at the levels of their core areas as well as their contact areas. The region extending from the Sarasvati Valley in the east to the banks of Indus in the west was the homeland of both the cultures. Still more important is the fact that in both the cultures river Sarasvati had played a greater role as compared to Indus. As I have shown elsewhere (Singh 1997-98b), the authors of the Vedic Culture, living in the Sarasvati Valley, were not acquainted with the river Indus in the early Rigvedic times. Of course, later on, in the Rigvedic period itself, they reached the Indus, settled in its valley and glorified it, but Sarasvati continued to be the most important river for them (*Rigveda* 2.42.16). This corresponds well with the importance of the Sarasvati Valley in the life of the Harappans. The Harappan sites in the Sarasvati Valley far outnumber those located in the Indus Valley. The latest counting done by B. B, Lal (2002:47-48) is a total of 50 sites (both Early and Mature) in the Indus Valley as against 177 Early and 283 Mature Harappan sites in the Sarasvati Valley. The archaeologists now agree that the cultural integration of several social groups that gave rise to the Harappan Culture had occurred in the Sarasvati Valley (Shaffer and Lichtenstein 1989:123).

A comparison of their contact areas also supports their identity. In the northwest, both extend up to Afghanistan. The discovery of a Mature Harappan site named Shortughai in northeastern Afghanistan and the references in the *Rigveda* to Rasa (Syr Darya), Anitabha (Amu Darya), Kubha (Kabul), etc., show this. In the southwest, the contact areas extend up to Gujarat as proved by the location of sites like Lothal, Surkotada and Dholavira in the case of the Harappan Culture, and the description of the shipwreck met by Bhujyu in the *Rigveda* (1.116.3-5) in the case of the Rigvedic Culture. Scholars like R.N. Nandi (1994-95:31-33) have already concluded that Bhujyu's shipwreck had occurred in the Kutch area. In my view, Bhujyu, as the name suggests, most probably belonged to the Bhuj locality of Gujarat.

Investigating the contact areas of the Rigvedic **Aryas** and the Harappans in the east I found them too to be identical. The journey of Videgha Mathava from the Sarasvati region to river Sadanira (modern Gandak in Bihar) described in the Sathpatha Brahmana (1.4.1.14-17) is rightly taken to be a clear evidence of the expansion of Vedic culture up to Bihar in the east. The question is: when did this journey take place? The historians place this event in about 8th-7th century BC when, according to them, this text was written. This is absolutely wrong for it goes against the very internal evidence of the text. The text clearly indicates that it is describing an episode of a hoary past and, therefore, the episode cannot be assigned to the time of the text. In fact, there is hardly any doubt that the episode relates to the Rigvedic period. Gotama Rahugas, who accompanied Videgha Mathava in the journey to Sadanira, is a famous Rigvedic Rishi of the Angira family who is seer of as many as 20 hymns of the *Rigveda* (1.74-93). That, the contact area of the Rigvedic people extended up to Bihar, is attested also by the Rigvedic reference to the Kikatas, a people of Magadh area.

The Harappan contact with Bihar has been attested by the excavations at a site named Senuwar situated in Rohtas district of the state. At this site the cultivation of barley, wheat and certain pulses was started for the first time in about 2000 BC. Earlier the farmers living there were growing only paddy. K.S. Saraswat, a scientist at the Birbal Sahani Institute of Palaeobotany, Lucknow, has examined the botanical remains from the site. He informs (personal communication) that barley, wheat and the pulses from Senuar are exactly of the same species which were being grown by the contemporary Harappans and, therefore, there is hardly any doubt that the people of Senuwar were in contact of the Harappans. These contacts couldn't have been made without passing through eastern U.P. which falls in-between the two areas. And, it is interesting to note, in this context, that Harappan micro-beads of steatite have been discovered from the site of Imlidih Khurd in Gorakhpur district of eastern U.P. attesting the contact of the Harappans with this area too.

The above discussion is sufficient, I hope, to convince any one that the geographical horizons of the Early-to-Mature Harappan and the Rigvedic cultures are one and the same in every respect. Not only the core areas but also the contact areas of the two in various directions coincide perfectly.

The latest limits of Rigvedic and Harappan chronological horizons coincide, proving their partial overlap

The various phases of the Harappan Culture have been firmly dated by Carbon-14 method and there is little controversy about Harappan chronology today. Though the beginning of the Early Harappan proper is placed in about 3200 BC, it is accepted that its roots go back to *cir.* 4000 BC. It is also agreed that the Mature or Urban Phase of the Harappan Culture came to an end in around 2000-1900 BC. As we are not concerned with the Late (i.e. Post-Urban Harappan) at the moment, it is this span of roughly 2000 years from about 4000 BC to around 1900 BC that is to be compared with the Rigvedic Period to find the relative chronological position of the two.

The Rigvedic chronology, on the other hand, has been and still continues to be a matter of controversy though during the last few years some significant light has been thrown on this problem. Linguistic, West Asian inscriptional, astronomical, archaeological, and other kinds of data and evidence have been used to fix the chronology (Singh 1997-98a). Efforts to reach acceptable conclusions have so far failed partly because of inherent limitations of certain sorts of data and partly because of a lack of mental clarity in some scholars who do not maintain a clear distinction between the antiquity of the language of the *Rgveda* and the antiquity of the hymns contained in the text, and sometimes even confuse the time of the composition of the hymns with the time of their compilation.

In any discussion on Rigvedic chronology, two issues are involved, one pertaining to its earliest limit and the other relating to its lowest limit. Fixing the lowest limit has not been so difficult as ascertaining the earliest limit, and so most of the scholars have concluded their discussions by stating that the *Rgveda* cannot be later than such and such date. To my knowledge, no body has ever claimed to have fixed the earliest limit of the Rigvedic period excepting, of course, the supporters of the AIT and AMT who believe that it began in around 1500 BC directly making a fool of Max Muller on whom they depend but who had stated that 'no power on earth will ever determine' how old the *Rigveda* is.

Ancient inscriptional evidence such as the names of

characteristically Vedic gods found recorded as witness deities on tablets of about 1400 B.C discovered at Boghaz-keui, a site some 145 kms east of Ankara in Turkey, names of kings like Suttarna, Yasdata, Artamanya, etc., occurring on tablets of about the same time discovered at El-Amama in Egypt, and the use of the word *Suriyas* for the sun god by the Kassites ruling over Babylon in 1760 BC prove the presence of Vedic Aryas in those areas at the mentioned times but they do not help us in fixing the limits of the Rigvedic time-span.

Linguistics too has miserably failed to provide any insight on this issue. I am not a linguist myself, but I am told that linguistics is now quite advanced and sophisticated. It is no longer in its primitive 19th century stage in which it was outright rejected by an eminent thinker like Shri Aurobindo as a discipline incapable of deciding what it aims at deciding. However, I feel surprised to find that using same methodology and similar data B. K. Ghosh (1952) thinks that the *Rigveda* cannot be earlier than 1500 BC and Satya Swarup Misra (1992) holds that it cannot be later than 5000 BC. Does it indicate any inherent imperfection in the discipline? I simply do not know.

Astronomical calculations, unlike linguistic considerations, have yielded uniform results. It is worth noting that B.G. Tilak in Mumbai and H. Jacobi in Bonn working simultaneously but independently of each other arrive at almost the same conclusion that the antiquity of the *Rgveda* goes back to at least 4500 BC (Winternitz 1933/91: 295-96). But under the spell of the AIT this fact was overlooked and this significant astronomical evidence was not given the importance that it deserved. Of late, when the spell has broken, some scholars like Subhash Kak (1994) have started working on Vedic astronomy and it may be expected that it would throw some significant light on Rigvedic chronology.

Unlike the archaeologists who have made serious attempts to know the causes that led to the extinction of Harappan cities, the vedicists have seldom probed the reason why the composition of the Rigvedic hymns came to an end. The Rigvedic creativity is no more present in the *Vedas* that follow. What was the catastrophe that killed the dynamic spirit of the Rigvedic Aryans? The recent investigations in the **Sarasvati** (modern Ghaggar-Hakra) Valley seem to provide an answer to this question. The drying up of the **Sarasvati** has long since been taken as a line of demarcation between the Early and Late Vedic periods. It is a matter of satisfaction, therefore, that the time when the river dried up is now known. The Mature Harappan settlement at Kalibangan, located on its bank, had to be abandoned because of scarcity of water in the river, and radiocarbon dates indicate that this abandonment occurred in 1900 BC. It has, therefore, reasonably been concluded that the river dried up 'some time at the beginning of the second millennium BC' (Lal 2002: 22). Thus, the drying up of the Sarasvati appears to be the main reason for the end of both, the urban phase of the Harappan Culture and the Rigvedic phase of the Vedic Culture though the work of hymn-compositions, needing serene atmosphere, must have stopped long before the abandonment of the cities.

Though the above conclusion can hardly be doubted, a different opinion in this connection must not be overlooked. Recently a few scholars like N.S. Rajaram, David Frawley and Subhash Kak have tried to prove that the *Rigveda* cannot be later than 3750 BC (Rajaram and Frawley 1995). Like K.D. Sethna (1981) they equate the Harappan and Sutra periods and push back the Rigvedic period to an age much earlier than the Harappan. Their arguments are: (a) the ancient Egyptian and Babylonian mathematics are derived from the *Sulbasutras* and (b) this mathematical evidence is supported by astronomical considerations relating to the pole star Alpha-Draconis, Krittika vernal equinox and the time taken in the shift of the cycle of seasons from the days of the *Sutras* to the present. Additional evidence for the proposed chronology is provided by the stand that the Rigvedic period ended with the Battle of Ten Kings that is calculated to have occurred in 3730 BC.

The arguments are quite emphatic, but the difficulty is that the cultural levels depicted in the *Rgveda* such as those indicated by organized battles and sea trade do not match with those brought to light so far by the archaeological assemblages of pre-3750 BC horizon. Although there is nothing final in archaeology since any new discovery any day may alter the entire perception, till such evidence is brought to light, an archaeologist would find it difficult to accept this early end of the Rigvedic period.

The mosaics of the Rigvedic and Harappan cultural contents have striking resemblance

Now, let us compare the cultural contents of the Rigvedic and Harappan cultures. The perception that the former is rural and illiterate and the latter urban and literate is wrong. First, the rural-urban dichotomy itself is incorrect for in every culture and especially so of ancient times, the number of people engaged in agriculture far exceeds the number of those who participate in non-agricultural production and trade. Then, the evidence now at hand shows that the Rigvedic Culture too had reached the stage of urbanization. Bhagwan Singh (1987/97; 1995) and R.S. Bisht (1988; 1999) have brought out enormous data from the *Rigveda* to show that some Rigvedic people lived in urban centers and carried on long distance trade by land and sea. Undoubtedly the Rigvedic Aryans destroyed their enemy *purs* (strongholds or fortified towns), but they also built purs and lived in them. They describe their own *purs* as metal-strong *(ayasi)*, multi-sided *(satabhuji)*, spacious *(Vipula)*, broad *(urvi)*, good-looking *(subhra)* and auspicious *(bhardra)*, etc. A large number of architectural terms and descriptions found in the text, specially references to covered *(surmi)* and un-choked *(sushira)* drains *(Rigveda,* 8.69.12) leading discharge water to pits *(kakuda)* immediately bring to our mind the Harappan drainage system.

Descriptions at various places in the text refer to business activities. The word ***vanij*** denoting a businessman or merchant is known. Words expressing the concepts like 'capital investment', 'profit', 'loan', 'tax', 'contract', etc., used in the business community are found (Bisht 1988:12). Trading was done by roadways as well as by waterways. Various kinds of land routes or roads like strait roads, deviant roads, waterlogged roads, etc., are referred to. Sea journey for trade is also referred to at several places. It was in such a sea journey for trade that Bhujyu, son of Tugra, had the misfortune of shipwreck. Bhagwan Singh has drawn our attention to a verse of the *Rigveda* (10.142.7) that reads: 'This is the reservoir of water, the house of all the waters. O Agni, now you can change your route and reach any destination you like.'

The literate-illiterate dichotomy is also untenable. Literacy was rare even in Harappan Culture limited only to a section of the society in the Mature Harappan phase only, the Early Harappans being totally illiterate. It was very limited in the Rigvedic Culture too, but not unknown. Bhagwan Singh (1987/97:266-72) quotes several Rigvedic verses indicating literacy and V.S. Pathak (1986) is of the opinion that the **Panis** are called *'granthinah* because they possessed account books.

Earlier, it was believed that the Harappans were peaceful people as against the Aryans who were warlike. Now, it is accepted by scholars that the Harappans too possessed weapons 'just like' Aryas (Elst 1999:253). The fact that the Mature Harappans had invaded and occupied several regions is well-attested by archaeological evidence (Lal 1997:91). If references to wars in the *Rigveda* lead one to believe that the Rigvedic **Aryas** were 'warlike' people, he or she will have to accept that the Mature Harappans too were equally 'warlike'.

Similarly, the perception that Harappans did not use horses, while the Aryans were fond of them, has been contradicted by the recovery of horse bones from Harappan settlements like **Harappa,** Ropar, Kalibanga, Lothal, Surkotada and Malvan. Though remains of horse bones have not been found at Mohenjo-Daro and Nausaro, the presence of the animal at these sites is attested by its terracotta figurines (Gupta 1996:159-61; Lal 1997: 285-86).

There are many more points of convergence between the Early-to-Mature Harappan and Rigvedic cultures. Several characteristic pottery types like knobbed and perforated varieties are mentioned in Vedic literature (Singh 1969). The population shift towards east concomitant with Mature Harappan decline, thoroughly documented by Shaffer and Lichtenstein (1999), tallies perfectly with literary information according to which the center of Aryan activities had shifted from the *Sapta Sindhavah* area to *Brahmdvarta* in the post-Rigvedic period. Thus, we find that Rigvedic and Harappan cultures are quite alike and the earlier notion of Vedic-Harappan dichotomy is yielding and giving place to Vedic-Harappan identity.

Do the geographical, chronological and cultural parities between Rigvedic and Harappan cultures prove their identity?

While comparing the Rigvedic Culture with the Harappan Culture, scholars generally conclude that in view of the above parities between them their identity is established. However, it may be noted that though these parities point to a strong probability of the two cultures being one and the same, they do not necessarily prove their identity. I have already referred to the processual difference between the two. These parities only prove that two distinct processes, the one urban represented by the Harappan Culture and the other ideological represented by the Rigvedic Culture, were at work in the same space-time context. In such a situation, one may argue that while some (or even most) of the social groups occupying the space-time under consideration might have participated in both the processes, some others (whatever their strength) may have been involved in only one of the two or even in none of the two processes. This shows that the problem needs a deeper probe.

Correlating the ideological and urban processes

The ideological and urban processes were, in fact, interconnected. Speaking in terms of Systems Theory, we may say that they were coupled in a stimulus-response relationship like sub-systems of a system. I have dealt with in detail elsewhere (Singh 1997-98b) and shown that the Rigvedic and Early-to-Mature Harappan ethno-geographic configurations too have a structural parity and that both the processes had originated in the Sarasvati valley from where they diffused first to the lower Indus valley and then to other places towards north, south and east.

The diffusion of the ideology from the banks of the **Sarasvati** to the lower Indus valley is attested to by the fact that while the Rigvedic hymn-composers are ignorant about the river Sindhu in the earliest portions of the *Rigveda,* in middle and late portions of the text many of them like Sindhukshit, **Sindhudvipa** and **Kakshivan** are found settled in the lower Indus area and composing hymns glorifying the river Sindhu and its bounties. A northeast to southwest diffusion of ideology is confirmed also by a somewhat late inclusion of the twin gods Asvins, originally gods of the coastal regions, in the Soma ritual that had originated in the Sarasvati valley. (Singh 1997-98b: 31 and fn 19). The urban process follows the same pattern. It too originates in the **Sarasvati** valley and diffuses first to lower Indus and then to other areas. This is shown by successive stages of diffusion of Early Harappan traits followed by the Urban Harappan expansion.

The ideology played a significant role in the rise and intensification of the urban process. This becomes clear when we consider variables causing transformation of the early (pre-urban) stage of the Harappan Culture into the mature (urban) stage. Earlier it was thought that trade, mainly external trade, brought about the transformation. D.K. Chakrabarti has contradicted this general belief and asserted that long-distance external trade was a concomitant of the urbanization, it did not antedate it. According to him, an ideology "which cannot yet be defined in concrete social and institutional terms" had played an important role in this transformation (Chakrabarti 1990:169). G.L. Possehl (1990: 276-79) too accepts the importance of ideology in this transition. The uniformity in Mature Harappan traits, especially the signs and symbols, over a large area demonstrate a kind of 'oneness', an evidence of the emergence of a sort of social identity fostered by an expanding ideology. The question is: what else this ideology was if not the Vedic? In literature, we find the optimistic and martial Rigvedic **Aryas** waging wars against their enemies and moving from the banks of the **Sarasvati** towards Indus and beyond. In archaeology, we see the Mature Harappans overrunning different peoples and burning down settlements at Kot Diji in the Indus valley and at Nausharo, Gumla and Rana Ghundai west of the Indus (Lal: 1997:91). Is this correspondence in literary and archaeological scenarios not significant? In my view, the Rigvedic and Harappan identity cannot be challenged on the basis of the notional distinction between ideological and urban processes. Their identity is proved not only by geographical, chronological and cultural parities between the two but also by the interdependence and similar developmental pattern of the urban and ideological processes that they represent.

The above discussions lead us to the point where we may ask a very significant question: since Vedic-Harappan identity is beyond doubt, and since indigenous origin of the Harappan Culture is accepted by all, how can one doubt the indigenous origin of the Vedic Culture? The fact, that the Vedic **Aryas** are sons of the soil, not aliens, cannot be challenged.

(The author, Prof. Shivaji Singh, is retired professor and head of the History Department, University of Gorakhpur. He is a scholar of great eminence in the field of ancient Indian history, culture and archaeology. Besides being author of several original books on the subject, Prof. Singh has contributed large number of research papers published in national and international journals. A recipient of Vakankar National Award for his outstanding scholarly contribution in the area of Vedic History and archaeology, Prof. Singh is credited with directing archaeological explorations bringing to light several ancient sites, including the hither to unknown site of Ramagram, the capital of the Koliyas, a republic during the Gautam Buddha era.)

REFERENCES:

India, 1800-800 B.C., in *Proceedings of Indian History Congress,* 52nd Session, New Delhi, 1991-92, pp. 72-97. Hemphill B.E., J.R. Lukacs and K.A.R. Kennedy 1991. Biological adaptations and affinities of Bronze Age Harappans, in R.H. Meadow (ed.):

Harappan Excavation 19861990: A Multidisciplinary Approach to Third Millennium Urbanism, pp. 137-82. Madison: Prihistory Press.

Kak, Subhash 1994. *The Astronomical Code of the Rigveda.* New Delhi: Aditya Prakashan.

Kenoyer, J.M. 1995. Interaction systems, specialized crafts and culture change: The Indus valley tradition and the Indo-Gangetic tradition in South

Asia, in George Erdosy (ed.): *The Indo-Aryans of Ancient South Asia,* pp. 213-57. Berlin and New York: Walter de-Gruyter.

Kivisild, T. e(*at* 1999. Deep common ancestry of Indian and Western Eurasian mitochondrial DNA lineages, in *Current Biology,* 9:1331-34.

Lal, B.B. 1997. *The Earliest Civilization of South Asia.* New Delhi: Aryan Books International.

Lal, B. B. 2002. *The Sarasvati Flows on.* New Delhi: Aryan Books International.

Manansala, P. K. 2000. A New Look at Vedic India, available online from the author, user name kekai@jps.net.

Misra, S.S. 1992. *The Aryan Problem: A Linguistic Approach.* New Delhi: Munshiram Manoharlal.

Nandi, R.N. 1994-95. Aryan settlements and the Rgveda, in *The Indian Historical Review,* 21(1-2):9-36.

Parpola, Asko 1988. The coming of the Aryans to Iran and India and the cultural and ethnic identity of the Dasas, in *Studia Orientalia* 64:195-302.

Parpola, Asko 2002. Pre-Proto-Iranians of Afghanistan as initiators of Sakta Tantrism: on the Scythian/Saka affiliation of the Dasas, Nuristanis and

Magadhans, in *Iranica Antiqua* 37:233-324.

Poliakov, L. 1974. *The Aryan Myth.* New York: Basic Books.

Possehl, G. L. 1996. *Indus Age: The Writing System.* New Delhi & Calctta: Oxford & IBH Publishing.

Rajaram, N.S. and David Frawley 1995. *Vedic "Aryans"and the Origins of Civilization.* Quebec: W.H. Press.

Sergent, Bernard 1997. Genese de I'Inde. Paris: Payot.

Sethna, K.D. 1981. *Karpasa in Prehistoric India: A Chronological and cultural Clue.* New Delhi: Aditya Prakashan.

Shaffer, Jim G. and D.A. Lichtenstein 1989. Ethnicity and change in the Indus valley cultural tradition, in J.M. Kenoyer (ed.): *Old Problems and*

New Perspectives in the Archaeology of South Asia, pp. 117-26. Madison: Dept. of Anthropology, University of Wisconsin.

Shaffer, Jim G. and D.A. Lichtenstein 1999. Migration, philology and South Asian archaeology, in J. Bronkhorst and M.M. Deshpande (eds.): *Aryan and Non-Aryan in South Asia,* pp. 239-60. Cambridge: Dept. of Sanskrit and Indian Studies, Harvard University.

Singh, Bhagwan 1987/97. **Harappa Sabhyata** aur Vaidika **Sahitya.** New Delhi: Radhakrishna Prakashan.

Singh, Shivaji 1997-98a. Dating the Rigveda archaeologically, in *Pragdhara,* Journal of the U.P. State Archaeology Department 8:137-47.

Singh, Bhagwan 1995. *The Vedic Harappans.* New Delhi: Aditya Prakashan.

Singh, Shivaji 1969. Vedic literature on pottery, in B.P. Sinha (ed.): *Potteries in Ancient India,* pp. 301-13. Patna: Patna University.

Singh, Shivaji 1997-98a. Dating the Rigveda archaeologically, *Pragdhara* 8:137-47.

Singh, Shivaji 1997-98b. Sindhu and Sarasvati in the Rigveda and their archaeological implications, in *Puratattva,* 28:26-38.

Singh, Shivaji 2004. ***Rigvaidika Arya*** *aur Sarasvati-Sindhu* ***Sabhyata.*** Varanasi: **Bharatiya Itihasa** Sankalana Samiti.

Srivastava, K.M.I 984. The myth of the Aryan invasion of Harappan towns, in B. B. Lal and S. P. Gupta (eds.): *Frontiers of the Indus Civilization,*pp. 437-43. New Delhi: Booka and Books.

Wheeler, R.E.M. 1947. Harappa 1946: The defences and Cemetery R37, in *Ancient India,* 3:58-130.

Winternitz, M. 1933/91. *A History of Indian Literature,* Vol. 1, New Delhi: Munshiram Manoharlal.

Witzel, Michael 1995. Rgvedic history: poets, chieftains and polities, in George Erdosy (ed): *The Indo-Aryans of Ancient South Asia,* pp. 307-52.

Berlin & New York: Walter de Gruyter.

16

Synthesize Science And Spirituality

Prof. V. G. Bhide

DURING the last two centuries, there has been an explosive creativity in science and staggering growth in technology in the West and these developments often tend to cloud the contributions made by ancient civilizations such as those of Persia, India and China. It is therefore necessary to remove the likely Impression on the minds of impressionable youth that science is an implant by the British in a language foreign to us, an activity foreign to our culture. Indeed India had a flourishing tradition in science and in a way the foundations of science, though not as an organized activity, as we understand today, were laid in India. Exploration of nature and the universe with an unbiased mind, the very soul of science, has been a part of our culture. However, one needs to be cautious that blind idolatory of the past should not lead us to a kind of a coma and to the condition of mental stupor and physical weariness. Science and Technology are increasingly moulding our view of the universe, conditioning our sojourn on this planet and shaping our ultimate destiny. For good or bad science has permeated deep in every walk of human endeavour.

Indeed Pandit Nehru, while presenting the Science Policy Resolution to the Parliament said "It is an inherent obligation of a great country like India with its tradition of scholarship and original thinking and its great cultural heritage to participate fully in the march of science, which is probably mankinds greatest enterprise". While these statements are as relevent today, if not more than when they were first made, problems of development and the nature of science itself have assumed greater dimensions and complexity and call for not only a restatement of our conviction to participate fully in the inexorable march of science but call for urgently evolving strategies for initiating a phase change wherein instead of pursuing and chasing others, we ourselves generate science and innovate technolgy which we can share with others in the world - a phase where we promote adventure of ideas, flights of imagination, sparks of creativity instead of being imitative and duplicative."

Science like religion originates in basic urges and deep aspirations of man. It is an endless quest, a quest to understand Nature, essentially outside that is the external world. There is no limit or ceiling to it. Increasing Knowledge reveals ever increasing areas of ignorance. In fact the pursuit of science rests ultimately on our deep conviction that Nature is understandable by the human mind. This conviction was first propounded in Rigveda in the form of Rta-the natural Laws. The Vedic seers conceived of this principle as the real governing force of the universe. Einstein gives expression to this conviction in a beautiful form when he says "The most incomprehensible". This conviction is similar to the conviction of the religious leaders who say that the most unrealised aspect of God is that he is realizable.

The history of science is a fascinating and glorious chapter in the book of human achievements. Science as we understand today has an indelible imprint of the Greek thought which emphasized more on the external world of atoms and molecules, matter and energy, keeping out of its purview the internal world of kindness, compassion, love, anger etc. What course would science have taken had it flourished, instead of in the individualistic West, but in harmony seeking India with its deep philosophical and spiritual background, is now only a matter of mere speculation. All the same, science as it has developed so far, has contributed to the artificial division between the external world of atoms and molecules, space and time, matter and energy and the inner world characterised by mind, soul etc.

Because of the method it follows, namely close observation, generalization based on these observations, predictions based on the generalization, further experiments to confirm predictions and so on, has made science truly objective and a common heritage of mankind. Science and objectivity are and must be recognized as inseparable. Within the realm of science, there is no place for mysteries or mysticism. Dogmatism of any kind whatsoever is totally inadmissable in science. Dogma is based on personal prejudices and not on reason but science is based on experiments, verifiable truth and is totally objective. Dogma is personal but science is communicable. It is, however, necessary to distinguish between dogma and faith. Faith in the fair play and justice of the supreme Lord, the natural laws, is even higher than the contemporary scientific reality. In April 1929 Goldstein cabled Einstein "Do you believe in God" Einstein cabled back saying "I believe in Spinoza's God who reveals himself in the harmony of all beings and not on God who concerns himself with fate and actions of men." Indeed it is lack of proper appreciation of the difference between dogma and faith in the Supreme Lord that led to the conflicts between science and religion in the West. Campenella was imprisoned, Bruno was burnt, Galeleo was humiliated, Darwin was ridiculed in the developed West but significantly there has not been a single instance where scientific truth, during the hayday of science in India, was opposed by any religious leader.

It is this objectivity of science that has made science a truly co-operative effort, participated in by people from various countries, belonging to various communities and professing different religions. Science, today, is what science has been thus far. It has been contributed to by every nation, every civilization and every community. More often, the recent contributions made to science in Europe and the USA tend to cloud the pioneering contributions made by ancient civilizations of Arabia, India, China etc. It is, however, true that the progress of science has been anything but uniform in space and time.

Periods of rapid advance have alternated with longer periods of stagnation and decay. In the course of time, the centres of scientific activity have been continuously displaced usually following rather than leading to the migration of the centres of culture, of commerce, and of industrial activity. Babylon, India, China have all been the focus of ancient science. Greece became their common heir where the rational basis of science as we know of it today, was developed. There was little place for science, in the Roman Empire and in the then barbaric kingdoms of modern Europe. The heritage of Greece returned to the East and we find in Syria, India and China, stirred new breaths of science and came together for a brilliant synthesis, on which the present edifice of science rests. We must recognize that the West inherited science from India, China, Persia etc. but it is undoubtedly true that in Europe it underwent a development which, though slow at first, was to give rise to great outbursts of creativity which resulted in modern science.

The earliest achievements in science and technology made by man anywhere in the world find documented in the impressive remains that have been discovered at Mohenjo - Daro in Sind and Harappa in Haryana, and Punjab. Sir John Marshall tells us "One thing that stands out clear and unmistakable, both Mohenjo - Daro and at Harappa, is that the civilization hitherto revealed at these two places is not an incipient civilization but one already age-old and stereotyped on Indian soil, with millenia of endeavour behind it. He says India must henceforth be regarded as the most important area where the civilization process and science were initiated. Cotton was used for textiles even at that time in India. The overall picture of this culture appears to be that it had reasonable agricultural surplus and farming economy, developed way of settled life and material culture enriched by many a craft and industry. The craft of pottery registered a technological progress. The Harappan pottery was mainly wheel made, turned various shapes and sizes out of the well levigated alluvium of the Indus. The unearthed pottery specimen with a number of designs and colour combinations, colours derived from plants, throw light on the fact that the production techniques were standardised to a high degree. During that time metal-smiths were well versed in the technique of making beads, sheet making, revetting, coiling and casting. The bronze figurine discovered at Mohenjo-Daro was probably cast by the tire-perdue process. A number of metallic tools mostly of copper and bronze found in this area reveal that Harappan metal-smiths had sound knowledge of cold working and annealing. Apart from metal working, the Harappans knew the use of number of minerals for ornaments, cosmetics and medicinal purposes. They had developed social sanitation and public hygiene to a high level as borne out by exquisite town planning, paved streets, water supply, public and private baths, hydropathic establishments, discharge and drainage system etc., in their urban living. They also knew spinning and weaving as well as brick and mortar construction. Doubtless, they had evolved a system of measurement and computational techniques. It is significant to note that at this dawn of India's and in a sense human story, India does not appear as a pulling infant but already grown up in many ways. She is not oblivious of life's ways, lost in dreams of vague and supernatural world but had made considerable technical progress in arts and amenities of life.

History of science in India is marked by intermittent spurts of creativity separated by considerably long periods of stagnation and decay. Inspite of this, throughout its chequered history, India made pioneering and profound contributions to science particularly in mathematics, astronomy, medicine and surgery, yoga etc. It is not possible to catalogue its numerous contributions but some illustrative examples would bring out the originality of mind, the sharpness of intellect and the power of abstract thinking.

Our approach to science is found in our civilization which has synthesis and adjustment as its cornerstones. Prof.

Childe remarks "Indian civilization represents a very perfect adjustment of human life to a specific environment that could have only resulted from years of patient effort. In the study of astronomy, our ancient seers were attempting to link the individual on this planet with the heavenly bodies. Not surprisingly these-studies led to the development of Astrology. In the contributions to mathematics is reflected unique synthesis in the then existing chaos and their creativity which has resulted in modern science.

Highly intellectual and given to abstract thinking, the ancient Indians excelled in mathematics. The astonishing progress that the Indians made in mathematics is now well known and it is recognised that the foundations of modern arithmatics and algebra were laid long ago in India. The clumsy method of using the counting frame and the use of Roman and such like numerals had long retarded progress when the ten Indian numerals including the zero sign liberated the human mind from these restrictions and threw flood of light on the behavour of numbers. These number symbols were unique and entirely different from all other symbols that had been in use in other countries. Hundred and fifty years ago, La Place, eminent mathematician himself wrote "It is India that gave us the ingenuous method of expressing numbers by means of ten symbols, a profound assertions like now known as Pythagorous theorem, Pascal triangle, and several others. There is reason to believe that these mathematical inventions were a result of demands of the time."

It is demand again which led to notable advances in Astronomy. The insistance of vedic society on the performance of sacrifical rites at auspicious times that led to the development of calendars, the observance and prediction of planetary, lunar and other heavenly body motion. The contributions of Aryabhatta, Varahmihira, Bhaskara I and II. Brahmagupta, Lilavati and several others to the field of astronomy and Mathematics are too well known to be recalled.

The Ayurveda, as a rational assemblage of methodical concepts and systematic theurapatic practices, occupies an honoured position in human achievements. Even though the celebrated classical texts of Ayurveda namely the Charak and Sushruta which have come down to us, took their present form probably in the early centuries of the Christian era, the thoughts and practices enshrined in these were doubtless in vogue from about the seventh century B.C. The prime object of the Ayurveda is preservation of human life, of plant life and of even animal life. Treatment in Ayurvdea is a two way process namely elimination of the deleterious ingradients and replenishment of the harmonious ones. All drugs, therapeautic procedures and even surgery are employed towards this end. Generally, plant products were preferred for both oral and non-oral medication, for it was believed that organic plants were composed of the five Bhutas while the inorganic materials were supposed to consist of only Prithvi Bhuta. In a sense herbal drug was considered a total drug taking care of the side effects of the main constitutent of the drug. Sushruta describes surgery under eight head, Chedna (incision), Bhedana (excision), Lekhana (sacrification), Vedhan (puncturing), Esana (exploration), Ahama (extraction), Visarvana (evacuation) and Sivano (stitching and saturing). Surgical instruments were highly developed. Indeed Dr. Guthrie rightly observes "It was in surgery above all that the ancient Hindus excelled." Another authority Neuberger says "The outstanding feats of the ancient Indian surgery related to Laparotomy, Lithotomy and plastic operations". Very few are aware that foundations of plastic surgery were well and truly laid in India. It is a great pity that this form of medicine, though becoming popular elsewhere, is suffering neglect in India. No efforts are made to standardise Ayurvedic medicine. Neither are any efforts made to study how the drugs act and to isolate an active component. In the wake of growing consciousness of eco-friendly medicines, perfumes, garments, dyes and paints in the West, India with its ancient rich tradition in these systems can be a leader. Our garment industry, perfumary industry will suffer heavily if attention is not devoted to obtain perfumes, dyes and paints from natural products. The yellow dye from cows milk is said to have no parallel in the dye industry.

Ancient Indians, right from the days of Harappa had excelled in metallurgy. The massive iron pillar, standing at the outskirts of Delhi having withstood the test of time without rust or blemish is an eloquent testimony to our achievements in metallurgy.

In practising Yoga, again the approach is wholistic. The Yoga system of Patanjali is essentially a method for the discipline of the body and mind leading to psychic, physical and spiritual upliftment. Yoga is a word Well known now in Europe and America, though little is understood and it is normally associated in foreign lands with quaint practices. The system is much more profound and is based on the psychological conception that by proper training of the mind certain higher levels of consciousness can be attained. It is a method for finding out things for oneself. It goes far beyond the scientific method. It raises a question where exactly must we search for the source of mystery that underlies the universe, in which man finds his being, his self and his consciousness. If you concentrate on the seen, the observable physical world, as science does, you have kept out of account the seer who undertakes the search. Similarly if you concentrate on the seer, then you ignore the material world. Yoga sutra, therefore, emphasises that the starting point of search for reality must be an inquiry into the nature of existential interaction that explodes into a vision of what is internally and externally. By the very nature of yoga, the seer has to forget the past, remove from his mind all ego, the 'I'ness. It is through the practice of Yoga, one can excite the higher states of consciousness, tone your physical body and derive spiritual bliss.

All these remarkable achievements, and many more, could not be due to freaks or accidents. To create the iron pillar or to fabricate complicated surgical instruments, not only deeper understanding of metallurgy is essential but it involves development of furnace technology, ceramic technology, casting and forging techniques, the deeper understanding of the mechanism of rusting etc. We must therefore conclude that these and several other pioneering contributions to science and technology were not just due to momentary outbursts of erratic genius but they were essentially the products of a social millieu, level of cultural attainment and response to demands of time. I am afraid, we do not yet have a fuller picture of our ancient culture and a fuller description of our contributions to science and technology. Views on this vital issue fluctuate normally between two extremes. One school would advocate that there was hardly anything worth the name that our forefathers contributed and that science is totally a product of Western thought and action. In contrast, at the other end of the spectrum there are people who fanatically argue that in Ancient India, we have had almost everything that has been only recently rediscovered by the West. Truth, however, lies in between the two extremes. Indeed, it is very unfortunate that even after years of independence, no serious effort has been made to objectively assess our contributions to science and technology. There is nothing like a detailed study of Prof. Joseph Needham on science in China documented in eight volumes, in relation to science in India. We should constitute multidisciplinary groups consisting of experts in natural sciences, Sanskrit, philosophy to authentically document our contributions to science and technology.

Although such a detailed study is not available even a cursory look will indicate that India had a flourishing tradition in Science and technology coupled with advanced civilization and elevating philosophy. It is almost beyond doubt that the early foundation of science, though not in an organised form as we have today, were laid in India. While recalling those, historical contributions is re-assuring and satisfying in the sense that it brings out that we are also capable of contributing to science, they call for a deep introspection into the psychological, cultural, social and philosophical reasons as to why those ancient cultures such as those of Persia, India, China have not been able to recapture so far this past glory and contribute to this storehouse of human knowledge proportionate to our population, potential and promise. Although this should not lure us into a coma resulting in mental stupor and physical weariness but on the contrary build confidence and spur us to action to match our past.

The search for the sources of India's strength and the causes for her deterioration and decay is long, arduous and intricate, yet the recent causes of the decay are obvious enough. She fell behind in the march of technique and Europe which had long been backward in many matters, took the lead in technical progress. Behind this technical progress was the spirit of science and a bubbling life which displayed itself in many activities and gave adventurous voyages of discovery, new techniques, military strength to spread out and dominate the East, including India.

Why this should have happened is more difficult to unravel, for India was not lacking in mental alertness and technical skill in earlier times. However, one senses a progressive deterioration during centuries. The urge to life and endeavour becomes less, the creative spirit fades away and gives place to the imitative and duplicative actions. Where triumphant and rebellious thought had tried to pierce into the mysteries of nature and the universe, the wordy commentators came with their gloss and long explanation. Originality and creativity were replaced by compilation and commentories. Magnificient art and sculpture gave way to carvings of intricate detail. The vigour and richness of language, powerful yet simple, were displaced by highly ornate and complex literary forms. The urge to adventure and for the outflowing life which led to vast schemes of colonization and transplantation of Indian culture in far off lands faded away and a narrow orthodoxy, tabooed even the crossing of the high seas. A rational spirit of inquiry so evident in the earlier times which would have led to further notable contributions to science, were replaced by irrationalism and blind idolatory of the past. Indian life became sluggish stream, living in the past, moving slowly through the dead centuries.

Why this should have happened needs to be explored and investigated. Some people argue that the seeds of stagnation and decay are to be found in our philosophy of life, centred round negation of the self, abstentation from life and concentrating on other worldliness or world-worthlessness. Even in philosophical language, the world is considered as the Maya, an illusion. But this perception was not absolute but was in relation to the ultimate reality. There was of course another stream of thought based on acceptance of life to be lived and enjoyed. These two streams of thought and action developed side by side with the emphasis on one or the other varying in different periods. We find that in every period, Indian civilization bloomed on intense joy in life and nature. This led to the development of art, literature, song, dance, theatre etc. It is inconceivable that a culture or view of life based on other worldliness or world-worthlessness could have produced those manifestations of vigorous and varied life. Indeed it should be obvious, that any culture that was basically other worldly, could not have survived for thousands of years as Indian civilization has.

Some people believe that the rigid caste system is mostly responsible for the stagnation and decay of Indian culture and the associated creativity and originality. In this pernicious system the learning and scholarship was restricted to a very small minority and this minority was reared in the philosophy of the Upanishads with its continued emphasis on the fitness of the body and clarity of mind because they felt that the discipline of the body and the mind are essential for acquisition of knowledge. They felt that any achievement requires restraint, self suffering, self sacrifice etc. It is obvious that these noble ideas of the authors of Upanishads were confined to a small body of the community (elected initially on the basis of merit but later on selected on the basis of birth) who were capable of understanding them. A creative minority is always small in number but if it is in tune with the majority and is always trying to pull the latter up and make it advance, so that the gap between the two is lessened, a stable and progressive culture results. Without that creative minority a civilization must necessarily decay. It may also decay if the bond between the creative minority and the majority is broken and the minority is selected by birth rather than on the basis of merit and capabilities. In such a situation there is invariably a loss of social amity and ultimately that minority also looses its creativity. Some people argue that the stagnation and decay of Indian civilization is essentially due to these factors.

It may not be out of place to mention that the present day India suffers from a similar syndrome. Speaking in the language of Physics, the Indian society seems today to be stratified in two distinct bands seperated by a large band gap. The top band, may be called the itinerant band, is populated by a small minority having very little interaction with the heavily populated hopping lower band. Unless one consciously, reduces the band gap, thereby simulating more interaction between the two bands, the present social structure might decay and deteriorate.

I personally feel that incisive investigations need to be undertaken as to what are the causes, philosophic, sociological, political etc, that are responsible for our stagnation and lackluster performance.

Science, one of the most successful enterprises of man, has had remarkable success in interpreting phenomenological world. Today, thanks to science, it is possible to trace the evolution of the universe from its origin some 15 billion years ago to the present time, frame by frame as it were. It has traced in finer detail the tradition of the universe from energy dominated to matter dominated universe leading to life-dominated universe. Nature is struggling, as it were, to evolve universal consciousness in the individual conscious life. This elucidation of the evolutionary process has unequivocally brought out that every specie and indeed every member of a specie attempts for perfection and harmony. Indeed, this natural evolutionary process has shown that each one of us is both a product as well as an instrument of evolution. Science has been equally successful in bringing out the nature of space and time, matter and energy. Developments in science have enriched our understanding of the galaxies on the one hand and that of an electron on the other. The development in science coupled with success achieved in Technology led to a feeling that matter is the only true reality, everything else, the mind, consciousness, soul etc. are secondary and eventually explicable in terms of quantifiable properties of matter. This view quite fashionable and generally acceptable at one time appears to be too naive and untenable in the light of new developments in science itself. The development of quantum theory, the concept of uncertainty principle, the theory of relativity have all struck at the very root of scientific thought. It suggested for the first time that time and space are relative and inter-related. It also brought out the distinction between the big and the small, and defined those objects small which get disturbed during the very process of observation. It further brought out the dual character of these particles, the two aspects being complementary. These particles can be localized in physical space whereas they behave as waves - probability waves not in physical space but in abstract mathematical space. These developments have given greater profoundity to science. Science essentially attempts to understand the external world of atoms and molecules, space and time etc. It is objective - neither subjective nor projective. The question - what is an electron - is important but to ignore still more basic question as to who is it that wishes to understand it, is bound to lead to catastrophic consequences. Today, we can say a lot about an electron as to what it is but suppose the electrons were to turn back and ask us, "who are we" what shall we say? Erwin Schroedinger says "I consider science as an integrating part of an endeavor to answer one great philosophical question which embraces all others, the one Plotinus expressed in his brief "Who are We". This is also the question Nachiketa asked of Yama, the Lord of death.

As I am talking, thousands of muscles and actions co-ordinate to make me speak the things I am speaking. The muscle cells are controlled by the electric pulses along nerve fibers linking muscles with the brain. The brain with its more than thousand million neurons is a fantastic network of electric currents in the brain. A basic question is who wills me to speak. Again the answer intuitively is 'I'. But who is this 'I'.

I see, I perceive, I sense the external world through my senses and I act in this world through my organs. For all practical purposes the human body is a machine, in fact the most miraculous aspect of the human body is that it functions miraculously. Science has attempted to explain the structure and functioning of every organ of the human body. Thus, for example, my eye works exactly as a photographic camera. The lens in my eye casts an image of an object on the retina in much the same way as the lens of the camera casts an image on the camera plate. However, my eye is different from the camera. On seeing a beautiful rose flower, I am inclined to pluck it, on seeing a ferocious beast, I tend to run away. The photographic camera also casts the image of a beautiful flower or an ugly beast but is unmoved by both. However, I respond. It is therefore clear that my eye is not 'I' but my eye belongs to me. Again the question is who that me is. In fact, 'I' is a grand synthesis of the external world in the form of organs and the physical today which follow the laws of physics and chemistry and the internal world in the form of mind, soul etc. whose action is determined by the value system. It is 'I' who controls the organs which obey laws of physics and chemistry and as Schroedinger put it 'I' am the God Almighty, a postulate of the Upanishadas.

Ours is a golden age of science, that is fine, but it is also the age of technology, business management, an age of over specialization and dehumanization that is ominous and degrading. Science is elevating for it is an endless quest to understand nature. Technology is the application of science to manipulate nature hopefully for the betterment of mankind. As man learns to apply his understanding of the physical world for practical purposes, he is in reality substituting a slow but effective process of natural evolution which produced man by a rapid and goal directed evolutionary process. By this drastic intervention in the natural evolutionary process man is greatly accelerating and expanding the range of possibilities, and it is for this reason that the role of technology and what it has done to man and nature needs to be looked at carefully. The beneficial role of technology in making life richer, fuller, healthier and happier, cannot be overemphasized. Take any aspect, it has profoundly changed my concept of the world and opened up new possibilities. The revolution it has brought about in the field of communication and transport has envisioned me to conceive for the first time that this really is one well-knit world. With the ushering in of atomic energy, it has opened the possibility of releasing tremendous amount of energy in the wombs of atoms for meeting our ever increasing demand for energy for the production of goods and services, space travel has enabled me to look at the earth from a distance and has made me realize that nowhere in the universe, I can find, such an hospitable atmosphere as I have on the earth. This has made man, we hope, to realize that he is and will remain earth bound and he must therefore preserve it. The remarkable developments in medicine and surgery have made it a distinct possibility of creating a desired form of life in a test tube. The precious human civilization that we have assiduously built with the help of science, technology and social institutions has varied things to offer to each one according to his liking. There is celestial music, fascinating dances, penetrating science, staggering technology, elevating philosophy etc.

As against these beneficial aspects of science, there is also an exponential depletion of fossil fuels, continuous depletion of raw materials not to mention ghastly creation of science, and technology namely atomic bombs and all that goes along with it. Killing always leads to callous disregard for life and the rights of an individual. The dehumanizing effects of war were apparent even in the days of bows and arrows. They have multiplied enormously through the advent of nuclear and other weapons of mass destruction. It is the impersonal killing by remote control which makes modern war the most degrading of human activity. The increasing military power and decreasing national security has no technical solution. The solution has to be found in the minds of men. Then, there is division of the world into the developed and developing nations resulting in unprecedented affluence in the midst of unimaginable poverty.

The picture is ghastly but essentially true. We find developed countries ranged against developing countries, terror matched by greater terror and so on. They basically tend to separate and pitch one man against another. Why is this? All this indicates a crisis of human spirit, the agony of the soul, but why? There has been unabated pursuit of power, national or individual, leading to greed, hatred, delusion in place of love, compassion and kindness. Man is facing man. I face myself.

All this has essentially been due to the fact that science has tended to concentrate on the external world without simultaneously understanding the inner world. It is time that we pause and cry a halt to this one sided development and initiate a process which synthesizes science and spirituality, atom and ahimsa. No other culture other than India and the Indian culture with its deep philosophical and spiritual tradition can show the path. The whole world, as it were, becons India to show the path and a sense of direction.

(The author, a renowned scientist, is the former Vice-Chancellor of Pune University.)

Appendix - I

प्रार्थना

नमस्ते सदा वत्सले मातृभूमे,
त्वया हिन्दुभूमे सुखव् वर्धितोऽहम्
महामङ्गले पुण्यभूमे त्वदर्थे,
पतत्वेष कायो नमस्ते नमस्ते ।।१।।

प्रभोशक्तिमत् हिन्दुराष्ट्राङ्गभूता,
इमे सादरन् त्वान् नमामो वयम्
त्वदीयाय कार्याय वद्धा कटीयम्,
शुभामाञिषन् देहि तत्पूर्तये
अजय्याञ्च विश्वस्य देहीश शक्तिम्,
सुशीलञ्जगद् येन नम्रम् भवेत्
श्रुतञ्चैव यत् कण्टकाकीर्णमार्गम्,
स्वयम् स्वीकृतम् नस् सुगङ्कारयेत् ।।२।।

समुत्कषं निश्श्रेयसस्यैकमुग्रम्,
परम् साधनम् नाम वीरव्रतम्
तदन्तम् स्फुरत्वक्षया ध्येयानिष्ठा,
हृदन्त प्रजागर्तु तीव्राऽनिशम्
विजेयी च नस् संहता कार्यशक्तिर्,
विधायास्य धर्मस्य संरक्षणम्
परव् वैभवन् नेतुमेतत् स्वराष्ट्रम,
समर्था भवत्वाशिषा ते भृशम् ।।३।।

।। भारत माता की जय ।।

RSS PRAYER

(Translation)

FOREWVER I how to Thee, O Loving Motherland O Mother-land of us Hindus, Thou hast brought me up in happiness. May my life. O great and blessed Holy Land, be laid down in Thy cause, I bow to Thee, again and again.

WE, the children of the Hindu Nation, bow to Thee in reverence, O Almighty God. We have girded up ear loms to carry on Thy work. Give us Thy holy blessings for its fulfilment. O Lord! Grant us such might as no power on earth can ever challenge, such purity of character as would command the respect of the whole world and such knowledge as would make easy the thorny path that we have voluntarily chosen.

MAY WE be inspired with the spirit of stern heroism, which is the sole and ultimate means of attaining the highest spiritual bliss with the greatest temporal prosperity. May intense and everlasting devotion to our Ideal ever inspire our hearts. May our victorious organised power of action, by Thy Grace, fully protect our dharma and lead this nation of ours to the highest pinnacle of glory.

VICTORY TO MOTHER INDIA

Appendix - II

Bhārata Ekātmatā Stotra

भारत एकात्मता स्त्रोतम

ॐ नमः सच्चिदानन्दरुपाय परमात्मने ।
ज्योतिर्मयस्वरुपाय विश्वमांङ्गल्यमूर्तये ॥१॥

प्रकृतिः पञ्चभूतानि ग्रहा लोका स्वरास्तथा ।
दिशः कालश्च सर्वेषां सदा कुर्वन्तु मङ्गलम् ॥२॥

रत्नाकराधौतपदां हिमालयकिरीटिनीम् ।
ब्रह्मराजर्षिरत्नाढ्यां वन्दे भारतमातरम् ॥३॥

महेन्द्रो मलयः सह्यो देवतात्मा हिमालयः ।
ध्येयो रैवतको विन्ध्यो गिरिश्चारावलिस्तथा ॥४॥

गङ्गा सरस्वती सिन्धुर्ब्रह्मपुत्रश्च गण्डकी ।
कावेरी यमुना रेवा कृष्णा गोदा महानदी ॥ ५॥

अयोध्या मथुरा माया काशी काञ्चि अवन्तिका ।
वैशाली द्वारिका ध्येया पुरी तक्षशिला गया ॥६॥

प्रयागः पाटलीपुत्रं विजयानगरं महत् ।
इन्द्रप्रस्थं सोमनाथः तथाऽमृतसरः प्रियम् ॥७॥

चतुर्वेदाः पुराणानि सर्वोपनिषदस्तथा ।
रामायणं भारतं च गीता सद्दर्शनानि च ॥८॥

जैनागमास्त्रिपिटका गुरुग्रन्थः सतां गिरः ।
एष ज्ञाननिधिः श्रेष्ठः श्रद्धेयो हृदि सर्वदा ॥९॥

अरुन्धत्यनसूया च सावित्री जानकी सती ।
द्रौपदी कण्णगी गार्गी मीरा दुर्गावती तथा ॥१०॥

लक्ष्मीरहल्या चन्नम्मा रुद्रमाम्बा सुविक्रमा ।
निवेदिता सारदा च प्रणम्या मातृदेवताः ॥११॥

श्रीरामो भरतः कृष्णो भीष्मो धर्मस्तथार्जुनः ।
मार्कण्डेयो हरिश्चन्द्रः प्रह्लादो नारदो ध्रुवः ॥१२॥

हनुमाञ्जनको व्यासो वसिष्ठश्च शुको बलिः ।
दधीचिविश्वकर्माणौ पृथुवाल्मीकिभार्गवा ॥१३॥

भगीरथश्चैकलव्यो मनुर्धन्वन्तरिस्तथा ।
शिबिश्च रन्तिदेवश्च पुराणोद्गीतकीर्तयः ॥१४॥

बुद्धा जिनेन्द्रा गोरक्षः पाणिनिश्च पतञ्जलिः ।
शङ्करो मध्वनिम्बार्कौ श्रीरामानुजवल्लभौ ॥१५॥

झूलेलालोऽथ चैतन्यः तिरुवल्लुवरस्तथा ।
नायन्मारालवाराश्च कम्बश्च बसवेश्वरः ॥१६॥

देवलो रविदासश्च कबीरो गुरुनानकः ।
नरसिस्तुलसीदासो दशमेशो दृढव्रतः ॥१७॥

श्रीमत् शङ्करदेवश्च बन्धू सायणमाधवौ ।
ज्ञानेश्वरस्तुकारामो रामदासः पुरन्दरः ॥१८॥

बिरसा सहजानन्दो रामानन्दस्तथा महान् ।
वितरन्तु सदैवैते दैवीं सद्गुणसम्पदम् ॥१९॥

भरतर्षिः कालिदासः श्रीभोजो जकणस्तथा ।
सूरदासस्त्यागराजो रसखानश्च सत्कविः ॥२०॥

रविवर्मा भारतखण्डे भाग्यचन्द्रः स भूपतिः ।
कलावन्तश्च विख्याताः स्मरणीया निरन्तरम् ॥२१॥

अगस्तयः कम्बुकौणिडन्यौ राजेन्द्रश्चोलवंशजः ।
अशोकः पुष्यमित्रश्च खारवेलः सुनीतिमान् ॥२२॥

चाणक्यचन्द्रगुप्तौ च विक्रमः शालिवाहनः ।
समुद्रगुप्तः श्रीहर्षः शैलेन्द्रो बप्परावलः ॥२३॥

लाचिद् भास्करवर्मा च यशोधर्मा च हूणजित् ।
श्रीकृष्णदेवरायश्च ललितादित्य उद्बलः ॥२४॥

मुसुनूरिनायकौ तौ प्रतापः शिवभूपतिः ।
रणजित्सिंह इत्येते वीरा विख्यातविक्रमाः ॥२५॥

वैज्ञानिकाश्च कपिलः कणादः सुश्रुतस्तथा ।
चरको भास्कराचार्यो वराहमिहिरः सुधीः ॥२६॥

नागार्जुनो भरद्वाज आर्यभट्टो वसुर्बुधः ।
ध्येयो वेङ्कटरामश्च विज्ञा रामानुजादयः ॥२७॥

रामकृष्णो दयानन्दो रवीन्द्रो राममोहनः ।
रामतीर्थोऽरविन्दश्च विवेकानन्द उद्यशाः ॥२८॥

दादाभाई गोपबन्धुः तिलको गान्धिरादृताः ।
रमणो मालवीयश्च श्रीसुब्रह्मण्य भारती ॥२९॥

सुभाषः प्रणवानन्दः क्रान्तिवीरो विनायकः ।
ठक्करो भीमरावश्च फुले नारायणो गुरुः ॥३०॥

संघशक्तिप्रणेतारौ केशवोमाधवस्तथा ।
स्मरणीया सदैवैते नवचैतन्यदायकाः ॥३१॥

अनुक्ता ये भक्ताः प्रभुचरणसंसक्तहृदयाः
अविज्ञाता वीरा अधिसमरमुद्ध्वस्तरिपवः ।

समाजोद्धर्तारः सुहितकरविज्ञाननिपुणाः ।
नमस्तेभ्यो भूयात् सकलसुजनेभ्यः प्रतिदिनम् ॥३२॥

इदमेकात्मतास्तोत्रं श्रद्धया यः सदा पठेत् ।
स राष्ट्रधर्मनिष्ठावान् अखण्डं भारतं स्मरेत् ॥३३॥

॥ भारत माता की जय ॥

(Translation)

OM NAMAḤ SACCIDĀNANDARŪPĀYA PARMĀTMANE I
JYOTIRMAYASVARŪPĀYA VIŚVAMĀṄGALYAMŪRTAYE II*1*II
Om Salutation to the Supreme Self, characterized as, Truth-Consciousness & Bliss with luminous nature (as that of the Sun), universal good (well being and beneficence) is whose very being.

PRAKṚTIḤ PAÑCABHŪTĀNI GRAHĀ LOKĀ SVARĀSTATHĀ I
DIŚAḤ KĀLAŚCA SARVEṢĀM SADĀ KURVANTU MANGALAM II2II
May Nature (Prakrti) with its t hree constitutive guna(s) (characteristics); Five Material Elements; Planets or Grahas; Regions or Spheres (habitats); Word (voice) & Musical Notes; Directions (held to be in ten in number) and Time do always good to all.

RATNĀKARĀDHAUTAPADĀṀ HIMĀLAYAKIRĪTINĪM I
BRAHMĀRAJARṢIRATNĀḌHYAṀ VANDE BHĀRATAMĀTARAM II3II
The mine of gems and jewels, the ocean washes whose feet, *Himālaya* (the great mountain) is whose crown, to such a Motherland – made prosperous, through their presence, by the gems-like Saints and Royal Sages – I bow.

MAHENDRO MAYAḤ SAHYO DEVATĀTMĀ HIMĀLAYAḤ I
DHYEYO RAIVATAKO VINDHYO GRIŚCĀRĀ VALISHTATHĀ II4II
1.(1) The *Mahendra* mountain, 2. (2) The *Malaya* mount (the *Nīlagiri*), 3. (3) The Sahyādri, 4.(4) The *Himālaya*, having the divine indentity, 5.(15) The *Raivataka* (*Girnāra*), 6.(6) The *Vindhyācala* and 7.(7) The *Arāvalī* are the mountains fit to be mediated upon.

GAṄGĀ SARASVATĪSINDHURBRAHMAPUTRASCA GANDARI I
KĀVERĪ, YAMUNĀ REVĀ KṚṢṆĀ GODĀ, MAHĀNADĪ II *5* II
1. (1) Gaṇgā, 2. (2) Sarasvatī, 3. (3) Sindhu, 4. (4) Brahmaputra, 5. (5) Gandakī, 6. (6) Kāverī, 7. (7) Yamunā, 8. (8) Revā (Narmadā), 9 (19) Krishnā, 10. (10) Godāvarī, 11. (11) Mahānadi.

AYODHYAMATHURA MAYA KASI KANCI AVANTIKĀ I
VAIŚALĪ DVARIKĀ DHYEYA PURĪ TAKṢAŚLĀ GAYĀ II*6*II

1. (1) Ayodhyā 2. (2) Mathurā 3. (3) Māyā (Haridwār) 4. Kāshī (4) 5. (5) Kānchi 6. (6) Avantikā (Ujjanyinī), 7. (7) Vaishālī, 8. (8) Dvārikā, 9. (9) Jagannāthapurī, 10. (10) Takshashilā, 11. (11) Gayā- these cities alongwith those mentioned in the next shloka and the river in the earlier shlokas are worth-contemplating.

PRAYĀGAḤ PĀTALĪPUTRAM VIJAYANAGARAM MAHAI I
INDRAPRASTHAṀ SOMANĀTHAḤ TATHĀMṚTASARAḤ PRIYAM II*7*II

1. (1) Prayāg 2. (2) Pātaliputra (Patnā) 3. (3) Vijayanagaram 4. (4) Indraprastha (Delhi), 5. (5) somanāth 6. (6) Amritsar.

CATURVEDĀḤ PURĀṆĀNI SARVOPANIṢADASTATHĀ I
RĀMĀYAṆAṀBHĀRATAṀCA GĪTĀ SADDARŚANĀNI CA II*8*II

1. (1) Four Vedas, 2. (2) (Eighteen) Purānas, 3. (3) All the Upanishads 4. (4) Rāmāyana, 5. (5) Mahābhārata, 6. (6) Gita, 7. (7) Virtuous Philosophic Systems (*Sānkhya, Yoga, Nyāya, Vaiśeṣika, Pūrva-Mīmāmsā and Uttara-Mimāṁsā or Vedānta*).

JAINĀGAMĀSTRIPIṬAKĀ GURUGRANTHAḤ SATYĀṀ GIRAḤ I
EṢA JÑĀNANIDHIḤ ŚREṢṬHAḤ ŚRADDHEYO HṚDI SARVADĀ II*9*II

1. (1) Jaināgama granthas 2. (2) Buddist Tripitaka, 3. (3) Guru Grantha Sahib and 4. (4) The utterances of the saints, these and all the works mentioned in the former sloka-aphorism are the excellent treasures of knowledge to be faithfully (admiringly) kept always in the heart.

ARUNDHATYANASŪYĀ CA SĀVITRĪ JĀNAKĪ SATĪ I
DRAUPADĪ KAṆṆAGĪ GĀRGĪ MĪRĀ DURGĀVATĪ TATHĀ II*10*II

LAKṢMĪRAHALYĀ CANNAMMĀ RUDRAMĀMBĀ SUVIKRAMĀ I
NIVEDITĀ SĀRDĀ CA PRAṆAMYĀ MĀTṚDEVATĀḤ II*11*II

1. (1) Lakshmī Bāī, 2. (2) Ahalyā Lāī, 3. (3) Channammā, 4. (4) Rudramambā, 5. (5) Sister Nivedatā, 6. (6) Mother Sāradā, all these (and those mentioned in the former shloka are divine mothers fit to be offered obeisance.

ŚRĪ RĀMO BHARATAḤ KṚṢṆO BHĪṢMO
DHARMASTATHĀRJUNAḤ I
MĀRKAṆḌEYO HARĪŚCANDRAḤ PṚAHLĀDO NĀRADO
DHRUVAḤ II*12*II

1. (1) Shri Ramā, 2. (2) Bharata, 3. (3) Shrī Krishna, 4. (4) Bhīshma, 5. (5) Dharamarāja (Yudhishthira), 6. (6) Arjuna, 7. (7) Sage Mārkaṇḍeya, 8. (8) King Harishchandra 9. (9) Prahlāda, the great devotee, 10. (10) the divine sage Narada and 11. (11) Dhruva.

HANUMĀÑJANAKO VYĀSO VASIṢṬHAŚCA ŚUKO BALIH I
DADHĪCIVIŚVAKARMĀṆAU PṚTHUVĀLMĪKIBHĀRGA VĀḤ II*13*II

1. (1) Hanumān, 2. (2) King Janaka, 3. (3) Sage Vedavyāsa, 4. (4) Muni Vasishtha, 5. (5) Shukadeva, 6. (6) King Bali, 7. (7) Sage Dadhīchi, 8. (8) Vishvakarmā 9. (9) King Prithu, 10. (10) Muni Vālmīkī, 11. (11) (Bhargava) Parashu Rama.

BHAGĪRATHAŚCAIKALA VYO MANURDHANVANTARISTATHĀ I
ŚIBIŚCA RANTIDEVAŚCA PURĀṆODGĪTAKĪRTAYAḤ II*14*II

1. (1) King Bhageeratha, 2. (2) Ekalavya, 3. (3) Manu 4. (4) Dhanvantari, 5. (5) King Shibi, 6. (6) King Rantideva all these whose praises have been sung in the puranas.

BUDDHĀJINENDRĀ GORAKṢAḤ PĀNINIŚCA PATAÑJALIH I
ŚAṄKARO MADHVANIMBĀRKAU ŚRĪ RĀMĀNUJA VALLABHAU II*15*II

1. (1) Buddhas, 2. (2) Tirthankaras, 3. (3) Guru Garakhnath, 4. (4) Panini, 5. (5) Patanjali, 6. (6) Shankaracharya, 7. (7) Madhvacharya, 8. (8) Nimbarkacharya, 9. (9) Ramanujacharya, 10. (10) Vallabhacharya.

JHŪLELĀLOATHA CAITANYAḤ TIRUVALLUVARASTATHA I
NĀYANMĀRĀLA VĀRĀSCA KAMBAŚCA BASA VEŚVARAḤ II*16*II

1. (1) Jhūlelāl 2. (2) Chaitanya Mahāprabhu, 3. (3), Tiruvalluvara, 4. (4) Nāyanmāra saints, 5. (5) Ālavāra saints, 6. (6) The poet Kamban, 7. (7) Basaveshvara.

DEVALO RAVIDĀSAŚCA KABĪRO GURUNĀNAKAḤ I
NARASSISTULASĪDĀSO DAŚAMEŚO DṚḌHA VRATAḤ II*17*II

1. (1) Devala, 2. (2) Saint Ravidas, 3. (3) Saint Kabirdas, 4. (4) Guru Nanak 5. (5) Devotee Narasi, 6. (6) Goswami Tulsidas, 7. (7) The strong-willed Tenth Guru Govind Singh.

ŚRĪMAT ŚAṄKARADEVAŚCA BANDHŪ SAYAṆAMĀDHAVAU I
JÑĀNEŚVARASTUKĀRĀMO RĀMADĀSAḤ PURANDARAḤ II*18*II

1. (1) Shankaradeva, 2. (2) Sayanacharaya, 3. (3) Madhavacharya (Vidyaranya Swami), 4. (4) Saint Jñānneshvara, 5. (5) Saint Tukaram, 6. (6) Samartha Swami Ramadas, 7. (7) Purandaradas.

BIRASĀ SAHAJĀNANDO RĀMĀNANDASTATHĀ MAHĀN I
VITARANTU SADAIVAITE DĀĪVIṀ SADGUṆASAMPADAM II*19*II

1. (1) Birasā, 2. (2) Swami Sahajananda, and 3. (3) Swami Ramananda, these great men and those mentioned in the earlier shlokas may always distribute the Divine Wealth in the form of virtues.

BHARATARHṢIḤ KĀLIDĀSAḤ ŚRĪBHOJO JAKAṆASTATHĀ I
SŪRADĀSASTYĀ GARĀJO RASAKHĀNAŚCA SATKA VIḤ II*20*II

1. (1) (Expert in dramatics) The sage Bharata, 2. (2) The great Poet Kalidas 3. (3) King Bhoja, 4. (4) Jakanacharya, 5. (5) Surdas, 6. (6) Tyagaraja, 7. (7) The Poet Rasakhan.

RAVIVARMĀ BHĀTAKHAṆḌE BHĀGYACANDRAḤ SA BHŪPATIḤ I
KALĀVANTAŚCA VIKHYĀTĀḤ SMARAṆĪYĀ NIRANTARAM II*21*II

1. (1) Ravi Varma, 2. (2) Bhatakhande and 3. (3) King Bhagya Chandra– the famous Artists (and those mentioned in the 20th Shloka) are fit to be remembered.

AGASTYAḤ KAMBUKAUNDINYAU RAJENDRAŚCOLAVAṀ ŚAJAḤ I
AŚOKAḤ PUṢYAMITRAŚCA KHĀRA VELAḤ SUNĪTIMAN II*22*II

1. (1) The sage Agastya, 2. (2) Kambu Swayambhuva, 3. (3) Kaundinya, 4. (4) Rajendra of the Chola dynasty, 5. (5) Ashoka, 6. (6) Pushyamitra of the Shunga dynasty, and 7. (7) Kharavela, known for his good policy.

CĀṆAKYA CANDRAGUPTAU CA VIKRAMAḤ SĀLIVĀHANAḤ I
SAMUDRAGUPTAḤ ŚRĪHARṢAḤ ŚAILENDRO BAPPARĀVALAḤ II23II

1. (1) Chanakya, 2. (2) Chandragupta Maurya, 3. (3) Vikramaditya, 4. (4) Shali vahana, 5. (5) Samudragupta, 6. (6) Harshavardhana, 7. (7) Shailendra, 8. (8) Bappa Raval.

LĀCID BHĀSKARA VARMĀ CA YAŚODHARMĀ CA HŪṆAJIT I
ŚRĪ KṚṢṆSADEVARĀYAŚCA LALITĀDITYA UDBALAḤ II24II

1. (1) Lachit Badfukan, 2. (2) Bhaskar Varma, 3. (3) Victor over the Hunas, Yashodharma 4. (4) King Krishna Deva Raya, 5. (5) The Brave Lalitaditya.

MUSUNOORINĀYAKAU TAU PRATĀPAH ŚIVABHŪPATIḤ I
RAṆAJITSIMHA ITYETHE VĪRĀ VIKHYĀTA VIKRAMĀḤ II25II

1. (1) Musunoori Heroes Kappaya Nayak and Pralaya Nayak, 2. (2) Maharana Pratap 3. (3) Chhatrapati Shivaji, 4. (4) Maharaja Ranjit Singh- these and those

VAIJÑĀIKĀSCA KAPILAH KANĀDAH SUŚRUTASTATHA I
CARAKO BHĀSKARĀCARYO VARĀHAMIHIRAḤ SUDHĪḤ II26II

Among the excellent intellectuals and great scientists are 1. (1) Kapila Muni, 2. (2) Sage Kanad, 3. (3) Sushruta, 4. (4) Charaka, 5. (5) Bhaskaracharya, 6. (6) Varahamihira.

NĀGĀRJUNO BHARADVĀJA ĀRYABHATTO VASURBUDHAḤ I
DHYEYO VEṄKATARĀMAŚCA VIJÑĀ RĀMĀNUJĀDAYAḤ II27II

1. (1) Nagarjuna, 2. (2) Rishi Bharadvaj, 3. (3) Aryabhatt, 4. (4) Jagadish Chandra Vasu, 5. (5) Chandrashekhara Venkataramana, 6. (6) Ramanuja (together with the scientists mentioned in the previous shloka) are the wise persons to be reckoned with.

RĀMAKṚṢṆO RAVĪNDRO RĀMAMOHANAḤ I
RĀMATĪRTHORVINDAŚCA VIVEKĀNANDA UDYAŚAḤ II28II

1. (1) Ramakrishna Paramahansa, 2. (2) Swami Dayananda Sarasvati, 3. (3) Ravindranath Tagore, 4. (4) Raja Ramamohan Roy, 5. (5) Swami

Ramatirth, 6. (6) Shri Aurobindo (Aravinda), 7. (7) Swami Vivekananda these (and those mentioned in the previous shloka) have been the persons highly praiseworthy.

DĀDĀBHĀĪ GOPABANDHUḤ TILAKO GĀNDHIRĀDṚTĀḤ I
RAMAṆO MĀLA VĪYASCA ŚRĪSUBRAHMAṆYA BHĀRATĪ II*29*II

1. (1) Dadabhai Nauroji, 2. (2) Gopabandhudas, 3. (3) Lokmanya Bal Gangadhar Tilak, 4. (4) Mahatma Gandhi, 5. (5) Ramana Maharshi, 6. (6) Maha Mana Madan Mohan Malaviya, 7. (7) Shri Subrahmanya Bharti–these have been honoured persons.

SUBHĀṢAḤ PRAṆAVĀNANDAḤ KRĀNTIVĪRO VINĀYAKAḤ I
ṬHAKKARO BHĪMARĀVAŚCA PHULE NĀRĀYAṆO GURUḤ II*30*II

ŚAṄGHASAKTI-PRAṆETĀRAU KEŚA VOMADHA VASTATHĀ I
SAMARAṆĪYĀ SADAIVAITE NA VACAITANYADĀYAKĀḤ II*31*II

The progenitors of Sangh Shakti (Rashtriya Swayamsevak Sangh) 1. (1) Dr. Keshavai Bali Ram Hedgewar, 2. (2) Madhavarao Sadashivarao Golwalkar and all the great men and women mentioned in this panegyric to the Integral Spirit of Bharat are the great beings who inspire a new awakenking and are worthy to be ever remembered.

ANUKTĀ YE BHAKTĀḤ PRABHUCARAṆASAMASAKTA KTAHṚDĀYAḤ
A VIJNATĀ VIRA ADHISAMARAMUDDHVASTARIPAVAH I
SAMĀJODDHARTĀRAḤ SUHITAKARA VIJÑĀNANIPUṆAḤ
NAMASTEBHYO BHŪYĀT SAKALASUJABEHYAḤ PRATIDINAM II*32*II

Those who mention has not been made (in the Panegyric) here but who are such devotees who dedicated themselves at the feet of the Bhagavān whole heartedly; there have been many such unknown brave persons who destroyed the enemies in the battle-fields; many such uplifters of society and many such competent scientists who worked for the good of the people and made valuable discoveries (or inventions)– to them all our homage of heart be paid every day.

Appendix - III

SHREE GURUJEE'S HOROSCOPE

Birth : February 19, 1906, 4.34 a.m. Nagpur Dashami joint with Ekadashi, Magh Vadya 11, Shaka 1827.

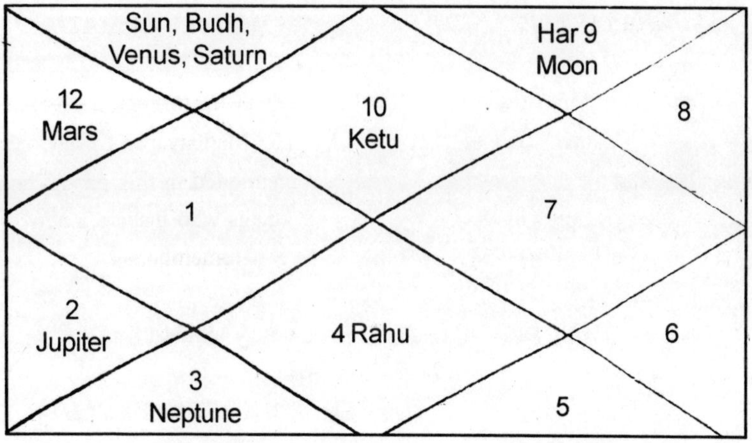

Appendix - IV

CHRONOLOGY OF SHREE GURUJEE'S LIFE

1906	Feb. 19 Monday, Magha Vadya 11, Shaka (1827) : Birth in Nagpur at 4.34 a.m.	
1915	Passed fourth standard examination. Stood first in Narmada Division (Pre-independence Madya Pradesh). Awarded Scholarship.	
1924	Passed Intermediate examination. Won prize for standing first in English. Entered Banaras Hindu University.	
1926	Passed B.Sc.	
1928	Passed M.Sc.	
1929	Research at Madras aquarium.	
1931	Entered Sangh.	
1930-33	Lecturer at Banaras Hindu University.	
1933	Law student at Nagpur.	
1934	Appointed *Karyawaha* (Secretary) at Tulsibagh Shakha of Sangh.	
	Stay in Mumbai for some time for Sangh work.	
	Appointed *Sarvadhikari* (Chief Executive Officer) of Akola (Vidarba) Sangh training camp.	
1935	Passed L.L.B.	
1936	Left for Sargachhi (Bengal) before Diwali.	
	Stay with Shir Akhandananda, President of Ramakrishna Sangh	
1937	Jan. 13 :	Accepted *Deeksha* (Initiation) on Makar Sankranti day.
	Feb :	Swami Akhandananda passes away.
	March end : Return to Nagpur.	
1938	*Sarvadhikari* of Sangh training camp in Nagpur.	
1939	Feb. end :	Attended prominent workers meeting at Sindi (Wardha district, Vidarbha).

	March 22 : Left for Calcutta for Sangh work.	
		Sarvadhikari of Sangh training camp in Nagpur.
	Aug. 13 :	Appointed *Sarkaryawaha* (General Secretary) on Bandhan Day.
	Jan. 21 :	Dr. Hedgewar Passes away.
	July. 3 :	Appointed as Sarsanghachalak.
	July 21 :	All Bharat convention on monthly *shraddha* day of Doctorji.
	Aug. 4 :	Government ban on Sangh activities like route-march, uniform etc.
1942-47	Big expansion of Sangh work.	
1946	Huge public programmes in Rawalpindi, Jhelum (Punjab) and Pashwar (NWEP).	
1947	March :	Extensive tour of Punjab.
		Punjab Relief Committee established; 3000 relief camps set up.
	Aug. 5-8 :	Big programmes in Hyderabad and Karanchi (Sindh).
	Aug. 15 :	Bharat Achieves Truncated Independence.
	Sept. 12 :	Meetings with Home Minister Sardar Patel and Mahatma Gandhi
	Oct17-19 :	Meetings with Maharaja Hari Singh in Srinagar, Kashmir.
		Meeting with Prime Minister Nehru.
1948	Feb. 1 :	Arrest in Nagpur
	Feb. 2 :	Ban on Sangh
	Feb.5 :	Sangh dissolved. Thousands of Sangh workers arrested.
	Aug. 6 :	Release from prison.
	Oct. 17 :	Leaves for Delhi.
	Nov. 12 :	Issues clarion call to re-start Sangh at the Instance of *Sarkaryawaha*, Shri Bhaiyaji Dani
		Arrest again in Delhi.

	Nov. 14 :	Brought from Delhi to Nagpur jail. Later shifted to Seoni jail.
	Dec. 9 :	Sangh starts again under the leadership of Bhaiyaji Dani. Country-wide *Satyagraha*.
1949	Jan. 21 :	*Satyagraha* suspended. Mediation by Shri G.V. Ketkar and Shri T.R.V. Shastri.
	July 12 :	Ban removed.
	July13 :	Unconditional release from Betul Jail. Arrival in Nagpur.
	July 19 :	Left for Madras to see Shri T.R.V. Shastri. All Bharat tour resumed. Meeting with Sardar Patel in Mumbai.
	Aug. 21 :	Unprecedented reception in Delhi.
1950	Feb. 8 :	*Vastuhara Samiti* set up in Calcutta.
	Aug. 11 :	Relief work for Assam earthquake sufferers begins
1951	'*Akal-grasta Sahayata Samiti*' set up in Bihar.	
1952	Anti-cow slaughter movement.	
	Dec. 7 :	Memorandum signed by nearly 2 crore citizen submitted to President Rajendra Prasad.
1954	March-April :	Prolonged meeting of nearly 250 prominen *pracharaks* at Sindi (Wardha district).
	July 21 :	Demise of father.
1956	Fifty-first Birthday of Shri Guruji celebrated all over the counry	
1960	March :	All Bharat workers meeting at Indore.
1962	April 6 :	Inauguration of *'Smriti Mandir'*, Dr. Hedgewar's Memorial at Reshimbagh, Nagpur, on Varsha *Pratipada Day* Impressive all-Bharat assembly of Swayamsevaks.
1962	Aug. 12 :	Demise of mother. Swami Vivekananda Birth Centenary Celebrations.

		Vivekananda Rock Memorial Committee set up.
1964	*Krishna Janmashtami* : Vishwa Hindu Parishad established at Sandipani Ashrama, Mumbai.	
1965	Sept. 6 :	Indo-Pak war. Attended meeting of national leaders convented by Prime Minsiter Lal Bahadur Shastri.
1966	Jan. 22, 23, 24 :	World Convention of Vishwa Hindu Parishad in Prayag.
1967	September :	*Atma-Shraddha* at Brahma Kapal.
1970	July 1 :	Cancer operation in Mumbai.
	July 22 :	Discharge from Hospital.
1972	Oct. 29 to : Nov. 2	Meeting of nearly 450 important workers from all over the country at Thane.
	Dec. 19 :	Dr. Moonjes portrait uneviled by Gen. Cariappa in Nagpur.
1972	Aug. 20 :	Inauguration of Deendayal Research Institute in Delhi.
	Feb. 4 :	Last public programme in Bangalore.
	Mar. 14 :	End of tour and return to Nagpur.
	March 24-25 :	Meeting of Akhila Bharatiya Pratinidhi Sabha in Nagpur, Last address- Victory is certain.
	April 2 :	Wrote three letters about future arrangements and sealed them.
	May 19 to 31 :	Group-wise meetings with Swayamsevaks attending the Third Year Training Camp at Nagpur.
	June 5 :	Shuffled off his mortal coil at 9.05 p.m.
	June 6 :	Last rites at Reshimbagh; Nagpur in the evening.

Appendix - V

Facsimile of Gurujee's writing (Hindi)

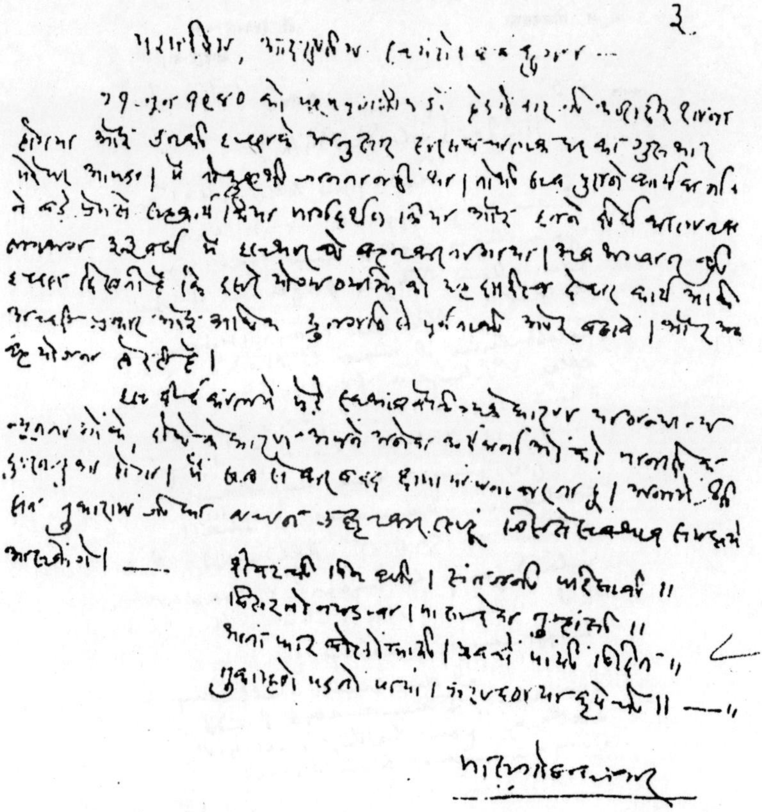

Appendix - VI

Facsimile of Gurujee's writing (Hindi)

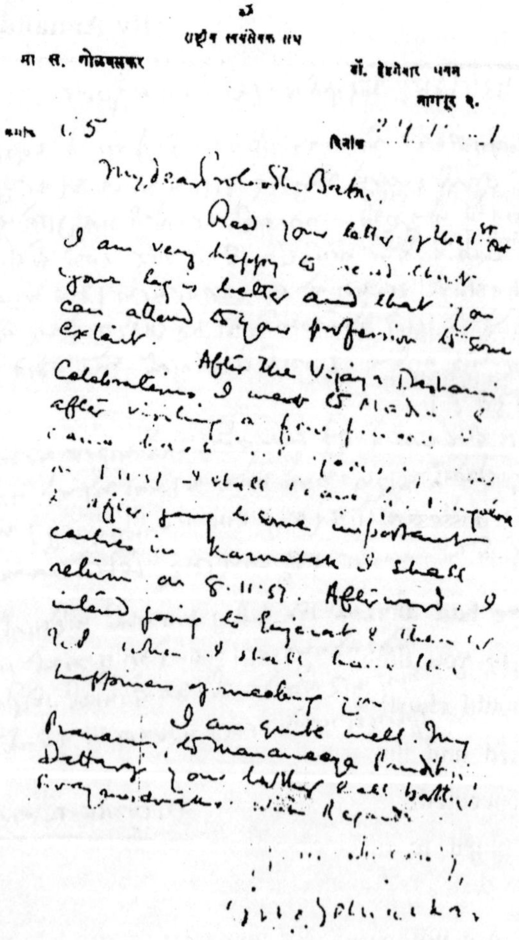

ॐ

राष्ट्रीय स्वयंसेवक संघ

मा. स. गोळवलकर

डॉ. हेडगेवार भवन

नागपुर १.

क्रमांक 1. 5

दिनांक [illegible]

My dear [illegible] Batra,

Read your letter of [illegible]. I am very happy to read that your leg is better and that you can attend to your profession to some extent.

After the Vijaya Dashami Celebrations I went to Madras & after visiting a few places [illegible] came back [illegible] on [illegible] I shall [illegible] After going to some important centres in Karnatak I shall return on 8.11.57. Afterwards I intend going to Gujarat & then [illegible] when I shall have the happiness of meeting you.

I am quite well. My Pranams to Mananeeya Pandit[illegible]. [illegible] your brother & all [illegible] [illegible] With Regards

[illegible]

[illegible]

Appendix - VII

Our Humble Submission

By Aanand Aadeesh

Revered Guruji
We cannot say of heart,
But from lips for sure,
During your stay here on earth
We could never dare address you as–
Maryada Purushottam Ram
or
Yogi-Raj Shyam!
Though you possessed all the attributes of both
And content;
Whereas we had all the intent.
We knew, to you the very idea was loath.
Lest you should chastise
We refrained and thought it wise–
To keep concealed,
What we ought to have revealed.
But now,
When you are not physically around,
And only your ideas resound
Cannot we afford to be a little bold and ask–
Sir,

How could you transform us–the sick and suffering lot–
Into men of steel,
Little water drops into oceans of unfathomable reach
And
Pebbles picked up from sandy beach into mighty mountain
Mere mortals into some one from divine domain,
Without the alchemy?
If you were not part of that supreme spark
That burns itself at both ends
Before it radiates the entire Universe
With its golden glow,
Infusing new life into sleeping graves
With His conch's powerful blow.
Now, your silent smile
Can no longer beguile.
Deny, if you can,
Revered Guruji!
Could this miracle be performed
Without Krishna's Karmyog
And Ram's vow (Raghukul Reeti...)
We mean your well earned Devattava!!
Is not your sublime silence
An eloquent admission
To our obstinate submission!!!

(Published in Organizer Weekly, dated February 19-26, 2006)